CAMBRIDGE COMPANIONS TO LITERATURE

The Cambridge Companion to Milton

The Cambridge Companion to Milton provides an accessible and helpful guide for any student of Milton, introducing readers to both the scope of Milton's work and the range of current approaches to it. The *Companion*'s eighteen contributors have written informative, stimulating, often argumentative essays that will provoke thought and discussion both in and out of the classroom.

The Cambridge Companion to Milton offers in a single volume the responsible and diverse introduction to Milton that undergraduate students, together with their professors, are looking for.

William Faithorne's engraved portrait of Milton for the frontispiece of *The History of Britain* (1670)

The Cambridge Companion to Milton

Edited by Dennis Danielson
University of British Columbia

CAMBRIDGE
UNIVERSITY PRESS

Published by the Press Syndicate of the University of Cambridge
The Pitt Building, Trumpington Street, Cambridge CB2 1RP
40 West 20th Street, New York, NY 10011–4211, USA
10 Stamford Road, Oakleigh, Melbourne 3166, Australia

© Cambridge University Press 1989

First published 1989
Reprinted 1992, 1994, 1995, 1996, 1997

Printed in Great Britain at the University Press, Cambridge

British Library cataloguing in publication data

The Cambridge Companion to Milton.
1. Poetry in English. Milton, John, 1608–1674
– Critical studies
I. Danielson, Dennis Richard, *1949–*
821′.4

Library of Congress cataloguing in publication data

The Cambridge Companion to Milton / edited by Dennis Danielson.
        p.   cm.
Includes bibliographies and index.
ISBN 0 521 33402 0 (hardback) ISBN 0 521 36885 5 (paperback)
1. Milton, John, 1608–1674 – Criticism and interpretation.
PR3588.C27 1989
821′.4 – dc 19   88-31181
CIP

ISBN 0 521 33402 0 hardback
ISBN 0 521 36885 5 paperback

WD

Contents

Illustrations

Contributors

Joan S. Bennett, University of Delaware
John Carey, Merton College, Oxford
Georgia Christopher, Emory University, Atlanta
Thomas N. Corns, University of Wales, Bangor
Dennis Danielson, University of British Columbia
J. Martin Evans, Stanford University
Roy Flannagan, Ohio University
James A. Freeman, University of Massachusetts
Dustin Griffin, New York University
Marshall Grossman, University of Maryland
Lee M. Johnson, University of British Columbia
William Kerrigan, University of Massachusetts
John Leonard, University of Western Ontario
Barbara Kiefer Lewalski, Harvard University
Diane K. McColley, Rutgers University, Camden, New Jersey
Michael Allen Mikolajczak, University of St Thomas, Minnesota
Mary Ann Radzinowicz, Cornell University
John T. Shawcross, University of Kentucky

Preface

This book, as its title suggests, is intended to provide friendly and helpful company for any student of Milton. Cambridge University Press began by asking me to plan a book – and a team of contributors – which would introduce readers of Milton to both the scope of his work and the range of current approaches to it. In response I put forward a list of chapters that I hoped might most nearly accomplish this challenging task, trying where I could to make individual chapters do more than one job – such as introducing a particular work, character, or theme *and* exemplifying a particular critical approach. I then accordingly recruited a mosaic of outstanding academics from three countries (the United Kingdom, the United States, and Canada), encouraging each one to practise his or her own scholarly or critical art on the assigned topic.

What follows, therefore, is not a series of homogeneous encyclopaedia articles but eighteen original essays by eighteen different human beings who care about Milton, who would (and do) disagree with each other about innumerable issues, and who seek in an informative, responsible, often argumentative way to say something important about a subject they love. Unfortunately, this book does not include discussion of all of Milton's works, nor does it exemplify every major critical approach; such are the limitations of a single volume. But each contributor has been asked to try to do in a modest way what Milton himself so consistently does: by means of a particular style, angle of vision, or argument to encourage critical thought, further study, and a process of understanding. Moreover, despite the fact that this book is intended primarily for the serious student approaching Milton for the first time, I have invited each author to speak in his or her own voice, and without condescension. As their interested first reader – and simply as a lover of Milton – I have found the resulting essays also to be most enjoyable, and I hope that others will enjoy them too.

Although readers may consult the contents list and select chapters to read according to their specific needs or interests, I have sought to organize the book so that it has some rough logical continuity. John Shawcross's informative chapter on Milton's life is followed by Roy Flannagan's thorough introduction to *Comus*, a work that played a signal role in Milton's early life as a poet. Martin Evans's stimulating essay on *Lycidas* similarly has biographical implications, as well as pointing to Milton's transition from the pastoral to the heroic. James Freeman pursues Milton's emphasis on individual and poetic heroism as both an element of continuity throughout Milton's works and as a ready way of access into them for the modern reader. Following this introduction to the heroic are four essays, by Lee Johnson, Barbara Lewalski, John Leonard, and myself, on the forms and purposes of Milton's great heroic poem: the style, genres, language, and theodicy of *Paradise Lost*. Two of the most perennially controversial topics related to *Paradise Lost* – Milton's Satan and Milton's treatment of the sexes – are introduced in lively essays by John Carey and Diane McColley respectively. *Paradise Lost* is likewise the focus of Marshall Grossman's discussion of Milton's rhetoric, the 'rhetoric of prophecy'. With Thomas Corns's chapter the focus shifts for a while on to some of Milton's prose and the stylistic developments it reveals. The chapters that follow, by Georgia Christopher, Mary Ann Radzinowicz, and Joan Bennett, bring our attention back again to the great poems, *Paradise Lost*, *Paradise Regained*, and *Samson Agonistes*, exploring (respectively) Milton's rich, complex relationship to the Reformation, to the Bible, and to the timeless issue of human freedom. Our historical perspectives on Milton are then lengthened and deepened by Dustin Griffin's chapter on Milton's literary influence and by William Kerrigan's on the place of Milton in intellectual history. Each of these chapters is accompanied by a reading list. These are followed, finally, by Michael Mikolajczak's helpful bibliographic essay.

I would like to thank contributors, whom one of their number dubbed the 'Cambridge Milton Companions', for being colleagues and companions indeed, our diversity notwithstanding. I thank the Press for graciously inviting me to undertake the project in the first place. And I am grateful to the Social Sciences and Humanities Research Council of Canada for a grant, administered by the Office of Research Services at the University of British Columbia, that has assisted me greatly in keeping up communications with contributors and in preparing the manuscript. I also offer sincere thanks to Doreen Todhunter and Peter Parolin for the role their keen eyes and minds have played in bringing this project to fruition.

If I were the sole author of this book I could here conclude by blaming myself for all its errors and shortcomings. But I am only its editor; and however much blame I may genuinely deserve, responsibility for both its failures and successes – like the pleasure of reading Milton – is happily something I can share with others.

Dennis Danielson

John Milton: significant dates and works

1608   Born Cheapside, London (9 December)

1620   Enters St Paul's School, London

1625   Admitted to Christ's College, Cambridge

1632   Takes MA degree, begins period of 'studious retirement' at his father's residence in Hammersmith

1634   *A Mask (Comus)* performed at Ludlow Castle

1635   Takes up residence at Horton

1638   *Lycidas* published

        (May) Sails for France and (June, July) travels on to Italy

1639   (July) Returns home to England

1641   *Of Reformation*, *Of Prelatical Episcopacy*, and *Animadversions upon the Remonstrants Defence, against Smectymnuus* published

1642   *The Reason of Church-Government* and *Apology against a Pamphlet* published

        (July?) Marries Mary Powell, who (in Aug.?) returns home to her mother in Oxfordshire

1643   *The Doctrine and Discipline of Divorce* published

1644   *Of Education* and *Areopagitica* published

1645   Mary Powell Milton returns

        Poems of Mr. John Milton registered (published Jan. 1646)

1649   (Jan.) Charles I executed

        (Feb.) *The Tenure of Kings and Magistrates* and (Oct.) *Eikonoklastes* published

        (March) Appointed Secretary for the Foreign Tongues

1651   *Pro Populo Anglicano Defensio* published

1652   Milton's blindness becomes almost complete

        Mary Powell Milton dies

1654   *Defensio secunda* published

1655   *Defensio pro Se* published

1656   Marries Katherine Woodcock

1658 Katherine Woodcock Milton dies

1659 *A Treatise of Civil Power* and *Considerations Touching the Likeliest Means to Remove Hirelings* published

1660 (March) *The Ready and Easy Way to Establish A Free Commonwealth* published

(May) The monarchy is restored in England

1663 Marries Elizabeth Minshul

1667 *Paradise Lost* (in ten books) published

1670 *The History of Britain* published

1671 *Paradise Regained* and *Samson Agonistes* published together

1673 *Of True Religion* published

1674 *Paradise Lost* (second edition, in twelve books) published

(8 Nov.) Milton dies

1823 Manuscript of *De doctrina christiana* discovered (published 1825)

Note on the text and abbreviations

References to works quoted or mentioned are given in the text, usually in an abbreviated form that cites the author's name, the date (where necessary), and the page. Fuller details of works thus cited may be found in the reading list that follows each chapter but the last. All biblical quotations, except as otherwise indicated, are from the Authorized (King James) Version.

Poems *The Poems of John Milton*, ed. John Carey and Alastair Fowler (London, 1968). All quotations of Milton's poetry are from this edition.
YP   *Complete Prose Works of John Milton*, 8 vols., ed. Don. M. Wolfe *et al.* (New Haven, 1953–82)
CM   *The Works of John Milton*, 18 vols., ed. Frank Allen Patterson *et al.* (New York, 1931–8)
CD   *Christian Doctrine* (original Latin title: *De doctrina christiana*)
PL   *Paradise Lost*
PR   *Paradise Regained*
SA   *Samson Agonistes*

1 The life of Milton

In comparison with the lives of most of his contemporaries, the life of John Milton is well documented and detailed. And even in the recent critical climate emphasizing the literary text, Milton's life has frequently been a source for the interpretation of his works. Some of his works are tied to historical events and Milton's relationship to them; others take on differing readings according to their presumed relationship to biographical elements such as their date of composition or our psychological understanding of the author at a particular time. Indeed, recent criticism has often found it difficult to revise earlier 'biographical' readings of Milton's works even where authentic biographical evidence indicates they are wrong. For this reason Milton's documented biography is more important for a reading of his work than are Shakespeare's or George Herbert's or Sir Thomas Browne's for a reading of their work.

John Milton was born at 6.30 a.m. on Friday, 9 December 1608, to Sara and John Milton, Sr, at their home, the Spread Eagle, in Bread Street, London. He was baptized at All Hallows, Bread Street, on 12 December, into the Protestant faith of the Church of England. He lived almost all his life within easy proximity of his natal home: his family may have moved briefly to Westminster, but certainly lived in Hammersmith from mid 1631 through mid 1635 (both then being western suburbs of the City of London) and in Horton, Buckinghamshire, from mid 1635 to early 1638. Milton's 'Horton period' as referred to by critics has meant the years after graduation from Cambridge in 1632 through his leaving for the Continent in April 1638, though we now know that the Horton period in fact began only in 1635. During his governmental service (1649–60), Milton resided in Westminster, no longer a suburb, with homes in Charing Cross, Scotland Yard (Whitehall), and Petty France. Other residences were in and around the City in St Bride's Churchyard, Aldersgate Street, the fashionable Barbican, High Holborn, Holborn near Red Lyon Fields, Jewin Street, and Artillery Walk, Bunhill Fields.

Milton's father was a scrivener and professional composer. His family came from Stanton St John, Oxfordshire, but sometime in the early 1580s he left his Roman Catholic home after disagreement over his espousing a Protestant, generally Calvinist, persuasion. His business, operated from his home, involved secretarial tasks, notary public work, real estate, and loans, and made him and his family financially well off. Many of these transactions can be traced in Chancery Court, and they provided the means for his son's livelihood in future years. (John Milton, son and poet, received only minimal compensation for subsequent services as a tutor, as secretary to the Council of State, and as an author.) Milton, Sr, was a successful composer, in acquaintance with some of the leading musicians of his day: he is said by his grandson, Edward Phillips, to have been rewarded with a gold medal and chain by a Polish prince for an *In Nomine* of forty parts, and he is remembered particularly for his five-part 'Fair Orian' in honour of Queen Elizabeth (1601). Paternal relatives, however, are little known and seem not to have played any strong part in Milton's life.

Milton's mother was Sara Jeffrey of St Swithin's parish, London. Among her relatives were people named Bradshaw, Caston, and Haughton, names that early biographers occasionally assigned to her. A few maternal relatives figure in Milton's life, particularly in the 1640s. Sara and John Milton, Sr, were married sometime between 1590 and 1600. Their children included an unbaptized child in 1601; Anne, who was older than John; John; Sara, who was born and died in July 1612; Tabitha, who was born in January 1614 and died in 1615; and Christopher, born in November 1615.

Milton's early education was with private tutors at home; Thomas Young, a Scotsman who became a dissenting minister and was sent to Hamburg in the 1620s, is the only one identified. Letters from Milton to Young are extant, and he wrote *Elegia quarta* to him. Young has been suggested both as the friend to whom Milton sent an undated letter known in manuscript, in which he explains his reasons for not pursuing the ministry and perhaps for now contemplating a poetic career, and as the one to whom Milton's first acknowledged prose tract, *Of Reformation*, is dedicated. (At least two other prose items of slightly earlier date have been ascribed to Milton, without general scholarly acceptance.) Even more importantly, however, Young is the 'TY' of the acronym SMECTYMNUUS, which stands for five ministers who argued in March 1641 against prelacy – church government by bishops – in the Church of England. Apparently through Young, Milton joined in the antiprelatical position, perhaps with 'A Postscript' (ascribed to Milton) to the Smectymnuan *An Answer to a Booke entituled, An Humble Remonstrance*, but certainly with his five tracts of 1641–2: *Of Reformation, Of*

Prelatical Episcopacy, *Animadversions upon the Remonstrants Defence, against Smectymnuus*, *The Reason of Church-Government*, and *Apology against a Pamphlet call'd A Modest Confutation*. Young may have served as tutor around 1618–20, after which Milton attended Alexander Gill's St Paul's School, only a few short blocks from his home. During this period he would surely also have heard sermons by the Dean of St Paul's Cathedral, John Donne. Here Milton remained until early 1625, when he went up to Christ's College, Cambridge, being admitted on 12 February, and matriculating on 9 April.

Through these years before he went up to Cambridge, Milton was studying for the ministry, and his study habits, it would seem, kept him reading late and long, which perhaps contributed to his poor eyesight later on. Of his writings during this period we know only two Psalm translations, some Latin verses, and a prose theme. Friends at St Paul's School included Alexander Gill, the younger, an instructor, although not one of Milton's, and Charles Diodati. Extant letters to both these men add to our knowledge of Milton's activities and hopes at significant points in his life. A Greek translation of Psalm 114 may have been prompted by correspondence with Gill, and *Elegia prima* and *Elegia sexta* were written to Diodati. Diodati's untimely death, apparently from the plague, in 1638 while Milton was abroad is mourned in the pastoral verse *Epitaphium Damonis*, which Milton wrote after his return to England, and in which he reveals more about himself than about Diodati.

His years at Christ's College, Cambridge (1625–32), were both happy and unhappy for Milton. We are not aware of many particular friends there. Most seriously, he ran into difficulty with his tutor William Chappell, perhaps being whipped, as later reported, and he was rusticated (that is, suspended) during the Lent Term of 1626. He returned to his London home, and *Elegia prima* discusses some of his activities and his feelings, although there is a bias of self-defensiveness in what he says. He returned to Cambridge on 19 April 1626, and was placed under Nathaniel Tovey, who remained his tutor through the rest of his college days. At Cambridge Milton was also known as 'The Lady of Christ's', a title to which he refers in his Sixth Prolusion. The sobriquet may comment upon his youthful good looks, but more probably on his dissociation from the usual social and athletic activities of male college students. On the other hand, he seems to have been known for his intellectual abilities and sought out for them. He was graduated fourth in the University honours list and first from Christ's. Milton received his Bachelor of Arts on 26 March 1629, and his Master of Arts on 3 July 1632, in both cases signing the Subscriptions Book, an act required of all those accepting degrees, and indicating one's acceptance of the religious and ecclesiastical regulations of the time. Presumably Milton still intended to become a minister, though he did not receive a preferment, either collegiate or parochial; and perhaps he sought none. Except for his period of rustication and the time during which Cambridge was closed down because of the plague (17 April 1630 through January 1631), Milton was at Christ's College from 1625 to 1632. His literary work of this period includes the seven Latin elegies, various other Latin verses, seven prolusions and some prose letters, *On the Death of a Fair Infant Dying of a Cough, At a Vacation Exercise, On the Morning of Christ's Nativity, The Passion, Song: On May Morning, On Shakespear,* the Hobson poems, the first six or seven sonnets (including thus the Italian poems), the *Epitaph on the Marchioness of Winchester,* and the companion poems. There may have been summer vacations, such as the Seventh Prolusion alludes to, in some country area, but the association of *L'Allegro* and *Il Penseroso* with a summer vacation demands a biographical context that may be non-existent and may also lead to misreading. The date of Sonnet 7 ('How soon hath time') has been variously placed in 1631, before graduation, and in 1632, after graduation. The dates offer differing psychological pictures of Milton in the poem.

During the years 1632 through 1638 Milton was at his parents' home, first in Hammersmith and then in Horton, in 'studious retirement', as he called it. He may have joined them because of their age and need of attention, which could not be supplied by his siblings. His sister Anne had been married to Edward Phillips, who died in 1631, leaving her with two children, Edward, born in 1630, and John, born in 1631. She married Thomas Agar in 1632, himself a widower with a young child. Milton's brother Christopher, not yet seventeen, was now a student at Christ's College. Alternatively, Milton may already have been disinclined to enter the ministry, particularly the kind of ministry that William Laud, the Archbishop of Canterbury, was demanding. In this studious retirement Milton pursued his studies according to the pattern laid out in the Seventh Prolusion, moving both chronologically and geographically through all matters of intellectual importance. By November 1637, we learn from a letter to Diodati, he had proceeded to 'the affairs of the Greeks as far as to the time when they ceased to be Greeks' and through 'the obscure business of the Italians under the Longobards, the Franks, and the Germans, to that time when liberty was granted them by Rudolph, King of Germany'. Further, Milton's decision not to pursue the ministry was now firm, as were his hopes for a poetic career.

The poetry Milton wrote during his Cambridge years has led many critics to conclude that he then already considered himself a poet by vocation; and his rejection of the ministry – his being 'church-outed' as he called it in *The Reason of Church-Government* – has been variously dated. However, it is probably more accurate to view his time of decision as coming near the end of his period of studious retirement, when Laud's actions would indeed have 'church-outed' one of Milton's ideals. We should in any case make a distinction between writing poetry, excellent though it may be, and writing poetry as one's career, life-work, bid to fame. These biographical matters are significant for the way one reads the works Milton produced during this period, including *Arcades*, now dated May 1634; *A Mask* (now popularly known as *Comus*), first performed in September 1634; the three English odes (*On Time, Upon the Circumcision,* and *At a Solemn Music*); *Lycidas*; and *Ad Patrem*. We would like to understand the relationship of each of these works to Milton's decision about his vocation. For example, are the texts of *Arcades* and *A Mask* that we now read the result of a vocational decision late in this period (that is, *reading* texts), or are they the texts presented in 1634 as performances? A similar question can be asked of *Lycidas*, dated November 1637; and both the interpretation and the dating of *Ad Patrem*, which has been placed variously from 1631 through 1638, depend upon questions of biography.

Milton's first published poem was *On Shakespear* in the Second Folio of Shakespeare's *Works* (1632); his second was *A Mask*, dated 1637 but more probably published in the first months of 1638; and his third was *Lycidas*, printed in a memorial volume for Edward King, the subject of the monody, called *Justa Edouardo King naufrago* (1638). The latter volume appeared after Milton had gone to the Continent.

During his time of studious retirement Milton also began what has become an important record of his writing activities. This 'Trinity Manuscript' (also known as the Cambridge Manuscript) is today in the Library of Trinity College, Cambridge. Daniel Skinner, Milton's last amanuensis, perhaps deposited it there in order to improve his chances of obtaining a fellowship. It was discovered in 1738 and reported extensively by Thomas Birch in his edition of Milton's prose works and in his revision of Pierre Bayle's dictionary (Volume VII, 576–88). The manuscript contains transcriptions of *Arcades*, the letter to an unidentified friend mentioned earlier (one draft includes Sonnet 7), *A Mask*, the three English odes, *Lycidas*, and later short English poems and plans and subjects for dramatic writing. It does not record foreign language poems or translations or long poems (other than the plans for what was to become *Paradise Lost*). *Arcades*, *A Mask*, and *Lycidas* show revisions made prior to 1638, and *At a Solemn Music* in the manuscript is not a transcription but a working out of the poem in various drafts. Most of the manuscript is in Milton's hand, and is clearly of major importance for any complete analysis of his style, prosody, imagery, and aesthetics.

On 3 April 1637, Milton's mother died in Horton, setting in motion events which would involve his moving away from home, travelling to France and Italy, and returning to London, where he would continue studying and writing and also begin tutoring. In his letter to Diodati of November 1637 he talks of perhaps moving to London and taking up residence at one of the Inns of Court. Whether he in fact did so is unknown, but the comment indicates an altered situation for him at home. It is speculated that his brother Christopher was married early in 1637 and that, although he was now a student at the Inner Temple, his wife and possibly infant son went to live with his father later in the same year, freeing John from the duty of caring for his parent. In any case, at least by the beginning of April 1638 Milton was able to plan a trip to the Continent, for which he consulted Sir Henry Wotton, former ambassador in Venice and now Provost of Eton College. Wotton's letter to him details places to visit and people to contact, and within the month Milton was off on his long-delayed *Wanderjahr*. He saw the trip as a means of being in touch directly with the cultures of which he had read; and we can well imagine the poet eagerly in search of new and vital ideas. Sometime during his studious retirement Milton had begun to keep what is known as the Commonplace Book, a compendium of references under Aristotelian divisions of ethics, economics, and political life. Here he records for possible future use some of the ideas that struck him as he read. Indeed, most of the entries find their way into his later prose works. Milton quotes or gives a summary or comment, almost always with exact references so that we can determine quite well which books and editions he was reading. And the Italian journey, as it is usually called, we can view as Milton's way of extending the studious explorations of his Commonplace Book into the realm of living history.

While some records have emerged from the trip, our knowledge of it is largely from Milton's own account in *Defensio secunda* (1654), written as a defence of himself against the personal attack by Peter Du Moulin in *Regii Sanguinis Clamor* (1652), itself a rebuttal of Milton's *Defensio prima* (that is, *Joannis Miltoni Angli Pro Populo Anglicano Defensio*, 1651). The translation of Milton's account by his nephew Edward Phillips in the life accompanying the translation of *Letters of State* (1694) is inaccurate but unfortunately employed by later writers on Milton. Milton visited Paris, Nice, Genoa, Leghorn, Pisa, Florence, Siena, Rome, Naples, Rome and Florence for a second time, Lucca, Bologna, Ferrara, Venice, Verona, Milan, Lake Leman, and Geneva. Most of his time was spent in Paris, Florence, Rome, Naples, Venice, and Geneva. In Paris he met Thomas Scudamore, King Charles's legate, and the famous Hugo Grotius, then Swedish ambassador to France; in Florence, he read his own poetry (apparently a Latin poem) at the Svogliati Academy and developed friendships with Jacopo Gaddi, Carlo Dati, Pietro Frescobaldi, Agostino Coltellini, Benedetto Buonmattei, Valerio Chimentelli, and Antonio Francini. Testimonies published with Milton's Latin poems in 1645 and personal letters from most of these Italian friends verify his statements. In Rome he met Lucas Holstenius, librarian at the Vatican, and probably Cardinal Francesco Barberini (whom he does not name). Here he spoke freely of religious matters, incurring anger from English Jesuits. But warnings of possible reprisals did not deter him from returning to Rome and continuing to defend, as he says, 'the orthodox religion'. In Naples he met Giambattista Manso, a well-regarded author and patron of Giambattista Marino and Torquato Tasso. During one of his stops in Florence, as Milton attests in *Areopagitica*, he also 'found and visited the famous Galileo, grown old, a prisoner to the Inquisition for thinking in astronomy otherwise than the Franciscan and Dominican licensers thought'. The visit reinforced Milton's dedication to the cause of his own nation's liberty. And Galileo indeed seems to have remained for Milton's imagination a type of the one who sees and reveals the true nature of things, such as the moon,

> whose orb
> Through optic glass the Tuscan artist views
> At evening from the top of Fesole,
> Or in Valdarno, to descry new lands,
> Rivers or mountains in her spotty globe.   (*PL* 1.287–91)

From the Italian peninsula Milton thought of proceeding to Sicily and Greece, which were obviously not on his original itinerary, but decided that would be merely personal, not in keeping with his educational aims, and thus frivolous, especially given the civil war in England, of which he had by now been informed. Phillips's inaccurate translation has led to other interpretations of Milton's actions.

In Venice he shipped home books he had collected in his travels, including works of music by such composers as Claudio Monteverdi. Venice was the port from which most English people returned to England, because of the embassy there, and it was also where mail was received. Whether it was here or elsewhere that he learned of the death of Charles Diodati, and possibly other news such as the death of his sister Anne, is debated. The evidence is that he learned of Diodati's death while abroad, and it was from Venice that he returned home by way of Geneva, where he saw Diodati's famous theologian uncle, Giovanni Diodati. We do not in fact know when Anne died. However, upon his return to London, Milton did not go to live at his father's home but instead took lodgings in St Bride's Churchyard for a few months, where his nephew John Phillips, Anne's son, very soon came to live with him. Shortly after this Milton moved to larger quarters in Aldersgate Street, where his nephew Edward, Anne's elder son, joined them. While abroad, Milton wrote a number of Latin poems that have been preserved: *Ad Salsillum poetam Romanum aegrotantem*, *Mansus*, *Ad Leonoram Romae canentem*, and two others to Leonora, entitled *Ad eandem*.

Milton began schoolteaching, it would seem, to provide for his nephews the kind of education he himself had had. Within a short time, however, he was taking in a few day students, continuing to do so through the 1640s, and tutoring sporadically even into the 1660s and 1670s. Among his students were Richard Barry (second Earl of Barrymore), William Davenant (son of Sir William), Thomas Ellwood, Richard Jones (third Viscount and first Earl of Ranelagh), and Cyriack Skinner. A record of the kind of programme presented to those who were with Milton in the 1640s is found in his *Of Education* (1644) and in Edward Phillips's account in the 'Life of Mr. John Milton' (1694). Other results from this tutoring period may include Milton's examinations of *Accedence Commenc't Grammar* (1669), *The History of Britain* (1670), *Artis Logicae Plenior Institutio* (1672), and *A Brief History of Moscovia* (1682). His nephews and some of his other students served as amanuenses, entering items in the Trinity Manuscript and in the Commonplace Book, and penning personal letters and documents for him. We know the names of only two other amanuenses: Jeremy Picard, who may be the 'Mr. Packer' noted by John Aubrey in his 'Minutes of Mr. John Milton's Life' as a student, and Daniel Skinner, who was no relation to Cyriack. Picard made entries in the Commonplace Book and the Trinity Manuscript, including the transcription of Sonnet 23, produced some personal documents, and probably wrote out the original manuscript of *De doctrina christiana*. Daniel Skinner was the autographer of the revised first part of *De doctrina christiana*, and seems to have acquired it along with copies of the state papers and the Trinity Manuscript upon Milton's death.

Soon after his return from the Continent, Milton became immersed in religious controversy on the side of those whose aim was to remove the bureaucracy of episcopacy from the church. His five antiprelatical tracts, already mentioned, brought his name before the public and brought down upon him the antagonism of the defenders of the church administration. Milton was later to cast these works as an attempt to bring liberty into ecclesiastical and religious life, and his next group of works, on divorce, he saw as an attempt to regain personal and domestic liberty. But at the time, his works on divorce caused him to be greeted generally by vilification and namecalling. *The Doctrine and Discipline of Divorce* (1643) was rewritten in 1644 to almost twice its previous length; *The Judgement of Martin Bucer* (1644) elicited the thoughts of a well-respected sixteenth-century German theologian on the side of divorce; and the twin tracts *Tetrachordon* and *Colasterion* (1645) took on opponents by arguing from interpretations of four texts in the Bible that divorce was not proscribed by God and by lampooning a weak critic of the first divorce tract with a 'scourge'. Milton's approaches in these works on church government and on divorce are usually historical and logical, although the logic sometimes plays upon the arts of rhetoric, and are sometimes vituperative. In the last two of the antiprelatical tracts, confessional statements of his own experiences and ideals provide a strong ploy that helps Milton to overcome antagonistic personal criticisms and to argue sympathetically for his ideals. However, neither group of writings seems to have caused the changes in fact or attitude that he hoped for; their effect was ephemeral, and after the end of the decade they left Milton only with the infamy of being a divorcer. *Of Education* and *Areopagitica*, written in 1644 in the midst of some of this controversy, received little immediate attention, although the former was to be important to John Locke and thence to eighteenth-century theories of education, and the latter was to be plagiarized in 1679 when questions of licensing again arose. *Areopagitica* also emerged as an important statement in the debates over censorship and liberty of the press in the eighteenth century. And yet few readers have seemed to understand that it argues against *pre*publication censorship, not for the full availability of all published or publishable matter.

With the strongly negative reaction to his views on divorce, Milton retreated to his own study more exclusively in 1645 through 1649. As well as attending to his teaching, to his own reading, and to other, personal matters, he was writing the four prose volumes already mentioned (*Britain* was not completed until later) and was engaged in planning other, poetic works. His schoolteaching in fact declined during these years, with students like Cyriack Skinner and Edward Phillips leaving sometime around mid 1647, though John Phillips remained until he reached his majority in 1652. Milton's first reaction to the discouraging reception of the divorce tracts was the sonnet 'I did but prompt the age'; and soon after that, the production of the first edition of his shorter poems, *Poems of Mr. John Milton, Both English and Latin Compos'd at several times,* entered in the Stationers' Register on 6 October 1645, and perhaps published in December of the same year. Included in it are all the known poems written by Milton to that date, except for the 'Fair Infant Elegy', which must have been mislaid and undiscovered until later (it is included in the 1673 second edition of the shorter poems); 'At a Vacation Exercise', probably because it was part of the sixth prose prolusion; 'Apologus de Rustico et Hero' (also published in 1673); and the few other Latin verses discovered in the nineteenth century with his Commonplace Book. 'I did but prompt' was not published in the collection probably because it was not written until about the time that copy was being prepared for the Stationers' Registry. The Latin poems have sometimes been separated and treated as a separate publication (which they are not) because there is a full title page for them.

Poetry that Milton composed during 1640–5 includes *Epitaphium Damonis,* Sonnets 8–10, and *In Effigiei Ejus Sculptorem,* a Greek epigram poking fun at William Marshall and his ludicrous portrait of Milton reproduced as the frontispiece of the 1645 *Poems.* Further, at this time Milton began to conceive the poem that was to become his masterwork. The outlines for what came to be *Paradise Lost* are entered in the Trinity Manuscript in late 1640 and early 1641, and Edward Phillips reported that he had read a section of Satan's apostrophe to the Sun in Book 4 around 1642. How much work Milton was able to accomplish on this drama, a morality type, we can only guess. Whether he was planning or writing any other dramas – the Trinity Manuscript contains short and long prose outlines for dramas on other biblical and historical subjects – we do not know. Poetry he composed during 1646–9 includes Sonnets 11–15, *On the Forcers of Conscience, Ad Joannem Rousium,* and translations of Psalms 80–8. (The date of the translation of the Fifth Ode from Horace has been argued anywhere from the 1620s through 1648.) Work may have been continued on 'Paradise Lost', and there have been speculations that early starts on *Samson Agonistes* and *Paradise Regain'd,* both as dramas, occurred during this period.

The 1640s also saw great alterations in Milton's personal life. In 1642 he married Mary Powell, the daughter of Richard Powell of Forest Hill, Oxfordshire, who was indebted to Milton's father. The occasion of Mary and John's meeting and marriage is unknown and confused. It would seem that Milton journeyed to Oxfordshire to collect payment on the debt for his father, stayed some while, and returned to London with his bride. Whether there had been preliminary discussions, whether this was an 'arranged' affair between the parents (and if so, whether that altered the indebtedness) are not known.

The wedding seems to have taken place in May of 1642, and the circumstances which Mary must then soon have faced could have offered little hope for an untroubled marriage. Milton was thirty-three and Mary was sixteen; she at once moved to London and became 'mother' to Edward Phillips, not quite twelve, and John Phillips, not quite eleven; and Milton, to add to her challenges, was a fairly settled and introverted person. Furthermore, he was inexperienced sexually, from all accounts, and the kind of person whom modern therapists might well consider in need of help. The fact that Mary's family was Royalist and living in Royalist Oxfordshire seems specious as a reason for difficulty in the marriage. A more probable inciter of cause seems to have been Mary's mother (as Mary herself is reputed to have claimed). Mrs Powell blamed Milton for the disruption. In any case, Mary returned to her family's home soon after the marriage, perhaps in July, and did not rejoin Milton until the summer of 1645, three years later. It is certainly possible that she originally intended merely a visit home and that the civil war (and her mother) created problems in effecting a return to London. We do not know whether reconciliation took place, or was even necessary. The difficulties of a sixteen-year-old's life with Milton and his two charges may have been cause enough for the continuance of the separation. Some talk occurred concerning the possibility of Milton's obtaining a divorce and remarrying, one candidate being a Miss Davis. John and Mary's three-year separation after only two months of living together hardly makes this an outrageous consideration. There is no validity, however, in the quip that Milton's wife left him and so he wrote in defence of divorce. For he had begun to explore the matter of divorce before his marriage, as the Commonplace Book shows, and in his tracts he nowhere offers desertion as a reason for divorce. His main argument revolves around incompatibility of the married couple, looked at from both points of view (a very modern approach). Incompatibility may have been at the root of the difficulty for Mary and John at the time, although such incompatibility eventually was overcome or else dissipated. Certainly, though, personal experience may have sharpened Milton's attitude toward divorce and caused him to focus more firmly on incompatibility as a let to both marriage partners' personal liberty.

With his father living with him (from 1643), in addition to his nephews, and with Mary returning to him in the summer of 1645, Milton soon moved to much larger quarters in the Barbican around September 1645. The next summer the Powells also moved in with them, and the Miltons' change of residence may have been in anticipation of that. Having his in-laws with him may have been part of the reconciliation. Or the move may have looked forward to their having a family, and the Powells' joining the household may have occurred specifically because of Mary's pregnancy. Daughter Anne was born on 29 July 1646. How many of the eleven Powell children were in the household is not known. Richard Powell died in December 1646, as noted before, and John Milton, Sr, in March 1647. Mrs Powell and her children were still there in mid 1647, but in autumn Milton moved to smaller quarters in High Holborn.

Whatever had been their marital difficulties in the past, there are no hints of disruption in Mary and John's married state henceforth. Their first child, Anne, was physically and perhaps mentally impaired; she seems to have been lame and sickly (spastic?) and mentally slow (retarded?). Their second child, Mary, was born on 25 October 1648; their third, John, on 16 March 1651 (though he died by 16 June 1652); and their last, Deborah, on 5 May 1652.

A second major alteration in Milton's life during the 1640s was the onset of blindness. Various causes have been argued over the years: detachment of the retina, a cyst or tumour, glaucoma. Stories have it that his eyesight was always weak (perhaps an inheritance from his mother) and yet that he abused his eyes by long hours of study, particularly by candlelight. The symptoms are best described in a letter to his friend Leonard Philaras, dated 28 September 1654, as information for Philaras to share with the well-known French eye-specialist François Thevenin ('Thevenot' in Milton's text). 'It is ten years, I think, more or less,' Milton writes,

since I felt my sight getting weak and dim, and at the same time my spleen; and all my viscera were oppressed and distressed by wind: in the morning, if I began, as usual, to read anything, I felt my eyes at once pained inwardly; I avoided reading, thereupon to be refreshed after moderate bodily exercise. When I looked at a candle, a kind of iris was seen to encircle it. Not very long after, a mist appearing in the left part of my left eye (for that eye became clouded some years before the other) was snatching away all objects which were lying on that side. Objects in front also, if I perhaps closed the right eye, seemed smaller. With the other eye also failing perceptibly and gradually through approximately three years, I observed, some months before because my sight was entirely decayed, that objects, though I myself was not moving, all seemed to swim, now to the right, now to the left. Inveterate mists now seem to have settled in my entire forehead and temples, which weigh me down and depress me the most with a kind of sleepy heaviness in the eyes, especially from mealtime continually to evening . . . But I should not omit that, while yet a little sight remained when first I lay down in bed, and turned myself to either side, there used to shine out an abundant light from my shut eyes; then, my sight growing less from day to day, colours, correspondingly duller, would burst out with force and a certain noise from within, but now, as if with clearness extinct, it is an unmixed blackness, or set apart, as if inwoven with an ashy colour, it is wont to pour itself forth. Yet the darkness which is perpetually to be seen, by night as well as by day, seems always nearer to a whitish than to a blackish, and when the eye rolls itself, there is admitted, as through a small chink, a certain little bit of light.   (Author's translation; see CM 12: 64–70)

We do not know Thevenin's diagnosis, if he did communicate one, but the account informs us that Milton's sight began to fail noticeably in autumn 1644, a time when antagonisms against his divorce tracts were surfacing, and also a time during which his wife was still away and he may have been considering divorce and remarriage. He lost sight in his left eye around 1650, a period beset with problems on account of his governmental position, and he was totally blind by February 1652, after personal attacks on his *Defensio prima*. His description in the letter should be compared with the claims made in Sonnet 22, in which he says his eyes are 'clear / To outward view of blemish or of spot'; in *Defensio secunda*, in which he wrote that his eyes 'have as much the appearance of being uninjured, and are as clear and bright, without a cloud, as the eyes of men who see most keenly' (p. 42); and in *Paradise Lost* 3.22–6, where his blindness is described in terms of 'a drop serene' (*gutta serena*, total blindness) and 'dim suffusion' (partial blindness). Milton's blindness may have been both physical and psychosomatic, a suprachiasmal cystic tumour aggravated by a condition of glaucoma, which flared up under stress (see Lambert Rogers, *Journal of the History of Medicine and Allied Sciences* 4 (1949), 468–71; and William B. Hunter, *ibid.* 17 (1962), 333–41).

With the victory of the Parliamentarians and the trial of Charles I in late 1648 and January 1649, Milton saw hope for political liberty for his country. He entered the antimonarchical argument with perhaps his most influential prose work, *The Tenure of Kings and Magistrates*, written while the King was under trial and just before sentence and execution. In it Milton does not specifically argue for regicide but does offer justification for such drastic measures. The work brought him to the attention of the Council of State being formed in February (when the first edition appeared). He was appointed Secretary for Foreign Tongues to the Council of State on 15 March 1649, a position requiring him to communicate with foreign powers through Latin letters and other documents, and to relay communication from foreign sources to the Council; to produce texts as occasion required on subjects of the Council's choosing; and, later, to act as licenser. Composing the state papers demanded little originality; often it became the reduction of ideas to Latin or simply the translation into Latin of an English text written by someone else. But Milton himself did author three commissioned works. *Eikonoklastes* (1649) attempted to stem the popular sentiment raised for the King by *Eikon Basilike*, allegedly written by the King while in prison but actually by his chaplain John Gauden with sections by Bishop Brian Duppa and based in part on some authentic writings by Charles. Included as one of the King's prayers was Pamela's prayer from Sidney's *Arcadia*; Milton's pointing out this forgery redounded in later years on him when he was accused of having had the prayer inserted in order to accuse Charles of forgery. *Observations on the Articles of Peace* (1650), the second commissioned work, was produced to expose Charles's and the Earl of Ormond's duplicity in the Articles of Peace with the Irish.

The third commissioned work became the talk of Europe (a fact with which Milton solaced himself in Sonnet 22) and spawned a series of counter-attacks and rebuttals. To present the Council of State's case against the monarchy and to correct statements and attitudes fostered by Claude Saumaise's *Defensio regia pro Carolo I* (1649), Milton over a two-year period (1650–1) wrote *Defensio prima*. The ensuing Salmasian controversy centred on personal matters as much as political convictions for or against Charles and for or against regicide. Among published reactions were John Rowland's *Pro Rege et Populo Anglicano Apologia* (1651), Claude Barthelemy Morisot's *Carolus I. Britanniarum Rex* (1652), Du Moulin's tract already cited (1652), Sir Robert Filmer's *Observations Concerning the Original of Government* (1652), Rowland's *Polemica sive Supplementum Ad Apologiam Pro Rege et Populo Anglicano* (1653), and various German examinations of the issues, by Christian Woldenberg (1651), Nahum Bensen (1651), Caspar Ziegler (1652), Jacob Schaller (1652), Erhard Kieffer (1652), and Martin Zeiller (1653). In response to Rowland's first anonymous work, Milton's nephew John published *Joannis Philippi Angli Responsio Ad Apologiam Anonymi Cujusdam Tenebrionis Pro Rege et Populo Anglicano infantissimam* (1652), apparently with much help from his uncle. At the time, Milton was ill and virtually blind, and so did not answer himself. He construed Du Moulin's work as being that of Alexander More (he probably knew differently but More had written and signed the dedication) and rebutted it with *Defensio secunda* (May 1654). Whether he was aware of all the other works on the subject, we do not know. More in turn answered with *Alexandri Mori Ecclesiastae et Sacrarum Litterarum Professoris Fides Publica, Contra Calumnias Ioannis Miltoni* (1654), which brought forth Milton's *Defensio pro Se* (1655) and then More's *Supplementum* (1655). *Defensio pro Se*, not published until August, includes at its end 'An Answer' to More's 'Supplement', which had appeared in April, after Milton had written his basic defence. Saumaise's reaction, *Ad Ioannem Miltonum Responsio, Opus Posthumum, Claudii Salmasii* (1660), was edited by his son. All of the works were written in Latin to reach a wide European audience. Milton defends both the Commonwealth and himself and argues again against monarchy, while his opponents defend Charles and monarchy and often charge Milton with dissolute character and life, his blindness thus being seen as punishment from a just God.

Understandably, blindness reduced Milton's position to what has been popularly, although not officially, called 'Latin Secretary'. He received assistance in his work; gradually he seems to have done less and less translation, and no commissioned work. He remained in his secretarial position under Richard Cromwell, after Oliver's death on 3 September 1658, and until at least 22 October 1659. From early 1659 onward the clear trend toward a restoration of the monarchy moved Milton to try to influence the monarchic settlement in some way. It is unlikely that he thought he could deter that settlement. What he published in 1659–60 should therefore be read in context, not as indicating philosophically ideal beliefs: *A Treatise of Civil Power* (1659), *A Letter to a Friend, Concerning the Ruptures of the Commonwealth* (1659; published 1698), 'Proposalls of certaine expedients for the preventing of a civill war now feard, & the settling of a firme government' (1659; published 1938), *The Ready and Easy Way to Establish a Free Commonwealth* (1660), *The Present Means, and brief Delineation of a Free Commonwealth* (1660; published 1698), and *Brief Notes on a Late Sermon* (1660). The emphasis in a reading of *The Ready and Easy Way* should surely be on *ready* and *easy*, not on any supposed 'ideal' free commonwealth Milton was proposing. Despite some printed reactions to the published works, these tracts had no discernible impact, although it has been cogently argued that they and Milton's governmental ideas generally (but in particular those in *The Tenure of Kings and Magistrates*) were instrumental in formulating Whig theories and programmes in the ensuing years, influencing most significantly the settlement of 1688. Milton's other tract of the period, *Considerations Touching the Likeliest Means to Remove Hirelings Out of the Church* (1659), provides the promised second volume to join *A Treatise of Civil Power*, though it is more likely an earlier work and does not really complement *A Treatise*. It is, however, an important volume historically, being concerned with tithing and with the remuneration of the ministry, issues that reared up frequently in the next century and a half, often with Milton's tract republished as part of the argument.

Eikonoklastes and *Defensio prima* had been publicly banned and burned in

Europe in 1651–2, and in 1660 King Charles II similarly ordered them banned and burned. It is no wonder then that following the Restoration some sentiment was antagonistic toward Milton, though he was not named in the Act of Oblivion (29 August 1660) and thus should have needed to fear no reprisals. An order to apprehend him had, however, been given, which in the confusion of the times seems to have been forgotten, and then enforced (perhaps in error). Milton had gone into hiding, staying with his friend Edward Millington, the bookseller. Later, around October, when the perhaps outdated order was finally acted on, he was imprisoned through 15 December. His release was effected by various friends, Andrew Marvell and Sir William Davenant among them, by payment of a small fine, an action Milton seems to have tried to resist.

This decade clearly, like the previous one, was not always happy. In addition to the onset of his blindness, his ill health, and the controversial issues in which he was embroiled, Milton had to bear the loss of his wife a few days after she gave birth to their daughter Deborah on 5 May 1652; and, as previously noted, his son too died shortly thereafter, in June 1652. On 12 November 1656 Milton married his second wife, Katherine Woodcock, who gave birth to a daughter, Katherine, on 19 October 1657. But tragedy again struck, his wife dying on 3 February, and their daughter on 17 March, of 1658. From June 1652 to November 1656, therefore, Milton lived alone with his three young daughters (his nephew John having left in early 1652), and so he did again from March 1658 to February 1663, when he married for a third time. Relatives and friends, and probably mainly a servant or two, sustained him during these troublesome years.

Aside from his prose writings and the edition, in 1658, of a work allegedly by Sir Walter Ralegh entitled *The Cabinet Council* (discovered among his manuscripts, perhaps from a period when he was beginning to think once more about writing 'Paradise Lost'), Milton composed the remainder of his shorter poems: Sonnets 16–23 and the translations of Psalms 1–8. The Psalms, translated in August 1653, a period reflecting relatively little governmental work and no writing of his own, have been prosodically linked with metrical experiments in the epic. They may accordingly indicate an earlier return to 'Paradise Lost', put aside again as controversy intervened.

After the troublesome years of the 1650s, we can well understand Milton's semi-retirement and devotion to completion of former projects. Paramount, of course, was the great epic, which may have been worked on in null periods in the years immediately preceding, and which Milton seems to allude to in a postscript to the slightly revised 1658 edition of *Defensio prima*: 'I am earnestly seeking how best I may show not only my own country, to which I devoted all I have, but men of every land and, particularly, all Christian men, that for their sake I am at this time hoping and planning still greater things, if these be possible for me, as with God's help they will' (YP 4:537). The shift from drama to epic may also have occurred around this time. In any case, as the rigours of 1660 died away Milton returned to finish and polish *Paradise Lost*, which was completed as we know it by mid 1665, when his friend and former student Thomas Ellwood reports having read it. The visitation of the plague in London in 1665 caused Milton, through the offices of Ellwood, to move his family to the cottage at Chalfont St Giles, the only Milton residence still standing. The ensuing great fire kept the Miltons in Buckinghamshire until February 1666. After the fire, the difficulty which presses had in reviving caused a delay in the publication of Milton's epic, and it did not appear until August (?) 1667.

Paradise Lost did not sell well for perhaps a number of reasons: its length, its subject, its blank verse, its narrative difficulty; the recovery of the times which was still going on; the generally altered literary climate during a time when Sir John Denham's *Directions to a Painter* and John Dryden's *Annus Mirabilis* and *The Indian Emperour* were more to the public's liking. *Paradise Lost* was reissued with a new title page (intended to help sales by implying a new edition) in 1667, and then again in 1668. In 1668 there was yet another reissue, but now with outdated prose synopses added to assist in the reading of this complex poem, and with a statement on the verse, in response to Dryden's *Essay on Dramatic Poesy*, published a year earlier. But still it did not sell well, and two additional issues appeared in 1669. A second edition altering the 'strange' ten-book form into a 'standard' twelve-book form was published in 1674; but it too failed to make any great impression, and had to be reissued the very next year. Indeed, it was not until 1688 when a magnificent fourth edition was produced that Milton's poetic star began to rise. This edition in three simultaneous issues with differing title pages, and on regular paper and large paper, some copies having gilt edges, made *Paradise Lost* the first English poem published by subscription and also the first to be published with illustrations (by John Baptista de Medina, Henry Aldrich, and Bernard Lens).

With the completion of *Paradise Lost* and its publication, Milton seems to have gone back and looked over his various manuscripts, publishing the early *Accedence Commenc't Grammar* in 1669, *The History of Britain* in 1670, and *Artis Logicae Plenior Institutio* in 1672. Perhaps at this same time he discovered the few additional early items published in the second edition of the minor poems in 1673, which gathered together all the known minor poems with the exception of four 'political' Sonnets (Nos. 15, 16, 17, 22, published later in garbled versions in Phillips's 1694 *Letters of State*). Added also was a second edition of the *Tractate of Education*. Other early items to appear in the 1670s or posthumously were *Epistolarum Familiarium Liber Unus* (1674; with seven college prolusions); *Mr. John Miltons Character of the Long Parliament* (1681; a section excised from *The History of Britain* either for political or aesthetic reasons); and *A Brief History of Moscovia* (1682). *De doctrina christiana* (1825) was still being worked up up until his death in 1674.

Arguments have been advanced for the revision during the 1660s of Milton's other two major poems, *Paradise Regain'd* and *Samson Agonistes*, published together in 1671, and it is possible that their earlier manuscript forms, if indeed there was any prior composition, were discovered along with the items just listed. The traditional dates of composition of the two works are 1665?–70, when the manuscript was ready for licensing. The only other 'new' compositions during this period were *Of True Religion, Haeresie, Schism, Toleration* (written and published in 1673) and *A Declaration, or Letters Patents* (really a translation of the Latin report of the election of John Sobieski as King of Poland in 1674). These last ten years of Milton's life, therefore, were largely a putting things in order and a looking back and saying 'I devoted all I have', and I have indeed achieved 'still greater things'.

During his years following governmental service, Milton was visited by various foreign dignitaries and by various friends and relatives, but with decreasing frequency. The picture is of a blind man, ill with recurrent gout, generally undisturbed by much outside activity, particularly after about 1667, with a few students, amanuenses, or family members reading to him and taking dictation. From all accounts, one of the joys of the period arose from his third marriage, on 24 February 1663, to Elizabeth Minshull, whom he met through her relative and his physician, Dr Nathan Paget. She was perhaps more housekeeper and governess than wife, but what reports are available all point to a fond and happy relationship between them. Difficulties of inheritance after Milton's death suggest that there were strains between his daughters and their stepmother, though antagonism toward her and toward him seems to have come mainly from the middle daughter, Mary. Milton had schooled both Mary and Deborah in reading and languages, and probably in other subjects as well; we know that both younger daughters knew languages in addition to English and that they read to their father. Anne, it seems, was illiterate. There is no substance, however, to the snide story that Milton forced his daughters to be his amanuenses for *Paradise Lost*. The manuscript of the first book, now in the J. Pierpont Morgan Library in New York City, is in the hand of an amanuensis, who made entries in the Commonplace Book fifteen years earlier. Perhaps part of the child/parent difficulty existed because of strictures placed by Milton on his children, though the presence of a stepparent alone often can cause friction; and Mary, who was twenty in 1668, may simply have shared the spirit of independence that characterizes so many of that age. Further, Deborah by all accounts was the favourite daughter, or maybe that is only how a middle child naturally perceives the youngest. All three daughters, in any case, left Milton's household by 1669 and seem not to have visited thereafter. All three had been taught a trade (the making of gold and silver lace or embroidery, a 'sexist' though commonplace occupation for a middle-class girl). References to Milton's talking of his unkind children and of their lack of duty toward him certainly do reflect some kind of strain in their relationship during the last ten years of his life.

Milton's death, probably caused by heart failure brought on by various other ills such as the gout, occurred after he had retired for the night on Sunday, 8 November 1674. He was buried on Thursday, 12 November, in St Giles, Cripplegate.

Reading list

Clark, Donald L., *John Milton at St. Paul's School* (New York, 1948; rpt. Hamden, 1964)

Darbishire, Helen, ed., *The Early Lives of Milton* (London, 1932; rpt. 1966)

Dorian, Donald C., *The English Diodatis* (New Brunswick, NJ, 1950)

Fletcher, Harris F., *The Intellectual Development of John Milton*, 2 vols. (Urbana, 1956–62)

French, J. Milton, compiler, *The Life Records of John Milton*, 5 vols. (New Brunswick, NJ, 1949–56; rpt. Stapleton, NY, 1966)

Masson, David, *The Life of John Milton*, 7 vols. (London, 1881–94; rpt. New York, 1946)

Parker, William Riley, *Milton: A Biography*, 2 vols. (Oxford, 1968)

2 *Comus*

Not the least of critical problems with *Comus* is what to call it. It is not properly called *Comus*, because Milton originally gave it the generic name *A Mask presented at Ludlow Castle, 1634*. When John Dalton rewrote the masque as an opera in 1738, he changed the name to that of its principal character and the name stuck, though calling *Comus* '*Comus*' may be tantamount to calling *Paradise Lost* '*Satan*'. Modern editors and critics would rather call the masque *A Mask*, but they are all forced by popular usage to call it *Comus*, if they want to be understood by a general audience.

Even if Milton did not want *Comus* to be his title, the name of his magician has an evocative etymology, one which he certainly wanted spectators or readers of his masque to use as a key to interpreting its central character. The Greek word *komoi* meant 'a revel' and was at least a cognate of the root of the word 'comedy'. For Reformation theologians the Greek word also has associations with sinfully gluttonous feasts.

The masque form was well known to aristocratic audiences of the first quarter of the seventeenth century. Masques were popular at the court of Charles I and his Queen, Henrietta Maria, they were performed for potential lawyers at the Inns of Court in London, they were underwritten by such wealthy or influential public figures as Sir Francis Bacon, and they were a major source of private and public entertainment at the country houses of the nobility. Before Milton's *Comus* became famous, the best-known writer of masques was Ben Jonson, although Shakespeare incorporated masque elements into *The Tempest*, *The Merchant of Venice*, and *Love's Labour's Lost*. Under Jonson and his co-worker and occasional rival, the architect and stage-designer Inigo Jones, the genre of masques became artful: at their worst merely ingenious, lewd (Ben Jonson's version of Comus was fat and nude on stage), and clever, and at best artistic and high-minded. The most high-minded masques were designed, like Milton's, to improve the morals of the audience.

Another ideal of the masque genre was to create beauty on stage, to combine the talents of painter, poet, and musician in a philosophical drama that would demonstrate world order and universal harmony. Plato was the philosopher of choice, lending the notion of musical harmony philosophical respectability. In practice, masques cost a great deal and flaunted the wealth of their patrons, and their authors usually flattered those patrons; masques were criticized for flattery and extravagance even in their own era.

A masque scheduled for only one performance would normally be considered ephemeral, topical, or occasional. Milton was probably the only poet ever to think of masque as a genre that could be used exclusively for high moral instruction, and to write a work of art meant more for eternity than for one occasion. Nevertheless, his commission was to write a masque for one performance only, on the Welsh border in Ludlow, on Michaelmas Night in 1634.

Though the performance itself was not reported on in what would today be called the local media, the text has been preserved in different versions. Apparently desiring to save all the states of his own early compositions, Milton kept the Trinity Manuscript version of *Comus* (so-called because the manuscript was donated to Trinity College, Cambridge), even though in its final corrected state it was not the version of the masque used by the printer to set type for the 1637 or 1645 printed texts. Milton apparently added to the manuscript *after* a printer had used it to set type with.

Another manuscript version, called the Bridgewater Manuscript because it is preserved at Bridgewater House, was apparently made without Milton's supervision. Some passages are mysteriously deleted, and the deletions may have been requested by the Bridgewater family for the original performance.

The masque was printed thrice during Milton's lifetime: anonymously but with the endorsement of Henry Lawes in 1637; as part of Milton's collected poetry in 1645; and again, with a few minor emendations, in 1673. Editors use one or the other of the printed versions to base a modern text on, but modern 'complete poetry' editions will at least print in notes the significant variants from the manuscript versions.

Written for the installation of the Lord President of Wales, *Comus* is at the same time an occasional piece designed for family entertainment and a state masque. The masque was written under the patronage of John, Earl of Bridgewater, and it was written for three of his children to perform in. Since its patron was an important man being installed in an important public office, the first performance of the masque was also a state occasion. The 1634 Ludlow performance of *A Mask* was for townspeople as well as for the Bridgewater family, and it used elaborate costuming and sophisticated stage machinery. Henry Lawes, the well-known court musician who was also music master for the Bridgewater family, was commissioned to write songs for the masque, and his musician brother William Lawes was probably employed to help compose music and possibly to perform in Milton's masque.

The Earl of Bridgewater, who commissioned the masque, was a member of King Charles I's Privy Council and was by all accounts a humane man: at home he seems to have been a good and liberal husband and father, and at work a fair-minded, independent, and honest administrator and magistrate. His family was cultured: the Earl employed excellent musicians and painters; his wife purchased first editions of George Herbert's work; and the children were quite used to performing in grand theatricals, even at the court of Charles I and Henrietta Maria. There is no evidence that the first performance of *Comus* was not taken seriously by the Bridgewater family, since such a masque would have been expensive to produce and there was nothing in the masque which did not dignify the family.

Though masques were usually performed once only and then forgotten, or printed only if the author had an established reputation, *Comus* became well enough known in manuscript for Henry Lawes to want it to appear in print, to save himself (he said) the labour of copying it over by hand. The Bridgewater family must have thought highly enough of it to allow it to be printed with a dedication to them.

Despite the apparent endorsement of the Bridgewater family, there has been a slight smell of public scandal around the masque. A year or so before the first performance of *Comus*, two of the Bridgewater children who were to act in it had been diagnosed by a reputable physician who was also a relative of the Bridgewaters as having been bewitched by a disgruntled family servant. (Seventeenth-century physicians as a matter of course took horoscopes and tested for demonic possession, as well as seeking physical causes, for mental or physical disease.) While it is tantalizing to believe that *Comus*, the story of black magic being rendered ineffectual, might have been occasioned by a family problem, there is no direct evidence in the masque itself that Milton believed that members of the Bridgewater family had been in danger of demonic possession.

Several years before *Comus* was produced, Lady Bridgewater's sister was guiltlessly involved in an infamous scandal of sexual misconduct involving sodomy, rape, and incest. This nationally publicized scandal, which focused on the behaviour of the Earl of Castlehaven, Mervin Touchet, and his wife, the sister of the Countess of Bridgewater, may possibly have had something to do with Milton's writing a masque on the theme of chastity, but again there is no conclusive evidence in the masque itself that would show that Milton was writing it to expiate a family guilt, or to exonerate the family from the scandal.

Ludlow, on the Welsh border, had a reputation even in the 1630s as a rowdy border town. Richard Baxter, who left Ludlow to become one of the most famous spokesmen of the Puritan movement, complained that so much time in Ludlow was wasted 'dancing under a maypole . . . where all the town did meet together' that he and his father 'could not read the Scripture in our family without the great disturbance of the tabor and pipe and noise in the street' (*The Autobiography of Richard Baxter*, abridged by J. M. Lloyd Thomas, ed. N. H. Keeble (London, 1974), 6).

We cannot prove that Milton was satirizing rowdy or dissolute Ludlow citizens in his 'oughly-headed monsters'. We do not know if Milton knew the Bridgewater family well, or even if he ever went to Ludlow or ever saw a performance of his masque. Therefore any topical references that may be in the masque – as with those to Sabrina as goddess of the Severn River – could be taken generically to refer to a Welsh border that existed in Milton's mind or in the books he read, rather than one that he had observed in person.

Topical references may be less important to understanding Milton's intentions than are the political positions or theological doctrines buried in this most moral of masques. *Comus* has been described as a 'Puritan masque', since it seems to contain at least oblique references to the Puritan mistrust of rowdy popular games, together with other references to empty and wasteful displays of luxury and even to unequal distribution of wealth. It is possible to read the masque as incipiently puritan in its religious or political sympathies, but such a reading must be tendered very cautiously, for in 1634 'Puritan' and 'Roundhead' camps were not fully formed nor even well-defined.

Politically speaking, Milton had been operating very close to the heart of the court itself when writing his *Arcades* for the well-connected Countess Dowager of Derby (*Arcades* is usually dated in 1633, the year before *Comus*) and he was again behaving like a Royalist when he wrote *Comus* for the Earl of Bridgewater, a member of Charles's Privy Council. Milton's collaborator Henry Lawes was a member of the King's Chapel, in effect a sometime court musician. Hence Milton, in writing the masque, was honouring a loyal and close servant of the King who in turn was patronizing him and his friend Henry Lawes.

Scholars studying the Earl's papers preserved in the Huntington Library in California have recently come to believe that the Earl was close to Milton's and the Puritan position in his resistance to the legal power of Archbishop Laud's ecclesiastical court system, but again it is difficult to prove that the Earl or John Milton were allied in subversive activity against the King or the bishops, at least not in 1634. The separation of church and state courts, however, came to be a hotly debated issue in England on the eve of the Revolution. It should be stressed, though it may seem trivial today, that dancing around a maypole, or visiting a water-well supposed to have connections with an ancient saint, or bowing toward the cross before entering one's pew in church were all potentially subversive and dangerous acts in Milton's day.

Though it does not have to be read politically, Milton's masque must be read theologically, especially because it interprets or glosses one of the most resonant phrases in the New Testament, 'faith, hope and charity' from 1 Corinthians 13, by substituting *chastity* for *charity*. A masque celebrating chastity in a fifteen-year-old girl would not seem such a literary curiosity in the seventeenth century as it might today. Milton was to define chastity as a state of purity that could exist either before marriage or within the state of matrimony (Milton in 1642 could use a phrase like 'the honour and chastity of Virgin or Matron' (YP 1: 891) with no apparent fear of contradicting himself).

The word *chastity*, loosely allied etymologically with words meaning civic care, charity, and domestic mutual support, would be extremely evocative amongst emerging Puritans. A female born to a Puritan family living in England in the 1640s might have been named Chastity, just as the children of Shakers, Ranters, or Quakers in England or America might later be named Prudence, Faith, or Hope. Those who wrote masques or public entertainments before Milton did occasionally personify virtues and vices (Envy was pictured as having snaky hair like Medusa) or even Virtue itself, but Chastity would have been a rare choice as the subject of an aristocratic public entertainment. Milton's choice of chastity as a theme does seem to indicate his religious and political leaning.

If political and theological tensions seem to be buried in the masque, they are complemented by generic tensions as well. The masque genre had most often been used to glorify established nobility or kingship, as in Aurelian Townshend's *Tempe Restored*, written for Charles and Henrietta Maria shortly before *Comus* was written for the Bridgewaters, but Milton seems to have used the masque genre for quite different purposes, which include such a comparatively rare, if not unprecedented, feature as a high-minded debate over the potential for good or evil in the earth's fecundity. To put it simply, Milton's characters, from Sabrina to Comus himself, strain the genre with their moral immensity. The threat of Satanic evil in the character of Comus is not characteristic of the masque genre: it is too dangerous and threatening. Jacobean masques written for the King and Queen have been discovered to contain satirical or reformist messages between their lines, but still there are no other masques quite like Milton's, and it is most probable that he was trying to do things that no poet, not even Jonson, had done with the frothy medium before.

Both in its genre and in its language, however, *Comus* is distinctively English. Even by 1634 Milton had high hopes for his literary career in his own country. He knew that he was part of a living tradition of distinguished English literature, since he was quite well acquainted with the works of Spenser, Shakespeare, and Jonson, and he respected Chaucer. In 1632 he had published his poem to the memory of Shakespeare in the Second Folio, and he had mentioned Shakespeare and Jonson by name in *L'Allegro*, as well as alluding to Chaucer's Chaunticleer. Milton is directly inspired in *Comus* by the heroic and sensuously beautiful poetry of Spenser's *Faerie Queene*, by Michael Drayton's poetic glorification of England in *Polyolbion* (1612), by Shakespeare's tender and evocative English comedy, which preserves the richness and magic of rural life, as in *A Midsummer Night's Dream*, by Sidney's English pastoral in *Arcadia* (Milton used a 1633 edition), and by Ben Jonson's poetic emulation of classical models and his moral control of pagan values in both his spare lyrics and his masques. Yet Milton builds on all the best of English poetry without abating his own creative force. He is not an imitator but an emulator.

While honouring English sources by emulation and continuing to take pride in being (as he signed himself on the Continent in 1639) 'John Milton, Englishman', Milton was far from being aggressively nationalistic, and he was well aware that the masque was, in his own era, an Italianate form. The first known English masque, performed for Henry VIII, was a conscious imitation of an existing Italian drama, and Jonson's collaborator Inigo Jones learned much about Italian stage-design while travelling and sketching in Italy.

Milton was even more aware, since he was as well informed musically as any poet of his generation, that his masque contained the seeds of a new art form, which would come to be known as opera. In 1608, the first great Italian opera, Monteverdi's *Orfeo*, was performed in Venice. Because Milton's father was a composer of vocal music and an associate of English composers such as Giovanni Coperario (John Cooper) who imitated current Italian fashions in music, the younger John Milton was quite up to date in his international knowledge about the masque genre, or what in Italian was called the *dramma per musica*. Henry Lawes emulated Italian music in his own settings of English songs, though occasionally growing tired of doing so, even to the point of making fun of the fashion by setting to music a meaningless Italian list. There may be more original music designed for *Comus* than has come down to us, but what we do have, in several different printed versions, are songs for the Lady, the Attendant Spirit, and Sabrina, all written by Henry Lawes. The vocal line of all the songs is monophonic and rhythmically simple, the songs not especially difficult to sing. Probably neither of the actresses who first played the Lady and Sabrina had received extensive vocal training, yet like the arias of Monteverdi, Henry Lawes's airs emphasize the poet's words – a characteristic which Milton expressed admiration for in his 1645 Sonnet 13, 'To Mr H. Lawes, on his Airs'. There he called Lawes 'Harry whose tuneful and well-measured song / First taught our English how to span / Words with just note and accent.'

Since he was as well versed in Italian poetry as he was in music, Milton emulated Spenser's favourite Italian poet, Ludovico Ariosto, whose fantastic heroic romance *Orlando Furioso* had been translated by Sir John Harington and published in 1591; and he was sensitive to Torquato Tasso's use of heroic poetry in *Jerusalem Delivered* (1580; translated by Milton's family friend Thomas Fairfax in 1600) to defend theological positions. However, the motif of the dark and dangerous enchanted wood is developed not only in the romantic epics of Ariosto and Tasso but in Dante's *Inferno* as well.

Milton was well trained too in the British academic tradition of translating and emulating Latin and Greek poetry. He had both of Homer's epics virtually by heart, and he took the character of Comus's mother Circe from the *Odyssey*, darkening the implications of her sorcery with Christian gloom. He likewise remembered his Ovid, from whom he borrowed the great theme of metamorphosis. If the character of Comus is like that of his mother Circe, then the Lady's character is like that of Odysseus, but only when he is strong enough to resist Circe's temptations. As Milton presents it, the genealogy of Comus is Ovidian, and his perverse character Comus is like Ovid's unpredictable and dangerous Bacchus, who causes the unbeliever Pentheus to be torn to shreds for doubting his power (*Metamorphoses* III). As a seventeenth-century Christian, Milton denied the validity of 'pagan' myths by turning Roman gods like Bacchus into demonic figures, what he was later to call 'Devils to adore for deities' (*PL* 1.373). Likewise, Circe is allied with Hecate, the Roman goddess associated by Christians with witchcraft.

The themes, the plot, and the style of *Comus* fit closely with Milton's other youthful pieces. The masque is as lyrical and lush in its imagery as the

Nativity Ode. It confronts a similar theme: the death of false pagan values when they are opposed by Christian virtues. The cessation of the oracles in the Nativity Ode becomes the defeat of Comus in the masque, and the imagery of the two works is closely allied because of the parallel pagan and Christian themes.

The masque can be compared with *Lycidas*, though it is not so abrasively or obviously political. *Lycidas* is much more of a radical political statement. There is nothing in *Comus* resembling the elegy's bitter allusions to negligent Anglican clergy or to innocent flocks of English parishioners being devoured by subversive Catholic wolves, but it may contain the seeds of Milton's reactions to royal or ecclesiastical prerogative. The character of Lycidas is remarkably similar to that of the Attendant Spirit/Thyrsis in *Comus*. Both shepherds resemble the prototype of the shepherd-singer, Orpheus.

Comus is as unashamed of its pastoralism, and as sensitive to English rural life, as are *L'Allegro* and *Il Penseroso*. The language of the twin poems in its exuberance and its appreciation of the pastoral and the georgic modes is close to the language of the Attendant Spirit when he describes the natural world; the rural English landscape is colourful, vital, and good, and the labours practised there are useful and instructive.

The themes of *Comus* can be easily compared with those of Milton's other mature works in poetry. Like *Paradise Lost*, *Comus* is concerned both with the process of temptation and with the power of evil to corrupt innocence. As a character, Comus is obviously the spiritual ancestor of Satan, though he may also be allied with other dissolute fallen angels, like Belial, who tempt by their sensuality and their subtle intellect. The character should probably be pictured not as Ben Jonson saw him, a 'fat Bacchus', but rather as an attractive man, perhaps like Satan disguised as a stripling cherub in *Paradise Lost* 3.636. Though Comus traditionally was god of mirth, he is not the 'heart-easing mirth' of *L'Allegro*. Rather he is a sinister and demonic mirth, if indeed Milton associated him with mirth at all.

Like *Paradise Regained* and *Samson Agonistes*, *Comus* has as one of its major themes the passive resistance of good people to evil ideas, and like all of Milton's major works it focuses on the process of temptation. As a character, the Lady is an obvious ancestor of Jesus in *Paradise Regained*; both are fixed in one spot and tempted passively. Samson, physically in a similar situation, has fallen before *Samson Agonistes* begins, but he too resists the various forms of temptation paraded before him.

The plot of the masque was influenced by Milton's recently completed education at Cambridge (he took his MA in 1632) in that it is structured in the form of a series of academic debates between several representatives of virtue and one representative of vice. The classical art form it seems closest to is the Platonic debate, and its principal personages – the Lady, Comus, and the two brothers – are all distinguished by their ability to debate well and to use the devices of rhetoric skilfully. There is no great amount of suspense in the plot of the masque, because the Lady's strength of character is never in doubt.

The plot employs a *dea ex machina*, Sabrina, who is the goddess of the river which borders Wales, the Severn, to help break the immobilizing spell which has been imposed on the Lady, yet the Lady's mind, unlike her body, is free to resist evil unaided. The Lady has no tragic flaw; the only time she is 'wrong' is when she is temporarily deceived by Comus's hypocritical disguise as a friendly villager – as anyone in the audience might have been – though as soon as she discovers his true identity as a necromancer she is as strong as Milton's Jesus in *Paradise Regained* in saying the equivalent of 'Get thee behind me, Satan.'

The poetic style of *Comus* is youthful, skilful, and exuberant. It is the poetry of a young and joyful virtuoso just discovering the power and the music of his poetry. Milton as always takes himself very seriously as prophetic poet in touch with divine forces of harmony, but he also knows the power of good poetry to influence its listeners or readers, as when Orpheus made stones weep or sang Eurydice out of Hades, and he knows, as did the Shakespeare of the sonnets, the power of poetry to confer immortality on the poet.

Milton was later to define good poetry as being 'simple, sensuous and passionate' (YP 2: 403); the poetry of *Comus* embodies all three qualities: it is direct and easily understood, it is as sensuous as the poetry of Shakespeare or Marlowe (there are no senses its images do not explore), and it is passionately full of the beliefs of the young poet, including what may have been his devotion to an ideal of chastity and an ascetic life for himself. Milton may well have identified with the Attendant Spirit, played by his friend Henry Lawes, as the embodiment of the prophetic singer, the descendant of Homer, but he also seems to identify with the Lady, who is both a singer and the embodiment of ideal chastity. Whenever the Attendant Spirit or the Lady speak, we are in the realm of good language. Good language may be complex and logical, but never is it cryptic or perverse.

The imagery, the colour, and the music of Comus's language, on the other hand, all give away its intent to corrupt, because they are too rich, or over-ripe; his language itself is seductive and evil:

> Meanwhile, welcome joy, and feast,
> Midnight shout, and revelry,
> Tipsy dance, and jollity.
> Braid your locks with rosy twine
> Dropping odours, dropping wine.   (102–6)

Such language is perverse in its imagery as well as its logic. A phrase like 'What hath night to do with sleep?' (122) is *logically* evil, suggesting that night-time, during which all creatures feel the natural need for sleep, should be perverted to become a time of feverish activity, licentiousness, and abandon. Comus's language evokes all the excesses of the least inhibited poetry of Rome or Greece: he worships Hecate or Cotytto, and, like some of the depraved creatures of Juvenal or Martial, he is a dipsomaniac. Like Shakespeare's Caliban, Comus is an unnatural creature born of witchery and darkness, but unlike Caliban he is an eloquent and seductive orator. Comus's language is consistently demonic, like Satan's or Belial's, and it is pagan in the worst possible sense of that word.

Milton's masque uses all the stylistic arsenal of Renaissance poetics in English to demonstrate the opposing forces of good and evil, and it celebrates a linguistic joy in the learning and practising of those languages which Milton had embraced in his study of the Bible or of classical literature. Like Milton's other dramatic production, *Samson Agonistes*, *Comus* is written mostly in blank verse, but it breaks into rhyme occasionally – as when Comus is casting an incantation in good Jonsonian or Shakespearean tetrameter, or when the Attendant Spirit is making a sententious or didactic point, or when lyrics must echo rhythm, as during a song.

The imagery of the masque can be spoken of in terms either of central images which seem to control the entire masque or of peripheral images, set like lights around the central images. The two opposing central images are those of light, embodied in the Lady, and darkness, in Comus. The central image of darkness is that of Circe as she is reincarnated in her son Comus: the figure of the dark sorceress who tempts men by magic potions or by their own evil inclination to become what Milton calls grovelling swine. The image of the sorcerer or sorceress is androgynous and archetypal. It has resonances in *The Epic of Gilgamesh*, in the biblical stories of Samson and Delilah and of David and Bathsheeba, and in the stories of Armida in Tasso's *Jerusalem Delivered* and Acrasia in Ariosto's *Orlando Furioso*. But Milton's departure from the norm is to make the sorceress into a sorcerer and the eager and weak victim into a strong and virtuous resister of evil.

Opposed to the image of darkness is the image of light, the Lady, who has archetypal connections with the moon-goddess Diana (without the proverbial fickleness of the moon), with Christ the Sun, or with Apollo the sungod. The Lady is also allied with Dante's Beatrice, through her power to inspire song and to inspire goodness in others. She is an emblem of holy chastity as well. Because the Christian God is seen in terms of light, the Lady is allied with all forms of holy light and inspiration, and she seems at least to *resemble* a goddess.

Below the level of pervasive central images of Holy Light or of the dark Circean tempter, however, Milton includes many other layers of imagery, all working at once in a baroque whirl. Some of the images may be identifiable as Platonic, some neo-Platonic, some classical and pastoral, some Christian, some apparently political, and some even deeply personal.

I will take just one common image in the masque as example, that of water. Water is so pervasive an image in the poem that some critics think Milton is punning on the name Bridge*water*. Sabrina represents the most important body of water in the west of England, the Severn River, the very border (in Milton's era) between England and Wales; but very conveniently the nymph Sabrina also avoided being raped through inner moral strength. Sabrina is thus connected with the image of the river Severn, but also with images of rape and metamorphosis. Sabrina and the Lady are also linked metaphorically with the nightingale, since the story of Philomela and Procne in Ovid's *Metamorphoses* is the story both of beautiful singing and of rape. Likewise, the nymph Syrinx in Ovid resists rape and is changed into a water reed. Milton skilfully weaves together a topical and national image of water, the river Severn, with the story of a nymph, Sabrina, who resists rape like the Lady, and becomes an inspirational example of beauty and virtue rising above sordidness, like Procne the nightingale. The nightingale, incidentally, became Milton's image for himself as inspired nocturnal poet (*PL* 3.38–40).

When the Lady or her brothers speak of chastity, the imagery surrounding the word is Christian, but, when they use Platonic key words like *form*, the images (as well as the logic and dialectic) correspond closely to those of the dialogues of Plato. The masque is full of nymphs, swains, shepherds, all from the classical and Italian traditions of pastoral poetry, but it also alludes to the Pythagorean and Platonic music of the spheres and it may be alluding to or even making fun of theories of courtliness or courtly love popular at the court of Charles I.

Two images have caused argument in twentieth-century criticism, some of it more important to the meaning of the masque and some less so. The best-known textual crux in *Comus* is the exact meaning of *haemony*. This name of the herb which the Attendant Spirit discusses briefly (628–40) has occasioned much discussion over whether it is the equivalent of Homer's *moly*, or whether it has an etymology diversely based on the name for Thessaly or the Greek word for blood. The herb has been discussed as a symbol of Platonic virtue on the one hand or of Christian grace on the other. According to recent speculations, it may well be that Milton had in mind a certain English herb usually called St John's wort and thought of as a *demonifugium*, a herb which exorcized evil spirits. Henry Lawes, not long before *Comus* was first performed, helped to exorcize a demon from a house in London (it was reported) by using a placket of St John's wort under his pillow.

Recent critical debate over images in *Comus* has centred on the phrase 'gums of glutinous heat' (917), which Milton scholars have discussed with great imagination, if not abandon. The phrase has been found to mean everything from the kind of resinous lime used to ensnare birds to something less dignified having to do with buttocks (L. *gluteus*) or even sperm.

The question of imagery in *Comus* is a very complicated one, but the reader of the masque can quickly see that there is a battle going on between Light and Darkness, between Truth and Error, between Temperance and Dissolution, and between Vice and Virtue. Beyond those simpler references, the images of Vice or Virtue are complicated by the appearance of good in evil and evil in good, as when the Lady is made by Comus to sound like a sour Stoic pedant, or when Comus starts talking about something good, the abundance of the earth, only to pervert it into excess or promiscuous fecundity. It should be remembered that Circe, though she is the personification of sensual corruption, is also daughter of the sun; her son Comus is also attractive in an evil way, mixing images of goodness with evil intentions, in the same way that the angel of light, Lucifer, becomes Satan.

As a masque *Comus* seems not to have been intended by its creator to be re-performed, since Milton leaves very few stage directions in the text of the masque itself. A scholar working in archives in Yorkshire has recently discovered that a masque centring on a character called Comus was performed, rather lavishly, at a country estate not long after Milton's masque had been staged on the Welsh border, but there is no way to prove that the Yorkshire list of stage properties refers to a refurbished production of Milton's masque. Since the 1738 gala, with music by Thomas Arne, author of 'Rule, Britannia', *Comus* has been performed infrequently, sometimes as reader's theatre in London, sometimes as civic celebration in Ludlow. Milton scholars, both in Britain and the USA, since 1966 have supported performances at Rochester University, Christ's College, Cambridge, and the State University College at Buffalo. One performance was even videotaped at the University of Delaware, and the city of Ludlow regularly schedules performances at Ludlow Castle. The masque holds the stage remarkably well, even today, reminding audiences of *A Midsummer Night's Dream* and charming them with its pageantry, its magic, and its music.

Reading list

Arthos, John, *On 'A Mask Presented at Ludlow Castle'* (Ann Arbor, 1954)

Barber, C. L., ' "A Mask Presented at Ludlow Castle": The Masque as Masque', in Diekhoff, ed., *A Maske at Ludlow*

Breasted, Barbara, '*Comus* and the Castlehaven Scandal', *Milton Studies* 3 (1971), 201–24.

Brown, Cedric, *John Milton's Aristocratic Entertainments* (Cambridge, 1985)

Creaser, John, ' "The present aid of this occasion": The Setting of *Comus*', in Lindley, ed., *The Court Masque*

Demaray, John G., *Milton and the Masque Tradition* (Cambridge, MA, 1968)

Diekhoff, John S., ed., *A Maske at Ludlow: Essays on Milton's Comus* (Cleveland, 1968)

Evans, Willa McClung, *Henry Lawes: Musician and Friend of Poets* (New York and London, 1941)

Finney, Gretchen, *Musical Backgrounds for English Literature: 1580–1650* (New Brunswick, NJ, 1962)

Fish, Stanley E., 'Problem Solving in *Comus*', in *Illustrious Evidence: Approaches to English Literature of the Early Seventeenth Century*, ed. Earl Miner (Berkeley, 1975)

Flannagan, Roy C., ed., *Comus: Contexts* (Binghampton, NY, 1988)

Fletcher, Angus, *The Transcendental Masque: An Essay on Milton's Comus* (Ithaca, NY, 1971)

Hughes, Merritt Y., and John Steadman, eds., *A Variorum Commentary on the Poems of John Milton* (New York, 1972–); see vol. 2, part 3 for *Comus*

Hunter, William B., *Milton's Comus: Family Piece* (Troy, NY, 1983)

Jayne, Sears, 'The Subject of Milton's Ludlow *Mask*', in Diekhoff, ed., *A Maske at Ludlow*

Kirkconnell, G. Watson, '*Awake the courteous Echo*': The Themes and Prosody of '*Comus*', '*Lycidas*', and '*Paradise Regained*' in World Literature with Translations of the Major Analogues* (Toronto, 1973)

Leishman, J. B., *Milton's Minor Poems* (Pittsburgh, 1969)

Lindley, David, ed., *The Court Masque* (Manchester, 1984)

McGuire, Maryann, *Milton's Puritan Masque* (Athens, GA, 1983)

Macrus, Leah, 'Milton's Anti-Laudian Masque', in *The Politics of Mirth: Jonson, Herrick, Milton, Marvell and the Defense of Old Holiday Pastimes* (Chicago, 1986)

Sprott, S. E., *John Milton, 'A Masque': The Earlier Versions* (Toronto, 1973)

Tuve, Rosamund, *Images and Themes in Five Poems by Milton* (Cambridge, MA, 1957)

Wilkenfield, Roger B., 'A Mask', in *A Milton Encyclopedia*, ed. William B. Hunter, Jr (Lewisburg, PA, 1978–83)

Woodhouse, A. S. P., 'The Argument of *Comus*', in Diekhoff, ed., *A Maske at Ludlow*

3 *Lycidas*

On 10 August 1637 a pious young Cambridge graduate called Edward King was drowned in the Irish Sea when the ship carrying him to Ireland to visit his family struck a rock off the Welsh coast and sank. The author of some rather undistinguished Latin verses, King had intended to take Holy Orders and pursue a career in the church, but in 1637 he was still a fellow at Milton's old college, Christ's, which he had entered when Milton was in his second year. He was evidently a well-respected and popular figure in the University community, so much so that when the news of his death reached Cambridge a group of his friends and colleagues decided to organize a volume of memorial verses in his honour. Although Milton does not appear to have been a particularly close friend of King's, he was nevertheless invited to contribute to the collection. Published in 1638 under the title *Justa Edouardo King naufrago*, the volume contained thirty-six poems in all, twenty-three in Greek or Latin followed by thirteen in English. Milton's contribution, the last in the collection, was *Lycidas*.

Unlike the other verse memorials in *Justa Edouardo King naufrago*, *Lycidas* is a pastoral elegy. It belongs, that is to say, to a long-established generic tradition characterized by a number of stylistic and structural conventions which enable the reader to recognize it as an heir to such works as Spenser's 'Astrophel', Moschus's 'Lament for Bion', Virgil's 'Eclogue X' and Theocritus's 'Idyl I' (see Hanford; Harrison; Kirkconnell). In poems written within this tradition the poet typically represents himself as a shepherd mourning the death of a beloved companion whose departure has afflicted the entire natural world with grief. After consigning his sheep to the care of another shepherd and invoking the assistance of the muses of pastoral poetry, he proceeds to sing a dirge to his deceased friend in which he recalls the idyllic days they spent together in the countryside.

According to the great eighteenth-century critic Dr Samuel Johnson, Milton's choice of the pastoral elegy as the vehicle for his tribute to Edward King was distinctly unfortunate. In a famous passage in his 'Life of Milton' he declared that *Lycidas* 'is not to be considered as the effusion of real passion; for passion runs not after remote allusions and obscure opinions. Passion plucks no berries from the myrtle and ivy, nor calls upon Arethuse and Mincius, nor tells of rough satyrs and fauns with cloven heel. Where there is leisure for fiction, there is little grief.' What possible point could there be in representing King and Milton as shepherds tending their flocks in the English countryside, Johnson asks, when we know perfectly well that they were both students pursuing their studies at Cambridge University? 'Nothing', he concludes, 'can less display knowledge or less exercise invention than to tell how a shepherd has lost his companion and must now feed his flocks alone, without any judge of his skill in piping; and how one god asks another god what is become of Lycidas, and how neither god can tell. He who thus grieves will excite no sympathy; and he who thus praises will confer no honour' (quoted in Patrides 60–1). What Johnson is objecting to, in short, is what he takes to be the essential artificiality of Milton's elegy and the consequent absence of natural human feeling. The author of *Lycidas*, he insists, simply does not sound like a man deeply afflicted with grief. The poem is insincere.

There are two main lines of defence against this charge. The first was most persuasively stated by the Cambridge critic, E. M. W. Tillyard. When Milton wrote *Lycidas*, he begins by noting, the poet was still a young man himself. Like King he had intended to pursue a career in the church, like King he nurtured literary ambitions, and like King he would shortly be undertaking a sea voyage. How then, asks Tillyard, could Milton have missed the analogy between King and himself? In considering King's premature death, how could he have failed to confront the possibility that he might complete the analogy by getting drowned as well? 'Most criticism of "Lycidas" is off the mark', Tillyard therefore concludes, 'because it fails to distinguish between the nominal and the real subject, what the poem professes to be about and what it is about. It assumes that Edward King is the real whereas he is but the nominal subject. Fundamentally, *Lycidas* concerns Milton himself; King is but the excuse for one of Milton's most personal poems' (Tillyard 79–80). At its deepest level, then, *Lycidas* is about Milton's anxieties concerning the possibility of his own premature death, akin perhaps to those expressed by John Keats in his sonnet 'When I have fears that I may cease to be / Before my pen has gleaned my teeming brain.'

The second line of defence against Johnson's charges takes exactly the opposite tack. Instead of arguing that the poem does express sincere human feeling (albeit about the author rather than about his ostensible subject), it insists that in real life grief is usually inarticulate, or at best monosyllabic like

Lear's 'Howl, howl, howl, howl'. Faced with an actual bereavement, we are simply incapable of translating our feelings into words with any great eloquence. Any completely articulate expression of grief, then, is bound to be 'artificial' simply by virtue of the fact that it is articulate. Traditional forms such as the pastoral elegy thus fulfil a deep human need. Like the ritual of the funeral service itself, they provide us with a way of giving shape and order to what otherwise might have been chaotic, fragmented, and unspoken. The artifice of the pastoral convention with its shepherds, nymphs, and pastoral deities can serve as a machine for feeling with, an apparatus of lament which, if used to contain any private sorrow, at once absorbs it into the timeless.

Lycidas, according to this view, is deliberately impersonal in nature. To accept Johnson's assumption that a poem must express 'real passion' in naturalistic terms is to misunderstand the kind of poem Milton was trying to write. For, like most of Milton's early works, *Lycidas* is an occasional poem. As such, it is public, ceremonial, and formal rather than private, personal, and spontaneous. As C. S. Lewis once observed in a lecture, to complain because Milton sounds unmoved by grief in *Lycidas* is like complaining because the organist playing the funeral march does not break down in tears during the burial service.

Both lines of argument seem to me inadequate in one way or another. The first ignores the essentially conventional nature of the form in which Milton chose to cast his tribute to Edward King, while the second takes no account of the reservoir of deep feeling at the centre of the poem. I would like to propose, therefore, a reading of *Lycidas* which recognizes the poem's relationship to the generic traditions lying behind it but also admits the presence of intense personal emotion lying just beneath the marmoreal formality of the surface. It was precisely through his dialogue with the tradition of the pastoral elegy, I shall argue, that Milton first came face to face with some of his most profound and personal anxieties about the future direction of his own life.

Of all Milton's poems, we may begin by noting, *Lycidas* is the most specifically imitative. It is closely modelled on Virgil's Tenth Eclogue commemorating the death of the famous soldier, statesman, and poet Cornelius Gallus. Set in Arcadia, the legendary landscape of pastoral, this poem depicts Gallus as a lover whose mistress, Lycoris, has deserted him for another man. After a short prologue setting the scene, the formal lament begins with the following question: 'What groves, what glades were your abode, ye virgin Naiads, when Gallus was pining with a love unrequited? For no heights of Parnassus or of Pindus, no Aonian Aganippe made you tarry.' Virgil then proceeds to describe a series of visitors who arrive to comfort or to admonish Gallus as he lies at the brink of death. Apollo, the god of poetry, urges him to forget his mistress: 'Gallus, what madness is this? Thy sweetheart Lycoris hath followed another amid snows and amid rugged camps.' A rustic deity called Silvanus arrives waving fennel flowers and tall lilies. And Pan, the god of shepherds, advises Gallus to stop grieving: 'Will there be no end? Love recks naught of this: neither is cruel Love sated with tears, nor the grass with the rills, nor bees with the clover, nor goats with leaves.' But despite these admonishments, Gallus continues to love the unfaithful Lycoris, and with his last words affirms the sovereignty of Eros: 'Love conquers all; let us, too, yield to Love.'

Together with Virgil's other Eclogues this poem was a standard fixture in the curriculum of seventeenth-century grammar schools, and most, if not all, of Milton's readers would have been intimately familiar with it. Virgil, they would have learned from their school texts, wrote the poem not to celebrate the value of love but to warn us against its insidious power. 'In this Eclogue', declared one contemporary authority, 'is set forth the picture of a foolish lover, so that by looking at this picture we may learn to avoid all the occasions and enticements by which this fire is wont to be aroused' (Philip Melanchthon, *Argumenta . . . in Eclogas Virgili*, 1568, sig. G8). According to the Renaissance schoolmaster, John Brinsley, Gallus could have cured himself 'by giving his mind to the studie of Poetrie' (*Virgil's Eclogues* (1620), 98). So when Virgil asked the nymphs where they were while Gallus was dying he was really rebuking the Muses 'that they were so careless of Gallus to let him so leave his studies and to perish in such unbeseeming love'.

Other commentators, noting Gallus's career as a statesman, found in him 'a memorable example of the kind of fortune one gets at court' (Melanchthon, sig. G6r) and interpreted Virgil's questions to the nymphs in political terms. Parnassus and Pindus, wrote William Lisle, 'were the places of Gallus his retrait amongst the Muses, and the study of sweete Poesie: wherein if hee had still retir'd himselfe . . . and had not aspired to the great Imployments, and Business of state, which caus'd his ruin, hee had still liv'd' (*Virgil's Eclogues* (1628), 184). According to this view of the poem, then, Virgil's lament for Gallus was a warning against the perils of politics.

Now the resemblances between 'Eclogue X' and *Lycidas* are striking and numerous. Phoebus Apollo appears at a crucial juncture in both poems. Silvanus, wearing 'rustic glories on his brow, waving his fennel flowers and tall lilies', is clearly the prototype of Camus with his 'mantle hairy, and his bonnet sedge, / Inwrought with figures dim' (104–5). Pan, the god of shepherds, has his counterpart in Peter, the founder of the church. Both poems ask the same question: 'Who would refuse verses to Gallus?' 'Who would not sing for Lycidas?' (10). Both poems appeal to Arethusa for aid. Both poems interrogate the nymphs, though Milton substitutes British for Arcadian landmarks in his adaptation of Virgil's lines:

> Where were ye nymphs when the remorseless deep
> Closed o'er the head of your loved Lycidas?
> For neither were ye playing on the steep,
> Where your old bards, the famous Druids, lie,
> Nor on the shaggy top of Mona high,
> Nor yet where Deva spreads her wizard stream. (50–5)

And both poems conclude with the image of a shepherd rising to his feet at evening and setting off home with his flock.

But striking as they are, these formal resemblances pale beside the fundamental substantive difference between the two elegies. Virgil is mourning a lover who died of unrequited passion. Milton is celebrating the memory of a studious young virgin *who died by accident*. In accordance with the advice of commentators like Brinsley and Lisle, Edward King had abstained from the allurements of love and politics, yet he had still been cut off 'ere his prime' (8). His death simply could not be attributed, as Gallus's could, to some fatal error on his part. It was morally meaningless. Small wonder, then, that after paraphrasing Virgil's questions to the Naiads, Milton comments so bitterly:

> Ay me, I fondly dream
> Had ye been there – for what could that have done? (56–7)

If chastity, retirement, and the study of poetry were no protection against the blind Fury and her shears, what was the point of sexual and political self-denial?

The primary allusive context within which Milton chose to lament the death of his fellow student, I would therefore suggest, may have served to trigger his anxieties not about the possibility of his own premature death, as Tillyard suggested, but rather about the validity of the 'fugitive and cloistered virtue' exemplified by Edward King, and still more to the point, about the validity of the kind of life Milton himself had been leading for the past five years.

When he composed the poem in November 1637, we should remember, Milton himself was almost twenty-nine years old. Since coming down from Cambridge in 1632 he had been living with his parents, first in Hammersmith and later in the rural village of Horton, where he had immersed himself in an intensive reading programme in theology, church history, and classical literature. Thanks to the ever-increasing pressure on Puritan clergy to conform to the rites and doctrines of the Anglican church, he had probably abandoned by now his earlier intention of making a career in the church. 'Church-outed by the prelates', unmarried, unemployed, and relatively unknown, he was preparing himself to be a great poet.

A Latin poem Milton wrote to his father (*Ad Patrem*) offers a convenient window into his state of mind during this period. Rejecting 'the golden hope of making piles of money' or a career dedicated to the study of 'our nation's ill-preserved statutes' (70–1), Milton declares that he has taken refuge from 'the din of the city' in 'this deep seclusion . . . amidst the leisurely delights of the Aonian spring' where he can walk 'by Phoebus's side' (74–6). In the Arcadian security of his studies at Horton, he assures his father, he will be invulnerable to the ills which afflict those who have chosen to pursue wealth or public office: 'Away with you, sleep-destroying worries, away with you, complaints, and the squinting eye of envy with its crooked goatish look. Do not stretch your snaky jaws at me, cruel calumny. Your whole filthy gang can do me no harm: I am not within your power. I shall stride on in safety with an unwounded heart, lifted high above your viperous sting' (105–10).

This boundless confidence in the Muse's capacity to protect her followers from the ills of the world must have been severely shaken by the death of Edward King. Hence, perhaps, the particular pastoral name which Milton chose to give his dead friend. For Lycidas is the protagonist of the bleakest of Virgil's Eclogues, the ninth, in which the power of poetry to shape events is called into serious question. At the beginning of the poem Virgil's Lycidas believes that poetry can preserve pastoral life from destruction, but he soon learns that 'amid the weapons of war . . . our songs avail as much as, they say, the doves of Chaonia when the eagle comes'. As he ponders the meaningless death of another Lycidas, Milton is brought face to face with the same question as Virgil: if the muse is not only thankless but powerless as well, then what is the point of serving her so strictly? Perhaps there was something to be said, after all, for the active life of sexual and political engagement. Far from recording Milton's discovery of his role as a divinely inspired epic poet, as some critics have recently argued (see, for example, Friedman, Wittreich), *Lycidas* calls into question the worth of the poetic vocation itself.

All three of the issues I have mentioned, chastity, retirement, and poetry, come into even sharper focus in Milton's treatment of Edward King's mythical surrogate within the poem: Orpheus. After chastising the nymphs for their absence from the scene of King's death, Milton goes on:

What could the muse herself that Orpheus bore,
The muse herself for her enchanting son
Whom universal nature did lament,
When by the rout that made the hideous roar,
His gory visage down the stream was sent,
Down the swift Hebrus to the Lesbian shore.   (58–63)

The allusion here is to an episode which haunted Milton's imagination for
the rest of his life, the legend of Orpheus's death, as recounted, for example,
by Ovid in the *Metamorphoses*. Saddened by the death of Eurydice, Ovid
relates, Orpheus shunned the company of women and devoted himself to
singing songs of such beauty that all nature was moved to respond. Enraged
by his rejection of their amorous advances, the female followers of Bacchus
drowned out Orpheus's music with their howls, and tore him limb from
limb.

In the Renaissance, Orpheus's power to move the natural world with his
song was interpreted as a symbol of the power of poetry to control both
physical and psychological reality (see, for instance, the song which opens
Act III of Shakespeare's *Henry VIII*). Like the angelic choir in the 'Nativity
Ode', the Muse's son had the power to restore the age of gold with his
redemptive song. In *Ad Patrem*, for example, Milton had assured his father
that there was virtually nothing that human eloquence could not accomplish
when divinely inspired. Poets, he claimed, were the acknowledged legis-
lators of the world, and their original prototype was Orpheus, 'who with his
singing . . . held streams spellbound and gave ears to the oak-trees and
moved lifeless phantoms to tears' (52–5).

It is a far cry from this majestic figure to the helpless victim of the 'rout
that made the hideous roar'. Even though they both derive from the same
original myth, the Orpheus whose song could make rivers stand still in *Ad
Patrem* and the Orpheus whose 'gory visage down the stream was sent' in
Lycidas are scarcely recognizable as the same character. We could hardly
have been given a more precise or vivid way of measuring the impact which
the death of Edward King must have had upon Milton's conception of the
poetic vocation. The youthful optimism which had animated the verse
epistle to his father has collapsed in a nightmare of senseless destruction
which even the Muse was powerless to prevent.

The bitter questions which immediately follow the Orpheus episode have
often been called digressive, as though they had little or nothing to do with
the rest of the poem (see French). But once the point of the Orpheus allusion

has been recognized, it should be readily apparent that Milton's misgivings about the worth of 'the homely slighted shepherd's trade' are anything but a sudden or unexpected interruption. After the allusions to Virgil's 'Eclogue X' and the Orpheus story, the questions Milton asks are not merely relevant; they are inescapable:

> Alas! What boots it with uncessant care
> To tend the homely slighted shepherd's trade,
> And strictly meditate the thankless muse?
> Were it not better done as others use,
> To sport with Amaryllis in the shade,
> Or with the tangles of Neaera's hair?   (64–9)

The sense of release in these lines is almost as powerful as the sense of angry bafflement they simultaneously express. The undercurrent of anxiety which has slowly been gathering strength beneath the allusions to Lycidas, Gallus, and Orpheus has finally broken through to the surface.

That it should prove to be such intensely sexual anxiety – Amaryllis and Neaera were the traditional names of the nymphs who alternately torment and gratify the shepherds in pastoral poetry – should come as no surprise after all the doubts that the Orpheus allusion in particular has tacitly directed at the ideal of chastity. For in the eyes of Milton and his contemporaries, Orpheus was an exemplar not only of poetic eloquence but also of the sexual abstinence necessary to achieve it. As Milton wrote in his *Elegia sexta*, the poet must live a life 'chaste and free from crime . . . In this way, so it is said . . . old Orpheus lived, when he tamed the wild beasts among lonely caves' (63–70). But the brutal scene on the banks of the Hebrus totally subverts this simple-minded faith in the efficacy of pastoral virtue. Despite their determination to scorn delights and live laborious days, both Orpheus and Lycidas have gone to a watery death anyway.

Small wonder, then, that Milton is led to question the fundamental principle upon which his whole conception of the poetic vocation had been based: the denial of the flesh. Perhaps, after all, the suppression of the sexual impulse was too high a price to pay for an art he might never survive to practise. In light of Orpheus's fate, would it not be more sensible to follow Volpone's advice and prove 'while we can, the sports of love' (Ben Jonson, *Volpone*, 3.7.167)? Better, surely, to risk gathering rosebuds too soon than to suffer the fate of the 'rathe primrose' (142) which, in an earlier draft of *Lycidas*, died 'unwedded', 'colouring the pale cheek of uninjoyed love'.

Milton's treatment of this issue owes a great deal of its power, I suspect, to the intimate connection that existed in his own mind between poetic productivity on the one hand and sexual abstinence on the other. For when the pursuit of one activity is made dependent upon the avoidance of some other, the first often turns out to be a sublimated version of the second. Alternatives, in other words, have a way of becoming substitutes. So by insisting that the poetic impulse could not be fulfilled unless the sexual impulse was repressed, Milton was in effect creating an equivalence between them. The Muse, Calliope, displaces Venus, and her followers make poems instead of love. It was only natural, then, that Milton should have equated the frustration of literary potentiality with the denial of sexual fulfilment. To cut off the possibility of great literary works was analogous to destroying the opportunity to beget children. As a result, the assault of the abhorred shears feels like nothing so much as a castration:

> Fame is the spur that the clear spirit doth raise
> (That last infirmity of noble mind)
> To scorn delights, and live laborious days;
> But the fair guerdon when we hope to find,
> And think to burst out into sudden blaze,
> Comes the blind Fury with th'abhorred shears,
> And slits the thin-spun life.   (70–6)

In response to this crisis, the poem initially offers two provisional solutions, neither of which, I shall argue, is entirely satisfying. The first of them is provided by the god of poetry, Phoebus Apollo, who intervenes to remind his disciple that true fame is to be found not on earth but in heaven. Dramatic as it is, the god's revelation completely misses Milton's point, which had to do not so much with losing fame as with losing the chance to earn it. Confronted with the possibility that he may never be allowed to run the race for which he has spent most of his adult life training himself, what possible consolation can Milton be expected to find in the announcement that the prize-giving will take place in heaven? Divine approval of the rigour of his preparations would no doubt be gratifying, but it would hardly compensate for the utter futility of undertaking them. The solution simply does not address the problem, and one is left with a sense of incompleteness, of answers yet to be given.

The same is true of the second solution, offered by St Peter shortly afterwards. The saint's enigmatic promise that corrupt ministers will be punished by 'that two-handed engine at the door' (130) postpones the reform of the church until the day of judgment. To a sensibility as passionately concerned as Milton's certainly was with the social and political realities of his immediate situation, an eschatological solution to a contemporary problem could scarcely have been satisfying. For Milton the most important question was always: what should be done *now*. Even granted that St Michael's sword will smite the faithless herdsmen on the last day, how is the flock to be protected in the meantime? Shouldn't some attempt be made to remedy the current condition of the church, to banish false shepherds from the fold and hunt down the wolf in his lair?

That Milton was troubled by such questions appears all the more likely when we consider one of his most significant departures from the pastoral tradition: his violation of the long-standing convention whereby the sheep are delegated to the care of a companion while the shepherd himself is performing the song. For the duration of *Lycidas* no one is tending the flock. Milton is warbling his Doric lay and Edward King is dead. In the meantime, the sheepfold has been left to the mercies of ignorant and greedy hirelings. Like the lambs in the *Epitaphium Damonis* who 'go home unfed' (18) because their master is too busy singing his song to attend to them, the 'hungry sheep' (125) are starving for want of adequate nourishment. The absence of the shepherd's traditional companion thus poses a further set of questions: instead of playing on his 'oaten flute' (33), shouldn't the uncouth swain be feeding the flock himself? Were it not better done, if not to sport with Amaryllis in the shade, at least to labour for St Peter in the sheepfold? Instead of writing poems, shouldn't John Milton be ministering to the religious needs of his fellow countrymen?

For many years, of course, that is exactly what he had planned to do. According to the autobiographical preface to Book II of *Reason of Church-Government*, Milton was destined for the ministry both 'by the intentions of my parents and friends' and 'in mine own resolutions' (YP 1: 822). As he goes on to explain, however, 'perceaving what tyranny had invaded the Church' he had subsequently abandoned his plans to enter Holy Orders and had decided to devote himself wholly to poetry, an activity which he believed to be an alternative priesthood (see *Elegia sexta*, 65ff.). The situation he describes in St Peter's speech must, surely, have given him some qualms about his decision. For as we have seen, the death of Edward King has brought Milton face to face with the possibility that he has been over-estimating the power of poetry. Suppose, after all, that the poet's voice was not capable of replacing the preacher's? If Orpheus's song could not allay the perturbations of the Bacchantes, what hope could Milton have of charming their seventeenth-century counterparts? Won't the lean and flashy songs of false shepherds drown out his music just as surely as the hideous roar of the Maenads overwhelmed the song of Orpheus? Perhaps Milton's mouth, too, is blind. The headnote added to the 1645 edition of *Lycidas* may affirm the prophetic efficacy of Milton's words, but in 1637 when the corrupted clergy was 'in their height' there was no reason to suppose that the Laudian church was destined to collapse so soon. St Peter's speech thus serves to intensify, not assuage, the anxieties which we saw earlier were implicit in the poem's title, and in the allusion to Orpheus. Far from being a digression, as it is still sometimes called, it touches on the central issue of Milton's entire career. In a land threatened by wolves, who will listen to the shepherd's piping?

All three issues that we have examined (chastity, retirement, and poetry) are finally resolved at two levels. So far as Edward King is concerned, the scene in heaven offers the answer:

> So Lycidas sunk low, but mounted high,
> Through the dear might of him that walked the waves;
> Where other groves, and other streams along,
> With nectar pure his oozy locks he laves,
> And hears the unexpressive nuptial song,
> In the blest kingdoms meek of joy and love.
> There entertain him all the saints above,
> In solemn troops, and sweet societies
> That sing, and singing in their glory move,
> And wipe the tears for ever from his eyes. (172–81)

Whereas Phoebus's speech failed to offer any genuine solace for the frustration of the homely slighted shepherd's sexual and poetic aspirations, this second account of divine reward restores the dead swain to an idealized landscape in which both impulses can be satisfied, albeit vicariously. For the 'blest kingdoms meek' are characterized by two qualities that were conspicuous by their absence in Jove's bleak court: 'joy and love'; joy expressed in the singing of the 'sweet societies', love in the 'nuptial' union they are celebrating. As the poem's original readers would have needed no reminding, Lycidas is attending the marriage of the lamb:

And I heard the voice of harpers harping with their harps: And they sung as it were a new song before the throne . . . and no man could learn that song but the hundred and forty and four thousand, which were redeemed from the earth. These are they which were not defiled with women; for they are virgins . . .

And I heard as it were the voice of a great multitude, and as the voice of the mighty thunderings, saying Alleluia! for the Lord God omnipotent reigneth. Let us be glad and rejoice, and give honour to him; for the marriage of the Lamb is come, and his wife hath made herself ready. (Rev. 14: 2–4; 19: 6–7)

But Milton's description of Lycidas among the saints is not only a Christian fulfilment of the scene originally adumbrated by Phoebus Apollo. It is also a celestial re-enactment of the events which took place still earlier in the poem on the banks of the Hebrus. The apotheosis of Lycidas, that is to say, bears a striking resemblance to the death of Orpheus. Orpheus's gory visage 'down the stream was sent'; Lycidas washes his oozy locks 'other streams along'. Orpheus's head was carried to 'the Lesbian shore'; Lycidas will henceforth serve as 'the Genius of the shore'. Orpheus was killed by 'the rout that made the hideous roar' because he resisted marriage; Lycidas is entertained by 'solemn troops, and sweet societies' singing a 'nuptial song'. The scene in heaven thus transfigures the scene in Thrace, harmonizing its dissonance, sublimating its violence, reviving its protagonist. In the final analysis it is the resurrection of Lycidas rather than the intervention of Phoebus that dispels the horror of Orpheus's and Edward King's deaths.

Yet for Milton himself the question remains: how is he to live out the rest of his life? At this terrestrial level, the solution comes in the final eight lines of the poem:

> Thus sang the uncouth swain to the oaks and rills.
> While the still morn went out with sandals grey,
> He touched the tender stops of various quills,
> With eager thought warbling his Doric lay:
> And now the sun had stretched out all the hills,
> And now was dropped into the western bay;
> At last he rose, and twitched his mantle blue:
> Tomorrow to fresh woods, and pastures new.   (186–93)

This is one of the most extraordinary moments in English poetry. For Milton's unexpected introduction of a third-person narrator at the end of a first-person poem violates one of the oldest and most fundamental covenants governing a writer's relationship with his reader: the implicit understanding that the genre of the work will remain constant, that a play will not turn into an epic half-way through, or vice versa.

Now *Lycidas*, the headnote informs us, is a 'Monody'. The term derives, as Milton certainly knew, from Greek tragedy, where it means an ode sung by a single character. The ensuing tribute to Edward King, we are thus led to expect, will be dramatic in nature. And indeed it reads very much like a soliloquy. Up to line 185, that is to say, we seem to be in the presence of a single speaker who is addressing us in the dramatic present. But in line 186 a second, unidentified speaker suddenly emerges from the wings and with a single preterite verb thrusts the original speaker (and his speech) back into the narrative past: 'Thus sang the uncouth swain . . . ' A work that began as drama has ended as narrative.

The immediate effect of this startling shift in the poem's modality is readily apparent. It establishes a clear distinction between the fictional *persona* who speaks the first 185 lines and the living poet who speaks the last 8. The question is: why does Milton suppress this distinction until the poem is almost over? Or, to put it another way, why is there no matching narrative introduction to warn us in advance that the 'uncouth swain' is a character in, rather than the author of, the elegy? Because, I would suggest, the distinction between the swain and the poet simply did not obtain at the beginning of *Lycidas*, because, initially at least, the two figures were identical. 'In this Monody', the headnote declares, 'the author bewails a learned friend', and there is nothing in the opening paragraphs of the poem to prevent us from taking this announcement quite literally. The voice we hear at the beginning of *Lycidas* is, unmistakably, the voice of John Milton himself, agonizing over his poetic immaturity, showing off his classical learning, recalling with evident nostalgia his days as a student in Cambridge.

As the poem proceeds, however, the owner of that voice gradually sheds his historical identity, and finally turns into a fictional character whose values and attitudes Milton no longer necessarily shares. The first major fissure in the speaker's identity comes with Phoebus Apollo's dramatic intervention in line 76: 'But not the praise, / Phoebus replied, and touched my trembling ears.' The tense here suddenly lapses from the dramatic present to the narrative past, and as the experience of lines 1–75 is thrust back into an earlier time-plane a gulf opens up between the speaker who remembers Phoebus's advice and the speaker who received it. The two figures are still recognizably the same person – the ears that Phoebus touches are 'my ears' not 'his' – but the second figure, enlightened by the revelations of the god of poetry, speaks from a perspective considerably broader than that of his earlier manifestation.

After St Peter's speech, the speaker's identity undergoes another transformation: it expands to include an undefined chorus of fellow mourners who share the speaker's 'false surmise' (153) and his subsequent disillusion as he remembers the true fate of Lycidas's body. The 'frail thoughts' and 'moist vows' (153, 159) belong now to a multiple consciousness – they are 'ours' rather than 'mine'. And a still more violent change occurs shortly afterwards when at line 165 the speaker dissociates himself from his fellow mourners in a change of viewpoint so extreme that more than one critic has attributed the lines that follow to a completely different character, St Michael (see Madsen). As we have seen, a yet more radical disjunction awaits us in line 186: what we took for fact turns into fiction, and the swain is transformed into a figment of Milton's poetic imagination. The entire poem, one might say, records Milton's emergence from the *persona* of the uncouth swain. *Lycidas* is one long act of disengagement.

The conclusion of *Lycidas* thus enacts in an extraordinarily vivid way an experience analogous to, though not, I think, identical with, the Christian conversion experience. As the old speaker fades away, a new speaker is born. Like a snake sloughing its skin, the singer withdraws from his song and in the final lines begins what is essentially a new song which contains the old one. It is as if the self of a dream had suddenly awakened into the self of everyday reality. The elegy and the swain who sang it recede into the distance, and we are left with the sense that we have witnessed a rebirth. In Pauline terms, Milton has cast off the old man.

But who is this new man, and what does he represent? As is so often the case with Milton's poetry, the verse form itself holds the key. Whereas the first 185 lines have been written in irregular stanzas modelled (as F. T. Prince has shown) on the Italian *canzone*, the concluding eight lines are in *ottava rima*, the major vehicle of the sixteenth-century romantic epic, the stanza not only of Tasso's *Gerusalemme Liberata* and Ariosto's *Orlando Furioso* but also of their English translations by Fairfax and Harington. As the verse form in which the amorous and military conquests of Roland and Godfrey had been celebrated, the *ottava rima* naturally invokes the turbulent world of heroic action and romantic love. The concluding stanza of *Lycidas* thus carries with it a set of values diametrically opposed to those associated with the pastoral as a genre or with Edward King as a character. After the meditative, loosely organized *canzoni* preceding it, it acts like a sudden burst of adrenalin, rousing the singer from his reverie and propelling him towards the wars of truth in which 'the true warfaring Christian' could show his mettle. The new verse form thus opens up the possibility of living an entirely different kind of life, animated no longer by the ideals of the pastoral eclogue but rather by those of the Christian epic. The course of Milton's life, it suggests, is about to undergo a drastic change.

And so, of course, it did. Rather than remaining in the cloistered calm of Horton, Milton travelled extensively in France and Italy and shortly after-wards plunged into public life in London. Rather than remaining chaste, he soon married Mary Powell. And rather than fulfilling his poetic ambitions, he devoted the next twenty years of his life to establishing himself as one of the principal public champions of the Puritan and Parliamentarian cause. *Lycidas* is thus a pivotal work in Milton's career. Like Marvell's 'Horatian Ode', it is about an epiphany. No longer content to sing his numbers languishing in the shades of Horton, Milton is about to abandon that part of himself represented by the swain, with his devotion to retirement, chastity, and poetry, in order to pursue an open-ended future of heroic and sexual engagement. For the fact is that, with the exception of a few sonnets, *Lycidas* is the last poem Milton wrote in English for the next twenty years. Not until the dying days of the Commonwealth when he was almost sixty would Milton reassume that part of his identity which he had discarded at the end of *Lycidas* and take up the mantle of the shepherd poet 'yet once more'.

Reading list

Alpers, Paul, 'The Eclogue Tradition and the Nature of Pastoral', *College English* 34 (1972), 352–71

Baker, S. A., 'Milton's Uncouth Swain', *Milton Studies* 3 (1971), 35–53

Berkeley, D. S., *Inwrought with Figures Dim* (The Hague, 1974)

Elledge, Scott, *Milton's Lycidas* (New York, 1966)

Evans, J. Martin, *The Road from Horton: Looking Backwards in 'Lycidas'* (Victoria, 1983)

Fairclough, H. R., *Virgil: Eclogues, Georgics, Aeneid 1–6* (London, 1967)

Fish, S. E., '*Lycidas*: A Poem Finally Anonymous', *Glyph* 8 (1981), 1–18 (and in Patrides, *Milton's 'Lycidas'*)

French, J. M., 'The Digressions in Milton's *Lycidas*', *Studies in Philology* 50 (1953), 485–90

Friedman, D. M., '*Lycidas*: the Swain's Paideia', *Milton Studies* 3 (1971), 3–34 (and in Patrides, *Milton's 'Lycidas'*)

Hanford, J. H., 'The Pastoral Elegy and Milton's *Lycidas*', *PMLA* 25 (1910), 403–47 (and in Patrides, *Milton's 'Lycidas'*)

Harrison, T. P., *The Pastoral Elegy* (Austin, 1939)

Hunt, Clay, *Lycidas and the Italian Critics* (New Haven, 1979)

Kirkconnell, W., *Awake the Courteous Echo* (Toronto, 1973)

Lambert, E. Z., *Placing Sorrow: A Study of the Pastoral Elegy Tradition from Theocritus to Milton* (Chapel Hill, NC, 1976)

Madsen, W. B., 'The Voice of Michael in *Lycidas*', *Studies in English Literature* 3 (1963), 1–7

Martz, L., 'Who is Lycidas?', *Yale French Studies* 47 (1972), 170–88

Mayerson, C. W., 'The Orpheus Image in *Lycidas*', *PMLA* 64 (1949), 189–207 (and in Patrides, *Milton's 'Lycidas'*)

Patrides, C. A., *Milton's 'Lycidas': The Tradition and the Poem*, rev. edn (Columbia, MS, 1983)

Pigman, G. W., *Grief and English Renaissance Elegy* (Cambridge, 1985)

Prince, F. T., *The Italian Element in Milton's Verse* (Oxford, 1954)

Ransom, J. C., 'A Poem Nearly Anonymous', in Patrides, *Milton's 'Lycidas'*

Smith, Eric, *By Mourning Tongues: Studies in English Elegy* (Ipswich, 1977)

Tillyard, E. M. W., *Milton* (London, 1930)

Tuve, Rosemond, *Images and Themes in Five Poems by Milton* (Cambridge, MA, 1957)

Wittreich, J. A., *Visionary Poetics: Milton's Tradition and his Legacy* (San Marino, CA, 1979)

Woodhouse, A. S. P. and D. Bush, *A Variorum Commentary on the Poems of John Milton*, vol. 2 (New York, 1972)

4   Milton and heroic literature

Readers of today who wish to appreciate John Milton sometimes resort to self-deception. He pondered, as we do, the use of knowledge, the relation of men and women, the remedies for loss, and the necessity of moral choice, but in idioms that demand familiarity with long tradition. Thinking as most of us do in terms of psychological, economic, or biological models does little to prepare us for Milton's assumptions. Because he refers to some 1,500 other authors, many now forgotten, we need those footnotes that make his pages more resemble foreign language texts than living classics. Our modern limits sometimes urge us to overvalue certain familiar references so that his work does not become (in the famous Victorian phrase) a monument to dead ideas. One recent commentator, for example, has compared Milton's imaginative flights through space to those of astronauts.

Certainly ideas regarding religion, history, and literary models have changed since the 1600s. But spotlighting differences can both enlarge our understanding of Milton's world and also demonstrate that he truly resembles us because he pays special attention to the individual. For his major characters live in at least two worlds, one of Christian humanism, and a second familiar to anyone craving independent heroes whose lives oscillate between predictability and idiosyncrasy. Reading Milton with this kind of binocular vision thus allows us to remain faithful to his assumptions and to ours.

Like many of his late Renaissance contemporaries, learned and not so learned, Milton accepted as absolute several religious premises that our culture usually entertains as merely possible. He knew, for example, that the Bible coexisted with non-theistic literature celebrating earthly love and secular activities, yet for him Scripture was the final arbiter of truth. He felt sure that God and Satan now contended for our souls on this earth, had already fought one another in approximately 4000 BC for possession of Heaven, and would at the end of time reassume their proper relationship as Creator and subject in some new realm freed from time. The great battle in

Luca Giordano (1632–1705), *The Archangel Michael*

all eras was not between id and ego or rich and poor or developing and senescent; rather, it pitted good against evil.

Further, Milton understood that this ancient and superhuman animosity was replicated daily in the life of each Christian. Everyone was expected to be Christ's soldier because the powers of blackness prowled the earth, hunting for unwary souls. James I ordered Reginald Scot's *Discovery of Witchcraft* (1584) to be burned because it questioned the existence of witches; Sir Thomas Browne believed in demons; Matthew Hopkins's working title was 'Witchcatcher General'; and judges in Salem, Massachusetts, sentenced witches to be hung. Alive to spiritual dangers, Milton agreed with Nicholas Remy that 'Satan seizes as many opportunities of deceiving and destroying mankind as there are different moods and affections natural to the human character' (Remy 1). Milton's *Christian Doctrine* gives primacy to Scripture, but he arranges his material in original categories, some suggested by pagan rhetoricians and none exactly foreshadowed by the Bible itself. As he says in his introductory 'Epistle': 'any man who wishes to be saved must work out his beliefs for himself' (YP 6: 118).

If questions of one's spiritual survival were asked daily, so too were queries we might label historical. The past never faded, even when current events roused people to passion. Germany suffered agonies during the Thirty Years' War; Galileo pointed to spots on the sun; and England executed a king. Yet partisan commentators felt compelled to justify their private views in terms of verities agreed upon in previous eras. Lurid propaganda, for example, claimed either that the German Lutherans were God's elect, extirpating the papacy just as biblical Hebrews had destroyed idolatry, or that they were barbarians once again threatening Rome. Contemporary 'proofs' of Catholic persecution such as Philip Vincent's *Lamentations of Germany*, whose shocking woodcuts showed cannibalism and torture, none the less alluded to happenings in the past to drive home their lessons. Guided by his faith in precedent, Milton offers his older contemporary Galileo as yet another victim of the Roman church's old repression, while he represents Charles I as still one more grasping autocrat.

Milton's trust in history allowed him to travel backward in time as well as laterally: defending the Puritan cause; codifying rules for logic or Latin grammar; compiling a history of Russia and reasons for divorce; as well as creating imaginative dramas about those far-off eras when the world began, Samson died, and Christ withstood temptation.

Milton's veneration for religion and history may strike a nostalgic chord in modern readers, but he had to deal with a third, more time-bound problem: pagan antiquity. Our own literary past resembles a series of spontaneous generations in which relationships to models are understood as interesting coincidences rather than parentages. 'Influence' usually implies the pressure of immediate predecessors: 'Hemingway admired the work of Stephen Crane.' Yet thinkers for more than one and a half millennia before Milton had preserved pre-Christian works in order to salvage truths useful to 'moderns'. As his beloved Ovid had said, 'it is right to learn even from enemies'. Milton's treatise *Of Education*, thoroughly in line with other humanist programmes, urges seventeenth-century students to master classical languages so they may understand agriculture from Cato, Varro, and Columella, morality from Plato and Xenophon, rhetoric from Phalerus and Cicero, and so on. This impulse to learn from the past typifies the formal education that Milton underwent at St Paul's School and at Cambridge as well as his own programme for his nephews Edward and John Phillips. His *Accedence Commenc't Grammar* taught Latin by showing the many forms of the verbs 'to be' and 'to praise': a reminder that for him actual and ideal always coexisted. He clearly set his works, written in so many genres, against a background of classical as well as continental and biblical models.

We moderns often read as if each work exists alone rather than as the sum of previous writings. Thus Milton's multi-referential poems may prompt us to skip religious, historical, and literary information and look for the familiar conventions that make authors as dissimilar as Wordsworth or Whitman or William Carlos Williams accessible. The speaker whom they put forward is a unique 'I', a Robinson Crusoe who guides us into private territory others have not seen. The speaker of many Miltonic compositions, however, insists upon the constant presence of literary models. Comus can speak with the sensuous plenitude of Ovid. The speaker of sonnets to Fairfax and Cromwell echoes moralists like Horace. *Retractatio*, or perfective imitation, counted for more in the Renaissance than the current attempt at unmediated contact between the poet and his hearer.

One example of Milton's dialogue with his predecessors may stand for many others. The ecstatic speaker of *Paradise Lost* 1.14–18 asserts that he 'intends to soar / Above the Aonian mount', to serve the Holy Spirit which prefers 'Before all temples the upright heart and pure'. He simultaneously echoes Old Testament prophets, who rejected empty ceremonies in favour of amended consciences, and Virgil. The bold Roman speaker of the Third *Georgic* promises to fly forever in men's imaginations because he will first bring captive Muses from their home on the Aonian mountain and then erect a marble temple in honour of the Emperor (lines 8–13). Virgil's speaker alludes to Pindar, who called a great poem a 'temple', and Ennius, who boasted that even after death he would fly by men's lips. Both Virgil and Milton honour as well as go beyond their literary fathers. But Milton is especially clever because he reminds his Christian reader how vain are metaphoric temples such as the *Aeneid* and physical ones such as Pandemonium.

Milton's learning is thus ambiguous, a two-handed engine that may initially seem too ponderous for us to wield. If used energetically, though, it clears a path for us through mental landscapes we seldom visit. One cultural bias links both our age to his: fascination with the individual. If we call to mind the way in which he portrays his heroes, then we need not dwell upon our innocence of seventeenth-century data. Milton's training in litera-ture accustomed him to follow the exploits of singular heroes. Classical epics dealt with the wrath of Achilles or the wanderings of one versatile fighter or the battles of a divinely led survivor of Troy. Continental epics such as Ariosto's *Orlando Furioso* began by promising that their sprawling adven-tures, 'never before recounted in prose or rhyme', would cluster around the love-maddened Roland. Even those other models known to Milton which pretended to talk of groups usually focused upon individuals. Dante involves us at the start of his *Inferno* with talk of '*our* life's road' but spot-lights a single pilgrim; Tasso begins *Jerusalem Delivered* by balancing talk of the Christian armies and of their leader Godfrey.

Similarly, St Paul predicated his theology of salvation for mankind upon two men, a first and a second Adam. The practical mysticism of the Nether-landish schools at Deventer and Zwolle, which led to *The Imitation of Christ* and Erasmus's meditations, took as its central activity the dialogue of the alone with the Alone, of unique humans with their Deity. Sermons from early Elizabethan preachers through John Donne to the most enthusiastic Ranters urged listeners to see their own lives as dramas in which the self is simultaneously the author, chief actor, and critic. No matter which 'influence' seems important for Milton, both secular and religious ideals habituated him and his audience to look at single characters rather than groups. One need only compare the three parts of Shakespeare's crowded history play *Henry VI* with the leaner, more effective *Macbeth* to realize how success in any medium demands that attention be paid to individuals.

The individual hero speaks with many voices in Milton's work. Words like 'alone', 'lone', 'lonely', 'sole', 'only', 'solitary', 'solitude', 'one', 'apart', 'single', 'unattended', 'individual', 'detached', 'separate', and 'unaided' occur in so many important passages that their presence should condition us to think, as Milton did, about the relation of the one to the many.

As a young man, he often chose to write farewells. His first surviving poem, a paraphrase of Psalm 114, commemorates the Hebrews' joyous exodus from Egypt. But most other verses lament deaths of people like the Vice-Chancellor, the Beadle, the Bishop of Winchester, the Bishop of Ely, 'A Fair Infant', Hobson, the university carrier, and the Marchioness of Winchester. Even though such elegiac exercises were common, he was intrigued by the disappearance of some valued person who moves away to a realm the survivor may visit only briefly and imaginatively. The lone speaker in these early compositions often glances backward, once to his own slow-ripening youth ('How soon hath time'), another time to his father's tolerant generosity (*Ad Patrem*). Throughout his life, Milton treated death and the passage of time with special fervour.

Even when Milton wrote of new beginnings, as in *On the Morning of Christ's Nativity*, he habitually dwelt upon those figures which receded from the viewer's eye. Milton's blessed child appears only briefly 'in smiling infancy' (151). He discomfits 'The old dragon' (168) and forces him to retreat with many of his outmoded devotees. However, the proportion of the ode suggests two separate foci: at one centre, the 'heaven-born-child' (30) who routs demons; but, crowded at the other centre, the many false gods, carefully catalogued and imaginatively presented. Despite the optimistic lesson of this triumph of quality over quantity (a favourite Renaissance topic), anyone familiar with Milton's concerns here recognizes the fascination with departure.

These speakers suffer partly because they learn that one cannot live forever in community with an adored paragon. A central mystery of Christianity informs any personal loss. The adored Christ, taken away before most humans could know him, promised to return but has not yet reappeared. Even though his benign plan of salvation demanded that he leave the earth, those who wait for him must continually balance sorrow and joy. Similarly, the deaths of notable people destroy that comforting illusion of *koinonía*, of community, that Milton sought throughout his life.

Other works deal with separation in various ways. The speaker of *Elegia prima* sounds much like the eighteen-year-old author as he tells his friend Charles Diodati what he has been doing while on leave from Cambridge during the spring of 1626. Fondly and bookishly, he organizes his material more mathematically than is usual among those using the ancient form of the familiar epistle. Maybe to compensate for some irregular behaviour that led to academic banishment, he talks in terms of controlled binary oppositions (his locale and Diodati's; London's attractions and the spartan world of Cambridge). More important, though, he employs stereotypes from antiquity to portray his current pastimes. The very use of Latin elegiacs justifies his alluding to Roman plays rather than to ones currently on English stages. The speaker implies that his current activities have validity because, rusticated though he may have been, he still conforms to recognizable behaviour patterns hallowed by generations of schoolteachers. Yet he does so independently, free from that compulsion which robs acts of their merit.

Likewise the speaker of *Elegia quarta* both resembles and transcends the author. He assures his former tutor Thomas Young in Hamburg that time has not erased his recollection of those many classical exempla which he presumably learned from the Scotsman at St Paul's. The speaker's command of his material implies a reversal of roles, a becoming-the-instructor. Just as he had reassured Diodati that exile, despite its bad connotations, did not irk him, so he informs the pastor that scholarly piety will protect him against war's horrors in distant Germany. The sense of being beleaguered, common perhaps in all ages but underscored by the German war, heightened the value of the friendship, tutelage, and encouragement contained in Milton's letter.

This trust that people can live virtuously in the present so long as they emulate some noble past may seem a dated credo. (Even Gilbert and Sullivan's comic Mikado sniffs, 'it's an unjust world, and virtue is triumphant only in theatrical performances'.) It contradicts the more recent idea that each person is privileged (or doomed) to create himself anew with little external aid. Choice during the Reformation often involved clear alternatives. Dr Faustus's two spirits, one urging godliness and the other impiety, typify the rigidly dualistic categories in which most Christians thought. Whether relatively humble like Milton in his epistle, or famous, like Faustus, each believer knew that the evil one's nimble malice might take advantage of any weak decisions.

Before his Italian trip of 1638–9, Milton continually repaired to the debate between withdrawal and integration. Once they have defiantly dismissed alternatives, both *L'Allegro* and *Il Penseroso* determine the degree to which each will become involved in society. *Comus* dramatizes the traditional quandary of whether to remain alone or to compromise one's values and join an alien community. Standing behind Milton's works are innumerable warnings to exercise one's options wisely. The first Psalm, which Milton translated in 1653, enjoins any who wish to be decent pilgrims on earth to avoid evil companions. The Psalmist encourages humans instead to take as their only partner the law of God. Adhering to the religious and aesthetic implications of such advice, Milton pursued a life whose outward sociability did not distract him from an inner pursuit of literary achievement.

Comus's conviviality conceals an emptiness which only the Lady may satisfy. But the Lady in the masque, rather like the Lady of Christ's College, although alone, neither seeks out the 'late wassailers' (178) nor, when captured, accepts Comus's serpentine invitation ('Be wise, and taste'; 812). The masque settles idealistically the perennial question of what price a decent person must pay for refusing to join a group. She chooses immobility and exclusion. The isolation of some more recent literary characters implies loss of humanity (George Eliot's Silas Marner, for one, or Melville's Bartleby the Scrivener). An inner hollowness forces others to demand membership in hostile or indifferent groups (Joseph K in Franz Kafka's *The Trial*). *Comus* insists that an integrated individual may rightly withdraw into a private world. The final words of the drama, spoken by the trustworthy Spirit, emphasize that genuine self-fulfilment may be earned by the determined individual who acts with moral intelligence: 'Love Virtue, she alone is free' (1018).

In contrast, *Lycidas* supplies a more complex experience of isolation. The speaker says goodbye both to Edward King and to Milton's young manhood. Nearing thirty, about to complete his education by touring the Continent, possessed of some success as an author, he none the less was pained by the death of another young poet/priest. Years before in an early school exercise, Milton had translated an ode by Horace. The young Roman speaker expresses relief for escaping from a *femme fatale* named Pyrrha and looks back on the affair as a shipwreck. But in 1637, there seemed to be little comfort for the English speaker who ponders an actual sinking. Lycidas's death initiates anguished queries, incomplete responses, and at least two climaxes. 'Lycidas sunk low, but mounted high' (172), has returned as the 'genius of the shore' (183). Relieved, 'the uncouth swain' (188) finishes his solitary lament and prepares to travel 'to fresh woods, and pastures new' (193). This harmonizing of many voices from pagan, Christian, and personal sources emphasizes how much control Milton had gained over material that could have been impassively typical or, in another age, merely private.

Exhilarated by warm receptions in Italy but concerned about the growing hostilities in Britain, Milton turned homeward in 1639. He inscribed a visitor's album at Geneva with two significant quotations, one from *Comus* ('If Virtue feeble were, Heaven itself would stoop to her') and another from Horace ('I change my sky but not my mind when I cross the sea') (Parker 1: 181). For the next decade and a half, his certitude that good people could remain steadfast was severely tested by civil and personal trials. Real conflicts delayed until the early 1650s his plan to write a national epic. Serving the Puritan cause in several literary capacities, dealing with marital

problems, becoming aware of his blindness – all urged upon him the significance of individual courage.

His busy involvement in public debates called forth brilliant prose. Often
the personas he creates to describe himself resemble speakers already
introduced in the early verse. In *Defensio secunda* he recalls that 'I would not
exchange the consciousness of my achievement for any deed of theirs'
because 'true and substantial liberty . . . must be sought, not without, but
within' (YP 4: 589, 624). One who knew his poetry or his Commonplace
Book would not have been surprised that the writer politicized theological
and psychological beliefs about individual responsibility.

Milton's major poems continue to examine personal heroism. *Paradise
Lost* introduces many characters who may be labelled 'heroes'. Some are
submerged. The Speaker promises 'Things unattempted yet in prose or
rhyme' (*PL* 1.16) and summons up ghosts of Ariosto and Boiardo for
listeners who could appreciate such necromancy. Although Milton vigorously confronted his predecessors on almost every page of the epic, we may
pass on to more available characters.

The Speaker himself emerges as more than a conventional device to tell
the story. He begins humbly in Book 1 by asking for supernatural help. Yet
he quickly assumes the role of evaluator. Satan's ringing words, he reminds
us, bear 'Semblance of worth, not substance' (1.529) and the Lemnians'
account of Mulciber's fall, while artful, is 'Erring' (1.747). When he must
recount activities in heaven, he again asks for aid, admitting that he is blind,
but trusting that his physical disability will be replaced by spiritual insight:
'that I may see and tell / Of things invisible to mortal sight' (3.54–5). As the
epic unfolds, he sometimes lectures ('neither man nor angel can discern /
Hypocrisy'; 3.683–4), othertimes begs ('O for that warning voice'; 4.1), at
points defines ('necessity, / The tyrant's plea'; 4.393–4), at other points
defies ('On evil days though fallen', he is 'yet not alone' because the spirit
Urania will protect him and his 'fit audience' from a hostile 'wild Rout';
7.26–34). His last extended address, the first forty-seven lines of Book 9,
summarizes his past, present, and future as Narrator. Although he was 'Not
sedulous by nature to indite / Wars', both his 'long choosing' and 'celestial
patroness' convince him that chivalric combat, hitherto the accepted subject
for serious poets, must be replaced by a 'better fortitude / Of patience and
heroic martyrdom'. Thus one may claim that the Speaker grows in bravery
as his poem progresses.

Announced characters in *Paradise Lost*, unlike the sophisticated Speaker
and his sometimes remote models, explode upon our consciousness. John
Dryden pointed to Satan as the 'Hero' because he seemed to be the most

active participant. Romantic readers, eager for ancestors of their own revolutionary energy, also concentrated upon Satan's vigorous intransigence. A convenient modern theory suggests that we are meant to admire Satan's dynamism and then, thanks to the author's many promptings, realize we have pledged allegiance to an unworthy hero.

Even if we do not feel like guilty readers, the epic undercuts Satan so routinely that admiration for his bustling should be temporary. During his last appearance, he boasts to his followers in hell: 'Him by fraud I have seduced / From his creator' (10.485–6). He implies that he chose fraud, the traditional military alternative to force, and bested Adam. We, however, realize Satan cozened only Eve and refused to face our common father in any duel of trickery or strength. If our knowledge of his lie does not diminish him here, circumstances do: he and his rebels metamorphose into snakes, now unable to disguise physical facts with specious rhetoric. Satan often spoke words once associated with heroes like Aeneas; now his ambitious monomania can be seen as only a delusion. Resembling all whom Milton scorned, Satan mistakes his private resentment of authority for a valid argument against it.

Adam and Eve also regress from dignity to disobedience. But they preserve a sombre nobility because they accept their roles in salvation history. Previous literature supplied few examples of a man–woman team engaged in momentous acts. The Adam and Eve of Genesis largely disappear from the rest of the Old Testament. (In their unfallen state, they reappear in the New Testament and later Christianity as Jesus and Mary.) Secular epics usually chronicle the male hero's journey toward his absent beloved in the manner of romance. Milton, however, carefully presents our parents as exemplars of mutual love. When Adam calls his wife 'Sole partner and sole part of all these joys' (4.411), we should appreciate the mingling of worldly and religious ('soul') awe which animates their relationship. Except for their fall and its all-too-recognizable results of rapacious carnality and 'mutual accusation' (9.1187), they remain consistent characters.

Even at the poem's conclusion, when Adam and Eve wend 'their solitary way' (12.649), they exit as tragic figures who have played crucial roles in a cosmic drama and not, like Satan, as parodies of themselves. Although we understand that they cannot exist apart from one another, such mutuality signals the start of conscious humanity. If Satan pretended to live 'farthest from' God (1.247), his actions proved that such independence had no theological or social validity. He thought constantly of heaven, denounced the sun because it reminded him of obligation and, thanks to an inner emptiness resembling that which drove Comus, had to return to his fellow conspirators. Like the sorcerers in Dante's inferno, Satan can only look behind him. Conversely, Adam and Eve set forth to initiate the great parade of subsequent history which Raphael and Michael have exhibited. The fiend's vague plans for future mischief pale when compared with the onward march of generations toward the birth of the Saviour.

Many other figures in the epic rise above a crowd, but few qualify as heroic. Moloch, Belial, and Mammon suggest self-serving schemes at the Great Consult and affront both Satan, who has other plans, and readers, who hear Abdiel declaim in Book 5. The former base their projects on inner needs for violence or indolence; Abdiel, on the other hand, whom Milton invented, passionately attacks Satan's confused assertions about hierarchy and, having stated that angels honourably rank beneath God and the Son in a community, withstands the rebels' sneering judgment that he is 'singular and rash' (5.851). His ostracism from the mutineers allows him to participate more fully in the fellowship of those whose energy is later directed to creation. Yet the Son himself furnishes our most powerful proof of noble individuality. Having overcome Satan in Book 6, in Book 7 he brings into being 'Another world' which will eventually produce 'out of one man a race / Of men innumerable' (7.155). Such fecundity might encourage any human to persevere during unjust isolation.

The archetype of victorious withdrawal is Jesus in *Paradise Regained*. 'This glorious eremite' (*PR* 1.8) duels alone in the wilderness with Satan who, having failed to capture heaven by armed rebellion, now seeks dominion of this earth. Their initial confrontation in 'A pathless desert' (1.296) allows each figure to loom large. Like the bare stage of medieval or Shakespearean drama, this *plataea* does not distract us from the personal confrontation between a dissembler and an authentic hero.

The combat in all four books involves words alone. Only Jesus, the incarnate Word, knows their meanings and thus can best Satan. Unlike the armour and cannon in Book 6 of *Paradise Lost*, objects such as 'A table richly spread' (2.340) exist passively, subject to naming and evaluation by the two antagonists. Both seek to discover and denominate essential truth as opposed to apparent truth. Jesus has the advantage of his opponent from their first meeting: 'I know who thou art' (1.356). Satan still insists upon his autonomy, even after the defeat in heaven. 'I enjoy / Large liberty to round this globe of earth, / Or range in the air, nor from the heaven of heavens / Hath he excluded my resort' (1.364–7), he rightly says, but argues by analogy that his emotions are similarly unrestricted: 'I have not lost / To love' (1.379–80). Jesus, however, destroys such fiction by announcing that 'henceforth oracles are ceased' (1.456). Milton thus emphasizes the optimistic lesson that some upright intellects can penetrate hypocrisy.

In subsequent books, Satan tries to pierce through Jesus' appearance. He peppers his speech with phrases like 'False titled' (2.179) and 'so fables tell' (2.215) which imply that he can winnow fact from fantasy. Yet he fails because he is 'self-deceived' (4.7). Satan's temptations of stone, mountain, and tower miscarry because they, like his words, exist apart from any essential value. Although neither being is coterminous with his guise on earth, Satan, the word-intoxicated scoundrel, assigns private meanings to phenomena, the habit of an involuntary outsider.

Ironically, Satan himself discerns his opponent's notable homogeneity: 'Thy actions to thy words accord, thy words / To thy large heart give utterance due, thy heart / Contains of good, wise, just, the perfect shape' (3.9–11). Jesus' consistency operates like Newton's laws. As the angelic choirs put it, he is 'True image of the Father whether throned / In the bosom of bliss . . . / . . . or remote from heaven, enshrined / In fleshly tabernacle' (4.596–9). His singularity complements that of previous heroes in Milton and conquers for a second time his most determined foe.

Samson Agonistes emphasizes the aloneness of Samson at the play's start but offers little indication that he will overcome his enemies. They include his own 'restless thoughts, that like a deadly swarm / Of hornets' torment him (19–20). His complete isolation from God, people, and mission harks back neither to the biblical tale nor, really, to classical precedents. (Epic heroes often first appear at the low point of their fortunes, yet authors such as Homer and Virgil reassure us that their quests will eventually succeed.) Unlike Milton's other main characters, Samson considers himself dead, 'a moving grave' (102). His connection to deity will not be explained by an omniscient Speaker nor angelic teachers nor self-knowledge. Rather, he will have to use each of his visitors as rungs on a ladder leading from despair to clarification. Whether Milton intended Samson's spiritual progress to represent his own or that of the normative Protestant or merely the Danite champion's seen through the lens of late Renaissance psychology matters less than the steps which the author envisions as vital for regeneration.

With a candour that initially paralyses him, Samson confesses one fact about himself: he caused his own misfortune. But his 'Whom have I to complain of but myself?' (46) accomplishes more than self-judgment. It makes credible his responses to the Chorus, Manoa, Dalila, and Harapha, whom he excuses from culpability. When the Chorus views him emblematically, a 'mirror of our fickle state' (164), they prompt a further refinement of his motives. He defends his dangerous liaisons with infidel women because God initiated them, thus reminding us that Samson has in the past been passive until moved for a holy purpose. His admission to the pious Danites ('She was not the prime cause, but I myself'; 234) frees him from any simple theory of 'we–they' conflict. The primary *agon*, or struggle, of this pugnacious hero will be against himself.

Manoa's visit also allows Samson to advance. Samson continues to insist upon his individual guilt ('I myself have brought them on'; 375) and dallies with the plausible theory that he no longer has a place in holy history: 'all the contest is now / 'Twixt God and Dagon'; 461–2). For him, virtuous combat is an impossible dream: 'What boots it at one gate to make defence, / And at another to let in the foe?' (560–1). Thus Manoa's news that he will try to secure Samson's release to his boyhood home should be welcome. Even *hors de combat*, though, Samson can pray for nothing except death. Such a descent into the soul's dark night, a solitary experience of what Thomas Carlyle would later call 'The Everlasting Nay', does not silence him. In Protestant scenarios, such emptying necessarily precedes a filling by the Holy Spirit. In the drama, Samson's exhaustion will open him to the possibility that he is mistaken about his past and his future.

Dalila, the cause of his present powerlessness, offers him a sensual alternative to slavery or Manoa's home. Here too Samson reacts differently from the way his visitor had anticipated he would. Instead of succumbing to her lascivious coaxing, he violently rejects her as a 'hyaena' (748) and sorceress (937) and 'viper' (1001). Perhaps the anger that he exhibits is merely metamorphosed lust. At any rate, he has passed beyond his former uxoriousness. His willingness to wait for easeful death with no companion suggests a new concern to exit with solitary dignity.

Harapha ends the parade of interrogators and supplies Samson with another chance to grow. Milton invented this aggressor, at once a boastful bully who wishes to fight and a psychological stimulus that helps Samson recapture his former physical confidence. By dismissing Harapha ('Go baffled coward'; 1237), Samson exorcizes the third of his chief dependencies. One may see structural patterns in Judges that repeatedly emphasize Samson's faculties of mind, sense, and muscle. Having cut off his hero from a rational escape to his father's home and an erotic retreat into Dalila's bower, Milton now eliminates the possibility of regeneration through single combat in 'Some narrow place enclosed' (1117). The Danite's words accomplish what his fists might or might not have done and strengthen him so that, after listening to the Chorus, he can cooperate with 'Some rousing motions' (1382).

We only hear of Samson's last moments. He lulls the Philistines with tricks of physical prowess so they do not perceive that his 'patient but undaunted' (1623) demeanour conceals a revitalized avenger. His penultimate action shows his new integrity. He threatens the giddy spectators with sardonically ambiguous words: his next feat 'with amaze shall strike all who behold' (1645). The unseen slaughter and obsequies may be considered as physical parallels to the miraculous ascent of Samson's inner condition from spiritual death to brief but brilliant life.

Samson's return to his community after death sums up the typical reward that Milton envisioned throughout his life for individuals who successfully battle evil in this world. The Lady in *Comus* withstood her trial in the dark forest and headed back to her 'father's residence' (947); after conquering Satan, Jesus 'Home to his mother's house private returned' (*PR* 4.639). So too the dead-but-triumphant Samson heads 'Home to his father's house' (*SA* 1733). Milton felt the persuasive pressure of depravity on solitary people. Yet he still preserved a magnificent hope that goodness somehow prevails and comforts those few who stand firm.

Reading list

Baker, Herschel, *The Image of Man* (New York, 1961)

Bowra, C. M., *From Virgil to Milton* (London, 1965)

Cook, Albert, *The Classic Line* (Bloomington and London, 1966)

Fish, Stanley E., *Surprised by Sin: The Reader in 'Paradise Lost'* (London, 1967)

Freeman, James A., 'Samson's Dry Bones: A Structural Reading of Judges 13–16', in *Literary Interpretations of Biblical Narratives*, vol. 2, ed. K. Gros Louis (Nashville, 1982), 145–60

Freeman, James A. and Anthony Low, eds., *Urbane Milton: The Latin Poetry, Milton Studies* 19 (Pittsburgh, 1984)

Greene, Thomas, *The Descent from Heaven* (New Haven and London, 1963)

Martindale, Charles, *John Milton and the Transformation of Ancient Epic* (Totowa, NJ, 1986)

Parker, William Riley, *Milton: A Biography*, 2 vols. (Oxford, 1968)

Remy, Nicholas, *Demonolatry* (London, 1595)

Steadman, John M., *Milton and the Renaissance Hero* (Oxford, 1967)

Tillyard, E. M. W., *The English Epic and its Background* (Oxford, 1966)

Vincent, Philip, *The Lamentations of Germany* (London, 1638)

5 Milton's epic style: the invocations in *Paradise Lost*

The style of Milton's verse, especially in *Paradise Lost*, is one of the great glories and problems of English poetry. As a subject for admiration and praise, Milton's epic style has received tributes from other poets such as Marvell, Dryden, Wordsworth, and Tennyson. Scholarly attempts to specify the nature of that style have led to the widespread use of distinctions between ornate and plain expressions, grand and conversational modes, and of epithets such as 'baroque' to describe the lavish splendour of Milton's language. More than perhaps any other major English work, *Paradise Lost* invites close and comprehensive examination of its style; and an additional benefit of all that scrutiny has been a general enhancement of our knowledge of style, no matter whose works we are considering, and a realization that metrical choices, as well as diction and syntax, must be taken into account in any thorough discussion of the subject. Remove *Paradise Lost* from the literary tradition, along with the thousands of pages devoted to its style alone which we find spread over more than three centuries, and our understanding of the possibilities of style in English verse would be greatly diminished.

There are those, of course, whose critical comments seem at times designed precisely to accomplish, if not the removal of *Paradise Lost* from the canon of poetry, at least a severe depreciation of its stylistic value. Along with his praise came the censure of Samuel Johnson, and John Keats also vacillated between wonder and dismay at the ways in which Milton did not keep up good English. In the twentieth century, Ezra Pound and T. S. Eliot have decried the style of Milton's epic and its bad influence on subsequent English verse, even though one cannot imagine how, among others, the major Romantic poets could have written so magnificently as they did without the example of Milton before them. The principal objection to Milton's epic style is that it does violence to the basic nature of English, that, in the memorable phrase of Samuel Johnson (who echoes Ben Jonson on Spenser), Milton 'wrote no language' at all (S. Johnson 442). In the *A B C of Reading* (51), Pound summoned up his usual dismissive manner in ridiculing the

following un-English lines from *Paradise Lost*: 'him who disobeys / Me
disobeys' (*PL* 5.611–12). It is such a phrase which elicits the charge that
Milton's style is sometimes awkwardly Latinate: in good English, there
would be no confusion over which verb takes which object. Yet the fact that
either verb can take either object or both, although syntactically odd, is from
another point of view poetically apt. Would it be possible to construct
another phrase which shows, in such a forceful and concentrated way, the
shared properties of the Father and the Son? Milton's syntax here
ingeniously dramatizes a key theological concept and, from his presumed
standpoint, fulfils his definition of decorum, which, as he said in his treatise
Of Education, 'is the grand master peece to observe' (YP 2: 405). Faced with
such sharply conflicting accounts of Milton's epic manner, we may be
tempted to say of style what Horace said of taste: that there is no use debating
it – which is essentially what C. S. Lewis means when defending Milton
against the onslaughts of F. R. Leavis, who hates the very thing that Lewis
loves (Lewis 130). The stylistic liberties of *Paradise Lost* will nevertheless
continue to provoke discussions of style, and we must address the question
of what constitutes style and how Milton's epic relates to that question.

   The range of what may be included in a consideration of style is itself, of
course, problematical. At one extreme are those who treat style as a virtually
separate addition to the basic, and much more important, substance of a
work. For such readers, to discuss style is essentially a mechanical matter of
identifying figures of speech, leading tropes, and grammatical behaviour.
At the other extreme is the view that style is inseparable from substance, that
it in fact is the means by which we apprehend, through textual intentions, a
writer's entire intellectual and emotional response to the world. Most of us
occupy a shifting middle ground, mixing together observations on the
mechanics of a phrase or image with our basic assumptions about the work
itself. Such an eclectic approach may indeed help us transcend the limitations of one particular writer's, or reader's, or era's narrow assumptions.
Historical considerations too can help us place in perspective the stylistic
expectations that may be brought to a work of literature. Although, in
Milton's case, the wrong expectations have led to much hostile criticism,
T. S. Eliot (one of Milton's evasive detractors) can help us fashion some
stylistically helpful ones. In his essay 'The Music of Poetry' Eliot dis-
tinguishes between verse that attempts to imitate the conversational mode of
the day and that which is developed artificially or musically away from
current speech. Thus, in comparison to Milton's 'musical' style, Dryden
took poetry back to the condition of speech and initiated a style brought to

its musical elaboration by Pope. And this style, in turn, was later countered by Wordsworth's lyrical ballads and the 'language really used by men'.

Let us, then, following Eliot's lead, distinguish between primary and secondary languages. A primary language, as Wordsworth and Eliot imply, is always that of current speech in common use. It is also, of course, always changing, so that one era's primary language will not be quite the same as another's; but within the bounds of modest linguistic developments it preserves enough features to explain why so many people can refer to 'good English' or ascribe a basic nature to a language. However, all literary expressions are by definition secondary languages. Unlike a dialect, which its practitioners use as if it were the primary language, a secondary language is more or less deliberately contrived in ways that inevitably involve concepts of style. In modern poetry, prevailing secondary languages usually try to give the illusion of being primary languages; conversational diction, short-winded syntax, imagism, and freedom of versification all contribute to a familiar manner which at its best can mean more than it seems to say. Eliot champions Donne, and Pound champions Browning, largely because of Donne's and Browning's successfully talkative style.

By contrast, Milton's secondary language is often far removed from common speech and does not so much talk as sing, and in such a carefully designed and elaborate way that our knowing the primary language is not enough to enable an easy comprehension; we must also learn another language, as it were, with its own special expectations, conventions, and rules. In varying degrees, older poetry often makes such demands; but Milton's or, say, Hopkins's, is an extreme instance. It is hardly possible, unless one is learning English as a second language, to miss the divergence of Milton's verse from the primary language. 'Where couldst thou words of such a compass find?' asked Marvell in his tribute, thereby indicating how unusual the epic seemed even to Milton's contemporaries (Marvell 65). To Thomas Gray's contemporaries, on the other hand, his *Elegy Written in a Country Church-Yard* seemed familiar from the outset and has endured as one of the most popular and best-loved of all poems despite Gray's insistence that the language of poetry should be as far removed as possible from the language of daily life. In Gray's case, the accessible diction engenders a deceptive simplicity which masks his use of artifice, particularly the prevalent bilateral symmetry in his patterns of sound and in his syntax, which relies heavily on the 'golden line' (the nature of which we shall note shortly with respect to *Paradise Lost*). Perhaps Gray's poem enjoys the best of both worlds by having a style that appeals to readers who prefer a fairly close approximation to the primary language and by simultaneously satisfying the poet's desire for a kind of architectural precision associated with the more advanced expressions of a secondary language. When, however, as in *Paradise Lost*, all elements of language and style seem unusual, it is important to define the kind of secondary language achieved and to appraise its success, at some point, on its own terms. It is not useful or perceptive to condemn Milton for failing to do something he never attempted in the first place.

Milton's attempt to develop an 'answerable style', as he calls it in the invocation to Book 9, involves a claim that it is obtained from his muse; but it is difficult to know how to give such a private claim a public and rational value. The mystery at the basis of his style is somewhat surprising because he characteristically writes in a decidedly logical way. As a religious poet, for that matter, he is unusual for being so rational and doggedly anti-mystical; on its surface, his verse abounds in careful explanations, distinctions, and arguments. Although it is probably not useful to address head-on the subjective relationship between a poet and his muse, it is possible to identify related issues which Milton accepts as given principles and which, unlike the muse, are relatively easy to discuss.

Among the given principles that establish the basis of Milton's inspiration and style, perhaps the foremost concerns what, for him, are two great and related events: the creation of the universe by the Son of God and the incarnation of the Son of God as the historical Christ. At the birth of the universe, the angels sing the same song that they bring to the shepherds at the birth of Christ:

> Glory they sung to the most high, good will
> To future men, and in their dwellings peace.   (7.182–3)

Milton's explicit association of the birth of the universe and the birth of Christ is unusual; religious tradition, so far as I am aware, does not emphasize such a link, although Milton earlier hinted at it in stanza 12 of the Hymn from *On the Morning of Christ's Nativity*. Equally significant, in *Paradise Lost*, is the Son's decision to be born as Christ, and it is a mark of Milton's excitement that the epic narrator joins the angels in singing of the Incarnation:

>   O unexampled love,
> Love nowhere to be found less than divine!
> Hail, Son of God, saviour of men, thy name
> Shall be the copious matter of my song

Henceforth, and never shall my harp thy praise
Forget, nor from thy Father's praise disjoin.   (3.410–15)

Such a personal intrusion by the epic narrator is rare outside of the four formal invocations, and it stands out simply because it is so unusual.

What the preceding two passages indicate is that, whether 'answerable' to the birth of the universe or answerable to that of Christ, Milton's epic style is fundamentally epiphanic and revelatory: his is an authentically personal reinterpretation of inherited religious material. At the same time, his style is remarkably logical and free of mystical confusions, and its rational character demonstrates a confidence in philosophical and rhetorical discourse, the medium without which, of course, the epic poet could never achieve a voice that is public and representative. The private and public demands on Milton's style, though thus obviously somewhat antithetical, combine with the cosmic grandeur of his material to yield a secondary language that is notably complex and symbolic, sensitive and coherent.

Because the invocations of *Paradise Lost* establish a close relationship between Milton's conception of style and his depictions of his muse, they also provide probably the most instructive case studies of Miltonic style. The first of them (1.1–26) immediately proclaims the revelatory mode of the epic by juxtaposing the advent of Christ and the birth of the universe: the narrator is to sing of 'one greater man' (4) just as 'that shepherd' – Moses – taught 'In the beginning how the heavens and earth / Rose out of chaos' (9–10). It has long puzzled me that Milton here calls Moses 'that shepherd' rather than 'that prophet', 'that father', or some other characteristic name. In addition to typological associations with the Good Shepherd and poets as pastoral figures, however, it seems likely that Milton is depicting Moses rather like the shepherds of Bethlehem: subject to a creative revelation, just as the epic narrator assumes himself to be in the nature of his poetic creation, which is modelled in turn on the creative act whereby the divine Spirit 'with mighty wings outspread / Dove-like [sat] brooding on the vast abyss' (20–1).

While themes of advent and birth account for much of the first invocation's content, Milton's style emphasizes 'man' as its key word: 'Of man's first disobedience', 'one greater man', and 'justify the ways of God to men' (1, 4, 26). As we shall see in other examples, it is typical of Milton to use certain words as keystones in building his verse paragraphs. In this case, the key words encircle the paragraph, calling attention to the first and second Adams and to the human race in general.

The metrical setting of the key words is also of interest. What we can call the metrical principle refers to the ways in which the poet's chosen metre and metrical line-length are approximated by the actual rhythms, movements, and sounds of words in a phrase. Metre is of course an abstraction, a formal pattern; all 10,565 lines of *Paradise Lost* have exactly the same metre, iambic pentameter; yet no two have exactly the same rhythms and sounds, and their actual versification therefore conforms to the metrical ideal in many different ways. Obviously, the more closely rhythms agree with metre, the greater is the sense of metrical order; the more the rhythms go their own way, the more the verse is expressive of variety, even of chaos. The accentual-syllabic pattern of iambic pentameter is precisely upheld only when the actual rhythmic impulses on odd-numbered syllables are relatively weak in relation to the stronger impulses on even-numbered syllables. Thus, 'Of man's first disobedience, and the fruit' shows clear dislocations between rhythm and metre in the third and eighth syllables, and these dislocations express a disorder befitting the actions of the first Adam.

By contrast, 'till one greater man / Restore us, and regain the blissful seat' reveals a generally strict alternation of weak and strong syllables in accordance with the metrical form and with the theme of restoration brought about by the second Adam. The strength of this phrase is reflected not only in its prosody, in the relationship of rhythm to metre, but also in its syntax, which is a variation of the 'golden line', described by Dryden as 'two substantives and two adjectives, with a verb betwixt them to keep the peace' (Dryden 6). The bilateral symmetry of the golden line (modifier–noun–verb–modifier–noun) is especially well suited to normal English word order, which is thereby graced with a dignified balance. So Gray, in his *Elegy*, uses the golden line repeatedly to ennoble descriptions of rural life, as does Keats in the final stanza of 'To Autumn' in conjunction with his ritualistic treatment of the deaths of the day and the season. Milton's phrase, if anything, strengthens the symmetry of the golden line by having two central verbs, 'restore' and 'regain', each alliterating with the other. Although the two verbs at the end of the verse paragraph are in a different syntactical construction, they uphold the metrical principle in another way and lead to the final instance of the key word 'man': 'I may assert eternal providence, / And justify the ways of God to men' (25–6). Here, the strength and clarity of the phrase are attributable partly to the regularity of their rhythmic impulses and partly to their containment by the metrical boundaries of line-length. Roughly three out of every five lines in *Paradise Lost* are enjambed; and a regularity of phrasing that harmonizes with the given line-length can therefore stand out, as it does here with Milton's announcement that he will attempt a theodicy and so account for the relationships among his key words.

The theme of establishing divine goodness in the face of so much evil in the world leads us to the final extension of the metrical principle: the nature of the verse paragraph itself and its function of embodying that theme. Just as we can examine small-scale relationships between metre and rhythm within a line, or between an entire line and the actual phrasing that occupies it, so we can study how actual blocks of language fulfil the design of an entire verse paragraph – a design that in some cases can be highly abstract and symbolic, as 'ideal' as the concept of metre itself and the order it represents.

The most important fact about the design of *Paradise Lost*'s opening invocation is that it divides asymmetrically into two parts: (1) a sixteen-line sentence on the beginning and ending of human history, as demarcated by the first and second Adams, followed by (2) a ten-line sentence on God's creative actions in cosmic history and the poet's desire to explain the implications of those actions in a human context. In the first sentence, the muse who inspired Moses is implored to help the poet rise above his classical predecessors: his fame is thus measured in relation to biblical and classical traditions. In the second sentence, the poet wishes to go beyond the limits of human history and fame and to participate, instead, in the divine viewpoint. The two sentences move from human to divine contexts and achieve a literary effect similar to the shift from terrestrial to celestial realms encountered between the octaves and sestets of many Petrarchan sonnets, including Milton's own. Just as the Petrarchan sonnet's asymmetrical form can suggest a symbolism based on numbers, setting the fourness of the octave against the threeness of the sestet, so the asymmetrical form of the first invocation expresses the symbolic value of what is known as the 'divine proportion', which is based not on numbers but on pure geometry.

The divine proportion gives a geometrical relationship between two parts such that the smaller (a) is to the larger (b) as the larger is to the whole (a + b). In Milton's invocation, the ten lines of the second sentence are proportionate to the sixteen lines of the first sentence as the first sentence is to the entire twenty-six lines of the verse paragraph – $10:16::16:26$. Why, in the Renaissance, was this proportion termed divine? A little quick figuring will show that $10:16$ is not quite the same as $16:26$; in fact, numbers can only imperfectly express the divine proportion, which is perfectly clear only as a purely geometrical concept. It is therefore, from the standpoint of numbers, unreachable and ineffable, which is one of the reasons why the Renaissance mathematician Luca Pacioli, whose *Divina Proportione* is an entire treatise on the subject, associated the proportion with the attributes of God and called it divine. Although the proportion has been significant throughout the histories of poetry, painting, music, and architecture, its particular symbolism depends on the era and the individual. To the ancients, it was the division of a form into 'extreme and mean ratio', to the eighteenth century it was 'continuous division', and to the modern age it is the 'golden section'. As the divine proportion to the Renaissance, its precise value in Milton's verse can be specified further.

A more detailed treatment of Pacioli and of Milton's use of the ratio is available elsewhere, but one point is worth repeating here: there are, to my knowledge, only three other instances of the divine proportion in Milton's poetry (L. Johnson 619–26). Two occur near the end of *Paradise Lost*. Michael concludes Adam's education by identifying and summarizing the life of the 'greater man' in a verse paragraph of eighty lines (12.386–465). The first fifty treat Christ's earthly ministry, and the final thirty outline His glory after the Resurrection, that is, after the transition from death to life which occurs at the end of line fifty, the point of divine proportion – 30:50::50:80. Adam's response is to proclaim the fortunate Fall, and his sixteen-line verse paragraph has two main parts – ten lines followed by six (6:10::10:16) – the symbolic form of his utterance mirroring Michael's and so demonstrating that Adam is now in harmony with his mentor, that his education is finally complete (12.469–84). The only other Miltonic example of the ratio is in the climactic tenth stanza of *Lycidas* (165–85). The stanza's twenty-one lines show their main division between the opening thirteen, in which the soul of Lycidas is taken from the ocean's depths to the height of a pastoral heaven presided over by the Good Shepherd, and the concluding eight, in which Lycidas is deified as a guardian of the shore (8:13::13:21).

In each of these three instances of Milton's use of the divine proportion, as in *Paradise Lost*'s opening invocation, the common subject is the 'greater man', the divine being whose incarnation represents the most radical form of apparently self-contradictory qualities and whose depiction therefore taxes the resources of an author's style. Milton's use of the divine proportion, which is restricted to these four passages, accordingly suggests a close correlation between the mathematical symbolism of his style and the theological nature of his subject. The relationship between divinity and humanity, heaven and earth, perfection and imperfection, even good and evil, has its stylistic counterpart in the divine proportion's relationship between perfect geometry and imperfect numbers, an ideal form and an actual structure which, although always falling short of the ideal, takes whatever meaning it has from its conjunction with that form.

The association of Christ with the divine proportion has implications for the degree to which Milton's art is deliberate, for the importance of Christ in his religious outlook, and for the nature of his muse. I have assumed that

Milton's use of the divine proportion is deliberate; were it not, it would occur frequently and fortuitously in association with a wide variety of themes and subjects, thereby defeating any inference concerning its symbolic value. But Milton in fact does use the divine proportion exclusively in connection with one subject; and that subject, as noted already, reflects the great epiphanic event which inspires the epic's revelatory style. The seminal importance of the 'greater man' and the conjoined geometrical symbolism of the divine proportion should accordingly give pause for thought to those who think that Milton denigrated the roles of the Son of God and Christ. Furthermore, the paradoxical nature of the 'greater man' is linked to the antithetical demands placed on Milton's muse. The direct address to the 'heavenly Muse' (1.6) in the first section's outline of the limits of human history gives way, after the point of divine proportion, to the simple word 'Spirit' (1.17) in the eternal context, thus constituting the most abstract and direct representation of the epic narrator's guide and the closest approach to its mysterious source that the poem affords. By contrast, representations of the muse in the three subsequent invocations are distanced by metaphorical and conventional literary means as they move overall from cosmic to terrestrial concerns. As a group, the four invocations show four different ways of depicting the muse: the initially close relationship between the confident poet and his muse becomes increasingly troubled as he comes to the sad task of describing the Fall. The changing relationship between poet and muse requires changes in expression which thereby reflect in miniature the large range of demands that the epic places on its style.

The muse as light organizes metaphorically the celebrated invocation at the beginning of Book 3. Although neither this nor the remaining invocations display the divine proportion, the non-verbal or structural significance of the invocation to light is notable. Here, Milton builds up the verse paragraph with simple binary divisions of his material but uses the key word 'light' to provide a symbolic touch. The first six lines address light as a metaphor for God and are balanced by the next six, in which light is couched in the further metaphor of a stream or fountain. The opening twelve lines show a strong conformity with the metrical principle and are balanced by the next thirteen (13–25), which are verbally bonded by the repetition of the verb 'revisit' (13, 21, 23) and which, through greater use of enjambed phrases, recount the poet's journey through the darkness of hell and Chaos. Now, the entire twenty-five lines are in turn counterbalanced by the next twenty-five (26–50), as Milton meditates on his blindness in relation to beautifully evoked terrestrial images and landscapes. Of particular stylistic interest are the last dozen or so lines (38–50), which display a sustained and poignant contrast in versification: between words capable of sonorous prolongation (for example, 'human face divine') and those terminated by consonants which immediately cut them off ('cloud in stead', 'quite shut out'). A similar effect is present in the choice of rhymes in Sonnet 19, and the related use of voiced and unvoiced consonants in a passage such as the one on the 'fair field of Enna' provides further evidence of Milton's acute sensitivity to the qualities of sound (4.268–72).

The simple binary divisions and balances which account for the internal architecture of the first fifty lines of Book 3 are characteristic of the way in which most verse paragraphs in the epic are constructed; in this case, however, the final five lines (51–5), which renew the poet's direct address to light, transform it into a symbol. Although the blank verse of *Paradise Lost* is by definition unrhymed, there are notable instances of rhyme such as the one here on 'celestial Light' (51) and 'mortal sight' (55) which, in brief, virtually summarizes the burden of the entire paragraph. Not only does the rhyme enclose the final five lines, but it circles back to the beginning of the invocation, linking up with 'holy Light' (1) and 'since God is light' (3). The invocation is thus ringed with a circle of rhyme based on the key word 'light', a circle which thereby encompasses the scale of creation in its extraterrestrial aspects in the first twenty-five lines and its terrestrial images in the next twenty-five. The symbolic enclosure of antithetical realms in the unending line of a circle reflects the complexity of Milton's conception of light, which systematically moves from transcendent to physical qualities. The circle motif here is stylistically reminiscent of the circle of rhymes which enclose the tenth stanza of *Lycidas* and, more astonishingly, run right back to the elegy's opening line which is unrhymed in its own stanza. In both the elegy and the invocation, therefore, expressions of distress and adversity are suddenly perceived to be (as the enclosing circles of rhyme indicate) but part of a larger design which originates in the spiritual realm.

Structural similarities between *Lycidas* and the first two invocations of *Paradise Lost* give way to a verbal parallel in the invocation to Book 7 with the reference to the death of Orpheus (7.32–9). The strongest associations, however, are among the invocations themselves. Book 7 recalls Book 3 both in its invocation's structure and in its disposition of content. It is a strong example of simple binary form, its thirty-nine lines dividing after line twenty with the phrase 'Half yet remains unsung', which calls attention to the two halves not only of the verse paragraph but also of the epic as a whole. As in Book 3, so here the content is split between the celestial and the terrestrial. In the first half, the muse is addressed directly as Urania; but the heavenly context leads to a discussion of how a conventional and classical name for the muse cannot embrace her significance in *Paradise Lost*. The effect of 'now you see Urania, now you don't' may prompt us to ask why Milton became entangled in such cumbersome distinctions in the first place. The usual, and quite correct, response is to point out that the poem's opening invocation asserts the superiority of the Christian epic over its classical predecessors; hence, the classical Urania cannot be invoked without being essentially transformed by her new context. By calling attention to names for his muse, however, Milton is perhaps also asking us to compare their differences throughout the poem. Thus far, the muse has appeared as a direct expression of 'Spirit' (1), through the metaphor of 'Light' (3), and in the traditional and conventional guise of 'Urania' (7), all of which reveals increasingly distanced epithets that suggest a descending sequence from the poet's closest proximity to heaven to his growing preoccupation with the earth. The division of the invocations of Books 3 and 7 into extraterrestrial subjects followed by terrestrial concerns even reproduces in miniature the larger movements of the epic and is commensurate with the graded evocations of the muse.

The invocation to Book 9 provides the final illustration of how the four invocations together constitute a downward sequence. It follows the lead of the invocation to Book 7 by showing two halves, but, instead of displaying a clear structure, it is a weak and troubled simple binary: its forty-seven lines have their main division after line twenty-four, but its clarity is reduced as heavy enjambment obscures the metrical principle and the absence of several main clauses obscures the syntax. All this is of course appropriate for an invocation which must introduce the sad events of the Fall. The muse is no longer directly addressed but is merely referred to in the third person as the 'celestial patroness' (21). The growing distance between God and mankind is played out not only by the relationship between the poet and the muse but also by the diction:

> foul distrust, and breach
> Disloyal on the part of man, revolt,
> And disobedience: on the part of heaven
> Now alienated, distance and distaste,
> Anger and just rebuke, and judgment given,
> That brought into this world a world of woe.   (6–11)

While praising Milton's poignant choice of the word 'distaste' as a perfect response to the tasting of the apple, Christopher Ricks has speculated that the imbalance between 'on the part of man' and 'on the part of heaven', where 'on the part of God' would normally supply the parallel, might be a

way of distancing language in accordance with the divine view of the Fall
(Ricks 69–70). The third-person treatment of the muse provides a strong
analogy to his supposition. Verbal echoes between this invocation and that
in Book 1, which is most distant from it in every sense of the word,
emphasize the great contrast between them. The line 'That brought into this
world a world of woe' recalls 'Brought death into the world, and all our woe'
(1.3). Yet what was merely a springboard to the heights of a revelatory style
at the beginning of the poem is here the prelude to a sustained tragic manner
and tone. Even the epic narrator's self-portraits follow suit: at the outset he
says little about himself except to express unbounded confidence in his
'adventurous song' (1.13); in Book 3, his blindness is turned from a topic of
complaint to the mark of a prophet who possesses internal sight; by Book 7,
he sings 'with mortal voice' (24) and worries about his fate in relation to the
violence that beset Orpheus; and the final invocation concludes with
depressing thoughts on historical and personal debilitation. The composite
portrait of the poet, as of his muse, represents a descent and suggests again
the benefits of treating the invocations as a sequence and therefore, too, as
a guide to the changing nature of the poet's style.

The invocations have, in literary criticism, come a long way from being
the beautiful 'superfluities' faintly praised by Samuel Johnson. It is now customary to take them seriously as a group, as work throughout the past half
century demonstrates (Tillyard 243; Fixler 961–2; Lewalski 31–6). Michael
Fixler has gone so far as to argue that Plato's 'four furors' or levels of
inspiration are respectively invoked in descending order in the four
invocations (Fixler 952–8). His argument is based on a careful consideration
of intellectual history; mine here is concerned more with style and structure,
though it nevertheless establishes a close parallel to his views. On the basis
of structure alone, the sequence of a divine proportion (Book 1), a symbolic
circle (Book 3), a strong example of a binary paragraph (Book 7), and a weak
or troubled one (Book 9) constitutes a descending order that affirms the
tragic development of the epic and lends credence to the notion that the Fall
is wholly unfortunate. As a counterbalance, however, we must recall the
reappearance of the divine proportion in speeches by Michael and Adam
near the end of Book 12 and the consequent emphasis on the fortunate Fall.
That is to say, although the invocations form a sequence, they must always
be seen as ways of approaching the larger dimensions of the poem.

But all such thematic issues tend to deflect attention away from our
immediate concern with the epic's style, a basis for which I have attempted
to establish by emphasizing the importance of structural or non-verbal
significance and symbolism in the invocations. One could, of course, devote

more space to the purely verbal aspects of Milton's style, but over the centuries many others have done precisely that, often at great length; and it is best simply to consult their works for further examples. A thorough discussion of comments on lines such as 'Erroneous there to wander and forlorn' (7.20) would itself require another essay.

By emphasizing the formal construction of Milton's invocations in *Paradise Lost*, we can perceive how essential his non-verbal artistry is to his verbal meaning, to the initially exalted and finally muted portraits of the epic's narrator and muse, and to the striking ways in which the invocations parallel the themes and styles that inspirit the epic overall. Milton's ability to create such a flexible style is impressive, all the more so because of the vast range of subjects it encompasses. Nor does he practise it only in *Paradise Lost*: as our references to *Lycidas* show, even before reaching the age of thirty Milton had worked out the metrical and geometrical symbolism of the divine proportion, which would become a keystone of his epic style. For that matter, the circle of rhyme and range of diction in *Lycidas*, as well as the daring enjambment of the latter sonnets, are further indications that his epic style evolved from a lifetime's experience. Milton is one of the best examples since Virgil of a poet who learned from his earlier works, and he is one of the few who has ever achieved an epic style whose building blocks, its individual verse paragraphs, are so worthy of the 'great argument' of an entire long poem.

Reading list

Dryden, John, 'Preface to *Sylvae*', in *The Works of John Dryden*, ed. Earl Miner, vol. 3 (Berkeley, 1969)

Eliot, T. S., 'The Music of Poetry', in *On Poetry and Poets* (London, 1957)

Fixler, Michael, 'Plato's Four Furors and the Real Structure of *Paradise Lost*', *PMLA* 92 (1977), 952–62

Johnson, Lee M., 'Milton's Mathematical Symbol of Theodicy', in *Symmetry: Unifying Human Understanding*, ed. Istvan Hargittai (Oxford, 1986)

Johnson, Samuel, 'The Life of Milton', in *Selected Poetry and Prose*, ed. Frank Brady and W. K. Wimsatt (Berkeley, 1979)

Lewalski, Barbara Kiefer, *'Paradise Lost' and the Rhetoric of Literary Forms* (Princeton, 1985)

Lewis, C. S., *A Preface to 'Paradise Lost'* (London, 1942)

Marvell, Andrew, 'Mr Milton's Paradise Lost', in *The Poems of Andrew Marvell*, ed. Hugh MacDonald (London, 1952)

Pound, Ezra, *A B C of Reading* (New York, 1960)

Ricks, Christopher, *Milton's Grand Style* (Oxford, 1963)

Tillyard, E. M. W., *Milton* (London, 1930)

Weismiller, Edward, 'Studies of Style and Verse Form in *Paradise Regained*', in *A Variorum Commentary on the Poems of John Milton*, vol. 4 (New York, 1975)

6   The genres of *Paradise Lost*

The Renaissance is a period of heightened genre consciousness in literary theory and poetic practice, and Milton is arguably the most genre-conscious of English poets. His great epic, *Paradise Lost*, is preeminently a poem about knowing and choosing – for the Miltonic Bard, for the characters, for the reader. One ground for such choices is genre, Milton's own choice and use of a panoply of literary forms, with their accumulated freight of cultural significances shared between author and audience.

Critics have long recognized and continue to discover in Milton's poem an Edenic profusion of thematic and structural elements from a great many literary genres and modes, as well as a myriad of specific allusions to major literary texts and exemplary works. Almost everyone agrees that *Paradise Lost* is an epic whose closest structural affinities are to Virgil's *Aeneid*, and that it undertakes in some fashion to redefine classical heroism in Christian terms (Bowra; Di Cesare; Hunter; Steadman 1967). We now recognize as well how many major elements derive from other epics. From Homer's *Iliad*: a tragic epic subject – here, the death and woe resulting from an act of disobedience; a hero (Satan) motivated like Achilles by a sense of injured merit; the battle scenes in heaven (Blessington 1979; Mueller). From the *Odyssey*: Satan's wiles and craft; and Satan's Odysseus-like adventures on the perilous seas (of Chaos) and in new lands (Aryanpur; Steadman 1968, 194–208). From Hesiod's *Theogony*: many aspects of the war in heaven between the good and evil angels (Hughes 1965; Revard). From Ovid's *Metamorphoses*: the pervasiveness of change and transformation – diabolic and divine – in the Miltonic universe (Harding 1946; Lewalski 1985, 71–6; Martz). From Ariosto's *Orlando Furioso*: the Paradise of Fools (Hughes 1967; Schumacher). From the *Faerie Queene*: the Spenserian allegorical characters, Sin and Death (Greenlaw; Hieatt; Williams; Quilligan). From Du Bartas's massive hexameron (creation epic), *The Divine Weeks and Works*: Milton's brief epic of creation in Book 7 (Evans; Snyder, 1: 82–8; Taylor). In more general terms, Milton's Eden is in some respects a romance garden of love in which a hero and heroine must withstand a dragon of sorts (Giamatti). Moreover, because heroic values have been so profoundly trans-valued in *Paradise Lost*, the poem is sometimes assigned to categories beyond epic: pseudomorph, prophetic poem, apocalypse, anti-epic, transcendent epic (Spencer; Steadman 1973; Wittreich 1975; Tolliver; Webber).

Many dramatic elements have also been identified: some vestiges of Milton's early sketches for a drama entitled *Adam Unparadiz'd*; some structural affinities to contemporary epics in five 'acts', such as Davanant's *Gondibert*; and tragic protagonists who fall from happiness to misery through *hamartia* (Barker; Rollin; Sirluck). Others include the tragic soliloquies of Satan and Adam, recalling those of Dr Faustus and Macbeth; the morality-play 'Parliament of Heaven' sequence in the debate of God and the Son (3.80–343); the scene of domestic farce in which Satan first vehemently repudiates and then fawns upon his reprehensible offspring, Sin and Death (2.643–883); the scenes of domestic tragedy in Books 9 and 10 which present Adam and Eve's quarrel, Fall, mutual recriminations, and (later) reconciliation; and the tragic masques or pageants of Books 11 and 12, portraying the sins and miseries of human history (Demaray; Gardner; Grossman; Hunter 72–95; Kranidas; Samuel).

The panoply of kinds includes pastoral: landscape descriptions of Arcadian vistas; pastoral scenes and eclogue-like passages presenting the *otium* (ease, contentment) of heaven and unfallen Eden; and scenes of light georgic gardening activity (Daniells; Empson 149–94; Frye 1965; Knott). Also, several kinds of lyrics embedded in the epic have received some critical attention: celebratory odes, psalmic hymns of praise and thanks-giving, submerged sonnets, an epithalamium (wedding song), love lyrics (*aubade*, nocturne, sonnet), laments and complaints (Summers 71–86; McCown; Johnson; Nardo; Blessington 1986). There are also many rhetorical and dialogic kinds which have not been much studied from the perspective of genre: Satan's several speeches of political oratory in Books 1 and 2; God's judicial oration defending his ways (3.80–134); the parliamentary debate in hell over war and peace (2.11–378); the Satan–Abdiel debate over God's right of sovereignty (5.772–895); a treatise on astronomical systems (8.15–178); a dialogue on human nature between God and Adam (8.357–451) and another on love between Raphael and Adam (8.521–643); Michael's lectures on Christian historiography in Books 11 and 12; Satan's temptation speech to Eve in the style and manner of 'some orator renowned / In Athens or free Rome' (9.670–732; Amorose; Broadbent; Burden; MacCallum; Steadman 1968, 241–62; Steadman 1969, 67–92).

If we ask why Milton incorporated so complete a spectrum of literary forms and genres in *Paradise Lost*, a partial answer must be that much Renaissance critical theory supports the notion of epic as a heterocosm or compendium of subjects, forms, and styles. Homer's epics, Rosalie Colie has reminded us (22–3), were widely recognized as the source and origin of all arts and sciences – philosophy, mathematics, history, geography, military art, religion, hymnic praise, rhetoric – and of all literary forms. Renaissance tradition also recognized the Bible as epic-like in its comprehension of all history, all subject matters, and many genres – law, history, prophecy, heroic poetry, psalm, allegory, proverb, hymn, sermon, epistle, tragedy, tragicomedy, and more (Lewalski 1966, 10–36; Lewalski 1979, 31–71; Wittreich 1979, 9–26).

Responding to this tradition, Renaissance poets devised epics on inclusivist lines. Tasso, whom Milton recognized as the premier epic poet and theorist among the moderns, observed that Homer and Virgil had intermingled all forms and styles in their great epics, but claimed for Renaissance heroic poems (with obvious reference to his own *Gerusalemme Liberata*) an even greater range and variety, imaging the entire created universe (Tasso 78). Moreover, the major sixteenth-century English narratives with claims to epic status – Sidney's *New Arcadia* and Spenser's *Faerie Queene* – were quite obviously mixtures of epic, romance, pastoral, allegory, and song. But if contemporary theory and practice gave Milton ample warrant to comprehend a very broad spectrum of literary kinds within *Paradise Lost*, he did not make of it a mausoleum of dead forms. On the contrary, all of Milton's major poems are invested with an imaginative energy which profoundly transforms the genres themselves, creating new models which profoundly influenced English and American writers for three centuries.

Attention to Milton's generic strategies can also highlight some important ways in which Renaissance poetic theory and practice intersect with contemporary critical concerns: intertextuality, the springs of poetic creativity and authority, the responses of the reader (Bloom; Greene; Kerrigan; Fish). In regard to genre, Milton's poem manifests several of the so-called 'novelistic' characteristics the Russian genre-theorist Mikhail Bakhtin finds in many Renaissance and post-Renaissance prose narratives: multiple genres, including extra-literary kinds, which create multiple perspectives upon the subject; the dialogic interaction of forms; the 'polyglossia' of several generic languages within the work; strong connectives linking the poem to contemporary reality; the valorization of process. Yet while these characteristics give Milton's modern epic enormous complexity, they do not produce the indeterminacy and inconclusiveness Bakhtin associates with them. In pursuing these and other suggestive connections between Renaissance and contemporary poetic theory we need to recognize some fundamental differences in assumptions about poetry and the poet, grounded chiefly in the Renaissance and Miltonic conception of the poet as teacher and rhetor.

Milton's complex use of the Renaissance genre system serves in part to enable his own poetic vision, since it is only through such literary forms, which embody the shared imaginative experience of Western man and woman, that the Miltonic Bard is able to imagine and articulate his vision of the truth of things. But also, it is only through such forms that he can accommodate that vision to readers present and future, educating them in the complex processes of making discriminations which are at once literary and moral. Milton's comments about poetry in *The Reason of Church-Government* and the pedagogic ideal he sets forth in *Of Education* suggest that as teacher and rhetor he wishes to advance our understanding through a literary regimen at once intellectually demanding and delightful (YP 1: 801–23; 3: 366–79). In *Paradise Lost* his method is to build upon and let his readers refine their responses to the cultural values and assumptions encoded in the genre system – about man and woman, God, nature, language, heroism, virtue, pleasure, work, and love (Lewalski 1985).

Since terms relating to genre have often been used inconsistently, we need a few definitions which accord with the concepts of major Renaissance and modern genre-theorists (Scaliger; Minturno 1559, 1564; Puttenham; Sidney; Frye; Fowler). In the Renaissance, the familiar triad of narrative, dramatic, and lyric normally carried meanings deriving from Plato's and Aristotle's three kinds of imitation or presentation, so I shall refer to them here as *literary categories* or *strategies of presentation*. The term *Genre* (or *kind*, the usual Renaissance word) is reserved for the historical genres – epic, tragedy, sonnet, funeral elegy, hymn, epigram, and many more – which are identified in classical and Renaissance theory and poetic practice by specific formal and thematic elements, topics, and conventions. Alastair Fowler (37–74) discusses these historical genres as families whose members share several (but not always the same) features, among them formal structure, metre, size, scale, strategy of presentation, subject, values, mood, occasion, attitude, style, motifs. *Subgenres* are formed by further specification of subject matter and topics – for example, the revenge tragedy is a subgenre of tragedy. The term *Mode* is appropriate for several expressive literary kinds – pastoral, satiric, comedic, heroic, elegiac, and tragic, among others – which are identified chiefly by subject matter, attitude, tonality, and motifs, and which interpenetrate works or parts of works in several genres.

For example, we may have a *pastoral* comedy or novel or song, a *tragic* epic, or short story, or ballad, a *satiric* verse epistle or epigram or essay.

Milton's 'Preface' to Book 2 of the *Reason of Church-Government* (1642) provides some indication of his complex approach to the Renaissance genre system. Referring to the epic–dramatic–lyric triad, he deliberates about a wide range of genre choices and notable models – classical, biblical, or contemporary – within each category:

> Time servs not now, and perhaps I might seem too profuse to give any certain account of what the mind at home in the spacious circuits of her musing hath liberty to propose to her self, though of highest hope, and hardest attempting, whether that Epick form whereof the two poems of *Homer*, and those other two of *Virgil* and *Tasso* are a diffuse, and the book of *Job* a brief model . . . Or whether those Dramatick constitutions, wherein *Sophocles* and *Euripides* raigne shall be found more doctrinal and exemplary to a Nation, the Scripture also affords us a divine pastoral Drama in the Song of *Salomon* consisting of two persons and a double *Chorus*, as *Origen* rightly judges. And the Apocalyps of Saint *John* is the majestick image of a high and stately Tragedy, shutting up and intermingling her solemn Scenes and Acts with a sevenfold *Chorus* of halleluja's and harping symphonies . . . Or if occasion shall lead to imitat those magnifick Odes and Hymns wherein *Pindarus* and *Callimachus* are in most things worthy, some others in their frame judicious, in their matter most an end faulty: But those frequent songs throughout the law and prophets beyond all these, not in their divine argument alone, but in the very critical art of composition may be easily made appear over all the kinds of Lyrick poesy, to be incomparable. (YP 1: 812–16)

Remarkably, Milton incorporates virtually the entire genre system in *Paradise Lost*, achieving effects which can only be suggested here through a few examples.

Milton employs specific literary modes in his epic to characterize the various orders of being: the heroic mode for Satan and his damned society; mixed for the celestial society of the angels; pastoral (opening out to georgic and comedic) for prelapsarian life in Eden; tragic (encompassing at length postlapsarian georgic, pastoral, and heroic) for human life in the fallen world. These modes establish the affective quality of the several segments of the poem, through appropriate subject matter, motifs, tone, and language, and each mode is introduced by explicit literary signals. As the narrative begins, the epic question and answer present Satan and hell in heroic terms, with reference to a range of epic passions, motives, and actions: 'pride', 'glory', 'ambitious aim', 'impious war in heaven', 'battle proud' (1.34–44). The Edenic pastoral mode is introduced by reference to the garden as 'A happy rural seat of various view' (4.247). The forthright announcement 'I now must change / These notes to tragic' (9.5–6) heralds the Fall sequence. And the claim that this tragic subject is 'not less but more heroic' than traditional epic themes (9.14) leads into the mixed modes of postlapsarian but regenerate human life.

These several modes import into the poem the values traditionally associated with them: great deeds, battle courage, glory (*aristeia*) for the heroic mode; love and song, *otium*, the carefree life for pastoral; responsibility, discipline, the labour of husbandry for georgic; the easy resolution of difficulties through dialogue and intellect for the comedic; the pity and terror of the human condition for the tragic. These contrasting modes and their modulations, together with the mixed modes which present life in the heavenly society, engage us in an on-going critique of the various perspectives on human life which they provide.

Within this structure of literary modes Milton incorporates a great many narrative, dramatic, lyric, and discursive genres. The longer narrative and dramatic kinds – epic and romance, tragedy and comedy – are incorporated through what I term generic paradigms, identified by characteristic themes, motifs, conventions, and structural patterns associated with the given genre. These generic paradigms are further reinforced by verbal allusions, plot analogies, and references to scenes, episodes, and motifs in major classical and Renaissance works in each kind. By this means we are invited to identify certain genres and certain poems as subtexts for portions of Milton's poem, and then to attend to the completion or transformation of those allusive patterns as the poem proceeds. Let us examine some of these paradigms.

Satan, we soon discover, enacts the generic paradigms of one after another of the heroic genres (epic of strife, quest epic, romance): he is thereby measured against the most notable heroes in all these kinds, promoting an exhaustive examination of the meaning of heroism. The opening scene in hell displays the distinctive topics and conventions of the epic of wrath and strife: Homeric catalogues of leaders, epic games, a council of war, addresses to armies. In relation to this paradigm, Satan reveals himself by degrees as a debased version of Achilles and Aeneas, the most notable heroes in that kind. Like Achilles (though without his justification) Satan prides himself on his obduracy, his 'fixed mind / And high disdain, from sense of injured merit' (1.97–8); and like Aeneas he escapes from a flaming city to seek a better kingdom. The *Iliad* pattern develops through several flyting matches (epic taunts), single combats, and epic battle scenes in heaven in which Satan, unlike Achilles, is ignominiously defeated. The *Aeneid* pattern continues through Satan's adventures and successful conquest in Eden, though (unlike Aeneas) he can find no new homeland because he brings hell with him everywhere: 'my self am hell' (4.75). The epic-of-wrath paradigm culminates in Satan's self-designed scene of epic triumph in Book 10, a triumph which turns to abject humiliation as Satan and his followers are abruptly transformed to serpents, enduring the thirst of a Tantalus in the Virgilian underworld.

Intersecting with this paradigm is that of the quest epic, which extends to include romance, the quintessential quest form. Milton incorporates a 'mini-Odyssey' into his epic as Satan is measured against the crafty Odysseus. The *Odyssey* pattern begins as Satan sets forth on his journey to earth through Chaos; it develops in Chaos and Eden as he continually proves himself a skilled rhetorician and a master of disguises (Steadman 1968, 194–208); and it finds completion when he returns to hell in Book 10, liberating his wife and son (Sin and Death) from captivity by his notable victory. But unlike Odysseus, whose entire adventure is a journey home, Satan at the very outset of his travels (in Book 2) is reunited with, but ironically fails to recognize, his reprehensible daughter–wife Sin, and the hideous offspring of their incestuous union, Death. And the honour they accord him at his return to hell in Book 10 soon gives way to the universal hiss of his followers turned into snakes.

Again, Milton's poem incorporates the basic narrative paradigm of romance: the continual wandering and multiple quests of knights-errant, as their ultimate goals or principal quests are almost indefinitely postponed or only partially achieved (Parker). In Satan and the fallen angels this romance paradigm is perverted as the wandering (intellectual and physical) becomes an absolute. In hell the fallen angels explore the hardest philosophical questions – 'Fixed fate, free will, foreknowledge absolute' – but find 'no end, in wandering mazes lost' (2.560–1). And instead of a wandering wood or labyrinthine landscape, Satan in Chaos traverses 'a dark / Illimitable ocean without bound, / Without dimension' (2.891–3), where he has no control whatsoever over his own motions or directions but 'swims or sinks, or wades, or creeps, or flies' (2.950) as he can, subjected entirely to the winds of chance.

Certain of Satan's adventures are specifically associated with episodes in particular romances or romantic epics, but again we recognize the perversions. Spenser's Red Crosse Knight defeats the serpent Error and (at last) the serpentine Duessa, but Satan embraces the Spenserian allegorical monsters he meets (Sin and Death) as his own progeny. Satan's journey to the Paradise of Fools is a darker version of Astolfo's journey to the Limbo of Vanities in Ariosto; however Satan comes on no rescue mission but because he is himself the source of all the vanities soon to be housed in that place. In

Eden, Satan perverts all the familiar romance roles of knights in gardens of love, for he cannot win love there, nor find sensual delight, nor enjoy sensuous refreshment: instead he sees 'undelighted all delight' (4.286) and feels more intensely than before the agony of his own loneliness, lovelessness, and unsatisfied desire. A perverse Guyon (*Faerie Queene* 2. Canto 12), he destroys in Eden not a wantonly sinful but a joyously innocent Bower of Bliss and Love. In Book 10 this romance paradigm also finds its fitting resolution, as Satan – a truly perverse St George – does not slay but turns into the dragon.

Milton also incorporates the paradigms of several forms of tragedy. Satan enacts at the outset a parodic version of heroic tragedy, portraying himself in Book 1, with particular reference to Aeschylus's *Prometheus Bound*, as the noble and indomitable victim of an irrational, tyrannical, and wrathful God (Werblowsky). But Satan himself admits that he was motivated to rebel by pride and ambition – not, like Prometheus, by an intention to benefit mankind. Satan's great soliloquy on Mount Niphates (4.32–113) casts him briefly as a Faustean tragic hero, voicing the spiritual agonies of the damned soul and forced to acknowledge his guilt – his paradigmatic scene of suffering, as John Steadman notes (1976, 103–4). In subsequent soliloquies in Book 4 Satan takes on first the posture of the villain hero driven by ambition (a Macbeth or a Richard III), and at length that of an Elizabethan revenge hero – a Barrabas or an Iago wracked with envy and jealousy, devising plots and exulting in evil plans: 'O fair foundation laid whereon to build / Their ruin!' (4.521). However, as he sets his revenge plot in motion in Book 9, he perverts the usual Elizabethan paradigm, for he cannot harm his true enemy, God, and the human beings he ravages have done him no wrong whatsoever.

When Satan imbrutes himself in the serpent he recognizes how radically he is reversing the usual tragic paradigm. He is not felled by fate or his own *hamartia* for seeking to soar above humanity; rather he here chooses to sink far below it:

> O foul descent! That I who erst contended
> With gods to sit the highest, am now constrained
> Into a beast, and mixed with bestial slime,
> This essence to incarnate and imbrute,
> That to the highth of deity aspired;
> But what will not ambition and revenge
> Descend to?   (9.163–9)

He also sees clearly that the revenge he seeks must be self-destructive:

'Revenge, at first though sweet, / Bitter ere long back on it self recoils' (9.171–2). Satan has now moved outside both the classical and Elizabethan paradigms of tragedy, since for him there can be no catharsis of any kind, not even the release of meeting the worst at last, but only a continual declining and falling. At last, when Satan's involuntary transformation into a serpent in Book 10 makes him the butt of scorn and derision, we see God rewriting the Satanic revenge tragedy as black comedy.

By contrast with Satan's parodic revenge tragedy, Milton devised the Fall of Adam and Eve to conform to Aristotle's prescriptions for the best kind of classical tragedy (Aristotle; Steadman 1976). The plot involves a change in the protagonists' fortunes from happiness to misery, precisely articulated in Adam's outcry – 'O miserable of happy!' (10.720). As Aristotle recommended, the protagonists are persons better than ourselves who fall through *hamartia* (in this case, culpable errors of judgment); and the plot is complex, developed through several highly dramatic scenes: the marital dispute, the two temptations, reactions to the Fall (9.192–10.862). There are several *peripeteia* (reversals) with attendant tragic ironies. There is an explicit *anagnorisis* (discovery) when Adam and Eve awaken from their lust-induced sleep and realize their loss: 'good lost, and evil got . . . naked thus, of honour void, / Of innocence, of faith, of purity' (9.1072–5). And there is a long scene of suffering as Adam and Eve voice shame, fear, guilt, remorse, torments of conscience, and mutual recriminations, culminating with Adam's poignant complaint, prostrate and paralyzed by despair, 'from deep to deeper plunged' (10.844).

At this point, the Aristotelian tragic paradigm gives way to the paradigm of Christian tragedy, drawn essentially from the Book of Revelation. Catastrophes in this paradigm are not averted: like Christ himself, the elect suffer trials, sicknesses, catastrophes, deaths, martyrdoms, but they are enabled through grace to endure their suffering in patience and to wait in faith and hope for the reversal which will occur only at the Apocalypse (King). In Milton's poem the turn from classical to Christian tragedy is the literary manifestation of the action of grace: God works a reversal by clothing Adam and Eve's physical and spiritual nakedness; and Eve's act of begging Adam's forgiveness does so on the human plane, restoring the community of human love. God's directive to Michael concerning the emotional state he is to induce in Adam and Eve defines precisely the catharsis appropriate to this new Christian tragedy: Adam and Eve are to go forth from the Garden, and we from the poem, 'not disconsolate', 'sorrowing, yet in peace' (11.113–17).

The lyric and discursive genres are present in Milton's epic through another strategy of inclusion. Rhetorical and dialogic kinds are embedded in *Paradise Lost*: rhetorical speeches in the three classical genres (judicial, deliberative, demonstrative); several kinds of dialogue (Platonic, Boethian, biblical); and also formal debates. These embedded discursive genres engage us in careful discriminations concerning the uses and the perversions of speech and language. Also, many lyrics are embedded in the narrative, set off by specific generic conventions, signals of commencement and closure, and integrity of structure, tone, and subject matter. Milton's epic employs a much more complete spectrum of lyrics, for a larger array of purposes, and in a more complex and conscious way, than does any previous epic. The Bard voices many apostrophes, four hymnic proems (to Books 1, 3, 7, and 9), and an epithalamium, 'Hail wedded love' (4.750–5). Satan and the fallen angels often fall into laments but cannot sustain them long, and they can only pervert lyrics of praise. The angels celebrate all divine activities with hymnic praises, but they produce their most elaborate and most exalted hymns when divine love and divine creativity are manifested (3.372–415; 7.182–91; 7.565–73; 7.602–32). And prelapsarian and postlapsarian man and woman exhibit their psychological and spiritual states through a great variety of odes, love lyrics, laments, complaints, prayers, and hymns, the most elaborate and eloquent of which is their magnificent morning hymn of praise (5.160–208). In *Paradise Lost* characters reveal their natures and their values through the lyrics they devise.

To illustrate how some of these embedded lyric forms function in Milton's epic, we might examine the rich significances which attach to Adam and Eve's love lyrics and laments. Eve devised the first love lyric in prelapsarian Eden, an exquisite, rhetorically complex, sonnet-like poem of eighteen lines, celebrating the sweetness and beauty of Eden through elaborate patterns of repetition, and building to the final half-line which proclaims Adam the essence of Eden for Eve:

> With thee conversing I forget all time,
> All seasons and their change, all please alike.
> Sweet is the breath of morn, her rising sweet,
> With charm of earliest birds; pleasant the sun
> When first on this delightful land he spreads
> His orient beams, on herb, tree, fruit, and flower,
> Glistering with dew; fragrant the fertile earth
> After soft showers; and sweet the coming on
> Of grateful evening mild, then silent night
> With this her solemn bird and this fair moon,

And these the gems of heaven, her starry train:
But neither breath of morn when she ascends
With charm of earliest birds, nor rising sun
On this delightful land, nor herb, fruit, flower,
Glistering with dew, nor fragrance after showers,
Nor grateful evening mild, nor silent night
With this her solemn bird, nor walk by moon,
Or glittering starlight without thee is sweet.   (4.639–56)

Lovely as this is, Adam's *aubade* or dawn song (5.16–22) is presented as a finer love poem, characterized by vibrant imagery, freer form, more intense feeling; verbal echoes identify it as a prototype of the Bridegroom's song to the Bride (Song of Sol. 2: 10–13), often said to be the most exquisite of all love songs (Lewalski 1979, 67):

Awake
My fairest, my espoused, my latest found,
Heaven's last best gift, my ever new delight,
Awake, the morning shines, and the fresh field
Calls us; we lose the prime, to mark how spring
Our tended plants, how blows the citron grove,
What drops the myrrh, and what the balmy reed,
How nature paints her colours, how the bee
Sits on the bloom extracting liquid sweet.   (5.17–25)

But in the fallen world the situation is reversed: Adam inaugurates the tragic lament-complaint while Eve transforms and perfects that kind. Adam voices several tragic lyrics: desperate laments for what is lost, and bitter complaints seeking some remedy or relief. His first sight of the fallen Eve evokes an anguished interior lament for her ruin and for the bleakness of life without her, 'O fairest of creation, last and best / Of all God's works . . . ' (9.896–916). His longest 'sad complaint' which begins 'O miserable of happy! Is this the end / Of this new glorious world' (10.720–844), vainly seeks relief in outcries, apostrophes, and agonized questions. In structure and tone, Adam's tragic lyrics most closely resemble such classical models as Ovid's *Heroides*, culminating in despair.

By contrast, Eve inaugurates a better kind of tragic lyric, the true archetype of the penitential psalms in substance and in structure. Echoing especially Psalms 38, 51, and 102, her prayer to Adam for forgiveness fully expresses the misery, grief, and agony of the fallen condition, but also voices repentance for sin, desire to make amends, hope of reconciliation:

> Forsake me not thus, Adam, witness heaven
> What love sincere, and reverence in my heart
> I bear thee, and unweeting have offended,
> Unhappily deceived; thy suppliant
> I beg, and clasp thy knees; bereave me not,
> Whereon I live, thy gentle looks, thy aid,
> Thy counsel in this uttermost distress,
> My only strength and stay: forlorn of thee,
> Whither shall I betake me, where subsist?
>
> .   .   .
>
> on me exercise not
> Thy hatred for this misery befallen,
> On me already lost, me than thy self
> More miserable; both have sinned, but thou
> Against God only, I against God and thee,
> And to the place of judgment will return,
> There with my cries importune heaven, that all
> The sentence from thy head removed may light
> On me, sole cause to thee of all this woe,
> Me me only just object of his ire.   (10.914–36)

Eve's eloquent psalmic prayer begging forgiveness of the husband she has wronged begins her redemptive role as type of the Second Eve whose seed is the Messiah, even as she echoes the Son's proposal in the dialogue in heaven to assume mankind's guilt unto himself (3.236–7). E. M. W. Tillyard was right to stress the importance of Eve's prayer, though not I think in his claim that it replaces the Fall as the true climax of the poem (8–44). Rather, Milton makes it the point at which the Fall as classical tragedy, eventuating in despair and death, gives way to Christian tragedy, in which catastrophes and suffering can be endured in hope. Eve's prayer prepares for the couple's repentant prayer to God at the close of Book 10, but at that point they can produce only mute sighs of remorse. Accordingly, Eve's psalmic prayer to her husband is the archetype for the highest form of tragic lyric in the fallen world.

In Book 12, Eve reclaims the genre of the love song from its Petrarchan perversions by Satan (5.38–47, 9.532–48). When Eve awakens from her prophetic dream and meets Adam returned from the mountain she voices a love poem appropriate to the fallen world. In substance and tone it echoes Ruth's loving and faithful promise to follow her mother-in-law Naomi to another homeland (Ruth 1: 16–17). Eve's postlapsarian love lyric is much simpler than her elegant poem in Book 4, but it retains some artful rhetorical schemes, and it develops the same theme – that Adam is her true Eden:

> In me is no delay; with thee to go,
> Is to stay here; without thee here to stay,
> Is to go hence unwilling; thou to me
> Art all things under heaven, all places thou,
> Who for my wilful crime art banished hence.   (12.615–19)

Along with their other rich significances, these embedded lyrics highlight Milton's portrait of Eve as lyric poet. Some feminist theory maintains that the foundation texts of our culture deny to women any place in literary creation, and exclude them particularly from the use of metaphoric language and poetry (Landy; Gilbert). *Paradise Lost*, sometimes cited as such a foundation text, does not inscribe that cultural myth. Milton's Eve 'invents' the love sonnet and also (in her story about her creation, 4.449–91) the first autobiographical narrative in Eden, as well as perfecting the tragic lament. Though in some respects inferior to Adam in the hierarchy of being, pre-lapsarian and postlapsarian Eve is imagined as sharing not only in all the georgic responsibilities and duties of the garden but also in all the arts of speech and song and dialogue which pertain to humankind. The final words spoken in Eden are Eve's, and in them she rises above lyric and above her role as tragic protagonist to become, along with Adam, a new kind of epic hero. Earlier, Adam affirmed the new ideal of Christian heroism (12.561–73); now Eve embraces her divinely appointed and even more central role in the epic of redemption: 'though all by me is lost, / Such favour I unworthy am vouchsafed, / By me the promised seed shall all restore' (12.621–3).

Paradise Lost is, then, an encyclopedia of literary forms which also affords a probing critique of the values those forms traditionally body forth. Most literary forms are present in *Paradise Lost* in several versions – celestial and infernal, prelapsarian and postlapsarian, Christian and pagan – inviting discriminations which are at once literary and moral. Some kinds are closely associated with the Satanic order and the diabolic consciousness – classical epic, deliberative rhetoric, soliloquy, Petrarchan sonneteering. However, this association is not exclusive. All these kinds have also their nobler versions: Christ is an Achilles-like hero in the battle in heaven; Christ's speeches in the dialogue in heaven have a persuasive dimension; Abdiel soliloquizes just before engaging Satan in battle; unfallen Eve composes a magnificent love sonnet to Adam. But some literary kinds and their values are not available to Satan – true dialogue, hymnic praise, the *otium* of pastoral – and that literary deprivation testifies to the impoverishment of the damned consciousness. By contrast, Milton suggests the plenitude and abundant life of the highest orders of being, the angels and most especially God, through the mixture and multiplicity of the genres and modes associated with them. And he indicates humankind's potential for growth and development both in the prelapsarian and the postlapsarian state as Adam and Eve take on the languages and the life-styles pertaining to one after another of the literary genres and modes.

The mixture and multiplicity of literary forms in Milton's epic are an index of its comprehensiveness and vitality. As cultural signposts common to author and reader, they also provide an important key to the interpretation of *Paradise Lost*. No poet has ever exploited them more extensively and more deliberately than Milton.

Reading list

Amorose, Thomas, 'Milton the Apocalyptic Historian: Competing Genres in *Paradise Lost*, Books XI–XII', in Wittreich and Ide, eds., *Composite Orders*

Aristotle, *Poetics*, translated by S. H. Butcher as *Aristotle's Theory of Poetry and Fine Art*, 4th edn (New York, 1951)

Aryanpur, Manoocher, '*Paradise Lost* and the *Odyssey*', *Texas Studies in Language and Literature* 9 (1967), 151–66

Bakhtin, M. M., *The Dialogic Imagination: Four Essays*, ed. Michael Holquist, translated by Caryl Emerson and Michael Holquist (Austin and London, 1981)

Barker, Arthur E., 'Structural Pattern in *Paradise Lost*', *Philological Quarterly* 28 (1949), 16–36

Blessington, Francis C., *'Paradise Lost' and the Classical Epic* (Boston and London, 1979)

' "That Undisturbed Song of Pure Concent": *Paradise Lost* and the Epic-Hymn', in *Renaissance Genres: Essays on Theory, History, and Interpretation*, ed. Barbara K. Lewalski, *Harvard English Studies* 14 (Cambridge, MA, 1986)

Bloom, Harold, *A Map of Misreading* (New York, 1975)

Bowra, C. M., *From Virgil to Milton* (London, 1944)

Broadbent, J. B., 'Milton's Rhetoric', *Modern Philology* 56 (1958–9), 224–42

Burden, Dennis, *The Logical Epic: A Study of the Argument of 'Paradise Lost'* (Cambridge, MA, 1967)

Colie, Rosalie L., *The Resources of Kind: Genre-Theory in the Renaissance* (Berkeley, 1973)

Daniells, Roy, 'A Happy Rural Seat of Various View', in *'Paradise Lost': A Tercentenary Tribute*, ed. Balachandra Rajan (Toronto, 1967)

Demaray, John G., *Milton's Theatrical Epic: The Invention and Design of 'Paradise Lost'* (Cambridge and London, 1980)

Di Cesare, Mario A., 'Paradise Lost and Epic Tradition', *Milton Studies* 1 (1969), 31–50

Empson, William, *Some Versions of Pastoral* (London, 1935), 149–94

Evans, J. M., 'Paradise Lost' and the Genesis Tradition (Oxford, 1968)

Fiore, Amadeus P., ed., *Th'Upright Heart and Pure* (Pittsburgh, 1967)

Fish, Stanley, *Surprised by Sin: The Reader in 'Paradise Lost'* (London and New York, 1967)

Fowler, Alastair, *Kinds of Literature: An Introduction to the Theory of Genres and Modes* (Cambridge, MA, 1982)

Frye, Northrop, *Anatomy of Criticism: Four Essays* (Princeton, 1957)
    The Return of Eden (Toronto, 1965)

Gardner, Helen, 'Milton's Satan and the Theme of Damnation in Elizabethan Tragedy'; rpt. in *A Reading of 'Paradise Lost'* (Oxford, 1965)

Giamatti, A. Bartlett, *The Earthly Paradise and the Renaissance Epic* (Princeton, 1966)

Gilbert, Sandra, 'Patriarchal Poetry and Women Readers: Reflections on Milton's Bogey', *PMLA* 93 (1978), 368–82

Greene, Thomas M., *The Light in Troy: Imitation and Discovery in Renaissance Poetry* (New Haven and London, 1982)

Greenlaw, Edwin, 'Spenser's Influence on *Paradise Lost*', *Studies in Philology* 17 (1920), 320–59

Grossman, Marshall, 'Dramatic Structure and Emotive Pattern in the Fall: *Paradise Lost* IX', *Milton Studies* 13 (1979), 201–19

Hanford, James Holly, 'The Dramatic Element in *Paradise Lost*'; rpt. in *John Milton: Poet and Humanist*, ed. John S. Diekhoff (Cleveland, 1966)

Harding, Davis P., *Milton and the Renaissance Ovid* (Urbana, 1946)
    The Club of Hercules: Studies in the Classical Background of 'Paradise Lost' (Urbana, 1962)

Hieatt, A. Kent, *Chaucer, Spenser, Milton: Mythopoeic Continuities and Transformations* (Montreal and London, 1975), 153–270

Hughes, Merritt Y., 'Milton's Celestial Battles and the Theogonies'; rpt. in *Ten Perspectives on Milton* (New Haven, 1965)
    'Milton's Limbo of Vanities', in Fiore, ed., *Th'Upright Heart*

Hunter, G. K., *Paradise Lost* (London, 1980)

Ide, Richard S., 'On the Uses of Elizabethan Drama: The Revaluation of Epic in *Paradise Lost*', in Wittreich and Ide, eds., *Composite Orders*

Johnson, Lee M., 'Milton's Blank Verse Sonnets', *Milton Studies* 5 (1973), 129–53

Kerrigan, William, *The Prophetic Milton* (Charlottesville, 1974)

King, John N., *English Reformation Literature: The Tudor Origins of the Protestant Tradition* (Princeton, 1982)

Knott, John R., *Milton's Pastoral Vision: An Approach to 'Paradise Lost'* (Chicago and London, 1971)

Kranidas, Thomas, 'Adam and Eve in the Garden: A Study of *Paradise Lost*, Book V', *Studies in English Literature* 4 (1964), 71–83

Landy, Marcia, 'Kinship and the Role of Women in *Paradise Lost*', *Milton Studies* 4 (1972), 3–18

Lewalski, Barbara K., *Milton's Brief Epic: The Genre, Meaning, and Art of 'Paradise Regained'* (Providence and London, 1966)

   Protestant Poetics and the Seventeenth-Century Religious Lyric (Princeton, 1979)

   'Paradise Lost' and the Rhetoric of Literary Forms (Princeton, 1985)

MacCallum, H. R., 'Milton and Sacred History: Books XI–XII of *Paradise Lost*', in *Essays in English Literature from the Renaissance to the Victorian Age, Presented to A. S. P. Woodhouse*, ed. M. Maclure and F. W. Watt (Toronto, 1964)

McCown, Gary M., 'Milton and the Epic Epithalamium', *Milton Studies* 5 (1973), 39–66

Martz, Louis L., *Poet of Exile: A Study of Milton's Poetry* (New Haven and London, 1980), 203–44

Minturno, Antonio Sebastiano, *De Poeta* (Venice, 1559)

   L'Arte Poetica ([Venice], 1563 [1564])

Mueller, Martin, '*Paradise Lost* and the *Iliad*', *Comparative Literature Studies* 6 (1969), 292–316

Nardo, A. K., 'The Submerged Sonnet as Lyric Moment in Miltonic Epic', *Genre* 9 (1976), 21–35

Parker, Patricia A., *Inescapable Romance: Studies in the Poetics of a Mode* (Princeton, 1975), 114–58

Puttenham, George, *The Arte of English Poesie* (London, 1589)

Quilligan, Maureen, *Milton's Spenser: The Politics of Reading* (Ithaca and London, 1983)

Revard, Stella P., *The War in Heaven: 'Paradise Lost' and the Tradition of Satan's Rebellion* (Ithaca and London, 1980)

Rollin, Roger E., '*Paradise Lost*: "Tragical–Comical–Historical–Pastoral"', *Milton Studies* 5 (1973), 3–37

Safer, Elaine B., 'The Use of Contraries: Milton's Adaptation of Dialectic in *Paradise Lost*', *Ariel* 2 (1981), 55–69

Samuel, Irene, 'The Dialogue in Heaven: A Reconsideration of *Paradise Lost* III.1–417', *PMLA* 72 (1957), 601–11

Scaliger, Julius-Caesar, *Poetices libri septem* (Geneva, 1561)

Shumacher, Wayne, '*Paradise Lost* and the Italian Epic Tradition', in Fiore, ed., *Th'Upright Heart*

Sidney, Philip, *The Defense of Poesie* (London, 1595)

Sirluck, Ernest, '*Paradise Lost*: A Deliberate Epic* (Cambridge, 1967)

Snyder, Susan, ed., *The Divine Weeks and Works of Guillaume De Saluste Sieur Du Bartas*, translated by Joshua Sylvester, 2 vols. (Oxford, 1979)

Spencer, T. J. B., '*Paradise Lost*: The Anti-Epic', in *Approaches to Paradise Lost*, ed. C. A. Patrides (Toronto, 1968)

Steadman, John M., *Milton and the Renaissance Hero* (Oxford, 1967)

Milton's Epic Characters: Image and Idol (Chapel Hill, 1968)

'Milton's Rhetoric: Satan and the "Unjust Discourse"', *Milton Studies* 1 (1969), 67–92

'The Epic as Pseudomorph: Methodology in Milton Studies', *Milton Studies* 7 (1973), 3–25

Epic and Tragic Structure in 'Paradise Lost' (Chicago, 1976)

Summers, Joseph, *The Muse's Method: An Introduction to 'Paradise Lost'* (Cambridge, MA, 1962)

Tasso, Torquato, *Discourses on the Heroic Poem*, translated by Mariella Cavalchini and Irene Samuel (Oxford, 1973)

Taylor, George C., *Milton's Use of Du Bartas* (Cambridge, MA, 1934)

Tillyard, E. M. W., *Studies in Milton* (London, 1951)

Tolliver, Harold E., 'Milton's Household Epic', *Milton Studies* 9 (1976), 105–20

Webber, Joan, *Milton and His Epic Tradition* (Seattle and London, 1979)

Werblowski, Zwy, *Lucifer and Prometheus* (London, 1952)

Williams, Kathleen, 'Milton, Greatest Spenserian', in Wittreich, ed., *Milton and the Line of Vision*

Wittreich, Joseph A., *Visionary Poetics: Milton's Tradition and his Legacy* (San Marino, 1979)

Wittreich, Joseph A., ed., *Milton and the Line of Vision* (Madison, 1975)

Wittreich, Joseph A. and Richard S. Ide, eds., *Composite Orders: The Genres of Milton's Last Poems*, *Milton Studies* 17 (Pittsburgh, 1983)

7   Language and knowledge in *Paradise Lost*

In Book 8 of *Paradise Lost*, Adam recalls his first experiences on waking into life:

> My self I then perused, and limb by limb
> Surveyed, and sometimes went, and sometimes ran
> With supple joints, and lively vigour led:
> But who I was, or where, or from what cause,
> Knew not; to speak I tried, and forthwith spake,
> My tongue obeyed and readily could name
> What e'er I saw. Thou sun, said I, fair light,
> And thou enlightened earth, so fresh and gay,
> Ye hills and dales, ye rivers, woods, and plains,
> And ye that live and move, fair creatures, tell,
> Tell, if ye saw, how came I thus, how here?   (8.267–77)

It is surprising to hear the newly created Adam speak so 'readily'; we might have expected him to take more time in finding words with which to express himself. We might even say that Adam takes speech and language for granted, but he is right to do so – precisely because they *are* granted to him. Unlike his descendants, Adam has no need to acquire language laboriously. In a word, Adam's language is natural, not conventional.

The distinction may become clearer if we turn from *Paradise Lost* to a different kind of text: Locke's *Essay Concerning Human Understanding*. In Book 3 of the *Essay*, entitled 'Of Language', Locke considers the case of an explorer encountering strange plants and animals in a newly-discovered country:

He that in a new-discovered Country, shall see several sorts of Animals and Vegetables, unknown to him before, may have as true *Ideas* of them, as of a Horse or a Stag; but can speak of them only by a description, till he shall either take the Names the Natives call them by, or give them Names himself.   (3.10.32)

At first sight, this explorer's situation might seem much like Adam's,

Medici Tapestries (*c.* 1550), *Adam Names the Animals*

though in fact it is quite different. Adam doesn't just follow – or even institute – a conventional usage: he recognizes the inherent appropriateness of a
certain name to a certain creature. For Locke, however, there is no necessary relation between names and their referents – all is a matter of custom and
convention. Where Locke's explorer has a licence to impose names at a
whim, Adam names 'readily' from a perfect understanding.

Milton's concept of Adamic language is largely indebted to Plato's
Cratylus, though it finds some biblical warrant in Adam's naming of the
animals in Genesis:

And out of the ground the LORD God formed every beast of the field, and every fowl
of the air; and brought them unto Adam to see what he would call them: and whatsoever Adam called every living creature, that was the name thereof.   (2: 19)

Like most of his contemporaries, Milton takes this text as sanctioning the
inherent correctness of Adam's names. Adam recalls how he saw 'each bird
and beast'

> Approaching two and two, these cowering low
> With blandishment, each bird stooped on his wing.
> I named them, as they passed, and understood
> Their nature, with such knowledge God endued
> My sudden apprehension.   (8.350–4)

The effortlessness of Adam's naming ('sudden apprehension') testifies to the
completeness of his understanding. In the *Christian Doctrine*, Milton
remarks that Adam 'could not have given names to the animals in that
extempore way, without very great intelligence' (YP 6: 324). He makes the
point still more forcefully in *Tetrachordon*: 'Adam who had the wisdom giv'n
him to know all creatures, and to name them according to their properties,
no doubt but had the gift to discern perfectly' (YP 2: 602). To name
creatures in Paradise was to know their essences, not just to assign convenient designations.

Adam's names bring him self-knowledge as well as knowledge about the
animals. He continues: 'but in these / I found not what me thought I wanted
still' (8.354–5). Seeing the animals grouped 'two and two', Adam becomes
suddenly aware of his own need for fit companionship. He goes on to employ
the animals' names carefully and deliberately in his request for a companion:

> of fellowship I speak
> Such as I seek, fit to participate
> All rational delight, wherein the brute
> Cannot be human consort; they rejoice

> Each with their kind, lion with lioness;
> So fitly them in pairs thou hast combined;
> Much less can bird with beast, or fish with fowl
> So well converse, nor with the ox the ape;
> Worse then can man with beast, and least of all.   (8.389–97)

Adam pairs the names of species and genera experimentally, by sound as well as sense, to attest to the fitness or unfitness of the creatures' possible unions. After the perfect fit of 'lion with lioness', the alliterations in 'bird with beast, or fish with fowl' reflect a less than perfect match, while the union of 'man with beast' does not even have alliteration to recommend it. Adam's concluding rhyme of 'beast' with 'least' resolutely dismisses any thought of fit society between himself, 'the master work' of Creation (7.505), and these, the least of sentient creatures. In this context of sound and sense, the rhyme of 'speak' with 'seek' – 'of fellowship I speak / Such as I seek' – affirms the bond between language and knowledge.

When he finally consents to Adam's request, God makes plain that his demurral had only been a test 'to see how thou couldst judge of fit and meet' (8.448). By giving 'fit and meet' names to the animals, Adam has gained knowledge of what is fitting for him. As God says:

> Thus far to try thee, Adam, I was pleased,
> And find thee knowing not of beasts alone,
> Which thou hast rightly named, but of thy self,
> Expressing well the spirit within thee free,
> My image, not imparted to the brute.   (8.437–41)

There are limits to Adam's powers of naming. He encounters the first and greatest limit to his language immediately after naming the animals:

> O by what name, for thou above all these,
> Above mankind, or aught than mankind higher,
> Surpassest far my naming, how may I
> Adore thee, author of this universe?   (8.357–60)

Adam cannot name or know God as easily as he had 'named . . . and understood' the animals, and yet his very inability to name here brings him the greatest recognition of all.

Names and naming are more important to *Paradise Lost* than at first appears. Adam's ability to call things by their proper names was one expression of the perfect wisdom which was his birthright in Paradise. Milton (unlike most of his contemporaries) even extends this wisdom to Eve, for she names the flowers (11.277). One consequence of the Fall was the loss of this ability to name things rightly, since reason was now clouded and the will perverted. The fallen angels fall so completely as to forfeit the names which had once befitted them:

> of their names in heavenly records now
> Be no memorial blotted out and razed
> By their rebellion, from the books of life.
> Nor had they yet among the sons of Eve
> Got them new names.   (1.361–5)

I have argued elsewhere (*Milton Studies* 21) that such names as 'Belial', 'Beelzebub', and 'Moloch' are 'new names' the fallen angels have not yet got at the time of their Fall. Suspended, as it were, in a limbo between their old and new identities, the devils do not yet have new names and are powerless to speak their old ones:

> If thou beest he; but O how fallen! how changed
> From him, who in the happy realms of light
> Clothed with transcendent brightness didst outshine
> Myriads though bright.   (1.84–7)

The 'he' here recognized by Satan is not yet 'Beelzebub'. Satan's followers are indeed quite nameless in *Paradise Lost*. No devil ever addresses another one by name.

Satan alone among the devils has a name. 'Satan' means 'enemy' in Hebrew. Before his followers have 'got them new names', before even the Fall of Man, Satan is the 'arch-enemy' and is 'thence in heaven called Satan' (1.82). But he is not called 'Satan' *in hell*. (The devils see God, not Satan, as their 'great enemy'.) Satan, like his fellows, had had a 'former name' (5.658), a name which Milton (following patristic tradition) associates with 'Lucifer', the morning star (5.760, 7.131, 10.425; the allusion is to Isa. 14: 12: 'How art thou fallen from heaven, O Lucifer, son of the morning!'). An awareness of this 'former name' brings out a pointed irony when Satan speaks his name for the first (and only) time:

> Fair daughter, and thou son and grandchild both,
> High proof ye now have given to be the race
> Of Satan (for I glory in the name,
> Antagonist of heaven's almighty king).   (10.384–7)

Is this just a casual gloss upon the name? Or is it an unprecedented recognition by Satan of who and what he has become? Satan had not been so forthcoming when the good angels had asked after his name in Paradise:

> Know ye not then said Satan, filled with scorn,
> Know ye not me? Ye knew me once no mate
> For you, there sitting where ye durst not soar.   (4.827–9)

It had been as 'Lucifer' that Satan had aspired to 'sit . . . upon the mount of the congregation' (Isa. 14: 13, *PL* 5.760–6). If 'Lucifer' is the name with which he now scorns his captors, the poet's 'said Satan' is not a neutral comment.

Milton builds into his poem a sustained distinction between prelapsarian and postlapsarian nomenclature. He often cites exotic and beautiful names in order to dismiss them. This is most apparent in the negative similes which recur throughout *Paradise Lost*:

> Not that fair field
> Of Enna, where Proserpine gathering flowers
> Her self a fairer flower by gloomy Dis
> Was gathered, which cost Ceres all that pain
> To seek her through the world; nor that sweet grove
> Of Daphne by Orontes, and the inspired
> Castalian spring, might with this Paradise
> Of Eden strive.   (4.268–75)

These place names with their mythical associations are drawn from a splintered, fragmentary, fallen world quite alien to the pristine clarity and passionate immediacy of Paradise. Introducing the names in a supposed attempt to apprehend Edenic beauty, Milton tactfully confesses that his own nomenclature is powerless to bring the kind of 'sudden apprehension' Adam had enjoyed before the Fall.

How, then, does Milton represent Adamic language? Latinisms play a part. In Book 7 Adam asks Raphael:

> what cause
> Moved the Creator in his holy rest
> Through all eternity so late to build
> In Chaos, and the work begun, how soon
> Absolved.   (7.90–4)

Christopher Ricks has drawn attention to the peculiar meaning of Adam's 'Absolved': 'before sin was, *absolution* was no more than completion' (115). By using words in their original, Latin sense, Milton 'takes us back to a time when there were no infected words because there were no infected actions' (110). Ricks sees the same kind of playing of fallen against unfallen meanings in the account of the river which moves 'with serpent error wandering'

(7.302): 'it is surely easier to believe in a slightly ingenious Milton than in one who could be so strangely absent-minded as to use both "serpent" and "error" without in some way invoking the Fall' (110). What, then, of 'Absolved'? Ricks asks: 'is Milton deliberately setting aside, and asking us to see that he has set aside, the application to sin because he is describing a sinless world?' (115). Milton is doing this, but Adam is not. Unlike the fallen poet, Adam remains unconscious of the ominousness we read into (and out of) his vocabulary. Milton's prelapsarian play at this point reaches 'back to an earlier purity' (Ricks), but it is free from the kind of melancholy or pejorative tone we hear in 'serpent error wandering'.

Adam's request to hear of Creation has implications for prelapsarian knowledge as well as language. Just what is Adam asking? Milton's early editors took 'late' ('expected so late to build / In Chaos') as meaning 'after the time'. Thus understood, Adam is asking why God created the universe at so late a date. Such a question, prying curiously into God's secrets, was felt to be impious. Here is Milton's first editor, Patrick Hume (from his edition of 1695):

Why God was not pleased to create the World 100,000 Years before he did, and how he employed his infinite Power, Wisdom and other unaccountable Perfections before the Creation, are some of those vain and Atheistical Enquiries of impertinent and daring Men, who, little acquainted with the turns and motions of their own frail and unruly Wills, would pry into the Secrets of the Eternal Mind, and ask an account of that *Almighty Will* which created all things how and when he pleas'd. Such Doubts are unresolvable, as not coming within the compass of Human comprehension, for the Question will at last run up to Eternity it self, and the Enquiry will come to this impious and absurd Demand, why God did not make the World co-eternal with himself? (214)

Hume's reading might be supported by an allusion to the Book of Job in 'magnify his works'. Elihu exhorts Job to

> Remember that thou magnify his work,
> Which men behold.
> Every man may see it;
> Man may behold it afar off.
> Behold, God is great, and we know him not,
> Neither can the numbers of his years be searched out.   (Job 36: 24–6)

On Hume's reading, Adam (unlike Job) is trying to search out the number of God's numberless years.

This interpretation continues to be delivered by Milton's modern editors. Alastair Fowler notes:

It is curious that Milton should put Adam's question so absurdly – as if he were to ask, like a child, what moved the prime mover. In *De Doctrina* 1.7 Milton calls it 'the height of folly' to enquire into 'the actions of God before the foundation of the world'. (*Poems*)

It would indeed be 'the height of folly' for Adam to ask the question his editors foist upon him; however, he does not ask it. Hume and Fowler have forgotten that 'late' can mean 'recently' (*OED* 4). Thus understood, Adam makes no enquiry about the timing of Creation. 'Late' most often means 'recently' in *Paradise Lost* – and this is its meaning on every other occasion where 'late' follows 'so' (compare 5.675; 10.721, 941; 12.642). This sense is surely uppermost in Adam's 'what cause / Moved the Creator . . . so late to build / In Chaos'. Milton is as aware as Jonathan Richardson (another early editor) that 'Eternal Ages pass'd makes This seem late, though had it been Millions and Millions of Ages Before, it had been Late with Regard to what was Past' (196). Adam might add (in effect he does add): 'though it had been millions of ages before, it would be late (recent) with regard to me'. Adam's question is accordingly both daring and humble. It is even more daring than Milton's editors recognize, for it amounts to 'Why Creation?' not just 'Why Creation now?'

Adam's whole speech is remarkable for the way in which it frees itself from curiosity while asserting a bold spirit of enquiry:

> Deign to descend now lower, and relate
> What may no less perhaps avail us known,
> How first began this heaven which we behold
> Distant so high, with moving fires adorned
> Innumerable, and this which yields or fills
> All space, the ambient air wide interfused
> Embracing round this florid earth, what cause
> Moved the creator in his holy rest
> Through all eternity so late to build
> In chaos, and the work begun, how soon
> Absolved, if unforbid thou may'st unfold
> What we, not to explore the secrets ask
> Of his eternal empire, but the more
> To magnify his works, the more we know.   (7.84–97)

Note that there is no question-mark anywhere in these lines. The positioning of 'ask' after 'not' (95) calls into question whether Adam is really asking a *question* at all. (The meaning would be different were he to say 'what we ask, not to explore'.) Placed at the line-ending, 'ask' assumes an emphatic boldness and directness, yet it also strengthens the implied antithesis between 'ask' and 'magnify' ('not to . . . ask . . . but to magnify his works'). Even the repeated 'how' ('how first began . . . how soon / Absolved') is not truly interrogative, for both 'how's follow on from the imperative 'relate'. Adam's whole speech is pregnant with curious questions, but between 'unfold' and 'magnify', it unfolds into a wondering celebration of the magnificence of God's works. Like the 'ambient air' which 'yields or fills / All space', Adam fills a space in his knowledge by yielding to it. He does not search out the number of God's years, but (anticipating Job), remembers to magnify his works.

The purity of Adam's prelapsarian request emerges when we compare it with Satan's very different way of asking about Creation:

> Chaos and ancient Night, I come no spy,
> With purpose to explore or to disturb
> The secrets of your realm, but by constraint
> Wandering this darksome desert, as my way
> Lies through your spacious empire up to light
>
> . . .
>
>   direct my course;
> Directed no mean recompense it brings
> To your behoof.   (2.970–82)

Where Adam asserts his will by setting limits to it, Satan is tactlessly blunt ('direct my course'). He tries to placate Chaos and Night by appealing to their self-interest, but it is clear that Satan's interest is not just in magnifying their works. Bentley's emendation of 'disturb' to 'disclose' (on the grounds that 'secrets' cannot be *disturbed*) even brings out a veiled threat. Satan promises not to 'disturb', not to breach the peace of, a realm which peals with disruption as 'loud and ruinous (to compare / Great things with small)' as 'if this frame / Of heaven were falling' (2.291–2, 924–5)! In surroundings which make redundant all talk of disturbing, Satan hints darkly at his own disruptive powers. Nothing could be further in tone and mood from the graceful amplification of Adam's bold humility.

Paradise Lost is a poem peopled with strong presences and many voices, each distinguished from the others, yet all distinctively Milton's. Adam's 'what cause / Moved the creator' picks up the voice of Milton's epic invocation six books earlier, and yet the two voices are quite different:

> Say first, for heaven hides nothing from thy view
> Nor the deep tract of hell, say first what cause
> Moved our grand parents in that happy state,

> Favoured of heaven so highly, to fall off
> From their creator, and transgress his will
> For one restraint, lords of the world besides?
> Who first seduced them to that foul revolt?
> The infernal serpent . . .   (1.27–34)

Here, as in Adam's lines, 'what cause' is placed at the line-ending and followed by 'Moved'. The presence of 'creator' also serves to tie the two passages together. In part, the cross-reference works to present Adam's lines as an epic invocation. But it also points to a contrast: our 'grand parents' were moved to fall off, whereas God (with the full weight of the paradox) moved in rest. To recall Fowler, 'it is curious that [Adam] should . . . ask, like a child, what moved the prime mover'. However, Adam does not ask 'what moved the prime mover'; he asks 'what cause / Moved the Creator in his holy rest'. God moved *in* his rest; he did not move *from* it. It is possible to see this too as an absurdity, but it is not the absurdity Fowler puts in Adam's mouth. Adam's version does not question God's identity as prime mover, but asserts a majesty and self-sufficiency of will which are absurd only when claimed by someone other than God.

The poet's invocation (as the repeated question-marks confirm) is a real question, not a seeming question magnified into something greater. Strictly, there are two questions, not one. Only the second question ('who first seduced them?') is fully answered: our 'grand parents' were seduced by the 'infernal serpent'. The question 'what cause?' is barely glanced at by this response. As Stanley Fish writes: 'the answer to the question, "what cause?" is given in the first line, "Of Man's First Disobedience" . . . The reader who finds a cause for the Fall denies it by denying its freedom' (259). The poet's 'what cause?' is finally unanswerable. Here, as in his negative similes and catalogues of proper names drawn from the fallen world, the poet quietly acknowledges his inability to arrive at first causes. Adam, however, arrives at the First Cause through a direct perception of the immediacy of Creation.

The question 'what cause?' is important to Satan's temptation of Eve. The serpent's argument takes a step forward when he claims to recognize (among other things) the cause for God's forbidding Adam and Eve to eat the apple:

> O sacred, wise, and wisdom-giving plant,
> Mother of science, now I feel thy power
> Within me clear, not only to discern
> Things in their causes, but to trace the ways
> Of highest agents, deemed however wise.
> Queen of this universe, do not believe
> Those rigid threats of death.   (9.679–85)

Satan's use of the plural in 'causes' and 'agents' prepares the way for his shift from 'God' ('Indeed? Hath God then said . . . ?') to 'gods': 'ye shall be as gods', 'And what are gods that man may not become / As they?' (9.656, 708, 716). Satan has always been reluctant to speak of 'God' in *Paradise Lost*. (In hell, the devils had used such circumlocutions as 'our supreme foe', 'he . . . whom I now / Of force believe almighty', or just 'he'). The effect here of the serpent's 'gods' is to offer the word as a title available to man: 'so ye shall die perhaps, by putting off / Human, to put on gods' (713–14). Soon it is dressed specifically for Eve: 'Goddess humane, reach then, and freely taste' (732).

While avoiding (so far as possible) any mention of 'God', Satan does sometimes drop a singular pronoun into his talk of 'the gods':

> What can your knowledge hurt him, or this tree
> Impart against his will if all be his?
> Or is it envy, and can envy dwell
> In heavenly breasts?   (9.727–30)

Discerning 'things in their causes', Satan here arrives most cunningly at his alleged cause for the prohibition. As Thomas Newton noted in 1749, Satan 'generally speaks of Gods when the sentiment would be too horrid, if it was spoken of God' (2: 186). Satan uses the plural to allege divine malevolence, and the singular to reassure Eve that God will not hurt her. To this end, he will even speak of 'God': 'will God incense his ire / For such a petty trespass?' (9.692–3). Eve must not feel too soon that she is being asked to repudiate the one God she has known and loved. Yet when (three lines later) Satan next speaks of 'God', it is to cancel the word: 'God therefore cannot hurt ye, and be just; / Not just, not God' (700–1). This is the last time 'God' passes Satan's lips in the poem.

What we witness throughout the temptation is a contest (unconscious on Eve's part) between herself and Satan for the authority to interpret pre-lapsarian language. The serpent first stakes a claim upon Eve's language through the seeming miracle of his ability to speak:

> he glad
> Of her attention gained, with serpent tongue
> Organic, or impulse of vocal air,
> His fraudulent temptation thus began.
> Wonder not, sovereign mistress . . .   (9.528–32)

Milton's demurral as to whether Satan actually employs the serpent's tongue is not mere pedantry. Satan finds words for his temptation, but it is not certain that he finds a tongue to speak them: his snake-speech might involve illusion within illusion ('impulse of vocal air'). Eve, however, believes herself to be hearing a 'serpent tongue / Organic' which obeys its owner as 'readily' as Adam's tongue had obeyed him when first giving names. She is amazed to hear a serpent speak.

Here Milton departs significantly from Genesis, which offers no explanation for the serpent's speaking. (It doesn't even identify the serpent as Satan, though this identification was made from pre-Christian times.) Milton's contemporaries were much interested in Eve's lack of surprise in Genesis. Thomas Browne inferred that Eve's own grasp of Adamic language must have been weak:

> She might not yet be certain that onely man was priviledged with speech, and being in the novity of the Creation, and inexperience of all things, might not be affrighted to hear a serpent speak: Besides she might be ignorant of their natures who was not versed in their names, as being not present at the generall survey of Animalls, when Adam assigned unto every one a name concordant unto its nature.   (1.238–9)

In *Paradise Lost*, Eve reflects directly on the serpent's name and nature: 'Thee, serpent, subtlest beast of all the field / I knew, but not with human voice endued' (9.560–1). Browne implies that for Eve to feel surprise would be an advantage. Yet surprise need not entail vigilance. When Milton's Eve replies: 'What may this mean? Language of man pronounced / By tongue of brute?' (553–4), she reacts in just the way Satan had hoped for. To be sure, her wonder creates a dangerous moment for Satan, an opportunity for Eve to exercise special vigilance. However, it is an opportunity Eve misses, and a moment that Satan turns to his advantage with what is a dramatic masterstroke by Milton: the serpent speaks specifically about his speaking and attributes this supposedly new power to some as yet unspecified fruit.

The serpent's most persuasive argument is his ability to argue. His seeming participation in language not only argues a miraculous change; in a world where names correspond to natures, language *is* knowledge. The illusion of a 'serpent tongue / Organic' implies Satan's whole case that the forbidden fruit confers knowledge. However, language on the serpent's lips becomes an instrument of deception and so a means of replacing knowledge with ignorance.

Throughout the temptation, Satan bestows names amiss so as deliberately to deceive Eve. We have seen how he abuses the terms 'God' and 'gods'. Another term, still more central to the serpent's argument, is the name of the forbidden Tree. As Arnold Williams has shown, the name 'Tree of

Knowledge of Good and Evil' received much attention from biblical commentators. Because God speaks the name at Genesis 2: 9 and 2: 17, it was most widely held that he had given it before the Fall. This is certainly the view incorporated in *Paradise Lost* (8.323–4). Milton agrees with Andrew Willet that the Tree cannot be 'so called because of the lying and entising words of Satan' (28). Thomas Newton noted that 'our first parents were created with perfect understanding, and the only knowledge that was forbidden was the knowledge of evil by the commission of it' (2: 59). Properly, the Tree's name is a warning against evil. Yet Satan speaks it as a promise of good. Eating, he claims, will lead

> To happier life, knowledge of good and evil;
> Of good, how just? Of evil, if what is evil
> Be real, why not known, since easier shunned?   (9.697–9)

Though many theologians have denied evil any real existence in Nature, none has thought it unimportant. Tucked away in a parenthesis, Satan's 'if what is evil / Be real' implies that evil is nothing to worry about. And yet the 'if' does not make for a complete dismissal. While reassuring Eve, Satan also excites her curiosity and suspicion by hinting that God has planted evil in Nature. Hume comments:

If what is Evil be real: if there be any thing really Evil in this World, wherein GOD the Creator made all, and acknowledged all that he made was *Good* . . . Eve had been forewarn'd of the dangerous Evil of Temptation and Sin, there was no other Evil in nature to be dreaded or avoided by her, though slyly here insinuated by Satan. (259)

Evil, in Milton's universe, is a vitiation of Nature; it is not a nature created by God. Satan manages to cast doubt upon the goodness of the Creator by insinuating that evil is created. He even implies that it would be dangerous for Eve *not* to know this evil. In just two lines Satan has (1) awakened Eve's suspicions about God, (2) titillated her curiosity about 'evil' (supposedly an unexplored part of Nature), and (3) reassured Eve that no harm will befall her if she eats the apple.

Twenty lines later, the serpent promises Eve knowledge of good and evil in the gods' (not God's) despite: 'if they all things, who enclosed / Knowledge of good and evil in this tree, / That whoso eats thereof, forthwith attains / Wisdom without their leave?' (9.722–5). Contemplating these words (and the serpent's ability to speak them), Eve then accepts Satan's interpretation of the Tree's name:

> Great are thy virtues, doubtless, best of fruits
>
> . . .
>
> Whose taste, too long forborne, at first assay
> Gave elocution to the mute, and taught
> The tongue not made for speech to speak thy praise:
> Thy praise he also who forbids thy use,
> Conceals not from us, naming thee the tree
> Of knowledge, knowledge both of good and evil;
> Forbids us then to taste, but his forbidding
> Commends thee more, while it infers the good
> By thee communicated, and our want:
> For good unknown, sure is not had, or had
> And yet unknown, is as not had at all.
> In plain then, what forbids he but to know,
> Forbids us good, forbids us to be wise?
> Such prohibitions bind not.   (9.745–60)

Eve thus comes to see the 'tree of knowledge, knowledge both of good and evil' as the tree of 'good'. 'Evil' drops quietly away. Governing 'good', the words 'not had at all' are dramatically ironic: Eve means that good must be known to be possessed, but her 'Knowledge of good' is to be 'bought dear by knowing ill' (4.222). Eve is to gain knowledge *of* good, but good itself is not to be had at all. As Adam later cries: 'our eyes / Opened we find indeed, and find we know / Both good and evil, good lost, and evil got' (9.1070–2).

Eve would have done well to heed the Tree's whole name, not just that part stressed by Satan. Despite the seeming miracle of 'language of man pronounced by tongue / Of brute', the serpent's language is not Eve's. He insinuates himself into her language in order to bestow names amiss and so deceive her. She surrenders her language too readily to him and so forfeits that pure and natural speech which Adam had spoken as a birthright on first waking into life. The corrupting of innocence begins with a corrupting of language.

Reading list

Bentley, Richard, *Milton's 'Paradise Lost'* (London, 1732)

Browne, Thomas, *Pseudodoxia Epidemica* (London, 1650)

Fish, Stanley E., *Surprised by Sin: The Reader in 'Paradise Lost'* (London and New York, 1967)

H[ume], P[atrick], *Annotations on Milton's 'Paradise Lost'* (London, 1695)

Leonard, John, '"Though of thir Names": The Devils in *Paradise Lost'*, *Milton Studies* 21 (1985)

Locke, John, *An Essay Concerning Human Understanding* (1690), ed. P. H. Nidditch (Oxford, 1975)

Newton, Thomas, *'Paradise Lost': A Poem in Twelve Books*, 2 vols. (London, 1749)

Richardson, Jonathan (father and son), *Explanatory Notes and Remarks upon Milton's 'Paradise Lost'* (London, 1734)

Ricks, Christopher, *Milton's Grand Style* (Oxford, 1963)

Willet, Andrew, *Hexapla: A Sixfold Commentary on Genesis* (London, 1608)

Williams, Arnold, *The Common Expositor: An Account of the Commentaries on Genesis, 1527–1633* (Chapel Hill, NC, 1948)

8   The Fall of Man and Milton's theodicy

Milton's presentation of his various literary characters can be controversial because so many people still believe in, or worry about, the actual existence of some of his most important ones: Adam, Eve, Satan, Jesus. But Milton's God is especially controversial. For all Milton's 'language of accommodation' (see *PL* 5.572–4, 6.893, 7.176–9), Milton never presents *his* God as if he is not really God, the eternal and almighty Being who created the heavens and the earth, who reveals himself in the Bible and in the life and person of Jesus Christ, and to whom all beings owe thanks and worship for his goodness and greatness. Moreover, to believe or not to believe in this God is such a fundamental thing that one cannot realistically join the conversation created by *Paradise Lost* and expect one's belief or unbelief to go unaddressed. Nevertheless, Milton does not force the issue concerning belief in God's mere existence, for that is something he simply assumes; for him God's existence is a premise much more than a conclusion (see YP 6: 130–2). In spite of the radical polarities of belief about God in *Paradise Lost*, its humans and devils and angels are united in this: they all believe that he is.

The theological apologetic that *Paradise Lost* does undertake concerns not God's existence but his nature, or character. Milton ends the first paragraph of his epic by asking the Muse to raise him 'to the highth of this great argument' so that he may 'assert eternal providence, / And justify the ways of God to men' (1.24–6). Milton thus announces that he will attempt a *theodicy*, a defence of God's justice. This attempt, in the course of the epic, requires that Milton perform a series of balancing acts. The so-called theological problem of evil – the problem that a theodicy sets out in some degree to solve – can itself be seen as a problem concerning how to balance three fundamental propositions to which virtually all Christians, and perhaps others, assent:

1 God is all powerful (or omnipotent).

Albrecht Dürer (1471–1528), *Adam and Eve*

2 God is wholly good.
3 There is evil in the world.

The question, some of whose formulations date from antiquity, is: if we assert any two of these three propositions, how can the remaining one make any sense? If God is all powerful and wholly good, how can there be evil in the world he created? But we know there *is* evil in the world, so how can we believe God to be both all powerful and wholly good? Is he able to remove evil but unwilling? Or is he willing but unable?

Historically there have been those who have 'solved' the theological problem of evil by tacitly abandoning its premises. Some 'dualists' have so defined and straitened God's power as to deprive omnipotence of its meaning. Some 'voluntarists' have defined God's goodness merely as a function of God's will, or power, so that a thing is good merely by virtue of the fact that God wills it – a manoeuvre whereby *goodness* as predicated of God loses its ordinary meaning. And still others, like the eighteenth-century 'optimists' mocked by Voltaire and Samuel Johnson, have defined evil in the world in such a way that it is not to be seen truly as evil after all but rather as a necessary part of some universal good. None of these wafflings, however, is acceptable to Milton, and it is a measure of his theodical courage that he sets out to tell the story of 'all our woe' in a way that none the less asserts God's power (his 'eternal providence') *and* justifies God's ways.

This philosophical balancing act that Milton knows he must perform also entails a rhetorical balancing act. For if God's ways are justifiable not only in the abstract but also to actual human beings ('justifiable to men'; *SA* 294), then part of Milton's job is to respect, and to avoid alienating, readers whom he must at the same time accuse of being sinful and limited in their understandings. To undertake a theodicy at all presupposes that we have *some* right or ability to arrive at judgments concerning God's nature and character. Yet no religious theodicist may ever forget that the God thus being 'judged' is himself the Author and Judge of all Things. Without the first assumption, an attempt to explain God's ways to human beings would be ridiculous. Without the second, it would be blasphemous. So Milton begins *Paradise Lost* by declaring our and his solidarity in the Fall of Man, in its effects, and in the need to be redeemed from its effects (1.1–5). He also confesses his own 'darkness' and 'lowness' and his need to be illuminated, raised, and supported before he can adequately tell his story and present his theodicy (1.22–6). Yet throughout his epic he not only provides us with repeated reminders that we are fallen creatures ourselves, but also presupposes and appeals to our ability truly to recognize that which is good. I will return to some of the ways in which Milton, by appealing to that recognition of good, draws his readers into his conversation. For now, it is enough merely to recognize how *Paradise Lost* as a theodicy demands of both its author and its reader a delicate balance between *chutzpah* and humility.

Now the Fall, or more precisely the Fall of Man, refers to the first human transgression of the divine command. It can be conceived narratively, embodied in an account of the transgression, including both the events leading up to it, and its consequences; or conceived in doctrinal terms concerning the cause and nature of humanity's wickedness, suffering, and estrangement from God. Although the narrative and the doctrinal may obviously influence each other, historically they have often not been particularly integrated, and *Paradise Lost* is remarkable for the extent to which Milton seeks to establish a balance between the interests of narrative and those of doctrine, with each enriching the other.

Biblically, the Fall narrative appears in Genesis 2 and 3: the Lord God, having created man (Adam) and placed him in the garden of Eden, commands him, 'thou shalt not eat' of the tree of the knowledge of good and evil, adding, 'for in the day that thou eatest thereof thou shalt surely die' (2: 17). After woman is created, the serpent speaks to her, denies that if they eat of the forbidden fruit they shall surely die, and ascribes to God a jealous motive for his interdiction: 'God doth know that in the day ye eat thereof, then your eyes shall be opened, and ye shall be as gods' (3: 5). The woman then eats of the fruit and gives some also to her husband, who likewise eats. This eating is followed immediately by their knowing themselves to be naked (3: 7), and not long after by the Lord God's arriving to curse the serpent with crawling upon its belly, the woman with sorrow in bearing children and in being dominated by her husband, and the man with sorrow and sweat in his obtaining food from the ground (3: 14–19).

Some modernist critics have viewed this story 'as a straightforward aetiological myth, designed to explain why a man cleaves to his wife and why he is the senior partner in the union, why he has to labour in the fields and she in childbirth, why we wear clothes, why we dislike snakes, and why they crawl on their bellies' (Evans 1968, 9), and, of course, also why we must die. In any case, the rest of the Old Testament makes no clear mention of the story of Adam and Eve, and its only biblical interpretation is given in the New Testament by St Paul, who reads it typologically, thus amplifying and universalizing the significance of Adam and of his transgression by seeing them as the backdrop for Jesus Christ's acts of redemption. Adam's sin and its effects are symmetrical with the non-sin and life-giving sacrifice of Christ, whom Paul calls 'the last Adam' (1 Cor. 15: 45): 'For since by man came death, by man came also the resurrection of the dead. For as in Adam all die, even so in Christ shall all be made alive' (1 Cor. 15: 21–2; see also Rom. 5: 19).

Although such doctrine, and such typology, play an important role in Milton's works, for him the narrative also informs doctrine. His epic medium is itself narrative; it must respect the details of its ur-narrative, and also inevitably impose some concrete, literary limitations of its own upon doctrine. Particularly because *Paradise Lost* vastly expands the biblical story of Adam and Eve, it brings into view narrative details which, when seen only from afar, might not even appear doctrinally significant. Milton's magnifying lens, however, focuses attention on a whole series of questions about the Fall story: How can we talk about *the* Fall when there really were two falls, Adam's and Eve's? How can we talk about Adam being tempted by Satan when Satan tempted only Eve? What motivations operated in each of their falls? How did it come about that they were tempted separately? Was Eve's fall inevitable? Once Eve had fallen, was Adam's fall inevitable? If they were ignorant of good and evil, how could they have been expected to avoid evil? If God knew they were going to be tempted, could he not have forewarned them? Why would the serpent have wanted to have Adam and Eve disobey God anyhow? These and many other questions which Genesis leaves in the background are brought by Milton's detailed narrative into the foreground where their answers can be inspected for both literary and doctrinal coherence.

One of the most notable difficulties Milton encounters in thus seeking to meld things narrative and doctrinal is the issue of divine foreknowledge and human free will. A vital component of Milton's theodicy is the 'Free Will Defence', the model or argument according to which God, for reasons consistent with his wisdom and goodness, created angels and human beings with freedom either to obey or disobey his commands. Such an act of creation represents a self-limitation on God's part: it means that he cannot manipulate the free choices of angels and humans, though this claim is no mark against his omnipotence, because the 'cannot' is a logical entailment of his own exercise of power. The Free Will Defence, furthermore, claims that, although innumerable such free creatures have in fact disobeyed God's commands and so created an immense amount of evil, the amount of goodness that presupposes the exercise of freedom ultimately *outweighs* the total amount of evil. For without freedom, what value would things such as honesty, loyalty, and love possess? From Tertullian on, freedom has been valued also theologically as an indication in human beings 'of God's image and similitude . . . the outward expression of God's own dignity', freedom being the 'primary postulate of goodness and reason' (*Adversus Marcionem* 2.6, 2.5). Milton himself stresses in *Areopagitica* that freedom is an essential quality for any moral or rational creature:

Many there be that complain of divin Providence for suffering *Adam* to transgresse, foolish tongues! when God gave him reason, he gave him freedom to choose, for reason is but choosing; he had bin else a meer artificiall *Adam*, such an *Adam* as he is in the motions [puppet shows]. We our selves esteem not of that obedience, or love, or gift, which is of force.   (YP 2: 527)

God of course could merely have created automata, puppets. But except in a depreciated, mechanical way, no honesty or loyalty or love could ever have been predicated of such beings. Therefore, it is at least plausible to claim that free will, though it is also the necessary condition of a huge amount of moral evil, is worth it – and therefore, too, that God's choosing to make creatures with that potential for going wrong is consistent with his being both all powerful and wholly good.

Accordingly, in *Paradise Lost* Milton's God declares:

> I made [man] just and right,
> Sufficient to have stood, though free to fall.
> Such I created all the ethereal powers
> And spirits, both them who stood and them who failed;
> Freely they stood who stood, and fell who fell.
> Not free, what proof could they have given sincere
> Of true allegiance, constant faith or love,
> Where only what they needs must do, appeared,
> Not what they would? What praise could they receive?
> What pleasure I from such obedience paid,
> When will and reason (reason also is choice)
> Useless and vain, of freedom both despoiled,
> Made passive both, had served necessity,
> Not me.   (3.98–111)

Most readers of *Paradise Lost*, I think, can accept, provisionally at least, the logic of the Free Will Defence – can accept it, in other words, as a reasonable *doctrine*. However, Milton has the doctrine appear in a speech delivered by God, as part of a larger scene, which in turn forms part of a narrative. The most obvious problem that results is that of anthropomorphism, of God sounding like a human being vociferously defending his own actions. The doctrine's dramatic context thus makes it very difficult for us not to feel the scepticism regarding the speaker's motivations that we would feel in any analogous human situation.

But even ignoring what might be called the dramatic problem – even if we can take God's words simply at face value – we encounter a more serious clash as we read on: a clash between doctrine and narrative. In Book 3, God carries on to say that angels and human beings were thus created truly free, so that if they fall, they cannot blame

> Their maker, or their making, or their fate,
> As if predestination overruled
> Their will, disposed by absolute decree
> Or high foreknowledge; they themselves decreed
> Their own revolt, not I: if I foreknew,
> *Foreknowledge had no influence on their fault,*
> *Which had no less proved certain unforeknown.*
> So without least impulse or shadow of fate,
> Or aught by me immutably foreseen,
> They trespass, authors to themselves in all
> Both what they judge and what they choose.   (3.113–23; italics added)

The doctrinal or philosophical question of whether God's foreknowledge and human free will can coexist remains an interesting and keenly debated one – as it was in Milton's day. For Milton and for many of his contemporaries, to accept any kind of determinism was to abandon free will, and to abandon free will was to abandon theodicy. One must conclude, says Milton in *Christian Doctrine*, that 'neither God's decree nor his foreknowledge can shackle free causes with any kind of necessity'. For otherwise, God himself is made 'the cause and author of sin'; and to refute this conclusion 'would be like inventing a long argument to prove that God is not the Devil' (YP 6: 166).

In so defending free will, however, Milton was not prepared to restrict God's omniscience. In the seventeenth century the Socinians, for example, argued that just as omnipotence can do only that which it is logically possible to do, so omniscience can know only that which it is logically possible to know; future free actions are in principle not knowable; and what is not knowable is therefore not *fore*knowable, even by God. By contrast, orthodox Calvinists saw God's foreknowledge as based on his decrees, so that if anything is said to be divinely foreknown, one can infer that it is also divinely decreed, and thus predetermined. Milton denies both of these extremes: 'We should feel certain that God has not decreed that everything must happen inevitably. Otherwise we should make him responsible for all the sins ever committed, and should make demons and wicked men blameless. But we should feel certain also that God really does foreknow everything that is going to happen' (YP 6: 164–5; CM 14: 84).

However, if God's foreknowledge implies no determinism, why does God in Book 3 of *Paradise Lost* say that humankind's fault 'had no less proved certain unforeknown' (119)? Seventeenth-century theologians carefully distinguished certainty from necessity, the latter relating to events in themselves, the former relating to knowledge of the events. Thomas Pierce complains about those writers who, failing 'to distinguish *necessity* from *certainty* of events . . . call that *necessary* which is but *certain* and *infallible*' (1657, 60; see YP 6: 165 and CM 11: 48–50). 'What God decreed to *effect*', says Pierce, 'will come to pass *unavoidably*, and by *necessitation* . . . But what he *only* decreed to *permit*, will *contingently* come to pass; yet . . . with a *certainty* of *event*, because his *foreknowledge* is *infallible*' (1658, 128). 'What is contingently come to pass', says Henry Hammond, 'being done, is certain, and cannot be undone, and God sees it, as it is, therefore he sees it as done, and so certain, yet as done contingently, and so as that which might not have been' (*Works* (1674), 586).

In this way, for Milton and some of his contemporaries, God's foreknowledge is no more indicative of any kind of determinism than is that certainty which an event proves to have once it becomes a *fait accompli*. That *we* know an event with certainty does not preclude its having occurred as a result of free choice. Boethius's *Consolation of Philosophy*, which contains what is still probably the most famous and influential treatment of divine foreknowledge, declares that indeed all of God's knowledge is analogous to our knowledge of things present – it is properly *scientia* rather than *praescientia*, since God dwells in an eternal present that transcends our categories of time and tense. 'Divine knowledge', says Boethius, 'resides above all inferior things and looks out on all things from their summit' (116). And in *Paradise Lost* Milton tells us that God looks down on the world, 'beholding from his prospect high, / Wherein past, present, future he beholds' (3.77–8).

One can thus recognize a Boethian element in Milton's presentation of divine foreknowledge, and one can accept the possible coherence of Hammond's and Pierce's and Milton's insistence that God foreknows with certainty human choices that are nevertheless genuinely free – and yet still have profound misgivings as one reads, in Book 3 of *Paradise Lost*, God's words about the Fall. For as Martin Evans points out, 'the abstract idea of an "eternal present" is simply not translatable into narrative terms' (Evans 1973, 178). The 'mistranslation' Milton thus has to settle for renders a view of things as temporally present or past and hence already accomplished. In Book 3, where we 'see God foreseeing', God's speech very quickly shifts into the past tense. We are told that man '*will* fall' (95), but then that he *had* sufficient means to avoid falling (97), that 'foreknowledge *had* no influence on their fault' (118), and so on. Accordingly, the notion of free will upon which Milton's theodicy is based takes on an ambiguity that it would not have possessed had God uttered his judgment only after the Fall, epic time. Because narrative is a time-bound medium, a God thus narratively presented cannot help but sound prejudiced when he speaks of the supposedly 'unnecessary' future Fall as if it were a *fait accompli*. Although the difficulty may be literary and not ultimately doctrinal, one cannot readily justify Milton for placing God in what appears such a doctrinally awkward situation.

Yet overall, Milton's intrepidity in trying to fuse narrative and doctrine produces much more clarity than confusion. Quite apart from the issue of foreknowledge, Milton in justifying God's ways must also render credible the claim that theologically, psychologically, sexually, and environmentally the Fall was not necessary. But he must also make credible the Fall's *possibility*. Though the latter claim may appear obvious, historically within Christianity there has been a tendency to glorify the prelapsarian condition in such superlative terms that one is made to wonder how the Fall could have happened at all. Clearly, if Adam and Eve's perfection before the Fall were defined in such a way that they appeared supremely and immutably good, then the Fall – especially when one tried to imagine it concretely and narratively – would appear utterly inexplicable. Yet historically within Christianity there has also been a separate, somewhat lesser tendency to see the Fall as inevitable (perhaps because of some innate, unavoidable flaw in human nature), or else as necessary to the greater glory of God and the fuller development of humankind. For Milton none of these alternatives is acceptable. If the Fall is in principle inexplicable, then a narrative account of it will lack credibility, and Milton's reader will either give up hope of hearing any rational theodicy, or even perhaps cultivate a suspicion that humankind did not fall but was somehow pushed. Similarly, if the Fall appears as inevitable, then Milton's reader, in spite of God's disclaimers, will indeed blame humankind's 'maker, or their making, or their fate' (3.113) – with similarly disastrous results for theodicy. Finally, of course, if the Fall appears desirable, then it will not be seen or lamented as a fall at all.

To put the matter technically, Milton had to build into his narrative both the necessary conditions for Adam and Eve's falling, and the necessary conditions for their standing. One of the main ways he does this is to expose Adam and Eve to some kind of trial or temptation before they must face *the* temptation. Eve, for example, almost becomes infatuated, Narcissus-like, with her own image in the lake; but she hears and responds to the Voice that leads her to Adam, and she moves from being attracted to a two-dimensional image to loving a real person whose image she shares (4.449–91). Some critics have thought that this episode and others like it – such as Eve's dream and Adam's flutterings of infatuation for Eve – are evidence that Adam and Eve are 'fallen before the Fall'. But what Milton is doing is presenting Adam and Eve's potential for falling, their *fallibility*, not their fallenness. Without that potential, nothing in the poem would make sense. And yet even given that potential, the Fall is not inevitable. Indeed, the discipline and moral exercise occasioned by that potential for evil are themselves good and help constitute Adam and Eve's potential for not falling. As Milton puts it in *Areopagitica*:

Wherefore did [God] creat passions within us, pleasures round about us, but that these rightly temper'd are the very ingredients of vertu? They are not skilfull considerers of human things, who imagin to remove sin by removing the matter of sin . . . *This justifies the high providence of God*, who though he command us temperance, justice, continence, yet powrs out before us ev'n to a profuseness all desirable things, and gives us minds that can wander beyond all limit and satiety. Why should we then affect a rigor contrary to the manner of God and of nature, by abridging or scanting those means, which books freely permitted are, both to the *triall of vertue*, and the exercise of truth . . . Were I the chooser, a dram of well-doing should be preferr'd before many times as much the forcible hindrance of evill-doing. For God sure esteems the *growth and compleating* of one vertuous person, more then the restraint of ten vitious.   (YP 2: 527–8; italics added)

In this passage Milton not only recapitulates the Free Will Defence, according to which the good that presupposes freedom outweighs the evil that restraint or a deterministic control of human behaviour could prevent; he here also adumbrates what is sometimes called a 'soul-making' theodicy, one that in part explains possibilities of both natural and moral evil as necessary ingredients in an environment for what Milton elsewhere in *Areopagitica* calls 'the constituting of human vertue' (YP 2: 516). In *Paradise Lost* Milton takes this dimension of theodicy much further, for here the demands of narrative for concreteness and coherence lead him to imagine a prelapsarian environment that is interesting, challenging, even at times frightening. Eve is tempted to fall for her own image, Adam is tempted to fall for his image, and both Adam and Eve are told the story of how Satan does fall for Sin, who is his image. They hear how Abdiel resists the temptation of Satan, who also enters Paradise and inspires in Eve a bad dream, which makes Eve cry and for which Adam and Eve must seek at least a partial explanation. They must work in the garden, organize their chores, and show hospitality to angels. They converse with, and compose poetry for, God, the angel, and each other. Adam must name the animals, and Eve the plants. And of course, again, there is one plant whose fruit, on pain of death, they are forbidden to eat. In this environment they thus face 'challenges, dangers, tasks, difficulties, and possibilities of real failure and loss' (Hick 1967; 3: 139) – which God is nevertheless justified in allowing them to face because of the conspicuous richness of life that such an environment makes possible. Milton imagines an unfallen life for Adam and Eve that seems very far indeed from what E. M. W. Tillyard unaccountably calls 'the hopeless position of Old Age pensioners enjoying perpetual youth' (quoted in Evans 1968, 244).

For Adam and Eve before the Fall, Paradise was a beginning, not a dead end. Their perfection was a perfection capable of enrichment and increase. One of the most exquisite examples of that perfection is provided by their sexual relationship with each other. Throughout history, many commentators have seen sexual intercourse as a result of the Fall, or have seen the Fall itself as resulting from sexual temptation. However, Milton not only assumes but also boldly presents prelapsarian sexual relations that take place fully within the divine plan of creation. The goodness Adam and Eve enjoy is from God. 'Their blissful bower . . . was a place / Chosen by the sovereign planter, when he framed / All things to man's delightful use' (4.690–2). And we are reminded by the couple's evening prayers, which immediately precede their gentle love-making, that their union is at once significant for the rest of humankind and conducive to the further declaration of the goodness of God, who has 'promised from us two a race / To fill the earth, who shall with us extol / [His] goodness infinite' (4.732–4).

The connection between sex and theodicy is clear: the abuses of sex may easily be seen as postlapsarian; but if also the glories of sex are seen as resulting from the Fall, then how can we look on the Fall as regrettable, and how can Milton declare the goodness of a Creator who would withhold so great a gift from his sinless creatures? In trying to depict the Fall and life before it concretely and narratively, Milton had to assume that if every good gift came from the very God whose goodness and power he was setting out to declare, then loving physical union between man and woman must be an essential component of Paradise.

Furthermore, though prelapsarian sex was good, and better than postlapsarian sex (compare 9.1011–58), it could have become better still – as could all of human enjoyment. As Milton presents it, the scope of unfallen experience was to expand as Adam and Eve grew and persisted in obedience.

Raphael tells them:

> Your bodies may at last turn all to spirit,
> Improved by tract of time, and winged ascend
> Ethereal, as we, or may at choice
> Here or in heavenly paradises dwell;
> If ye be found obedient, and retain
> Unalterably firm his love entire
> Whose progeny you are.   (5.497–503; see also 7.155–61)

This unfallen scenario includes a great increase in humankind's mobility and spirituality. And part of what Raphael implies is that Adam and Eve's bodies may become more like his body and those of the other angels, who even as spiritual beings enjoy all the pleasures of the body – eating, for example, and also sexual union.

In one of the most remarkable scenes in *Paradise Lost* Adam asks Raphael how angels express their love. And Raphael,

>   with a smile that glowed
> Celestial rosy red, love's proper hue,
> Answered. Let it suffice thee that thou know'st
> Us happy, and without love no happiness.
> Whatever pure thou in the body enjoy'st
> (And pure thou wert created) we enjoy
> In eminence, and obstacle find none
> Of membrane, joint, or limb, exclusive bars:
> Easier than air with air, if spirits embrace,
> Total they mix, union of pure with pure
> Desiring; nor restrained conveyance need
> As flesh to mix with flesh, or soul with soul.   (8.618–29)

Contrary to popular idiom, human beings in coitus do not go all the way. But Milton's angels do – and so eventually might Adam and Eve and their progeny, were it not for the Fall.

In constructing his theodicy, then, Milton's imagination is at work seeking to present recognizably good things – both actual joys and prospects of even greater – as the Creator's gifts, and so also to establish the undesirability of humankind's falling. 'Soul-making' and Free Will Defence work together to explain how the relative riskiness and decision-dependence of Adam and Eve's perfection create the necessary (though not the sufficient) conditions of their falling; the Fall is conspicuously possible. And at the same time, through Milton's dynamic presentation of life in Eden, they provide grounds for believing that the risk may have been worth it.

Yet the Fall did take place – as God knew it was going to. Was God thus simply thwarted? Or was the Fall really, at some secret level, something he willed? Perhaps the most famous response to these questions is the so-called paradox of the Fortunate Fall, according to which the sin of Adam and Eve was a happy fault, a *felix culpa*, because 'if it had never occurred, the Incarnation and Redemption could never have occurred' (Lovejoy 164). Without fully entering the debate here I would simply suggest that this theory has become an unfortunate cliché of Milton criticism. When Adam in Book 12 hears of the Redemption and glorious future that God will make available to the fallen human race, he confesses:

> Full of doubt I stand,
> Whether I should repent me now of sin
> By me done and occasioned, or rejoice
> Much more, that much more good thereof shall spring,
> To God more glory, more good will to men
> From God . . .   (12.473–8)

To read Adam's confession of doubt as a normative expression of doctrine, and to read the rest of *Paradise Lost* in the light of that doctrine, is highly uncritical. For here too Milton performs a balancing act. The future that God will provide is a glorious one, and he is much to be praised for providing it. That future may even offer something more glorious and happy than Adam and Eve's original condition (12.464–5). Yet the unfallen scenario Milton presents in *Paradise Lost* suggests that, however great our future, it will never match the still greater future that Adam and Eve and their offspring might have enjoyed in a world without sin. God in his mercy and might does bring good out of evil, but 'the alternative might have been *more* glorious' (Mollenkott 3). For man, as the words of God himself indicate in *Paradise Lost*, things would have been still 'Happier, had it sufficed him to have known / Good by it self, and not evil at all' (11.88–9).

Nor should the Fall be seen as necessary to God's greater glory. For, as Milton's contemporary John Goodwin puts it:

God is not so poorly or meanely provided, in, and of himself, for the exaltation of his Name and Glory, as to stand in need of the dunghill of sin to make a foot-stoole for him whereby to ascend into his Throne. If the *goodnesse* and *righteousnesse* of man be nothing unto God, *profit* not him, much lesse can the sins of men claime *part and fellowship* in such a businesse. So then the sins of men [are] . . . contriveable to his glory, but no wayes requisite or necessary hereunto. (*Redemption Redeemed* (1651), 40)

God is to be glorified. He is all powerful. He is wholly good. But there is evil in the world – evil that no juggling with optimistic paradoxes can rationalize away.

For Milton, a large proportion of the evil that persists in the world is represented by the loss of real human beings who will not accept the salvation that God offers them by grace through the work of his Son. Although free will is impaired by the Fall, Milton, in accordance with his belief in God's justice, declares that 'prevenient' grace (11.3) 'to all / Comes unprevented, unimplored, unsought' (3.230–1), grace that enables the fallen will to turn to God. Some, of course, will 'neglect and scorn' God's sufficiently and universally offered grace, though 'none but such' will be excluded from mercy (3.185–202). In this way Milton suggests that God, both before and after the Fall, does everything he can for the sake of humankind short of violating free will or the conditions necessary for 'the constituting of human vertue'.

In this way too Milton confronts the problem of evil at the practical level. His theodicy responds not only to the concrete demands of narrative, but also to the spiritual needs of human beings. The goodness of God has to be asserted not simply out of a kind of theological purism, but out of a recognition that one's actual worship of God, if it is to have any integrity, is predicated on a conviction that the object of one's worship is wholly worthy of it. To the extent that such worship, along with obedience, is a necessary part of human felicity, then to encourage it is also to perform a pastoral ministry. The preface to *God's Goodness Vindicated*, a pastoral theodicy published by Richard Baxter in 1671, puts the issue thus:

How much the Glory of God and the Salvation of Men is concerned in the right understanding of his Goodness . . . is evidently seen by all that have any true Notion of the Divine Excellency and Mans Felicity. God's Goodness is his most solemnly proclaimed Name and Glory. It is his Goodness duly known, that leads Sinners to Repentance, and unites their Hearts to fear his Name, and excites . . . that Love which is our Holiness and Happiness to Eternity. It is also too well known, how much this amiable Divine Goodness is denied or doubted of. (*The Practical Works* (1707), 2: 923)

Milton's theodicy too is thus evangelical and pastoral. It performs this role not merely by declaring the goodness of God, but by doing so in the face of evil, which experientially is theodicy's first datum, as it is of *Paradise Lost*: 'first disobedience', 'mortal taste', 'death', 'woe', 'loss'. Poetically and actually, we are thrust not only into the midst of things but into the midst of evils – including, of course, the evil of sin.

Integral with Milton's theodicy, therefore, is his attempt to help us to come to grips with sin. Moreover, in this attempt his narrative and pastoral and rhetorical skills are all essential. As Baxter says in *God's Goodness Vindicated*, 'with the Melancholy' – with those worried about the problem of evil – 'the greatest Difficulty lieth in making them capable to receive plain Truths: For [the truth] will work, not as it is, but as it is received' (2: 924). Theodicy therefore needs to address the problem of evil not just from above, abstractly, but also from below, from the point of view (so to speak) of the consumer, addressing what Stanley Fish has called the 'defects' of the reader (1–22). Again, that is one of the reasons why those last two words of the first invocation are so important. For, at least in Milton's theodicy, the job is to 'justify the ways of God *to men*' – to human beings with real needs and real sins.

Finally, Milton provides us with literary models, pastoral examples, of characters who in the midst of their fallenness come to remember the benevolence of the one who created and judged them. But just as a recognition of God's benevolence facilitates Adam and Eve's confession of sin, so the confession of sin enhances their freedom also to confess God's goodness. The first words we hear Adam speak in Book 11, after his and Eve's prayers of repentance are heard, emphasize the divine benevolence. 'Eve', says Adam,

> easily may faith admit, that all
> The good which we enjoy, from heaven descends;
> But that from us aught should ascend to heaven
> So prevalent as to concern the mind
> Of God high-blest, or to incline his will,
> Hard to belief may seem. (11.141–6)

If Adam was earlier surprised by sin, he is here also in a sense surprised by forgiveness. Clearly, the spontaneity of the unfallen Adam – who leaps to his feet, in Book 8, and declares at once God's 'goodness and power pre-eminent' (279) – is gone, but then so is ours. We *recognize* this more tentative Adam and perhaps also feel with him that, after the acknowledgement of our own sin, the next hardest thing is to believe that a holy God would forgive it.

Here then, once more, is the balancing act between *chutzpah* and humility. In a peculiar way, in Milton, these two apparently opposed attitudes end up nurturing each other. As Job's demand to put his case to God ends with his repenting in dust and ashes, and as Charles Wesley's 'And can it be that I should gain an interest in the Saviour's blood' leads to 'Bold

I approach th'eternal throne', so Adam's recognition of divine goodness leads to an astonishment at the gulf that separates us from it; and so an acknowledgment of humankind's fallen condition, as in the first paragraph of *Paradise Lost*, can eventuate in a project of theodicy. The two attitudes – like doctrine and narrative, like the potential for evil and the potential for good, like prelapsarian innocence and experience – can be integral. Perhaps naturally, a consideration of the Fall humbles, whereas theodicy emboldens. But as we know, Milton undertakes the two simultaneously. And it is an indication of the wholeness he aims at, that in concerning himself with the justification of God, he is also concerned with the justification of sinners.

Reading list

Boethius, *The Consolation of Philosophy*, translated by Richard Green (New York, 1962)

Burden, Dennis, *The Logical Epic: A Study of the Argument of 'Paradise Lost'* (London, 1967)

Danielson, Dennis, *Milton's Good God: A Study in Literary Theodicy* (Cambridge and New York, 1982)

   'Timelessness, Foreknowledge, and Free Will', *Mind* 86 (1977), 430–2

Empson, William, *Milton's God* (London, 1961)

Evans, J. Martin, *'Paradise Lost' and the Genesis Tradition* (Oxford, 1968)

Evans, J. Martin, ed., *'Paradise Lost': Books IX–X* (Cambridge, 1973)

Fish, Stanley Eugene, *Surprised by Sin: The Reader in 'Paradise Lost'* (London, 1967)

Hick, John, *Evil and the God of Love* (London, 1966)

   'Evil, The Problem of', *Encyclopedia of Philosophy*, ed. Paul Edwards (New York, 1967)

Kirkconnell, Watson, *The Celestial Cycle: The Theme of 'Paradise Lost' in World Literature with Translations of the Major Analogues* (Toronto, 1952)

Lewalski, Barbara Kiefer, 'Innocence and Experience in Milton's Eden', in *New Essays on 'Paradise Lost'*, ed. Thomas Kranidas (Berkeley, 1969)

Lovejoy, Arthur O., 'Milton and the Paradox of the Fortunate Fall', *ELH* 4 (1937), 161–79; rpt. in *Critical Essays on Milton from ELH* (Baltimore, 1969)

McColley, Diane Kelsey, *Milton's Eve* (Urbana, 1983)

Mollenkott, Virginia R., 'Milton's Rejection of the Fortunate Fall', *Milton Quarterly* 6 (1972), 1–5.

Pierce, Thomas, *The Divine Philanthropie Defended* (London, 1657)
   Self-Condemnation (London, 1658)

Plantinga, Alvin, *God, Freedom and Evil* (London, 1974)

Radzinowicz, Mary Ann, ' "Man as Probationer of Immortality": *Paradise Lost*

XI–XII', in *Approaches to 'Paradise Lost': The York Tercentenary Lectures*, ed. C. A. Patrides (Toronto, 1968)

Ulreich, John C., Jr, 'A Paradise Within: The Fortunate Fall in *Paradise Lost*', *JHI* 32 (1971), 351–66

Williams, Norman Powell, *The Ideas of the Fall and of Original Sin* (London, 1927)

9 Milton's Satan

The controversy about Milton's Satan provides an opportunity to inspect the relationship between a literary text and critical reaction to it. This is instructive because it shows how literature works (or has worked), and how it should not be expected to work.

A word, first, about the generation of Milton's Satan. There is very little in the Bible about Satan. In *Christian Doctrine* Milton collects all the available biblical evidence in a few sentences. It amounts to little more than that Satan is the author of all evil and has various titles (YP 6: 349–50). As Kastor has shown, it was not until about AD 200 that official Judaism began to absorb popular concepts of Satan. From then on appearances of Satan in literature, sub-literature, and theology multiplied. Scores of literary Satans evolved, and some of them – notably those created by Du Bartas, Andreini, Grotius, and Vondel – possibly influenced Milton. However, no convincing single source for Milton's Satan has been found.

The need to create a Satan figure arises from a Manichaean view of the moral universe. Within this mentality, as Jung has pointed out (Werblowsky x–xii), the evolution of God as a *summum bonum* necessitates the evolution of an *infimum malum*, to account for the presence of evil in the world. It was to combat Manichaeanism that the early church launched its doctrine that evil had no real being but was merely *privatio boni* (privation of good).

This sophistical tenet had no appeal for Milton. He presents evil as real and traceable to a single Evil One. The wish to isolate evil in this way argues a particular mental configuration which seems to be associated with the belief that, once isolated, evil may become containable or punishable. Hence has arisen the urge to locate evil in a single kind of being, which has borne fruit throughout history in pogrom, ghetto, and racial massacre. In Freudian terms it may be identified as an effort of the severe and critical superego which subjugates the recalcitrant id. From a literary viewpoint, the isolating effort of the purifying and punitive will is the opposite of the mentality we think of as Shakespearean, which accepts the fact that evil is inextricably enmeshed in collective human experience.

Milton's effort to encapsulate evil in Satan was not successful. That is, those readers who have left their reactions on record have seldom been able to regard Satan as a depiction of pure evil, and some of the most distinguished have claimed that he is superior in character to Milton's God. It is sometimes supposed that critical support for Satan began with the Romantics, but this is not so. Sharrock (463–5) has shown that the notion of Satan as the true hero of Milton's epic goes back to Dryden and was a commonplace of eighteenth-century literary opinion both in France and England. Barker (421–36) finds that eighteenth-century admirers of the sublime praised Satan's 'high superior nature', and so came into conflict with Addison and Johnson, who declared Satan's speeches 'big with absurdity'. Among Romantic critics, Blake, Byron, Shelley, and Hazlitt championed Satan, whereas Coleridge identified him with Napoleonic pride and sensual indulgence (see Newmeyer). These critics certainly intensified and politicized the controversy, but they did not start it – nor, of course, did they finish it. In the twentieth century, anti-Satanists such as Charles Williams, C. S. Lewis, S. Musgrove, and Stanley Fish have been opposed by A. J. A. Waldock, E. E. Stoll, G. Rostrevor Hamilton, William Empson, and others.

The correct critical reaction to this dispute is not to imagine that it can be settled – that either Satanists or anti-Satanists can be shown to be 'right'. For what would that mean but ignoring what half the critics of the poem have felt about it – ignoring, that is, half the evidence? A more reasonable reaction is to recognize that the poem is insolubly ambivalent, insofar as the reading of Satan's 'character' is concerned, and that this ambivalence is a precondition of the poem's success – a major factor in the attention it has aroused. Other texts generally recognized as 'great' literature manifest similar ambivalence in their central characters. The critics who strive to prove that Shakespeare 'really meant' Shylock to be essentially bad, or essentially good, would, supposing either side could prevail, destroy much of the play's power and interest. A similar ambivalence characterizes Isabella, Prospero, Othello, Lear, Falstaff, and so on. Within liberal bourgeois culture, disputability is generally advantageous to a text since it validates individual reinterpretation and so functions, from the consumer viewpoint, as an anti-obsolescence device.

To recognize that the character of Satan is essentially ambivalent is not to say that we must agree with everything the Satanists or the anti-Satanists propose. Both sets of critics misrepresent or over-state in their bid to strengthen their case. Among anti-Satanists there is a tendency to jeer at Satan and become sarcastic at his expense, as if he really existed. Williams and Lewis both manifest this. Pro-Satanists are likewise seduced into anger and indiscretion – as when E. E. Stoll (124), replying to Lewis, deplores the fact that criticism is nowadays 'complicated by scholarship'. The power to entangle and excite readers is an observable feature of the Satan figure.

Satanist critics generally emphasize Satan's courage, anti-Satanists his selfishness or folly. These simplified versions of Satan ignore or evade the evidence within the poem that fails to square with them. If we wish to find a single term for the character attribute which Satan's ambivalent presentation, taken as a whole, generates, then the most suitable term seems to be 'depth'. Depth in a fictional character depends on a degree of ignorance being sustained in the reader. The illusion must be created that the character has levels hidden from us, the observers. By comparison with Satan, the other characters in *Paradise Lost* – Adam, Eve, even God – exist simply and transparently at the level of the words they speak. Satan does not – partly because his habitual mode is dissimulation, partly because, unlike the other characters, he exists, or has existed, within the historical span the poem covers, in a number of different modes.

These different modes are partly inherent in the biblical and post-biblical Satan material. The traditional Satan story, as it eventually took shape, involves Satan in three separate roles – an Archangel, before and during the war in heaven; a Prince of Devils in the council in hell; a serpent-tempter in the garden. Satan is thus not a single concept, but a trimorph. In the earliest records of the Satan myth, the pseudepigrapha and apocrypha of the Old Testament, the three roles were, as Kastor notes (1–17, 69–71), performed by three different figures. The ambivalence of Milton's Satan stems partly from his trimorphic conception; pro-Satanists tend to emphasize his first two roles, anti-Satanists his third.

Further, Milton has compounded the ambivalence by making the division between the roles uncertain. Satan as Archangel, before his fall, is never shown by Milton, but this stage of his existence is often alluded to, as is the fact that some of his archangelical powers remain, though we cannot be quite sure which. Hence Satan, as fictional character, gains a hidden dimension and a 'past'. Also, Satan as Prince of Devils is still present within Satan-as-Tempter, as is shown when Ithuriel touches the toad with his spear, and Satan springs up 'in his own shape' (*PL* 4.819). This means that Satan's bestial disguises need not be regarded as debasement or degradation, as some critics have viewed them, since he retains his inner consciousness despite his disguises – or seems to. This qualification has to be added, for the precise state of Satan's consciousness at various points in the action is problematic (for example, at the point where, in the debate with Abdiel, he denies that he and the other angels were created by God; see below). The reader cannot solve these problems, because no textual evidence is available which will provide him with access to Satan's 'true' state of mind. By this device of narrative occlusion, Satan gains depth; whereas with the other characters no such interesting possibility of discrepancy opens up between inner state and outward profession or appearance.

The one part of the poem where access is provided to the 'true' Satan is his soliloquy at the start of Book 4 (32–113). The impression of depth is maintained throughout this because, although Satan's mind is no longer hidden, his inner debate and self-criticism reveal him as a creature of dynamic tensions, such as the other characters of the poem notably lack. This is partly because the soliloquy is a generic transplant. Edward Phillips, Milton's nephew, tells us it was written as part of a drama, not an epic, at a time when Milton intended to write a tragedy on the Fall. The soliloquy has the immediacy of drama, not the distance of epic. In it, Satan concedes his own criminality, and his own responsibility for his fall. He vacillates between remorse and defiance. He confesses that his rebellion was completely unjustifiable, that he had the same 'free will and power to stand' as all God's creatures, and that he therefore has nothing to accuse but 'heaven's free love dealt equally to all'. Since heaven's love means his own damnation, he curses it ('Be then his love accursed'), but then, rationally, turns his curse against himself ('Nay, cursed be thou'). Satan could be called evil at this point in the poem only in some attenuated sense, since he speaks the truth and curses himself as God curses him. He and God are in accord. The function of the speech within the poem's argument is to justify God; even Satan, we are meant to see, admits God was right. But paradoxically this admission redeems Satan in the reader's eyes, so that the response elicited is, as usual with Satan, ambivalent.

As part of his 'official' task of exculpating God in the soliloquy, Satan explains that even if he could repent and get back to heaven 'by act of grace', it would do him no good, since, once back there, he would grow proud again ('how soon / Would highth recall high thoughts'), and this would lead to a 'worse relapse' and 'heavier fall'. The intent of this argument, within the poem's apparent didactic strategy, is to make it seem merciful of God not to have mercy on Satan and allow him back. However, ambivalence once more surrounds the issue. For it is reasonable for the reader to ask why Satan should not learn from his fall, and be forgiven without any risk of his falling again. Why should a hypothetical but inevitable recurrence of his fall be built into his nature as part of the poem's case? The question is important, since whether Satan might ultimately be forgiven was a doctrinal issue; one church father, Origen, had opined that he would, though Milton disagreed (see Robins). Patrides argues that at this juncture in the poem the dramatic context demands that Satan's redemption should be entertained at least as a possibility, and it is of course true (within Christian doctrine) that Satan's redemption could not be regarded as impossible for God, since this would infringe God's omnipotence. To retrieve the situation, Milton has to make Satan's irredeemability his own fault, and the soliloquy effects this. He emerges as a creature trapped within his own inevitably and repeatedly fall-prone nature. But this means, of course, that he is trapped within Milton's fiction, of which that 'nature' is a part. The fiction leads him towards a doom from which he sees a way of escaping ('But say I could repent'). Hence Satan appears to possess, from the reader's viewpoint, an autonomy which is another attribute of fictional 'depth'. The illusion is created that he is independent of the fiction that contains him, and unfairly manipulated by that fiction.

The most obvious sense in which Satan is trapped within an alien fiction is that the fiction requires him, though an archangelically rational creature, to take up arms against a God who is axiomatically omnipotent. Much has been made of this by anti-Satanist critics, who take Satan's hostility to Almighty power as a sign of folly. The pro-Satan critics, on the other hand, produce it as evidence of his supreme courage, since even his adversary's omnipotence does not daunt him. Neither response can, of course, be pronounced 'right'; the potential of Satan to elicit both is simply a product of his habitual ambivalence. Folly and courage are, however, strictly inadequate terms for describing the behaviour of Satan and the rebel angels in relation to God's omnipotence, since these terms relate to human behaviour, and the fiction places Satan and his followers in a situation for which we can find no precise human counterpart.

Comparison with Napoleon and other earthly conquerors (such as Coleridge suggests) is inaccurate, since Satan's situation is more curious than any such parallel would allow. The situation the devils are in is clearly enunciated by Belial during the council in Pandaemonium in Book 2. Belial acknowledges that God is not only omnipotent, and therefore proof against any attack the devils can make, but also omniscient, so that he cannot be out-witted. Neither force nor guile, Belial concludes, can be effective against such an adversary. God 'views all things at one view', and 'sees and derides' the devils' council even while it is in progress. The devils are performing before God as their audience, and are aware of his presence even as they discuss outwitting him. This means that their behaviour is not just 'foolish' or 'courageous'; it has an inherent fictive improbability. In order to make their behaviour credible, the reader has to assume that the devils make an at least temporarily successful effort at self-deception or willed oblivion: that they forget, or pretend that they are ignorant of, the predicament Belial has described. Otherwise it is not evident how they could keep up the momentum of their action.

Milton indicates that this is how he requires us to read the processes of diabolic intelligence by the way he writes about Satan at the start of Book 4. As Satan flies up from hell to earth, we are told that he does not rejoice in his speed. 'Horror and doubt distract' his thoughts when he remembers that 'of worse deeds worse sufferings must ensue'. But if Satan knows his mission is bound to make things worse for him, why, we may ask, does he undertake it? The answer, strictly, is that he cannot escape the terms of the fiction he finds himself in. He is the victim of a breakdown of fictional logic inherent in the terms of the myth Milton is transcribing. For he is cast in a poem with an axiomatically omniscient and omnipotent God, and this means that every hostile move he makes must be self-defeating. Yet his fictional function is precisely to make hostile moves: he is the fiend, the enemy.

The unlikelihood of Satan's rebellion against God had worried biblical commentators. They were especially puzzled by Isaiah 14: 14 where 'Lucifer, son of the morning' is depicted as saying 'I will ascend above the heights of the clouds; I will be like the most High.' This text was generally taken as a reference to Satan, but it caused difficulties since it would have been irrational for Satan to aspire to be equal in power with God. As Stella Revard shows (45–6), both Anselm and Aquinas argued that Satan could not, despite the apparent meaning of the text, have wished directly for equality with God, for as a rational and perfect being he would have known this was impossible. Partly because of these interpretative problems, Protestant theologians tended to deny that the Isaiah text referred to Satan at all. Calvin and Luther both read it as alluding to the King of Babylon.

Milton, however, could not evade the terms of the story by an exegetical manoeuvre of this sort. In the narrative he adopts, the omnipotence of God, which must have been evident to an archangelically intelligent Satan, coexists incongruously with a Satanic rebellion. Milton disguises this insuperable narrative difficulty partly by omitting any depiction of the unfallen Satan from his account. In this way he sets aside the problem of showing perfect intelligence operating imperfectly. He also makes the story seem more likely by adapting the fallen Satan's psychology. Satan's states of awareness, we are given to understand, are murky and changeable. Thus his realization, at the start of Book 4, that worse deeds will lead to worse sufferings, is presented as something he managed previously to forget. 'Now conscience wakes despair / That slumbered' (4.23–4). Satan, then, manages genuinely to hope at times, though after these respites despair reasserts itself. The fallen Satan is, we gather, a creature of moods, apprehending reality through mists of self-deception and forgetfulness. This wavering, slumbering, deceptive state of consciousness is another factor that gives Satan fictional depth, concealing him from our full knowledge. It also lends credibility to his unlikely story, since the reader tends to assume that the fallen Satan's indecisiveness about God's omnipotence (perhaps, he sometimes thinks, God is only 'Almighty styled' (9.137) not really Almighty) also characterized the unfallen Satan, and led to his revolt. In fact, of course, the unfallen Satan could not, by definition, have been fallible in this way. But Milton's narrative strategy conceals the logical flaw.

The fallen Satan's ability to dismiss unattractive facts from his consciousness is a feature which complicates the interpretation of his argument with Abdiel about the creation of the angels in Book 5, lines 835–64. In response to Abdiel's declaration that the angels were created by the Son, Satan insists that they were, on the contrary, 'self-begot, self-raised', and that Abdiel's theory is a 'strange point and new'. When soliloquizing, however, in Book 4, lines 42–4, he admits to himself that it was 'heaven's matchless king' (meaning, presumably, God the Father not the Son) who created him. Some critics (Lewis, for example) have seen this later admission as proof that Satan was simply lying in the Abdiel episode. Others (such as Waldock and Empson) have interpreted it as a new perception by Satan, or a resurgence of something he has chosen to forget. We cannot adjudicate between these interpretations with any confidence, since either would be reconcilable with Satan's mental processes as the poem elsewhere shows them. It is certainly odd that the other angels present at the debate accept Satan's, not Abdiel's, version of the creation. Presumably this means either that they never had any intuitive knowledge of their creation by the Son, or that they have wilfully suppressed or simply lost it. Steadman (166) suggests that Abdiel, like Adam, may have worked out by means of reasoning the fact that God created him. But Abdiel would have intuitive, not discursive, reason, so would not need to work things out. The crux remains insoluble. Satan may be lying, he may be deceiving himself, he may have genuinely lost touch with the truth. That he never knew the truth does not seem a probable interpretation, since it would contradict his archangelical knowledge (though, of course, archangels did not know everything, nor, even, did the Son, according to Milton in *Christian Doctrine* (YP 6: 227) – full knowledge was the Father's alone).

The depth and ambivalence Satan gains from this episode issue from an uncertainty of interpretation. The facts are not fully ascertainable. More often it is the moral evaluation of his actions which generates disagreement among readers. Three episodes have proved particularly divisive. The first occurs in Book 1, when he weeps at the sight of his fallen followers, and cannot speak for tears:

> Thrice he essayed, and thrice in spite of scorn,
> Tears such as angels weep, burst forth.   (1.619–20)

Pro-Satanist critics interpret the tears as magnanimous compassion. But anti-Satanists point out that angels were not supposed, in orthodox theology, to weep, since tears were a sign of passion, which angels were not subject to. Fowler annotates the lines with a quotation from Marvell ('only humane Eyes can weep'). The tearlessness of angels certainly seems to be emphasized by Milton in Book 11, where Michael shows Adam the effects that death and disease will have upon mankind in the future. Adam weeps, but Michael remains composed and dry-eyed, and Milton remarks rather pointedly on the contrast between them. The future fate of mankind was

> Sight so deform what heart of rock could long
> Dry-eyed behold? Adam could not, but wept,
> Though not of woman born; compassion quelled
> His best of man, and gave him up to tears.   (11.494–7)

'Though not of woman born' echoes *Macbeth* (V.vii), and, as Fowler notes, the echo is more than just a verbal reminiscence, for one of the chief themes of *Macbeth* is the evil that ensues from a drying up of compassion – the 'milk of human kindness'. This point does not, of course, redound to the credit of Michael or other tearless angels, and, though Fowler fails to note it, Milton's phrase 'Tears such as angels weep' in the description of Satan weeping also has a Shakespearean original. In *Measure for Measure* Isabella proclaims that

> man, proud man,
> Dress'd in a little brief authority,
> Most ignorant of what he's most assur'd,
> His glassy essence, like an angry ape,
> Plays such fantastic tricks before high heaven
> As makes the angels weep; who, with our spleens
> Would all themselves laugh mortal.   (II.ii.117–23)

This Shakespearean original might be taken (by a pro-Satan critic) as removing any culpable passion from Satan's weeping. Weeping, it seems, is what angels do in situations where men, being coarser and more splenetic, would laugh. Anti-Satan critics might point out, on the other hand, that the 'proud man' in Isabella's speech is remarkably like Satan, an 'angry ape' of God, so that if the echo is to be taken as more than a chance reminiscence, it would become anti-Satanic in its reverberations, and would, indeed, highlight the ambivalent responses Satan's 'tricks' evoke – laughter in some readers, tears in others. As usual there is no deciding between these evaluations of Satan's action, which remains essentially disputable – though the Shakespearean echo, coming from such a context, probably enhances his depth for most readers. By weeping 'tears such as angels weep' he seems more grief-stricken than mere human weepers. A second instance of Satanic action – or reaction – which seems at first creditable, but can be claimed as evidence by both Satanists and anti-Satanists, occurs when he sees Eve in Eden and is so enraptured by her beauty that he becomes momentarily good (9.460–79). He is deprived of his 'fierce intent' as he watches her, 'abstracted' from his own evil:

> and for the time remained
> Stupidly good, of enmity disarmed,
> Of guile, of hate, of envy, of revenge.					(9.464–6)

But he snatches himself back from the brink of innocence, 'recollects' his hatred, and 'excites' himself to evil once more:

> Thoughts, whither have ye led me, with what sweet
> Compulsion thus transported to forget
> What hither brought us, hate, not love.					(9.473–5)

The passage seems to indicate that Satan's natural tendency, when caught unawares, is to love. Beauty and delight are his natural element. Hatred is an effort of his will. This could be seen as making him either more, or less, sympathetic. Like his angelic tears, it shows his capacity for a role different from the one the fiction assigns him to. From the viewpoint of his function within the plot, the incident is extraneous. Milton did not need to include it to advance his narrative. It is a gratuitous piece of 'characterization', and seemingly favourable. On the other hand, since Satan chooses not to escape his diabolism, although he has the opportunity, he could be seen as the more damnable. The incident shows that he is not a destructive automaton, but a creature who chooses to destroy the human race against the promptings of his better nature. Milton echoes, in the passage, both himself and Shakespeare. 'Sweet compulsion' is from the vision of universal harmony described by the Genius in *Arcades* ('Such sweet compulsion doth in music lie . . . '; 68); and 'whither have ye led me' echoes the ruined Antony after Actium ('O, whither hast thou led me, Egypt?'; *Antony and Cleopatra* III.xi.51). Both echoes can be seen as 'lifting' Satan, setting him in the context of tragic love and the music of the spheres, which is what the Genius is listening to. But both echoes are also, by implication, critical of Satan, since Antony chooses to lose the world for love, whereas Satan does the opposite, and the music of the spheres signifies universal harmony, which Satan is about to destroy. As usual, he moves within a cloud of ambivalence.

A third prominent example of Satan's attaining depth through ambivalence occurs earlier in the poem's action than his 'stupidly good' response to Eve, and is (if read as pro-Satanists read it) the most surprising and poignant of his utterances. When he first sets eyes on Adam and Eve in Eden he is stricken with wonder at the human pair – not spirits, he perceives, yet 'little inferior' to heavenly spirits – and feels, or says he feels, an inclination to love them. They are creatures

> whom my thoughts pursue
> With wonder, and could love, so lively shines
> In them divine resemblance.   (4.362–4)

Satan's reason for feeling he could love Adam and Eve – that they look so like God – naturally surprises the reader, since we have been led to suppose it is God Satan hates. Though there is nothing here so clear as an echo, there seems to be a recollection of the incident in Marlowe's *Doctor Faustus* where Mephistophilis, asked by Faustus how he comes to be out of hell, replies:

> Why, this is hell, nor am I out of it.
> Think'st thou that I, who saw the face of God,
> And tasted the eternal joys of heaven,
> Am not tormented with ten thousand hells,
> In being deprived of everlasting bliss?

The similarity lies in the unexpected revelation of love or desire for God in a figure we believed to be wholly committed to the opposition. Not all critics are prepared to grant that Satan really feels any inclination to love at this point. Whereas pro-Satanists (Raleigh, Stoll, Hamilton) take his response to 'divine resemblance' to be sincere, anti-Satanists (Lewis, Musgrove) interpret his words as brutal irony. Since he is soliloquizing, irony is perhaps unlikely – but not impossible. As usual, we cannot take the simple step of declaring one reading correct. But we can see that Satan gains fictional depth from the dubiety surrounding the point, as well as from the possibility of his underlying love for God.

These three examples all help to make Satan seem inscrutable. So, too, does his imaginativeness. As a dissimulator, he displays imagination in ways that are unavailable to God or the other good characters. Unlike him, they do not depend on lies, so the constant imaginative effort by which Satan sustains himself is foreign to them. They remain, from the viewpoint of imagination, relatively undeveloped beings. It is no doubt true, in a doctrinal sense, that God 'imagined' the universe, since he created it out of his mind. But he is not presented, in the poem, as an imaginative being. Satan is – as we note, for example, when the snake tells Eve how he found the forbidden fruit:

> Till on a day roving the field, I chanced
> A goodly tree far distant to behold
> Loaden with fruit of fairest colours mixed,
> Ruddy and gold: I nearer drew to gaze;
> When from the boughs a savoury odour blown,
> Grateful to appetite, more pleased my sense
> Than smell of sweetest fennel or the teats
> Of ewe or goat dropping with milk at even,
> Unsucked of lamb or kid, that tend their play.
> To satisfy the sharp desire I had
> Of tasting those fair apples, I resolved
> Not to defer; hunger and thirst at once,
> Powerful persuaders, quickened at the scent
> Of that alluring fruit, urged me so keen.
> About the mossy trunk I wound me soon,
> For high from ground the branches would require
> Thy utmost reach or Adam's: round the tree
> All other beasts that saw, with like desire
> Longing and envying stood, but could not reach.
> Amid the tree now got, where plenty hung
> Tempting so nigh, to pluck and eat my fill
> I spared not, for such pleasure till that hour
> At feed or fountain never had I found.   (9.575–97)

This is all lies, of course. Satan does not like milk or apples; he never climbed a tree. But he has imagined himself into the snake's existence so vividly that we almost forget he is lying. He even takes the trouble to make the tree 'mossy', imagining that would make it more comfortable for a snake to wind around. (Is this where Keats got his 'mossed' apple trees in 'To

Autumn'?) Of course, being inside a snake may have enabled Satan to take over the snake's sensibility, which would aid his imagination. We cannot tell. Nor can we tell whether his rapt musing on unsucked teats and fair apples is prompted by the naked woman he is gazing at. (Some critics have suggested that 'ewe' is a Freudian slip: 'the teats / Of you'.) Maybe. As usual we cannot locate Satan's state of consciousness within a firm reading. But however we read him, his imaginativeness is impressive, and allies him, of course, with the creator of the poem, Milton, who had to imagine it all.

Satan's imagination is crucial because it inaugurates the whole divergent history which is *Paradise Lost* and the story of the human race – a narrative divergent from God's original perfect creation, and a narrative which began when Sin, Satan's imagining, jumped out of his head. The episode with Sin and Death at the gate between Hell and Chaos (2.648–870) is one of the most puzzling in the poem, and the one that seems to carry us furthest into the half-light of Satan's subconscious. As he talks to Sin she reveals a buried phase of his life, and one which, even when she has recounted it, it seems he has no recollection of. He is, she tells him, her father, but also her mother. He went through birth pangs in heaven and she sprang from an opening in the side of his head. She became his accomplice against God, but she was also his image, as the Son is the image of the Father. He had a child by her, Death, who, once born, pursued his mother and raped her. That rape begot the 'yelling monsters' that now surround her.

We can recognize in all this a perverted rewriting of several of the poem's motifs. Adam is father and mother to Eve, since she was taken from his side, as Sin from Satan's head. He pursues her and unites sexually with her, as Death does Sin. In this murk of rape and incest and male birth pangs, the themes and actions of the poem swim about guiltily transformed. We have here, as it were, not just Satan's but the poem's subconscious. Its myths of origin are here released from narrative decorum, and parade in spectral shapes. The theme of lethal eating (the deadly apple) finds its counterpart in this underworld sequence in cannibalism. Death wants to eat Sin, but she warns him she would 'prove a bitter morsel, and his bane' (2.808). What adds to the strangeness and profundity of the sequence is that it has not only perversion to offer but also wifely and (as nowhere else in the poem) motherly love, shown when Sin rushes between Satan and Death to prevent their fighting.

Of course, readers are at liberty to insist that the sequence is 'just allegory', and that we should not bother with any of its deeper shades. However, even readers who take this line need to explain what it is an allegory of – what are the actual events that its various details correspond to? It does not take much thought to see that we are in no position to answer such a question. The status of the sequence in terms of the poem's 'reality', and the level on which we are to read it, are not matters about which we can obtain any firm directives. This means that, in this strange episode as in much else, Satan slips from our knowledge. We can see that he is implicated in depths, but the nature of them eludes our understanding.

The emergence of Sin from Satan's head was Milton's way of dealing with the poem's (and Christianity's) most difficult question – how evil originated. The problem of how evil could have been created spontaneously from good exercised, as Revard points out (35–6), the minds of the church fathers, and Manichaeanism grew from the belief that the evil factor, Satan, was created from a kingdom of darkness over which God had no authority. Christianity could not allow this solution, since it had an omnipotent God. But the church fathers who, like Cyril of Jerusalem, simply asserted that Satan became evil of his own free will, though created good, did not have to show it happening. Milton, too, found this impossible, and retreated into the cloudy region at hell's gate where Sin tells of events which took place somewhere other than in the poem's usual narrative mode, though we cannot tell where.

Finally, the relation of Satan to Milton's intentions (was Milton of the Devil's party? or not? or only subconsciously so?) has interested critics. Such questions are all clearly unanswerable since we have no access to Milton's mind, let alone his subconscious, at the time of writing. That does not, of course, prevent speculation about them. We can, moreover, be sure that Satan was originally the product of Milton's psychology (he was certainly, that is, not the product of anyone else's psychology), and critics who oppose the psychological approach are usually participating in it without realizing they are doing so. Merritt Hughes, for instance, asserts that the interpretation of Satan must be cleared of all 'modern psychologism' that makes him a reflection of irrational depths in Milton's nature. Milton created him, Hughes lays it down, 'as an example of the self-deception and the deception of others which are incident to the surrender of reason to passion' (177). Hughes's interpretation is of course flatly intentionalist, since it assumes access to Milton's mind, and is therefore an instance of the 'psychologism' he believes himself to be opposing.

Though originally the product of Milton's psychology, Satan, as he is read and interpreted, is also the product of the reader's psychology. *Paradise Lost*, like other texts, reads the reader, and Satan, as I have shown, divides readers into opposed camps. Most readers, probably, can feel sympathy with both the Satanists and the anti-Satanists. We feel that by suppressing a part of ourselves we can disown and denounce Satan, but we also feel the power of that part of us which is having to be suppressed. This situation has encouraged critics to see the character of Satan as built over a dichotomy in Western – or human – consciousness. Werblowsky (53) associates Satan with the drive towards science and rationalism in Western culture, and away from the female womb chaos (the Jungian *mater devorans*). Maud Bodkin (38–44) sees *Paradise Lost* as rendering in symbol the conflict between aspiration and a sense of one's own nothingness, basic to human experience. Isabel MacCaffrey (182–3) maintains that all arguments about where our sympathies lie in *Paradise Lost* are vain, since they lie both with the fallen and with the rigours of discipline necessary for our survival as reasonable beings.

Freud's analysis of the modern psyche seems particularly applicable to Satan's disputable nature, as well as to the recognition that Satan is a 'great' (that is, widely significant) creation. At the end of *Civilization and Its Discontents* Freud speaks of the exorbitant development of the superego in modern culture, and particularly the ethical demands the superego makes on the individual. It requires the individual habitually to suppress his aggressiveness and his hunger for self-satisfaction:

In the severity of its commands and prohibitions it troubles itself too little about the happiness of the ego . . . It, too, does not trouble itself enough about the facts of the mental constitution of human beings. It issues a command and does not ask whether it is possible for people to obey it. On the contrary, it assumes that a man's ego is psychologically capable of anything that is required of it, that his ego has unlimited mastery over his id. This is a mistake; and even in what are known as normal people the id cannot be controlled beyond certain limits. If more is demanded of a man, a revolt will be produced in him, or a neurosis.   (80–1)

Freud goes on to argue that the unappeasable commands of the civilized cultural superego in modern man lead to whole civilizations, 'possibly the whole of mankind', becoming neurotic. The controversy about Milton's Satan – what I have called Satan's essential ambivalence – is, I would suggest, evidence of that neurosis.

Reading list

Barker, Arthur E., ' " . . . And on His Crest Sat Horror": Eighteenth-Century Interpretation of Milton's Sublimity and his Satan', *University of Toronto Quarterly* 11 (1942), 421–36

Bodkin, Maud, 'Literature and the Individual Reader', *Literature and Psychology* 10 (1960), 38–44

Darbishire, Helen, ed., *The Early Lives of Milton* (London, 1932)

Empson, William, *Milton's God* (London, 1961)

Evans, J. Martin, *'Paradise Lost' and the Genesis Tradition* (Oxford, 1968)

Fish, Stanley E., *Surprised by Sin: The Reader in 'Paradise Lost'* (London and New York, 1967)

Freud, Sigmund, *Civilization and Its Discontents*, translated by Joan Riviere, revised and newly edited by James Strachey (London, 1979)

Hamilton, Rostrevor, *Hero or Fool? A Study of Milton's Satan* (London, 1961)

Hughes, Merritt Y., *Ten Perspectives on Milton* (New Haven and London, 1965)

Kastor, Frank S., *Milton and the Literary Satan* (Amsterdam, 1974)

Kirkconnell, Watson, *The Celestial Cycle: The Theme of Paradise Lost in World Literature with Translations of the Major Analogues* (Toronto, 1952)

Langton, Edward, *Satan, A Portrait: A Study of the Character of Satan Through All the Ages* (London, 1946)

Lewis, C. S., *A Preface to 'Paradise Lost'* (Oxford, 1942)

MacCaffrey, Isabel Gamble, *'Paradise Lost' as 'Myth'* (Cambridge, MA, 1959)

Milton, John, *Christian Doctrine*, ed. Maurice Kelley, translated by John Carey (YP vol. 6)

Musgrove, S., 'Is the Devil an Ass?', *Review of English Studies* 21 (1945), 302–15

Newmeyer, Edna, 'Wordsworth on Milton and the Devil's Party', *Milton Studies* 11 (1978), 83–98

Patrides, C. A., 'The Salvation of Satan', *Journal of the History of Ideas* 28 (1967), 467–78

Revard, Stella Purce, *The War in Heaven: 'Paradise Lost' and the Tradition of Satan's Rebellion* (Ithaca and London, 1980)

Robins, Harry F., *If This Be Heresy: A Study of Milton and Origen*, Illinois Studies in Language and Literature 51 (Urbana, 1963)

Rudwin, Maximilian, *The Devil in Legend and Literature* (London, 1931)

Sharrock, Roger, 'Godwin on Milton's Satan', *N&Q*, New Series 9 (1962), 463–5

Steadman, John M., *Milton's Epic Characters: Image and Idol* (Chapel Hill, 1968)

Stoll, E. E., 'Give the Devil His Due: A Reply to Mr Lewis', *Review of English Studies* 20 (1944), 108–24

Waldock, A. J. A., *'Paradise Lost' and Its Critics* (Cambridge, 1947)

Werblowsky, R. J. Zwi, *Lucifer and Prometheus: A Study of Milton's Satan*, with an introduction by C. G. Jung (London, 1952)

Williams, Charles, ed., *The Poetical Works of Milton* (Oxford, 1940)

10   Milton and the sexes

When the Archangel Michael, toward the end of *Paradise Lost*, foresees the church attacked from without by persecution and from within by 'specious forms' so that 'truth shall retire / Bestuck with slanderous darts' (12.534–6), he summons along with the figure of Truth a picture of St Sebastian stuck full of arrows: who, however, did not die of those wounds but had to be murdered by temporal power all over again. Milton's *Paradise Lost*, addressed to the 'church' of learned believers, is similarly susceptible to recurrent volleys; and his figure of Woman brought to life in Eve, who is a type of the church and perhaps of the poem, has (for being too free, or for not being free enough) been a primary target, with similar resurgent vitality.

In current discussions of Milton's treatment of 'the two great sexes', especially the one supposed less great, most of the darts adhere to his enactments in Eve of the Pauline analogies of marriage, both to the human body (with the husband as head), and to the spousals of Christ and the church – analogies that the modern mind does not perceive as complimentary to womanhood. Of course Milton's Adam and Eve are dramatic characters, not only types or allegories, but Milton does incorporate into their marriage the fusion of divinity and humanity that for him was the prime hope of the world. Like the apostles, he considered it his calling to prepare for 'an extraordinary effusion of *Gods* Spirit upon every age, and sexe' (YP 1: 566; Acts 2: 17–18). And although his hope of spiritual rebirth for the body politic was disappointed, he never abandoned his hope for the rebirth of the specific men and women who would read his poem.

One measure of the power of Milton's poetry is that readers so often either love it or hate it, and that those who hate it nevertheless go on writing about it. Recently in the vanguard of anti-Miltonists have been feminist critics offended by Milton's masculine outlook, his acceptance of the Genesis story and the Pauline tradition concerning the submission of wives, and the misogynous diatribes he allows some of his dramatis personae, such as fallen Adam in *Paradise Lost* and the chorus of Danites in *Samson Agonistes*. They

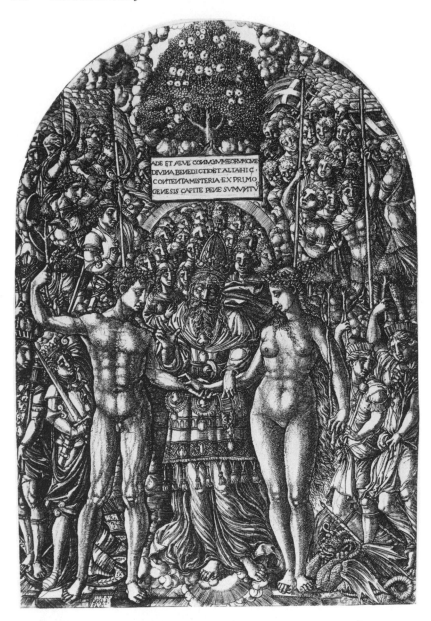

Johannes Duvet, *The Blessing of the Marriage of Adam and Eve* (*c*. 1540–55)

join other politically oriented critics in urging that literary scholars eschew indiscriminate apologetics and cast a cold eye on whatever misognyist, xenophobic, homophobic, or elitist stereotyping of 'the other' the canonical literary 'masters' have, advertently or inadvertently, given warrant for. At the same time, many who love Milton's poems, including many women, find that his regard for the *quality* of human beings of both sexes offers more toward mutual respect than the problem of equality can undo.

In seventeenth-century England, women did not hold civil or ecclesiastical offices, attend universities, or engage in the major professions. Milton shared some of the assumptions that caused these limitations, but provided a method for interpreting scriptural precedents meant to expand the disciplined liberties of a regenerate people. He rejected the double standard of sexual conduct, arguing not that women should be promiscuous, but that men should be chaste: since chastity, like all temperance, liberates one's power of apprehension (especially of 'celestiall songs') and since, he added to the fury of some later readers, the man 'sins both against his owne body which is the perfeter sex, and his own glory which is in the woman, and that which is worst, against the image and glory of God which is in himselfe' (YP 1: 892). He did not, however, deny to women perfectibility in any spiritual or moral gifts; and he insisted on the spiritual compatibility of husband and wife and defined marriage as mutual assistance in all *'the helps and comforts of domestic life'*. He did not think wifehood coextensive with womanhood, finding 'the properties and excellencies of a wife set out only from domestic vertues; if they extend furder, it diffuses them into the notion of som more common duty then matrimonial' (YP 2: 612–13).

Milton's views on the relations of the sexes may be found in a series of tracts on domestic liberty; in his *Christian Doctrine* 1.10, 'Of the Special Government of Man before the Fall' – which adds a defence of patriarchal polygamy – and 2.15, of 'Private Duties'; and in certain of his poems, pre-eminently *Paradise Lost*. All are are rooted in the biblical creation story and hold marriage in extraordinarily high regard. The crux of Milton's account of the relations of the sexes, then, is his interpretation of Genesis 1–3 taken together with the rest of the Scriptures, and especially of the words of the Creator in Genesis 2: 18. 'And the Lord God said, It is not good that the man should be alone; I will make him an help meet for him.'

Although Milton's works may be read on their own merit, their flavour is more distinct and more complex if we know something of their cultural contexts: the conflux of classical and Christian thought and art which we call the Renaissance; and the effort to return the church to something closer to its scriptural origins which we call the Reformation. As a participant in both these movements, Milton looked to the first marriage, as recorded in Genesis, as his source of first principles; and he interpreted that story with a Renaissance regard for human dignity and the goodness of the visible creation, including sexuality, as a divine gift.

In Hesiod's *Theogony*, Zeus creates Woman in revenge for Man's acquisition of forbidden knowledge from Prometheus; her name is Pandora, and she comes equipped with a box of evils. The Hebrew book of origins differs from the Greek in radical ways: instead of gods of both sexes who are a part of nature, and hence unreliable and sometimes hostile to humankind, it represents a transcendent maker of nature who 'created man in his own image . . . male and female created he them' (Gen. 1: 27), pronounced this whole creation good, and blessed it; and instead of providing Woman as punishment, it represents her as meet help: that is, as a fitting aid and companion in the care of the world and the procreation commended in the callings to dress and keep the garden and to increase and multiply. That little word *help*, however, supported by the graphic description in Genesis 2 of God making Eve from Adam's rib, suggests a sex that is subordinate, perhaps created only secondarily in God's image and so spiritually inferior. Coupled with the story that Eve was the first to disobey God and enticed her husband to do likewise, Genesis thus affords excuses for misogyny in spite of its ameliorations in comparison with other accounts of human origins, including those of our own age.

The Hebrew Bible continues with the epic of the monotheistic and patriarchal Israelites who established a theocracy ordered by holy laws amidst enemies who worshipped deities of both sexes and of undependable moral character, some of whom required child sacrifice, mutilation, ritual prostitution, and other violations of civil rights, which Milton abhorred and personified as Moloch, Mammon, and Belial. This process, once seen as unifying the human family under one 'Father' and freeing it by divine law from the inequities of human power, is now viewed by some feminists as establishing the rule of invisible (paternal) over visible (maternal) power.

The leaders of the Reformation, by treating the Old Testament typologically as the prefiguration of the New and as the pattern of their own experience, encouraged patriarchal language. In addition, they removed from the liturgy and from church decoration much of the feminine imagery associated with the Virgin Mary and other women saints. On the other hand, they improved the status of women by diminishing the authority of the early 'Fathers of the Church' with their sceptical attitudes toward women and marriage, by insisting on women's spiritual equality, by commending marriage to all (including priests) as the source of holy offspring and civic virtue, and by regarding the family as a 'little church and a little state', hierarchical to be sure but giving each member dignity and importance. Writers of conduct books stressed St Paul's teaching that the husband should love his wife as Christ loved the church and cherish her as his own body – advice meant to honour and protect women but couched in metaphors that now sound demeaning and have been outstripped as women have moved increasingly into arenas 'more common . . . th[a]n matrimonial'.

Milton believed that the Bible was true, but that the individual conscience guided by the Holy Spirit had a good deal of leeway in interpreting it, measured always by the rule of charity: trust in the goodness of God and commitment to the well-being of humankind. He believed also that next to the relation between each person and God, the relation of husband and wife was the chief source of personal happiness or misery. His task both in his polemical and his poetic works on marriage was to adhere to the spirit of his primary source while interpreting it with the greatest charity. By contrast with many classical analogues and with interpretations of Scripture that Milton thought tyrannical, his matrimonial ideals and especially his representation of the first marriage in *Paradise Lost* reflect a libertarian belief in the original goodness – now wounded by sin but recoverable by grace and hard work – of the whole creation, including man, woman, and sexuality. And the *quality* of this goodness depends partly on Milton's sense that to be a 'help' is not servile but a calling and pleasure that men, women, and angels share with their maker.

Thanks to three centuries of progress toward liberty, which Milton helped to promote, the idea that woman was made for man, or that any segment of the human family is subordinate to any other, has been discredited. Milton himself narrowed the gender gap considerably. The emphasis in his 'divorce' tracts is on mutuality and spiritual likeness, with a reservation of superior authority to the husband. His acceptance of patriarchal stances is now under attack, with reason. I would suggest, however, that what Milton does (especially in his poems) toward revising the attitudes of his contemporaries, short of repudiating Judaic and Christian tradition with its manifold contributions toward civility and charity, is on the whole on the side of human liberty and dignity; and that if we indiscriminately repudiate *him*, and that tradition with him, we are likelier to get an increase of barbarism than of justice. To follow out the paths Milton mapped is usually to proceed toward fuller awareness of the plenitude of potentiality for goodness and blessedness in each human soul.

Milton was born into an age when poets spent a great deal of ink and breath on the proposition that although some women are unattainable divinities, few are both 'true, and faire'. John Donne (who is Milton's most diverse and prolific recent predecessor in poetic exploration of the relations of the sexes) either echoes or parodies this and other proverbial views in early comic songs and elegies that advise men to 'hope not for minde in women' but make directly for 'the Centrique part' (90, 127, 66). Milton, however, set himself early to celebrate those in whom 'good and faire in one person meet', preferring above all poets Dante and Petrarch, 'the two famous renowners of *Beatrice* and *Laura* who never write but honour of them to whom they devote their verse, displaying sublime and pure thoughts, without transgression' (YP 1: 890). Milton did not publish any erotic poems of the cynical, frivolous, enticing, complaining, or repining kinds with which the early seventeenth century teemed. In fact, apart from 'O nightingale' and the sublime and pure love lyrics within *Paradise Lost*, he published no English poems in the usual amorous genres at all. A few of Milton's seventeenth-century predecessors, however – most notably, again, Donne – had begun to address women not only as wives, mothers, and objects of erotic desire but also as examples of more virtues than the one of 'honesty' or chastity usually assigned to them, and as spiritually and intellectually equal and eloquent friends. Milton is of their party.

Several of Milton's English poems address women in non-erotic ways. His first, written when he was seventeen, undertakes the delicate task of consoling his sister on the death of her infant daughter. His early 'Epitaph on the Marchioness of Winchester' places the Marchioness 'high . . . in glory' next to Rachel, who similarly died bearing her second child, and whom Dante seats next to Mary in a heaven well populated with women. 'Methought I saw my late espoused saint' commemorates a wife of whom he trusts to have 'full sight . . . in heaven . . . vested all in white, pure as her mind'; although in his blindness he cannot see her face, 'Love, sweetness, goodness in her person shined / So clear, as in no face with more delight'. Other sonnets, too, contain 'nothing but praise'. 'Lady, that in the prime of earliest youth' encourages a young girl whose 'growing virtues' have evidently aroused annoyance, as virtues sometimes do, and who has nevertheless serenely continued to 'labour up the hill of heavenly truth' with only compassion for her detractors. 'Daughter to that good Earl' commends a woman in whom he sees reborn all the virtues of her father, a leading jurist Milton deemed of the highest integrity. 'When faith and love which parted from thee never', in memory of a woman he calls 'my Christian friend', assures her that her good endeavours, led and clad by Faith, 'speak the truth of thee in glorious themes / Before the judge'. These commendations of the spiritual victories of actual women, with in some cases a Dantean gorgeousness of heavenly imagery, are a refreshing change from the prevailing poetry of amorous or courtly compliment.

In addition, Milton wrote six Italian sonnets and three Latin epigrams on women largely in praise of their speech and their singing – they are fellow artists in Milton's own vocation of reharmonizing Heaven and earth – and an accolade, in *Arcades*, to the Dowager Countess of Derby for her patronage of this vital function of the arts. *A Mask Presented at Ludlow Castle* (*Comus*) gives its young heroine vigorous moral views, a spirited resistance to evil, and a receptivity to grace that embody and adumbrate Milton's most serious and consistent themes. Moreover, Milton's graces and muses, especially the Muse of *Paradise Lost*, link what might be called the feminine principle to the act of poetic creation itself. The Celestial Muse appears to be a female persona of the Holy Spirit – supposing that all 'spirits when they please / Can either sex assume' (*PL* 1.423–4) – or perhaps an offspring of the inspiring Spirit and the aspiring mind, the matrix wherein the divine begetting and the human conception of the poem fuse.

A good deal of attention has been given to Milton's female horrors, though only one of them is human: the loathsome biform figure of Sin, and Dalila, if you read her as the embodiment of meretricious female sexuality used to exploit and entrap. But there are plenty of male horrors, too: Satan, Death, Moloch, Belial, Mammon, Chemos, Comus, and the like all caricature male forms of cruelty, deception, and sexual rapacity in at least an even-handed way.

Milton's definitions of marriage – the only sexual relation his chaste ardour admitted – are found in five tracts written in the 1640s as a part of his programme to advocate religious, civil, and domestic liberty for sober and religious men – and, to an extent, women – but also, one supposes, under some pressure from his own difficult marital situation. He had married in 1642 (in spite of the civil war between the King and the Parliament which Milton supported) seventeen-year-old Mary Powell, of an Oxfordshire Royalist family, who after a month of marriage went home for a visit and neither came back nor answered Milton's letters, Oxford having become the headquarters of the King, and Mary's family (as Edward Phillips comments in his *Life of Milton* (1694)) beginning 'to repent them of having matched the eldest daughter of the family to a person so contrary to them in opinion'. The first of these tracts was *The Doctrine and Discipline of Divorce: Restor'd to the Good of Both Sexes, From the bondage of the Canon Law, and other mistakes, to Christian freedom, guided by the Rule of Charity*, published unsigned and unlicensed in 1643, during the deliberations of the Westminster Assembly, and again, augmented and initialled, in 1644. His proposals were rejected and attacked in print, in Parliament, and from the pulpit – without, Milton complained, being carefully read or answered with reasoned argument. Shortly after the publication of the second edition, Milton learned that the respected reformer Martin Bucer had expressed similar views. Expecting to be 'fully justified' by so notable an authority, he translated the large portion of Bucer's *Judgment* that concerned divorce and published it, this time with the licenser's authorization but still with little success, in 1644. In 1645 he produced *Colasterion*, an angry reply to his detractors, and *Tetrachordon*, whose title means a four-stringed instrument, the four strings being the four chief places in Scripture concerning marriage: Genesis 1: 27–8 and 2: 18, 23–4; Deuteronomy 24: 1–2; Matthew 5: 31–2 and 19: 3–11; and 1 Corinthians 7: 10–16. The purpose of *Tetrachordon* is to show that despite canonical interpretation of the words of Christ in Matthew as stricter than the law of Moses, these four 'strings' are really in tune with each other. The hostility with which this closely reasoned exercise in case divinity was received elicited two sonnets, 'I did but prompt the age to quit their clogs' and 'A book was writ of late called *Tetrachordon*; / And woven close, both matter, form and style' – a proceeding Milton never lost hope would attract intelligent readers.

The arguments in these tracts are both close-woven and extensive, but their gist is that Christ did not abrogate the law of Moses permitting divorce, which would put God in the position of having colluded with sin, but spoke specifically to the arrogance of the Pharisees. Marriage was given by God for the good of man; a marriage that fulfils none of its purposes is not 'what God hath joined together'. Since the spiritual relation of husband and wife is its true form, followed by the procreation of children and, as a lesser though important cause, the 'mutual benevolence' of the marriage bed, to allow divorce for physical infidelity but not for fundamental spiritual discord turns upside down the purposes of the marriage covenant. To the charge that liberalizing divorce laws would give trivial and licentious persons an excuse to change partners at whim, Milton replies characteristically that the liberties of good and serious persons are more important than the restraint of the vicious, who are unfaithful to their marriage vows anyway, while good people in intolerable marriages are robbed of the energy to serve their families, callings, and countries.

In the course of these arguments Milton indulges in passages of what we would now call 'sexist language', especially where he addresses Deuteronomy 24 (which unlike Milton's proposal allows only a *man* to put away his wife) or canonists who thought that the divorce laws were only for 'afflicted wives': 'Palpably uxorious! who can be ignorant that woman was created for man, and not man for woman; and that a husband may be injur'd as insufferably in mariage as a wife[?]' (YP 2: 324). He explicates Genesis 1.27 by agreeing with St Paul that 'the woman is not primarily and immediatly the image of God, but in reference to the man. *The head of the woman*, saith he, 1 *Cor*. 11. *is the man: he the image and glory of God, she the glory of the man*: not he for her, but she for him.' Then, with only partial mitigation, he adds:

Nevertheless man is not to hold her as a servant, but receives her into a part of that empire which God proclaims him to, though not equally, yet largely, as his own image and glory: for it is no small glory to him, that a creature so like him, should be made subject to him. Not but that particular exceptions may have place, if she exceed her husband in prudence and dexterity, and he contentedly yeeld, for then a superior and more naturall law comes in, that the wiser should govern the lesse wise, whether male or female.

This habit of taking with one hand while giving with the other at least leaves the tracts with some openings for discourse; but the passage continues with perhaps the most stereotypical of Milton's observations, that

seeing woman was purposely made for man, and he her head, it cannot stand before the breath of this divine utterance, that man the portraiture of God, joyning to himself for his intended good and solace an inferiour sexe, should so becom her thrall, whose wilfulnes or inability to be a wife frustrates the occasionall end of her creation, but that he may acquitt himself to freedom by his naturall birthright, and that indeleble character of priority which God crown'd him with . . . She is not to gain by being first in the transgression, that man should furder loose to her, because already he hath lost by her means.   (YP 2: 589–90)

Yet in spite of this stung resort to the convention of attributing inferiority, and the first sin, to all women, Milton redefines marriage in language of thorough mutuality as 'meet and happy conversation' in 'conjugall fellowship' with 'a fit conversing soul', conferring the 'dignity & blessing' of the 'mutual enjoyment' of a love 'begot in Paradise by that sociable & helpful aptitude which God implanted between man and woman toward each other'. Each is 'the copartner of a sweet and gladsome society', fed by a 'coequal & *homogeneal* fire' which 'cannot live nor subsist, unlesse it be mutual'. Marriage was ordained by God 'in the beginning before the fall, when man and woman were both perfect' and is still meant to fulfil God's promise of 'meet help' though 'not now in perfection, as at first, yet still in proportion as things now are' (YP 2: 246, 251–5, 308–9). In marriage 'there must be first a mutuall help to piety, next to civill fellowship of love and amity, then to generation, so to household affairs, lastly the remedy of incontinence'; it is a covenant 'the essence whereof . . . is in relation to another, the making and maintaining causes thereof are all mutual, and must be a communion of spiritual and temporal comforts' (YP 2: 599, 630).

In *Paradise Lost* the 'essential form' of marriage becomes live experience, represented as it was 'in the beginning before the fall, when man and woman were both perfect'. Writers on Genesis in the century after the poem's publication wistfully echo Milton on the happiness of married life before the Fall; but the echoes extend to Eve as delightful pleasure, not the intellectual and spiritual companion or the free and responsible member of the human community Milton shows her to be. An anonymous *History of Adam and Eve* (1753), for example, waxes Miltonic about nuptial bliss but reverts to the old misogynist notion that the prohibition itself attracted Eve to the Tree, without benefit of Serpent: 'The Prohibition makes Eve curious; for it is awakening the curiosity of a Woman to forbid her anything. The Prohibition excites and inflames her desires, which are generally violent for things which are permitted, but insatiable for those forbidden. Prevail'd upon by that Impatience, which dug the Grave of their Happiness, she forsakes *Adam*, to enjoy without witness or reproach the Sight of a Fruit, which she esteem'd the most exquisite of all; only because it was forbidden' (2). One of Milton's most extensive revisions of traditional misogyny is his invention of motives more provident of Eve's dignity and of ours.

Many women who have recently written about Milton – Barbara Lewalski, Joan Bennett, Mary Ann Radzinowicz, Stelle Revard, Irene Samuel, Kathleen Swaim, and Joan Webber, to name a few – read his poem as addressed to their humanity, unhaunted by anxieties of influence. At the same time, 'resistant' readers who read from the point of view of gender – for example, Jackie DiSalvo, Sandra Gilbert, Christine Froula, Marcia Landy, Mary Nyquist, Patricia Parker, and, without being what she calls a terrorist of the text, Maureen Quilligan (178) – challenge sympathetic readings or historicize the text in diverse ways (see Shullenberger). Like the women's movement itself, feminist critics divide into differing camps: some want women (and women literary characters) to have the same power and privileges men (they believe) have always had, while others find 'women's' values worth extending and suggest radical re-evaluation of the concepts of power that have prevailed. The latter are more akin to Milton himself. For however many of Milton's epic voices call Eve 'the inferior', the poem as a whole gives at least as much praise to qualities often considered 'feminine' as to those considered 'masculine'. His major poems cast a great deal of scorn on the traditional epic hero's self-assertiveness and will to power, represented by Satan and his fellow vandals and terrorists; and they commend as more heroic the 'feminine' virtues of gentleness, patience, humility, mercy, and devotion, 'by small / Accomplishing great things, by things deemed weak / Subverting worldly strong, and worldly wise / By simply meek' (12.566–9), making it impossible to assign these qualities according to the stereotypes of gender. Milton satirizes showy competition and violent displays of strength, ridicules the male notion that one can pursue fame and glory by flinging hardware and maiming flesh, and makes – as Genesis does – the nurturing 'woman's work' of dressing and keeping the garden, together with increasing and multiplying, the shared and dignified concern of both sexes: the health and beauty of the earth and the growth of souls become in *Paradise Lost* clearly worthier of human effort than acquisition and exploitation.

The truer 'manly' virtues such as fortitude, clear-headed justice, fidelity to principle, and reason unswayed by passion, and 'womanly' ones like sympathy, responsiveness, and the desire to keep relationships reciprocal, are not strictly divided between Adam and Eve: although they do not always exercise all, both are capable of all. In the separation colloquy it is Eve's adherence to principles very like Milton's own that moves her to decline to let Satan's threat interfere with their liberties and the pursuit of their callings; it is Adam's respect for open dialogue and his sense of true relation, needing freedom, that move him to accede to her wish. But at the Fall these qualities run to excess in Eve's ambition and Adam's 'effeminacy' or uxoriousness, when he puts the immediate concerns of personal relations above the long-term claims of truth.

If Milton is to present these virtues in their perfection 'before the fall' in a drama of two human characters, the obvious way is to let the woman exemplify the by no means inferior qualities that are linked to the feminine. If he wants to bring man and woman closer to a 'conjugall fellowship' of beings who are more 'like' than convention considered them, he can show Eve and Adam both capable, in proportion, of both sorts of virtue, altering the stereotype of women in the direction of equality, not by a sudden assertion that his contemporary male readers (and he himself) would find hard to swallow, but by an intermingling and infusion of thought and imagery that will open the imagination and dispel the hardness of heart that mere confrontation often exacerbates. This it seems to me is what Milton does, or what happens to him at the hands of the Celestial Muse.

The imagery of *Paradise Lost* gives at least equal and sometimes superior value to constructs of the feminine. The masculine perspective of the text is everywhere balanced by its openness of form. Its style combines a sinewy firmness of structure with an infinitely penetrable music. Its language mates linear logic with radiant consciousness; the design is sturdily architectural, but the radiant consciousness so suffuses that form with dance that subsequence and precedence are constantly transposed. Its male and female imagery is distinguished by reciprocity and exchange, inscribed especially in Raphael's astronomical discourse (8.66–178) just before Adam's uneasy though delighted attempt to square Eve's theoretical inferiority with his sense of her 'greatness of mind' (8.521–59). What Raphael says about heavenly bodies should free Adam and us from oversimple assumptions about the domestic hierarchy, such as that the 'greater should not serve / The less':

> consider first, that great
> Or bright infers not excellence: the earth
> Though, in comparison of heaven, so small,
> Nor glistering, may of solid good contain
> More plenty than the sun that barren shines,
> Whose virtue on it self works no effect,
> But in the fruitful earth; there first received
> His beams, unactive else, their vigour find.   (8.87–97)

Even for 'him' it is not good to be alone. If, in fact, the whole heavens circle the earth, their swiftness serves 'thee earth's habitant', but 'What if the sun / Be centre to the world, and other stars / By his attractive virtue and their own / Incited, dance about him various rounds?' What if the earth 'industrious of her self fetch day', and her light be 'as a star' to the moon, their light 'Reciprocal', and the whole universal dance be so too, 'other suns perhaps / With their attendant moons . . . Communicating male and female light, / Which two great sexes animate the world'? (8.99, 122–5). This discourse on the 'new philosophy' throws in doubt ancient mythic sexual stereotypes and opens the concepts of inferiority and service to 'various' interpretations. As Stevie Davies, Michael Lieb, Joseph Summers, and Kathleen Swaim, among others, have variously and abundantly shown, the two sexes, both great, both in their natural innocence communicating light, constitute the universe and the fabric of the poem. Its characters and its bardic voice are sexually distinct, but the *poem* is androgynous.

With these matters in mind, let us examine four critical cruxes – a tetrachord, or perhaps tetradiscord, of places in *Paradise Lost* most likely to disturb people who read in a gender-conscious way. And as we do, let us imagine, following out James Turner's suggestion of the couple-reader, a serious yet lively witted seventeenth-century family reading aloud together, considering and debating the implications of these passages on the internal model of Adam and Eve themselves, who read the book of nature and discuss its implications in a traditionally gendered yet radically open way, Eve asking imaginative questions and Adam, intellectually stimulated by them, exercising his reasoning mind.

The first, in which we look over Satan's shoulder as he gets his first glimpse of Adam and Eve, begins by assuming a greater physical, spiritual, and moral equality for Eve than she had ever enjoyed before; but it ends with the lines that have, perhaps, most offended gender-oriented women readers:

> Two of far nobler shape erect and tall,
> Godlike erect, with native honour clad
> In naked majesty seemed lords of all,
> And worthy seemed, for in their looks divine
> The image of their glorious maker shone,
> Truth, wisdom, sanctitude severe and pure,
> Severe but in true filial freedom placed;
> Whence true authority in men; though both
> Not equal, as their sex not equal seemed;
> For contemplation he and valour formed,
> For softness she and sweet attractive grace,
> He for God only, she for God in him.   (4.288–99)

Both are 'lords of all', full of divine attributes, and placed, both *filius* and *filia*, in filial freedom. Eve is included, even, in 'true authority', though the qualification that follows (at least to Satan's seeming) reserves 'greater authority' to the husband: Milton attributes dominion, the divine attribute women were thought to lack, less largely to Eve than to Adam, though later he shows the animals of Eden 'duteous at her call' (9.521). We should note, too, his improvement on the 'he not for her, but she for him' of *Tetrachordon*. Some of us might be better pleased if Milton had written 'Both equal, though their sex not equal seemed' and 'Both for God and for God in each other', concocting a sort of Leveller's fantasy on Genesis and demolishing domestic hierarchy in one blow, much to the jeopardy of his credibility among his peers. Since he did not, we might ask whether his 'two' represent two kinds of goodness that can in each reader go, like Adam and Eve, hand in hand.

Equality under the law is a remedial idea – invented for a fallen race not much given to rejoicing in the goodness, much less the superiority, of others – needed to rectify injustices that no one in a state of sinless blessedness would consider committing. If we are to read Milton's poem with pleasure we need to get rid of Satan's dreary habit of thinking himself impaired by another's goodness. Postlapsarian wrongs occur when a sex or other group thinks itself superior, or any one person is exploited or scorned. Does Milton's poetry contribute to these injustices, or work to dissolve them by joyful reception of each person? What seems to matter most to him is the *each*ness of each. Each angel is a separate *kind* or species, like Dante's 'angeli festanti, / Ciascun distinto de fulgore et d'arte' (*Paradiso* 31.132–3); each human soul is a special making, jointly fashioned by herself or himself and God. This celebration of particularity – Ingram and Swaim's *Concordance* lists 151 uses of *each* in *Paradise Lost* – cries out for the highest regard for each created being regardless of place. We have since discarded some of the considerations of place Milton had to deal with, but we need not discard love of the distinct lustre of particular persons where each self is fuller of light the more it rejoices in other selves.

The second string of our chord or discord is Adam's perplexed avowal that though he knows Eve 'the inferior, in the mind / And inward faculties',

> Authority and reason on her wait,
> As one intended first, not after made
> Occasionally; and to consummate all,
> Greatness of mind and nobleness their seat
> Build in her loveliest, and create an awe
> About her, as a guard angelic placed.   (8.541–59)

Adam's state in this passage is more complex than either Raphael or psychologists of 'erotic valuation' give him credit for. Clearly, he needs to retrieve his 'wisdom' and balance. Yet a passage from Paul, less often observed than the notorious ones on the obedience of wives, exhorts 'all the saints' to be 'of one accord, of one mind', as Adam says he and Eve are (8.603–5); and, Paul continues, 'in lowliness of mind let each esteem other better than themselves' (Phil. 1: 1; 2: 2–3). Although there is a good deal else going on in their separate confessions of admiration for each other, Adam and Eve are 'all the saints' and their marriage is the type of the early church to be re-formed. So Milton is in the tricky position of needing to express through them both the scriptural not-quite-equality of husband and wife and the scriptural more-than-equality of a holy community – and on top of that, the erotic delight and mutual exaltation of lovers, with the risk of idolatry and the need for a responsive relation to the rest of creation by those who enjoy that 'sum of earthly bliss' (8.522). Insofar as they are a family, Adam and Eve participate in a hierarchy that gives the male 'greater authority'. Insofar as they are a church, each esteems the other 'better'. A world in which each person cares 'for the things of others' (Phil. 2: 4) and rejoices in *each* other's goodness must be a feast of splendours.

The third string is a double one. Eve's own views of her position shift even more radically than unfallen Adam's as she moves from naively innocent fallen perceptions. 'My author and disposer', she says to Adam in Book 4, 'what thou bid'st / Unargued I obey; so God ordains, / God is thy law, thou mine: to know no more / Is woman's happiest knowledge and her praise' (635–8). (Is this allegation to be taken as the true sentiments of a poet who thought that 'all believers' are 'living temples, built by faith to stand, / Their own faith not another's' (12.520–8) and that 'fellowship ... fit to participate/ All rational delight' (8.389–91) is the true form of marriage?) But after she bites the fruit, Eve reverses her earlier over-simplification, wondering whether to 'keep the odds of knowledge in my power':

> So to add what wants
> In female sex, the more to draw his love,
> And render me more equal, and perhaps,
> A thing not undesirable, sometime
> Superior; for inferior who is free?   (9.820–5)

If we set aside the fact that Eve is entirely deluded about the nature of the fruit, does her question have any validity? One answer to it is 'everybody', since in a universe constituted of plenitude and gradation (for the sake of diversity and unity) every being is 'inferior' in some sense to someone, yet all are free 'Till they enthrall themselves' (3.125). But in fact Eve is as self-governing as Adam. He needs her, she consents; and she (quite naturally and regularly) goes off alone on errands of art or mercy. Moreover, Milton often calls attention to the moral power of subordinates: Eve; Abdiel; the mocked, blind and imprisoned Samson; the politically powerless young Hebrew hero of *Paradise Regained* – none are impeded while they keep intact their will to goodness. Does anything in Milton's poem prevent any-one (as Gilbert says it does women writers) of either sex from feeding her or his own exuberant creativity from Milton's world of light?

Apart from eating the fruit of one tree – which God has forbidden in order to remind them that 'it is he who hath made us, and not we ourselves' – it is hard to think of any honest and non-violent activity or pursuit of knowledge that Adam and Eve cannot both enjoy. *Neither* can engage in the professions, because law, medicine, and the clergy all treat the effects of the Fall. But they can create good government, health, liturgy, and pastoral care. They cannot, without the Fall, engage in armed warfare, but spiritual valour is surely requisite to both sexes, with the Spirit of Darkness aping animals and entering through mists unseen. Unlike many predecessors, Milton did not think that sensuous pleasure was wicked nor that Adam and Eve fell because of erotic love. Their sexual bliss is matched by the spiritual intimacy of their prayers; and these set to music, along with their work and conversation, represent all wholesome arts and sciences. It is hard to think of anything worth doing that Adam and Eve do not, both, actually or tropologically do. Their work is mutual – only once does it fill typical gender roles, when Eve 'within, due at her hour / Prepared . . . dinner' while Adam 'sat' (5.299–304) – and unfallen Eve's love of fruits and flowers that 'at her coming sprang' is as needful as Adam's 'studious thoughts abstruse' (8.40–7) to ensure that their employments keep earth glorious. Their shared interests in work and coming children fit Carolyn Heilbrun's ideal modern symmetrical family. Sin can do nothing but impede these freedoms. When Satan perverts Eve's 'feminine' open, generous sympathy she loses both that ('Shall I . . . keep the odds') and her growing 'masculine' integrity learned from Adam, Raphael, and Abdiel. And when Adam colludes in the Fall he loses both that integrity and his growing 'feminine' bond with nature learned from Eve.

The fourth string, because it issues from their maker, redeemer, and judge, is the 'fundamental' of the chord, and so least susceptible of apologetics on grounds of context, multiplicity of voices, or the gradual education of the reader. The Judge asks Adam,

> Was she thy God, that her thou didst obey
> Before his voice, or was she made thy guide,
> Superior, or but equal, that to her
> Thou didst resign thy manhood, and the place
> Wherein God set thee above her made of thee,
> And for thee, whose perfection far excelled
> Hers in all real dignity [?]   (10.145–51)

These are salient lines for the reading family to wrestle with, then or now. What husband who had got this far in the poem would dare to gloat at them? Clearly, Milton agrees that it is the husband's 'part / And person' to 'bear rule' – at least this husband's, since his wife does not surpass him in prudence. We should not make the mistake of supposing, though, that the Judge is alluding to Adam's lack of 'government' in allowing Eve to leave his side: the 'filial freedom' in which both are created would then have been a lie in all its ramifications as a pattern for human institutions. The Judge censures Adam 'Because thou hast hearkened to the voice of thy wife, / And eaten of the tree concerning which / I charged thee' (10.198–200). Adam's mistake is making Eve his 'God' and his 'guide' at the moment of the Fall, and so both losing his chance to be a means of grace to Eve and transmitting sin to all posterity. This passage, like the first, improves the language of the divorce tracts, in which he 'lost by her means'; here the responsibility belongs to both, though more to him. Yet if we take Milton's Creator–Redeemer to say (as he does not in Genesis) that men are by immutable nature far more excellent 'in all real dignity' than women, then we will each have to decide what this passage means for the value of the whole poem. If we acknowledge the biblical, Dantean, Miltonic patterns for the perfection of all protagonists, whatever their gender – that status has no effect on fullness of joy, that humility exalts, that service frees – we will not see or use this passage as a statement authorizing male arrogance. If we have noted Milton's dramatic decorum, his sense of limitless process in the works of this very Creator–Redeemer, and the interchange of attributes Eve and Adam have experienced in their unfallen lives together, we will not suppose that these words dashing Adam's disastrous dependency on the opinion of fallen Eve apply to all people through all time. Yet for male readers looking for ways to justify tyranny or female ones looking for reasons to abandon charity – which either could do only by ignoring the rest of the poem – this passage is prime grist, and we would do Milton an injustice if we did not point out the misuses that can be made of it in new contexts, or the ways in which both the failures and the graces of both characters can apply to all of us. The epic poet, 'with his many voices' as Homer says (*Odyssey* 22.393), lets us not only hear but *be* each character in turn. While each of us is mimetically being Eve and Adam, we gather in the possibilities of both.

Curiously, some people object to Eve's derivation from Adam, in spite of her original splendour in truth, beauty, wisdom, and sanctitude, who are unalarmed by the news that we are all derived from hairy bipeds called *Australopithecus afarensis*. Some resent her service of 'God in him' who recommend the narrower confines of 'self-servience' and have no interest in service of God at all. Some censure the slight imparity of perfections of Eve and Adam without lamenting our general inferiority to them both. Some think Eve unfree who do not protest the massive oppression of psychological theories that put each person and all action and affection into a few sexual categories and locate the genesis of all creativity in the vicinity of that portion of the male body on which 'Adam sat'. Some denounce Milton's fidelity to the scriptural idea of the family who accept the stupendous repression of spirit with which much criticism ignores the wellspring of holiness from which all value issues in *Paradise Lost*.

The 'woman question' in Milton will never be *decided*; good poems never end. He was probably more serious about the relations of the sexes, more careful of their resonances, than any poet of or before his time, and of the happiness and holiness not only of a *Beatus vir* (Ps. 1 and 112), but also of a *Beata mulier*, a woman joyous in plenteous gifts, perhaps than any other poet of any time. He was radical in his insistence on women's spiritual complete-ness, responsibility, and fitness for 'all rational delight' and in his celebration of erotic bliss in the morning of creation. Perhaps no one else has depicted sexual happiness at once so lavishly and so purely. His loving portrait of Eve, not excusing her sin on any grounds, certainly not incapacity, but portraying her as a person of delightful mind as well as beautiful form, honour as well as charm, sanctitude as well as radiant looks and graceful gestures, moral searching as well as artistic creativity, asperity as well as gentleness, and a capacity for repentance and forgiveness as well as dutiful domesticity, raises her immeasurably above other Eves of art and story, opening new possibilities of dialogue for the reading family at every turn. To the small degree that Adam and Eve are 'higher' and 'lower' they are as two strings tuned to different pitches, to make harmony. It would be rude to ignore Milton's primary interest, and sad to miss his harmonies, in showing how good Adam and Eve are, and how many ways they are good, in an argument about precedence, as if jostling for a high place at the table kept us from enjoying the feast. The last shall be first, in any case. But it would be untrue to Milton, as well, not to give him the honest argument, based on thorough and thoughtful reading, that he looked for in vain from his early opponents. Such a reading can bring reader and text together in 'meet and happy conversation'.

Reading list

Aers, David, and Bob Hodge, ' "Rational Burning": Milton on Sex and Marriage', *Milton Studies* 13 (1979), 3–33

Barker, Arthur, 'Christian Liberty in Milton's Divorce Pamphlets', *Modern Language Review* 35 (1940), 153–61

Benet, Diana, 'Abdiel and the Son in the Separation Scene', *Milton Studies* 18 (1983), 129–43

Bennett, Joan S., ' "Go": Milton's Antinomianism and the Separation Scene in *Paradise Lost*, Book 9', *PMLA* 98 (1983), 388–404

Davies, Stevie, *The Feminine Reclaimed: The Idea of Woman in Spenser, Shakespeare, and Milton* (Lexington, KY, and Brighton, 1986; published in the UK as *The Idea of Woman in Renaissance Literature*)

DiSalvo, Jackie, *War of Titans: Blake's Critique of Milton and the Politics of Religion* (Pittsburgh, 1983)

Donne, John, *The Complete Poetry*, ed. John T. Shawcross (Garden City, 1967)

Evans, J. M., *'Paradise Lost' and the Genesis Tradition* (Oxford, 1968)

Farwell, Marilyn R., 'Eve, the Separation Scene, and the Renaissance Idea of Androgyny', *Milton Studies* 16 (1982), 3–20

Fleming, Ray, '"Sublime and Pure Thoughts Without Transgression": The Dantean influence in Milton's "Donna leggiadra"', *Milton Quarterly* 20 (1986), 38–44

Fresch, Cheryl H., '"And brought her unto the man": The Wedding in *Paradise Lost*', *Milton Studies* 16 (1982), 21–33

Froula, Christine, 'When Eve Reads Milton: Undoing the Canonical Economy', *Critical Inquiry* 10 (1983), 321–47

'Pechter's Specter: Milton's Bogey Writ Small; or, Why is He Afraid of Virginia Woolf?', *Critical Inquiry* 11 (1984), 171–8 (a reply to the reply of Edward Pechter to 'When Eve Reads Milton')

Frye, Northrop, 'The Revelation to Eve', in *'Paradise Lost': A Tercentenary Tribute*, ed. B. Rajan (Toronto, 1969), pp. 18–47

Gallagher, Philip J., 'Milton's Bogey', *PMLA* 94 (1979), 319–21 (reply to Gilbert) 'Creation in Genesis and in *Paradise Lost*', *Milton Studies* 20 (1984), 163–204

Gilbert, Sandra M., 'Patriarchal Poetry and Women Readers: Reflections on Milton's Bogey', *PMLA* 93 (1978), 368–82

Gilligan, Carol, *In a Different Voice: Psychological Theories and Women's Development* (Cambridge, MA, and London, 1982)

Hagstrum, Jean, *Sex and Sensibility: Ideal and Erotic Love from Milton to Mozart* (Chicago, 1980)

Halkett, John G., *Milton and the Idea of Matrimony* (New Haven and London, 1970)

Haller, William and Malleville, 'The Puritan Art of Love', *Huntington Library Quarterly* 5 (1941–2), 235–72

Heilbrun, Carolyn G., *Reinventing Womanhood* (New York, 1979)

Homer, *The Odyssey*, translated by Robert Fitzgerald (New York, 1963)

Kelso, Ruth, *Doctrine for the Lady of the Renaissance* (Urbana, 1956)

Kerrigan, William, *The Sacred Complex: On the Psychogenesis of 'Paradise Lost'* (Cambridge, MA, 1983)

Landy, Marcia, 'Kinship and the Role of Women in *Paradise Lost*', *Milton Studies* 4 (1972), 3–18

'"A Free and Open Encounter": Milton and the Modern Reader', *Milton Studies* 9 (1976), 3–36

Le Comte, Edward S., *Milton and Sex* (London and New York, 1978)

Lewalski, Barbara K., 'Milton on Women – Yet Once More', *Milton Studies* 6 (1974), 3–20

Lieb, Michael, *The Dialectics of Creation: Patterns of Birth and Regeneration in Paradise Lost* (Amherst, 1970)

Miller, Dorothy Durkee, 'Eve', *JEGP* 61 (1962), 542–7

Mollenkott, Virginia, 'Some implications of Milton's Androgynous Muse', in *Bucknell Review: Women, Literature, Criticism*, ed. Harry R. Garvin (Lewisburg, PA, 1978)

McColley, Diane K., *Milton's Eve* (Urbana, 1983)

Nyquist, Mary, 'Textual Overlapping and Dalilah's Harlot Lap', in *Literary Theory/ Renaissance Texts*, ed. Patricia Parker and David Quint (Baltimore, 1986)

    'Gynesis, Genesis, and Milton's Eve', in *Cannibals, Witches, and Divorce: Estranging the Renaissance*, ed. Marjorie B. Garber (Baltimore and London, 1987)

Parker, Patricia, 'Eve, Evening, and the Labor of Reading in *Paradise Lost*', *English Literary Renaissance* 9 (1978), 319–42

Pechter, Edward, 'When Pechter Reads Froula Pretending She's Eve Reading Milton; or, New Feminist Is But Old Priest Writ Large', *Critical Inquiry* 11 (1984), 163–70

Peczenik, F., 'Fit Help: The Egalitarian Marriage in *Paradise Lost*', *Mosaic* 17.1 (1984), 29–48

Quilligan, Maureen, *Milton's Spenser: The Politics of Reading* (Ithaca, 1983)

Radzinowicz, Mary Ann Nevins, 'Eve and Dalila: Renovation and Hardening of the Heart', in *Reason and Imagination: Studies in the History of Ideas, 1600–1800*, ed. J. A. Mazzeo (New York and London, 1962)

Revard, Stella P., 'Eve and the Doctrine of Responsibility in *Paradise Lost*', *PMLA* 88 (1973), 69–78

    '*L'Allegro* and *Il Penseroso*: Classical Tradition and Renaissance Mythography', *PMLA* 101 (1986), 338–50

Samuel, Irene, *Dante and Milton* (Ithaca, 1966)

Shawcross, John, 'The Metaphor of Inspiration', in *Th'Upright Heart and Pure*, ed. Amadeus P. Fiore (Pittsburgh, 1967)

Shullenberger, William, 'Wrestling with the Angel: *Paradise Lost* and Feminist Criticism', *Milton Quarterly* 20 (1986), 69–85

Summers, Joseph H., *The Muse's Method* (London and Cambridge, MA, 1962), especially chapter 4, 'The Two Great Sexes'

Swaim, Kathleen, 'Flower, Fruit, and Seed: A Reading of *Paradise Lost*', *Milton Studies* 5 (1973), 155–76

    '"Hee for God Only, Shee for God in Him": Structural Parallelism in *Paradise Lost*', *Milton Studies* 9 (1976), 121–49

Thickstun, Margaret Olofson, *Fictions of the Feminine: Puritan Doctrine and the Representation of Women* (Ithaca, NY, 1988)

Turner, James Grantham, *One Flesh: Paradisal Marriage and Sexual Relations in the Age of Milton* (Oxford, 1987)

Walker, Julia, ed., *Milton and the Idea of Woman* (Urbana, 1988)

Webber, Joan Malory, 'The Politics of Poetry: Feminism and *Paradise Lost*', *Milton Studies* 14 (1980), 3–24

Wittreich, Joseph, *Feminist Milton* (Ithaca, NY, 1987)

11   Milton and the rhetoric of prophecy

And such discourse bring on . . .   (*PL* 5.233)

Rhetoric enters the composition of Milton's poetry in three not always distinct ways: as the conscious craft of persuasion, acquired through the study of classical models and contemporary commentaries with their lexicon of tropes and schemes; as a structure that mediates between language and culture while accommodating new historical experiences to existing literary conventions; and as a set of formal expectations for the representation of argument. My main interest in this chapter will be the second of these: the process of rhetorical mediation and its effect on the design and execution of Milton's major poems. But in order to facilitate an appreciation of how rhetoric affects the design of these poems, I shall begin by trying to situate the three aspects of Milton's rhetoric in the historical imagination of the later seventeenth century.

In a famous passage from the tractate *Of Education*, Milton, spelling out a sequence or *paedeia* of studies by which young boys are to be formed into governors, counsellors, and clergymen, cites the sources of a rhetorical poetics, to which he accords a curiously ambiguous place in the curriculum of his ideal school:

Logic therefore so much as is usefull, is to be referr'd to this due place withall her well coucht heads and Topics, untill it be time to open her contracted palm into a gracefull and ornate Rhetorick taught out of the rule of *Plato, Aristotle, Phalareus, Cicero, Hermogenes, Longinus*. To which Poetry would be made subsequent, or indeed rather precedent, as being lesse suttle and fine, but more simple, sensuous and passionate. I mean not here the prosody of a verse . . . but that sublime art which in *Aristotles poetics*, in *Horace*, and the Italian commentaries of *Castelvetro, Tasso, Mazzoni*, and others, teaches what the laws are of a true *Epic* poem, what of a *Dramatic*, what of a *Lyric*, what decorum is, which is the grand master peece to observe. This would . . . shew them, what Religious, what glorious and magnificent use might be made of Poetry both in divine and humane things.   (YP 2: 402–6)

Milton uses the commonplace analogy of the closed fist and the open hand

to relate logic to rhetoric, the tools by which Truth is respectively determined and explained (Howell 4). But anyone wishing to implement Milton's
programme might well stumble over the words 'To which Poetry would be
made subsequent, or indeed rather precedent'. Do the boys read poetry after
studying logic and rhetoric, or before? The question of when in the mould-
ing of a citizen the poets are to be read is answered elsewhere in the tractate
– as soon as sufficient language has been acquired. But the rhetorical
reversal in Milton's 'subsequent or indeed precedent' involves a question
which is not wholly pedagogical: is poetry logically prior to the theories that
ostensibly govern its practice – logic, rhetoric, and poetics? This very broad
question conceals within it the question of whether the laws of discourse are
immanent in the particular examples from which they are induced, or logical
in the Platonic and Thomistic sense of being prior to, and enabling of,
discourse as such.

Milton makes an understanding of the divine and humane uses of poetry
the keystone of his educational programme, arguing that only when the
young scholars appreciate the uses of poetry can they attain the 'universall
insight into things' that will enable them to become the poets, orators, and
preachers of Milton's ideal republic (YP 2: 406). But how, precisely, does an
understanding of the uses of poetry open into a universal insight into things,
and through what sort of process? Milton's very practical response to
Hartlib's query on the reform of education would seem to engage, when it
touches on rhetoric, some very fundamental philosophical issues, and
necessarily so. For, as Milton says,

The end . . . of learning is to repair the ruins of our first parents by regaining to know
God aright, and out of that knowledge to love him, to imitate him, to be like him, as
we may the neerest by possessing our souls of true virtue, which being united to the
heavenly grace of faith makes up the highest perfection. But because our understanding cannot in this body found it selfe but on sensible things, nor arrive so cleerly
to the knowledge of God and things invisible, as by orderly conning over the visible
and inferior creature, the same method is necessarily to be follow'd in all discreet
teaching. (YP 2: 366–9)

When we consider that the end of learning is to return to the beginning –
that is, to the unmediated knowledge of God that preceded the Fall – and
that the method of this return must be through the body and its sensory
understanding of things, we may begin to appreciate the importance of the
ambivalence between priority and origin and between logical and temporal
sequence that surfaces in Milton's discussion of rhetorical poetics. This
ambivalence informs his work on two levels: (1) It represents the distinction

of two dialectically related kinds of knowing, both necessary 'to repair the ruins of our first parents' and 'know God aright' and (2) it represents the intersection of logical and temporal priority in such a way as to accommodate the view, gaining ground in the seventeenth century, that human history is an arena in which a revelation of God's eternal design unfolds in time.

The notion that there are two distinct kinds of knowledge, one available through the body, the other apprehended by a higher, rational faculty, descends, of course, from Plato's distinction between sense and intelligence. What is interesting in Milton's particular version of the doctrine is the way in which his insistent monism overcomes Platonic dualism by envisaging a dialectical linkage between sense and intelligence, so as to represent *knowledge of worldly things* as a historical route to a universal and atemporal insight. By situating Christian man at the intersection of historical retrospection and divine revelation, Milton allows the particularity of human experience to participate in a revelation of universal design. The process that underlies this exchange of qualities between the eternal and the historical is, strictly speaking, a rhetorical one, and Milton's assertion of a poetic practice at once subsequent and precedent to theoretical knowledge opens the way to a rhetoric of prophecy.

An outline of this rhetoric is implicit in the personal remarks that preface the second book of *The Reason of Church-Government* in which Milton asserts that a 'burden of mind . . . more pressing than any supportable toil, or waight, which the body can labour under' must be borne by anyone who, having 'obtain'd in more then scantest measure to know anything distinctly of God, and of his true worship, and what is infallibly good and happy in the state of mans life', undertakes to improve 'these his entrusted gifts'; for anyone so privileged with revelation must open the hand of rhetoric, deciding 'how and in what manner he shall dispose and employ those summes of knowledge and illumination, which God hath sent him into this world to trade with' (YP 1: 801).

The burden that Milton describes here in prose is represented as an angelic mission in the epic poem. In Book 5 of *Paradise Lost*, when, in their morning prayers, Adam and Eve ask God to disperse any evil left by the dream Satan had inspired in Eve during the night, God responds by sending Raphael to visit Adam, with the command 'such discourse bring on, / As may advise him of his happy state' (233–4). Deciding just what sort of discourse to bring on is certainly something of a rhetorical homework assignment; and when Raphael executes his mission he twice remarks the difficulty of such discursive revelation and comments on the rhetorical methods

to which he must resort. Before he answers Adam's query about the nature
and possibility of evil by recounting the war in heaven, he says:

> High matter thou enjoinest me, O prime of men,
> Sad task and hard, for how shall I relate
> To human sense the invisible exploits
> Of warring spirits . . .
>   how last unfold
> The secrets of another world, perhaps
> Not lawful to reveal? Yet for thy good
> This is dispensed, and what surmounts the reach
> Of human sense, I shall delineate so,
> By likening spiritual to corporeal forms,
> As may express them best, though what if earth
> Be but the shadow of heaven, and things therein
> Each to other like, more than on earth, is thought?   (5.563–76)

Later, in Book 7, when he has completed his cautionary tale of heavenly warfare, and Adam asks him to narrate the creation of the world, Raphael again
pauses to meditate on the difficulty of imparting 'high matter' and the
purpose that justifies the effort:

> This also thy request with caution asked
> Obtain: though to recount almighty works
> What words or tongue of seraph can suffice,
> Or heart of man suffice to comprehend?
> Yet what thou canst attain, which best may serve
> To glorify the maker, and infer
> Thee also happier, shall not be withheld
> Thy hearing, such commission from above
> I have received.   (111–19)

During his visit to Eden, Raphael narrates about one third of *Paradise Lost*;
when he does, he assumes the same burdens of prophetic narration borne by
the poem's human narrator, the same burdens Milton had assessed in *The
Reason of Church-Government*. Therefore, if I may sustain here, without
undue confusion, the pattern established in *Of Education*, I should like to
use Raphael's prefaces to his narratives of warfare and creation in *Paradise
Lost* as subsequent precedents of Milton's preface in *The Reason of Church-
Government*.

By the time Milton wrote Raphael's words, he seems to have answered,
for himself, a question about which he is still defensive in *The Reason of
Church-Government*: is poetry work? – work in the sense of socially pro-

ductive labour. When Milton begins his personal remarks in the preface to
the second book, he hesitates for a moment about their appropriateness –
drawing a distinction between the 'Poet soaring in the high region of his
fancies with his garland and singing robes about him' and the pamphleteer
'sitting here below in the cool element of prose, a mortall thing among many
readers of no Empyreall conceit – before going on to recount that, although
he was adept from an early age in both prose and verse, his teachers found
his verse especially possessed of a 'stile . . . [that] was likely to live' (YP
1: 808–9). Considering the evidence of his teachers' opinions, the praise he
received during his Italian journey, and 'an inward prompting' which 'grew
daily upon' him, Milton conceived the hope that 'by labour and intent study'
he 'might perhaps leave something so written to aftertimes, as they should
not willingly let it die' (YP 1: 810). He makes clear that the intent study
through which he hoped to learn to shoulder the burden of disposing and
employing 'those summes of knowledge and illumination' which God had
'sent him into this world to trade with' included the study of both classical
and contemporary rhetoric:

I apply'd my selfe . . . to fix all the industry and art I could unite to the adorning of
my native tongue; not to make verbal curiosities the end, that were a toylsom vanity,
but to be an interpreter & relater of the best and sagest things among mine own
Citizens throughout this Iland in the mother dialect. That what the greatest and
choycest wits of *Athens*, *Rome*, or modern *Italy*, and those Hebrews of old did for
their country, I in my proportion with this over and above of being a Christian, might
doe for mine. (YP 1: 811–12)

The studious labour invoked in *The Reason of Church-Government* accords
well with the nightly activities of the Penseroso, illuminating his expectation
that 'old experience' will eventually 'attain / To something like prophetic
strain' (*Il Penseroso* 173–4). Yet one must recognize that the abilities necessary to do what 'the greatest and choycest wits' have done are

the inspired guift of God rarely bestow'd, but yet to some (though most abuse) in
every Nation: and are of power beside the office of a pulpit, to imbreed and cherish
in a great people the seeds of vertu, and publick civility, to allay the perturbations of
the mind, and set the affections in right tune . . . (YP 1: 816–17)

The comment about the common abuse of divine inspiration suggests
Milton's awareness of the compounding, in his theory, of mundane and
divine sources of poetic truth, of work and grace. For the divine afflatus
without which the poet may create no more than 'verbal curiosities' can also

be abused, and so must be received with and dispersed through an austere collaborative effort: a life of 'labour and intent study'.

Had Milton not commented upon this collaboration of divine inspiration and dogged human labour, the recipient of Platonic *furor poeticus* and the rhetorical craftsman would have remained side by side, an internal contradiction in Milton's explanation of his own genius and of poetic genius as such. But by insisting that study and labour must develop a 'genial nature', and act on 'inward promptings', Milton turns this potential contradiction into a fruitful rhetorical crossing that can be usefully related to standard rhetorical theory. Rhetoricians from Cicero on often divide their art into five parts: invention, disposition, elocution, memory, and delivery (Howell 66–115). When the muse inspires an 'unpremeditated verse', its assistance is felt principally with invention; that is to say, divine revelation supplies the poet with the material about which he writes. Its arrangement and presentation are the poet's province, the province, in fact, of poetry, conceived as a self-consistent art, with its own integral history and immanent laws. Although the ability to master these laws is a God-given gift; attaining and developing such mastery is hard, socially productive, work. It is these workaday aspects of poetry that Milton calls style and for which he rather proudly takes credit and, rather diffidently, takes responsibility.

Thus, if we return for a moment to Raphael's visit to Eden, we may say that Raphael has been charged by God to fashion a discourse that will achieve a specified end. To do so, he must arrange certain remembered events in an illustrative and coherent order, put them into human language, and deliver them in such a way as to achieve his goal. He is indeed an angelic poet and his task is, as he twice insists, neither easy nor simple.

Milton proposes, as the alternative to producing 'verbal curiosities', to interpret and relate the 'best and sagest things'. Both his poetic practice and the procedures of scriptural exegesis common in his day suggest that the work of recognizing and interpreting the 'best and sagest things' at once presupposes and produces (is subsequent and precedent to) divine revelation. To attain a *universal* insight into things, one needs to know not just what they mean at the moment, but also what they have meant in the past and what they will mean in the future. Similarly, a rhetorician gifted with a divine revelation must dispose it in such a way as to represent the eternal through the sequential unfolding of language. As Raphael puts it:

> Immediate are the acts of God, more swift
> Than time or motion, but to human ears
> Cannot without process of speech be told,
> So told as earthly notion can receive.   (*PL* 7.176–9)

What unfolds sequentially in language, especially in the form of narrative, has a beginning, a middle, and an end. What is universal and divine is a design that encompasses that end from the beginning, a logical end that predestines the temporal one. In order to dispose a prophetic rhetoric, one must comprehend sequence as consequence, read the beginning through the end; and it is in this very specific sense that Milton's rhetorical poetics are at once subsequent and precedent to knowing God aright.

Milton finds the theoretical warrant for his practice of prophetic rhetoric in the confluence of the ancient distinction between the icastic and the phantastic imagination (Stevens) and the Reformation tendency to use typology to interpret not only the Hebrew Scriptures but contemporary historical events as well (Lewalski).

Though Milton was doubtless aware of the division of the imagination into phantastic and icastic faculties in Plato and Isocrates, a more immediate source was certainly Tasso's *Discourses on the Heroic Poem*, and this text provides a convenient statement of the claim for icastic representation as it concerns the content of heroic poetry in the Renaissance. Briefly stated, the argument for icastic poetry begins with the Aristotelian doctrine that all poetry is imitation and then divides poetry which imitates non-existent things – that is, figments of the poet's *phantastic* imagination – from poetry which imitates true things, as they are conceived through the faculty of the *icastic* imagination. The important thing about icastic poetry, however, is that although it imitates true things, it differs from history in so far as the true things it imitates *need never have been apprehended by the senses*. Icastic poetry is most properly the sensible sign of a truth that exceeds the senses and may be grasped only with the intellect. It is, therefore, a sensible stimulus to intellectual progress:

If images are of existing things, this imitation belongs to the icastic imitator. But what shall we say exists, the intelligible or the visible? Surely the intelligible, in the opinion of Plato too, who put visible things in the genus of non-being and only the intelligible in the genus of being. The images of the angels that Dionysius describes are of existences more real than all things human. So too the winged lion, the eagle, ox, and angel, which are the images of the evangelists, do not belong principally to phantasy and are not its proper object, since phantasy is [a faculty] in the divisible part of the mind, not the indivisible, which is the intellect pure and simple, unless besides the phantasy which is the faculty of the sensitive soul there were another which is a faculty of the intellective.   (Tasso 32)

Although, according to Tasso, the poet may imitate 'things that are, were, or may be' (30), it is the movement from intellectual idea to poetic expression that extends the scope of poetry from imitation of historical events to the instrument through which the poet's socially productive labour puts 'God's entrusted gifts' to use:

We should say that [the poet] is a maker of images in the fashion of a speaking painter, and in that is like the divine theologian [God] who forms images and commands them to be. And if dialectic and metaphysics, the divine philosophy of the pagans, have such similarity that the ancients thought them the same, no wonder that the poet is almost the same as the theologian and the dialectician. But divine philosophy, or theology as we may prefer to call it, has two parts, each of them fitting and proper to one part of our mind, which is composed of the divisible and the indivisible, according to not only Plato and Aristotle, but the Areopagite also, who wrote . . . that the part of the most occult theology *which is contained in signs and has the power to perfect,* belongs to the indivisible mind, which is intellect pure and simple. The other part, eager for wisdom, which uses demonstration, he assigns to the divisible mind, much less noble than the indivisible. *Now to lead to the contemplation of divine things and thus awaken the mind with images, as the mystical theologian and the poet do, is a far nobler work than to instruct by demonstration, the function of the scholastic theologian.* (Tasso 31–2; italics added)

The scholastic theologian appeals, through speculative concepts, to the intellectual faculty alone; but the poet, like the mystical theologian, appeals to the senses and links them to the intellect, thereby conducting his reader from sensible signs to a 'universall insight into things'. Poetry, then, is a medium through which the indwelling spirit is expressed and communicated, and since its immanent rules must be mastered before it can be effectively employed, it is at once the product and the source of the dialectical arts of logic and rhetoric. Mastery of the rhetoric of prophecy allows the discovery (or, in the terms of classical rhetoric, invention) of intellectual truth and the disposition of that truth in the form of sensible signs whereby it can be transmitted to a reader.

This elevation of poetry to the Spirit is less strange, less radical, than it seems. Words are the medium of poetry, and words do indeed mediate mental concepts among the participants in a conversation. Modern linguists like Ferdinand de Saussure divide every linguistic sign into a material signifier or acoustic image and the concept or mental image it invokes (Saussure 66). Moreover, every particular use of language relies upon and brings into play some part of the system of rules that make up a given language in much the way that Tasso's poetic image is a particular and sensible event that puts in play, derives its 'true' significance from, the divine design in its eternal completeness. The system of relations among sounds that is language precedes and underlies any meaningful discourse, but, at the same time, it is through the audible expressions, which we recognize as intelligible speech, that the system of language is known (Saussure 14–20). This state of affairs is reflected in the mimetic mirror of Tasso's poetry of the icastic imagination. Human life is a historical episode encompassed by and expressing itself within the universal and eternal design of divine providence. Each episode becomes meaningful, becomes legible, only with respect to the whole design; each historical event speaks as an episode in the advance of history toward the apocalypse, at which time its meaning will be fixed.

The rhetoric of prophecy places mundane events within this all-encompassing frame. Just as the rhetoric of tropes and schemes may exceed the grammar of language to introduce meanings that may be stated only through metaphor, or only through some other method of deforming a word or sentence from its normal use, so the rhetoric of prophecy transcends or exceeds the cause-and-effect grammar of mundane history by investing events with a final cause that integrates them into a design that can be grasped only immediately, all at once (Kerrigan 219–24). In the last books of *Paradise Lost*, Michael presents Adam with icastic images, first visible, then merely auditory and linguistic, to lead him to just this realization:

> How soon hath thy prediction, seer blest,
> Measured this transient world, the race of time,
> Till time stand fixed: beyond is all abyss,
> Eternity, whose end no eye can reach. (12.553–6)

Thus, when in *Of Education* Milton stutters over the subsequence or precedence of poetics, he brings to the surface the intimate connection between the medium of poetry and the way in which Christianity assimilates the unfolding sequence of historical events to an always already-completed providential design. Logic and rhetoric govern the discovery and the exposition or representation of this design from within the sequence of temporal discourse. But the poetic image, deployed according to a prophetic rhetoric, may reach back or forward, may reach, as it were, behind the scenes of logic, to attain a less mediated 'universal insight into things'. The question we now must ask is: where did Milton get the words that Michael spoke in order to lead Adam and Milton's readers to such an insight?

Granted the active participation of the Holy Spirit, Milton has but two sources, two routes along which the divine afflatus may travel: his experience of life in the fallen world; and the completed history of that world to be found in Scripture. The role of typology in joining these two sources to form a continuing and progressive revelation will form the last chapter in this story of Milton's rhetoric of prophecy.

Typology begins as a method of reading the Hebrew Scripture. It performs the necessary function of appropriating the Hebrew Bible to the Christian religion by reading it as an Old Testament, interpreting the true history of the Jews as also a prophetic prefiguration of the events recounted in the Gospels and predicted in Revelation. As long as typology remained one aspect of a four-fold system of Scripture interpretation, the knitting together of the two very different scriptural texts was its principal function. But when, as part of its commitment to biblical literalism, the Reformation radically questioned the allegorical and tropological traditions of Scripture interpretation, typology, because it was grounded in the incontrovertible 'history' of Israel, came to be regarded as a mode of literal reading (YP 6: 581) and to assume the social functions tropology or *moralitas* had formerly borne.

Tropology or moral allegory allowed the Christian, usually with the help of a clerical exegete, to draw guidance from Scripture in making choices that would affect human history and reveal the individual's moral nature. The tropological reading of Scripture distils from the text a universal moral that everywhere and always reveals the divine orderliness of the universe. It seeks insight into the eternal decrees of God as they are reflected in the immutable law of creation. In the seventeenth century, this atemporal universality comes under pressure from changes in agriculture, commerce, and social organization, changes that favour a less homogeneous experience of time, and also place more emphasis on the future fulfilment of current actions (Grossman 12–21).

The growing feeling that history is itself man-made coincides with the Reformation's doctrinal preference for literal and historical interpretation. The historically conditioned emphasis on the type in the seventeenth century displaces the tropological emphasis on the divine order with a typological search for order as it is revealed in time, with a picture whose details are constantly being filled in by contemporary historical experience. As typology takes over the function of moral evaluation, revelation comes to be appreciated as a process whose completion will occur only at the apocalypse. Just as the New Testament reveals the true meaning of the historical events narrated in the Hebrew Bible, so the in-dwelling Holy Spirit will eventually reveal the meaning of contemporary historical events. Whereas tropology imagines the unfolding of events according to underlying laws, set down by God before creation, typology imagines events as unfolding toward those laws, as achieving their divine meaning in time, until their fulfilment abolishes time itself. Whereas moral allegory had led from biblical text to universal law, typology leads from text to text, from Old

Testament type to New Testament antitype. Informed by the rhetoric of types, Milton's narratives lead us from episode to episode until the temporal unfolding of events is collected, from the vantage point of a completed story, into a fully integrated design in which every action derives its meaning from every other action (Mink). Meaning is thus shifted from the origin to the end, from eternally prescriptive laws to a dynamically revisionary design.

Milton's rhetoric of prophecy transcends historical time by using the icastic imagination and the revelation of history in Scripture to represent historical events and sensible things in a way that suggests how they would appear from God's throne or to a man or woman who gazed back from the apocalypse. By substituting a set of narrative patterns for traditional moral allegory, Milton thus responds to man's increased power over the natural world, representing the present and future history of humankind as a collaborative movement toward a universal insight into the meaning of all things.

I began this chapter by isolating three ways in which rhetoric enters Milton's poems, and we have now seen how the mastery of the craft of rhetoric, with its tropes and schemes and its division of discourse into the procedures of Invention, Disposition, Elocution, Memory, and Delivery, must be acquired by 'labour and intent study'. We have also seen how Milton adapts the divine rhetoric of typology, through which God uses historical persons and their acts to reveal his providential design, to a narrative rhetoric that accommodates the older, allegorical forms of heroic poetry in keeping with a newly developing sense of the importance of human history and the sequence of events unfolding in time. If we see Milton's later poems as mimeses of God's typological rhetoric, then the emergence in them of characters whose speeches *and* actions may be understood within the categories of classical rhetoric should come as no surprise. With this expectation in mind, we may now look briefly at some of the ways in which Milton uses rhetorical models of argument to dramatize the struggle of 'free-standing' individuals to enact the rhetoric of prophecy in their lives and their discourse.

We have already remarked the rhetorical tasks undertaken by the two angelic narrators in *Paradise Lost*. Raphael provides Adam with a narrative representation of past events, the war in heaven and the creation of the world. Michael provides a narrative disposition of future events: death's exploits on earth and his apocalyptic defeat. Adam's decisive historical acts occur between these two narrations, as the pivotal present of the poem. After the Fall, to which Eve is tempted by the rhetoric of Satan, Adam and Eve are unable to act. Their discourse, like Satan's, represents 'the hateful siege / Of contraries' (9.121–2). They are rescued from this impasse when, through the intervention of prevenient grace, Eve calls for the judgment to fall upon her alone:

> that all
> The sentence from thy head removed may light
> On me, sole cause to thee of all this woe,
> Me me only just object of his ire.   (10.933–6)

Eve echoes the language used by the Son when he offers to assume man's guilt, 'Behold me then, me for him, life for life / I offer, on me let thine anger fall' (3.236–7), and her example recalls to Adam the demeanour and words of the Son when he judged them after the Fall. In these words, Adam finds an argument, the promise that Eve's seed shall bruise the head of the serpent, who shall bruise his heel (10.179–81), which he then uses to prophesy their future reparation, to reject the alternatives of celibacy and suicide, and to restore their faith (10.1028–1104). It is possible to summarize this crucial episode in terms of rhetoric in general, and as an application of the rhetoric of prophecy in particular.

Since Eve was not present at the conclave in heaven to overhear the language with which the Son voiced the wish to accept man's guilt, we may assume that it is the icastic imagination which enables her to echo him. More precisely, it is the imagination of an unheard voice, found (or, in rhetorical terminology, invented) by repairing (still in the imagination) to a *place*, what the rhetoricians would have called, after Aristotle, a *topos*: 'And to the place of judgment will return, / There with my cries importune heaven' (10.932–3). By returning, in thought, to the place of judgment, Eve finds her memory of the Son and learns to speak the words of God's Word. Her voice then becomes the audible sign of God's grace, calling forth Adam's memory of the Son's promise, which he then interprets typologically as a prefiguration of Satan's ultimate defeat by Eve's seed. Later Michael confirms and completes this reading of God's living Word with his prophecy of Christ's death and resurrection:

> this Godlike act
> Annuls thy doom, the death thou shouldst have died,
> In sin for ever lost from life; this act
> Shall bruise the head of Satan, crush his strength
> Defeating Sin and Death, his two main arms,
> And fix far deeper in his head their stings
> Than temporal death shall bruise the victor's heel.   (12.427–33)

Having found the argument of faith, Adam and Eve are able to display, through behaviour, the new understanding they have achieved. Their acts and choices are founded on invention and memory, judged (or disposed) according to their understanding of the structure of divine narrative, and pronounced at once in the world of temporal actions and in the eternal design of divine providence. Accepting responsibility for their actions and expressing faith that God's mercy will bring good out of evil, they re-enact, visibly, on earth, the invisible action of the Son in Book 3. Milton puts this scene, which he has seen in his mind's eye, into words. He expects his readers to use those words to reconstruct it in their own imaginations and, through it, to learn to dispose their actions according to a revealed and revealing memory of the past and anticipation of the future.

It should be noted, however, that through the perfection of his faith, the Son knows from the beginning what Adam and Eve learn through a painful passage of time:

> thou hast given me to possess
> Life in my self for ever, by thee I live,
> Though now to Death I yield, and am his due
> All that of me can die, yet that debt paid,
> Thou wilt not leave me in the loathsome grave
> His prey, nor suffer my unspotted soul
> For ever with corruption there to dwell;
> But I shall rise victorious, and subdue
> My vanquisher . . .   (3.243–51)

Paradise Lost represents Adam's education in the rhetoric of typology as a way of joining his acts in time to God's eternal design, but the poem ends with Adam and Eve at the very beginning of human history. *Paradise Regained* and *Samson Agonistes*, published together in a single volume, present two characters, traditionally, though not always simply (Wittreich), linked as type and antitype, each acting within the temporal unfolding of events. In each of these poems, Milton addresses the difference between knowledge accumulated, collectively, over time, and the sudden insight that may be both the cause and the effect of a timely perfection of faith.

Although there is not space here to elaborate a rhetorical reading of *Paradise Regained* and *Samson Agonistes*, I want to conclude this discussion of the rhetoric of prophecy with the suggestion that in these poems Milton once again reproduces his own situation as a prophetic rhetorician, by representing and contrasting two characters who stake their lives and the destiny of their people on 'inward promptings' and who, in their need to

make these promptings visible, face the 'burden of mind . . . more pressing
then any supportable toil, or waight, which the body can labour under', and
strive to learn 'how and in what manner [they] shall dispose and employ
those summes of knowledge and illumination, which God hath sent [them]
into this world to trade with'.

Such a reading would note that Samson's rhetorical words and acts are
directed to his fellow Israelites, while the Jesus of *Paradise Regained* speaks
and acts in private transactions between himself and God the Father, and
between himself and the 'father of lies'. It would take Milton's unexpected
displacement of the regaining of Paradise from the Passion to the temptation
in the Wilderness as an invitation to explore the difference between attaining
knowledge and communicating it. And it would see the defeat of Satanic
rhetoric by Christian truth as the victory of the Spirit over evil and corruption, and the Passion as the sacrificial theatre through which this invisible
victory becomes 'doctrinal to the nation'. In contrast, Samson's spectacular,
and deadly, destruction of the Temple of Dagon might be understood as
marking man's inability to free the Spirit through the mastery of the law
(that is, the temporal government) and before the fullness of time:

> What wise and valiant man would seek to free
> These thus degenerate, by themselves enslaved,
> Or could of inward slaves make outward free?
> Know therefore when my season comes to sit
> On David's throne, it shall be like a tree
> Spreading and overshadowing all the earth,
> Or as a stone that shall to pieces dash
> All monarchies besides throughout the world,
> And of my kingdom there shall be no end:
> Means there shall be to this, but what the means,
> Is not for thee to know, nor me to tell.   (*PR* 4.143–53)

Reading list

Grossman, Marshall, *'Authors to Themselves': Milton and the Revelation of History*
    (Cambridge, 1987)
Howell, Wilbur Samuel, *Logic and Rhetoric in England, 1500–1700* (Princeton, 1956)
Kerrigan, William, *The Prophetic Milton* (Charlottesville, VA, 1974)
Lewalski, Barbara K., *Protestant Poetics and the Seventeenth-Century Religious Lyric*
    (Princeton, 1979)
Mink, Louis O., 'History and Fiction as Modes of Comprehension', *New Literary
    History* 1 (1970), 541–58

Saussure, Ferdinand de, *Course in General Linguistics* (New York, 1966)

Stevens, Paul, *Imagination and the Presence of Shakespeare in 'Paradise Lost'* (Madison, 1985)

Tasso, Torquato, *Discourses on the Heroic Poem*, translated by Mariella Cavalchini and Irene Samuel (Oxford, 1973)

Wittreich, Joseph, *Interpreting 'Samson Agonistes'* (Princeton, 1986)

12   Milton's prose

Milton was a major prose writer in a golden age of English prose. John Donne was preaching at old St Paul's and elsewhere in London throughout Milton's adolescence and young manhood. That leviathan of literary eccentricity and exhilarating style, Robert Burton's *Anatomy of Melancholy*, was published when Milton was thirteen, and had reappeared in seven editions by 1660, each longer and richer than its predecessor. Among even closer contemporaries of Milton were the devout scientist, subtle ideologue, and master stylist Sir Thomas Browne, and Gerrard Winstanley the Digger, whose radical voice can range from visionary ecstasy to poignant satire. Thomas Sprat, so widely acclaimed as a stylist in his own age, and John Bunyan, undoubtedly the most widely read seventeenth-century prose writer today, were Milton's juniors by two or three decades.

Furthermore, Milton's prose offers the modern reader pleasures quite comparable to those of reading Donne or Browne. Consider the potent felicity of Donne:

No man is an *Iland*, intire of it selfe; every man is a peece of the *Continent*, a part of the *maine*; if a *Clod* bee washed away by the *Sea*, *Europe* is the lesse, as well as if a *Promontorie* were, as well as if a *Mannor* of thy *friends* or *thine owne* were; any mans *death* diminishes me, because I am involved in *Mankinde*; And therefore never send to know for whom the *bell* tolls; It tolls for *thee* . . .   (Donne 101)

No doubt part of the power of this passage resides in its elevation of sentiment, but we respond, too, to the assured, declarative enunciation and the extended, controlled analogy of death and erosion. But just as this passage recommends itself to the anthologist, so does much of Milton's prose, and for similar reasons. Witness this passage from *Areopagitica*:

as good almost kill a Man as kill a good Book; who kills a Man kills a reasonable creature, Gods Image; but hee who destroyes a good Booke, kills reason it selfe, kills the Image of God . . . Many a man lives a burden to the Earth; but a good Booke is the pretious life-blood of a master spirit . . .   (YP 2: 492–3)

Here, too, the sentiment – an assertion of what may be perceived as liberal principle – impresses, and we are likewise struck by the tone. Like Donne, Milton offers what is really a subtle and rather remote analogy as if it were an apparent fact: a book shares important properties with human life, and censorship resembles a summary killing. And, as in the passage from Donne, the image is controlled, extended, persistent, and convincing.

The present discussion, however, will presuppose, not argue for, the pleasures of reading (as one does in Donne and Milton) large truths expressed with high decorum. My aim here, rather, will be to define more precisely some of the changing characteristics of Milton's prose – for critics often write as if his style admits neither variety nor development – and to suggest ways in which such changes relate to his probable perception of his audience and of the exigencies of debate.

All of Milton's earliest vernacular prose, that is, his five antiprelatical tracts of 1641–2, and some of his pamphlets of 1643–5, including what is currently his most popular, *Areopagitica* (1644), are characterized by a flamboyant style, rich in imagery and lexically innovative to the point of playfulness. In it, metaphors and similes abound, often in great elaboration. Thus, near the start of his first pamphlet, *Of Reformation* (1641), we encounter this wholly typical paragraph, in which Milton is talking about how the Reformation revitalized Christianity after the error and torpor of Catholicism:

But to dwell no longer in characterizing the *Depravities* of the *Church*, and how they sprung, and how they tooke increase; when I recall to mind at last, after so many darke Ages, wherein the huge overshadowing traine of *Error* had almost swept all the Starres out of the Firmament of the *Church*; how the bright and blissful *Reformation* (by Divine Power) strook through the black and settled Night of *Ignorance* and *Antichristian Tyranny*, me thinks a soveraigne and reviving joy must needs rush into the bosome of him that reads or heares; and the sweet Odour of the returning *Gospell* imbath his Soule with the fragrancy of Heaven. Then was the Sacred Bible sought out of the dusty corners where prophane Falshood and Neglect had throwne it, the *Schooles* opened, *Divine* and *Humane Learning* rak't out of the *embers of forgotten Tongues*, the *Princes* and *Cities* trooping apace to the new erected Banner of *Salvation*; the *Martyrs*, with the unresistable *might* of *Weaknesse*, shaking the *Powers* of *Darknesse*, and scorning the *fiery rage* of the old *red Dragon*.   (YP 1: 524–5)

With every sentence and almost every clause interwoven with simile or metaphor, the passage seems a riotous profusion. And the passage is profuse, though there is also in it something of an organizing principle that we can identify. The central image – of the darkness of ignorance and the light of truth – is familiar, perhaps to the point of triteness. But note how Milton revitalises it, invoking, brilliantly reworked, an image from the Book of Revelation: the 'train' of Error plainly invites identification with the 'great red dragon' whose 'tail drew the third part of the stars of heaven, and did cast them to the earth' (Rev. 12: 3–4). Milton, however, strengthens and makes more concrete the image he adopts. The 'tail' or 'train' (the words are synonymous in seventeenth-century English) is rendered 'huge' and 'over-shadowing'; the rather flaccid 'drew' (the translation favoured also by the Geneva Bible) gives way to the vigorously precise 'almost swept'. Such embellishment is wholly characteristic of the way in which biblical imagery is transformed into a livelier Miltonic idiom in the early prose. As we shall see, Milton later becomes more restrained, and more deferential to the minutiae of biblical phraseology.

The polarity of light and darkness is jostled before and after by diverse images, of the organic growth of *'Error'* and of 'the sweet Odour of the . . . *Gospell'*. However, the clash of allusion here is perhaps more apparent than real. Once more, the biblical intertext is at work, and again the imagery is millenarian or chiliastic. The image, *'Depravities* [which] . . . sprung, and . . . tooke increase', has its remote origins in the parable of the tares (Matt. 13), with its promise of the 'furnace of fire' for the nefarious. Again, the perfume metaphor evokes another image from Revelation, of the 'four and twenty elders' who fall down before the Lamb with 'golden vials full of odours, which are the prayers of saints' (Rev. 5: 8).

Thereafter the schema peters out, overwhelmed by the fertility of the Miltonic imagination. Milton, especially in his early prose, develops a way of speaking about abstract notions as if they were concrete and even living things. Here, 'Falshood' and 'Neglect', which are abstract nouns, have 'throwne' (a verb usually used only with concrete agents) the Bible into 'dusty corners'. Similarly, *'Learning'*, also abstract, is conceptualized as a still-glowing coal, to be 'rak't' from the remains of ancient languages. Milton, especially in the early 1640s, seems reluctant to argue his case at levels of high abstraction. Instead, his imagination clothes the concepts and sets them in action. Good and evil, learning and ignorance, appear as mighty forces in physical conflict.

The next image is biblical, but not apocalyptic. *'Princes* and *Cities* troop-ing apace to the new erected Banner of *Salvation'* is a vigorous reworking of the psalmist's 'We will rejoice in thy salvation, and in the name of our God we will set up our banners' (Ps. 20: 5), once more with a characteristic refinement of detail. The paradox – a less common figure of speech and habit of thought in Milton than, for instance, in Sir Thomas Browne – of 'the unresistable *might* of *Weaknesse'* is Pauline (2 Cor. 12: 7–10), as is the phrase

'*Powers* of *Darknesse*' (Col. 1: 13). The paragraph then ends with a further reference to the apocalyptic image with which we started, the 'old *red Dragon*' of Revelation (12: 3).

The function of the biblical allusion is complex. Obviously, Milton's imagination is shot through with the language and images of the Bible, and his perception of recent history and current affairs is shaped by its models and archetypes. Among Protestants in an age of faith this is not surprising, though such an insistent iteration of biblical reference is probably commoner among those of Puritan leanings. We recall, perhaps, how Ben Jonson, a generation earlier, had satirized this habit in the speeches of Zeal-of-the-Land Busy, who denounces puppet shows in the frenzy of echoes and citations:

I wil remove *Dagon* there, I say, that *Idoll*, that heathenish *Idoll*, that remaines (as I may say) a beame, a very beame, not a beame of the *Sunne*, nor a beame of the *Moone*, nor a beame of a ballance, neither a house-beame, nor a Weavers beame, but a beame in the eye, in the eye of the brethren.   (*Bartholomew Fair* V.v.4–9)

But of course Milton's practice is at a massive remove from such hysterical and affected nonsense. His imagination functions in a fertile dialectic with the Scriptures. As biblical images and expressions shape and inform his perception of the present world, so too his creative genius transforms them into material appropriate to the brilliant texture of his early prose. Moreover, the crises of mid-century England, rendered in terms of the abiding struggles between the godly and the impious, and of the final struggle of the apocalypse, present one phase of the larger conflict – one phase, and yet, perhaps, the final phase: the millenarian perspective, so common among his revolutionary contemporaries, is central to much of Milton's excited thinking of the early 1640s.

Modern readers are often staggered by the length and complexity of the sentences in Milton's prose. However, we must beware of over-reacting to an element of style which is fairly commonplace in serious, erudite prose of the middle of the seventeenth century. The first sentence of the quoted paragraph from *Of Reformation*, from 'But to dwell no longer' to 'the fragrancy of Heaven', is well over a hundred words long. Such sentences are quite frequent in Milton's vernacular prose. In most of his pamphlets, roughly twenty or twenty-five per cent of the sentences have over a hundred words each, a remarkably large proportion by modern standards. However, many learned prose writers contemporary with Milton show a similar predilection for length. And their style, of course, is sometimes labelled 'Latinate' or 'periodic' or 'Ciceronian'. But such categorization is of dubious usefulness.

[But to dwell ... increase]

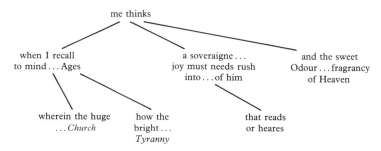

Diagram 1

A consciousness of Ciceronian stylistic practices may in some way have seemed to legitimize such syntactical copiousness. Long sentences, however, are so much the norm for serious English prose of the time, and are so pervasive among such a diversity of authors, that a specific, foreign, literary influence or model seems improbable.

Nor can the actual structure of such sentences composed by Milton accurately be termed 'Ciceronian' or 'periodic' in the sense of following a Latin rather than early-modern-English word-order or clausal organisation. For, in complex sentences, Milton rarely postpones completion of his main clause to the end; nor does he in the example here being considered. Rather, in a wholly English way, the sentence grows through the accretion of phrases and subordinate clauses, which are appended to the material on which they depend either in front (sometimes termed 'left-branching'), behind (right-branching), or in the middle (embedded). And subordinate material often supports further subordinate clauses or phrases.

Thus, the sentence we are considering, though it contains some minor elements of syntactical ambiguity, can probably best be conceptualized as in diagram 1. The main clause, the impersonal verb 'me thinks', supports, to its left, one immediately dependent clause, and to its right a further two. (The complex syntactical structure 'But to dwell . . . increase' can probably best be regarded as ancilliary to 'me thinks'.) Two of the subordinate clauses in turn support yet further subordinate material, the effect being a sort of pyramid of syntactical subordination. Such constructions are by no means uniquely Miltonic, but statistics show that he is likelier than his contemporaries to produce main clauses which support a multiplicity of directly subordinate clauses and that these clauses in their turn are likelier to support further subordination. However, the distinctiveness of these features, as characteristics of Miltonic prose, should not be overstated. Syntactical complexity is widespread among prose writers contemporary with Milton, and I would suggest that much of our pleasure in reading many of them comes as we appreciate their muscular syntactical control – the ways in which they achieve expressions of causality and purpose, temporal precision, and refined definition by means of such subordinate structures.

Milton's prose vocabulary, like his syntax, has sometimes been regarded as Latinate, that is, characterized either by frequent use of Latin loanwords, or else by the use of 'naturalized' but etymologically Latinate words in non-English senses redolent of their Latin significations. But neither aspect of this view about his vocabulary can be substantiated. Milton himself is openly critical of what he considers to be the redundant or affected coinage of words from classical languages (Corns 1982, 69–70). For example, when, in *Eikon Basilike* (a pamphlet offered to the public as the executed Charles I's apologia) Milton finds the newly coined 'Demagogues', he indignantly objects to 'the affrightment of this Goblin word; for the King by his leave cannot coine English as he could Money, to be current' (*Eikonoklastes*; YP 3: 393). In this instance, of course, the word proved a useful addition to the English wordstock.

Milton himself neologizes fairly freely, and he readily extends the signification of established vocabulary, but displays no affected classicism or inkhorn enthusiasm for learned ostentation. Most of his coinings come through the usual processes of word-formation in English, through prefixation and suffixation and through compounding. Much of it is quite unremarkable. In *Of Reformation* we find, for example, 'griffonlike', 'Africanisms', and 'unmonopolizing' (YP 1: 543, 568, 613). But sometimes the neologizing is to brilliant stylistic effect, as in the following ironic flourish against the appetitiveness of the prelates, in which Milton wonders how a bishop's lifestyle in the primitive church would be perceived by a Caroline bishop: 'what a rich bootie it would be, what a plump endowment to the many-benefice-gaping mouth of a Prelate, what a relish it would give to his canary-sucking, and swan-eating palat' (549). There is something strikingly absurd, grotesque, overblown in Milton's compounds here, but it is appropriate to his decorum of abuse. Moreover, by coining words for the bishops' conduct, Milton cleverly suggests the habituation of their actions: sybaritic feasting and mawing down pluralities are what they persistently do; so there ought to be words for their practices.

When Milton does borrow directly from classical tongues, it is usually either a technical term or else a word that he coins to connote the outlandish fustiness of a concept. In the first category, in *Of Reformation*, we find the phrase 'coming to the Bishop with *Supplication* into the *Salutatory*' (607). 'Salutatory' is coined directly from medieval Latin *salutatorium*, an audience chamber attached to a church or monastery. Even here, there may be something of a hostile flavour to the word, perhaps suggestive of the obscurantism of monasticism; Milton makes the contrast by appending his own gloss in plain English: 'some out Porch of the Church'. Elsewhere in *Of Reformation*, Milton is concerned to dismiss the efforts of those seeking to validate episcopalian government by reference to the records of the early Christian church, and he does so by postulating a choice between the opaque writings of the church fathers and plain Scripture truth. He asks which is better,

to dote upon immeasurable, innumerable, and therfore unnecessary, and unmerciful volumes, choosing rather to erre with the specious name of the Fathers, or to take a sound Truth at the hand of a plain upright man that all his dayes hath bin diligently reading the holy Scriptures, and thereto imploring *Gods* grace, while the admirers of Antiquity have bin beating their brains about their *Ambones*, their *Diptychs*, and *Meniaia*'s? (568)

The unfamiliarity of the concluding vocabulary contributes considerably to our response to this passage. 'Ambones', the plural of 'Ambo', the special name for the pulpit or reading desk of the early Christian church, is Milton's coining from late Latin. The 'meniaia' (unrecorded in the *OED*) are the books containing offices for the immoveable feasts of the Byzantine rite. As the Yale editor observes, we should note Milton's contemptuous use of the double plural, Greek and English. 'Diptychs', a word borrowed from Greek in the 1620s, had only recently been used in the technical sense of the tablets of wax on which, in the early church, the names of the orthodox, both living and dead, were recorded. Brilliantly, through his choices of vocabulary, Milton points up the distinction between the sterility, obscurity, and alienness of antiquarianism, and the forthrightness of the approach, described in simple English, of the 'plain upright man'.

Milton, as already noted, has sometimes been thought of as using words with Greek or Latin etymologies in senses not current in English. We must beware, however, of ignoring the dynamics of semantic change. When words become English, it is often in senses close to the original. Later, other meanings may develop and the original ones fall into disuse. It is easy, if we do not consult a historical dictionary (such as the *OED*), to attribute to Milton's prose a Latinism and a semantic atavism which, in the context of seventeenth-century linguistic practice, it does not truly possess. For example, in *The Reason of Church-Government*, a slightly later antiprelatical pamphlet, Milton observes that churchmen 'should be to us a pattern of temperance and frugal mediocrity' (YP 1: 856). The Yale editor notes that 'mediocrity' has the Latin sense of moderation or temperance. Quite so, but we must not be misled. That was also a normal *English* signification of the word from the early sixteenth century to the later eighteenth century. It is quite rare for Milton – and quite rare generally for mid-seventeenth-century writers of serious prose – to use words with classical etymologies in genuinely un-English significations.

The kind of writing I have been analysing, characterized by a high incidence of simile and metaphor, a vigorous assimilation of biblical material, and considerable lexical creativity, is uniformly present in Milton's antiprelatical pamphlets of 1641–2. In the next two or three years, however, while retaining this style for the elevated oratory of *Areopagitica* and the heated vituperation of *Colasterion* (1645), Milton develops another voice, one that uses imagery much more sparingly, for other kinds of writing, such as *Tetrachordon* (the careful exegetical justification of his thesis on divorce, 1645) or *Of Education* (1644), which is scarcely more than a list of proposals about how education ought to be organized. Then, after being silent in print from 1646 through to 1648, Milton in 1649 produces three pamphlets in defence of revolutionary independency, *The Tenure of Kings and Magistrates*, *Observations upon the late Articles of Peace*, and *Eikonoklastes*; and these works are yet further subdued in their imagery, though they retain some of Milton's earlier lexical vigour.

For the next ten years Milton writes no more vernacular prose pamphlets. But when, in 1659, he breaks his silence to consider issues concerning church funding and the relationship between church and state – in *A Treatise of Civil Power* and *The Likeliest Means to Remove Hirelings out of the Church* – it is a still different voice we hear. Consider the following:

Seeing then that in matters of religion, as hath been prov'd, none can judge or determin here on earth, no not church-governors themselves against the consciences of other beleevers, my inference is, or rather not mine but our Saviours own, that in those matters they neither can command nor use constraint; lest they run rashly on a pernicious consequence, forewarnd in that parable *Mat. 13.* from the 26 to the 31 verse: *least while ye gather up the tares, ye root up also the wheat with them. Let both grow together until the harvest: and in the time of harvest I will say to the reapers, Gather ye together first the tares & c.* whereby he declares that this work neither his own ministers nor any els can discerningly anough or judgingly perform without his own immediat direction, in his own fit season; and that they ought till then not to attempt it.   (*A Treatise of Civil Power*; YP 7 (rev. edn): 244–5)

Syntactically, we are on familiar ground – a sentence of well over a hundred words, organized in a hierarchy of subordination which can be sche-

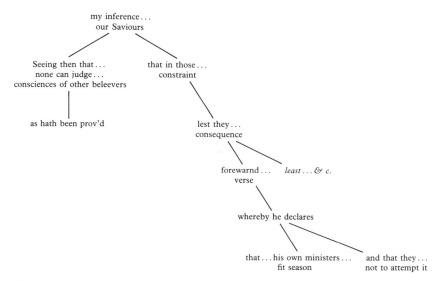

Diagram 2

matically represented by diagram 2. The main clause, 'my inference . . . our Saviours own', supports, to the left, a clause of circumstance, in which another clause is embedded. To the right of the main clause, subordinate clause supports subordinate clause, which supports subordinate clause, through a long chain of dependency. Milton's predilection for such structures remains constant throughout the prose *œuvre*, save for his last tract, *Of True Religion*, written, after a long intermission, in 1673, by which time the norms of the genre may well have changed in favour of a greater syntactical simplicity.

But our example shows how other characteristics of Milton's earlier style have been expunged. Note the use of the biblical material. Previously, Milton had freely reworked it into his own idiom. Now the biblical allusion – once more, to the parable of the tares – stands adjacent to his own discourse in the status of a proof text. He follows the Authorized Version verbatim, and even gives (albeit a little inaccurately) reference to chapter and verse. In the purely Miltonic part, there is neither simile nor metaphor, nor any creative deviation from the customary lexical usages of seventeenth-century English. What had been flamboyant, even pyrotechnic, prose has given way to a sober functionalism.

Inevitably, we must wonder why Milton changed. There is little external evidence. Although, as we shall see, Milton makes some useful observations on style, he gives no explicit account of his own development. Yet he is not simply following stylistic trends. Certainly, the prose style of the Restoration tended to be less figurative and its artistry was less obtrusive. Thus, in 1673, Samuel Parker, no lover of Milton's politics, takes exception also to his prose style, citing a passage from *Areopagitica* very similar to the one quoted earlier and remarking with heavy irony, 'Such fustian bumbast [*sic*] as this past for stately wit and sence in that Age of politeness and reformation' (French 5: 51). But in the period 1641–60 no general trend towards a plainer style is evident. The developments in Milton's prose must therefore be seen as resulting from changes in his own stylistic preferences rather than from any mere conformity with the practices of his contemporaries.

Why, then, should brilliance have given way to an (albeit elegant) functionalism? We may only hypothesize. Certainly, though, arguments about failing literary creativity must be discounted. As Milton produces his least exciting prose, he is simultaneously writing his greatest poetry. Perhaps those who favour a psychological explanation may see a connection. Maybe in the 1640s, when the polemical responsibilities he assumed precluded writing major poetry, the creative impulse found deflected expression in his prose works. Milton's early prose style may thus be perceived as the rechannelling of that creative mental energy which later found a proper discharge in *Paradise Lost*. Such an argument has its attractions, though I am not sure how by itself it could explain, for example, the variations in the pamphlets of 1643–5. The changes in Milton's prose style should probably be seen instead as part of his complex response to the polemical context in which he wrote and to his own perceptions of his role within it.

In his earlier prose, Milton constructs an image of himself as a poet who has turned to the prose genre both temporarily and a little reluctantly, out of a love for his country and an enthusiasm for its thoroughgoing reformation, and he seems troubled by the decorum of elevated, creative writing in this medium. In his fifth and final antiprelatical tract, *An Apology against a Pamphlet* (1642), he interrupts an elaborate, apocalyptic image about the 'fiery Chariot' of 'Zeale' with a defensive parenthesis: '(that I may have leave to soare a while as the Poets use)' (YP 1: 900), thus suggesting that his is a poetic impulse, ill-confined in the medium of prose. Once more on the defensive, in *The Reason of Church-Government*, he counters the charge that he writes controversial prose only to win notoriety, and he does so by asserting his own sense of poetic calling. He is 'led by the genial power of nature to another task' (that is, to poetry), and he glances with apparent envy at the 'Poet soaring . . . with his garland and singing robes about him'. By contrast, prose, that 'cool element', is something Milton writes with his 'left hand' (YP 1: 808). And yet the prose of 1641–2 is not really that much 'cooler' than poetry. Rather, it represents the efforts of a writer who still thinks of himself as a poet who happens to be writing, though only temporarily, in prose.

The *variety* of styles Milton develops over the next three years obviously does not reflect major changes in personality or a restriction of ability, since the variety subsists in closely contemporary works. Instead, Milton seems to be looking ever more closely at the nuances of genre and at how various styles of writing are appropriate to various rhetorical situations. The close exegesis of biblical texts invites a kind of exposition quite different from the lofty or impassioned enunciation of high principle or the vehement assailing of one's opponents. At the same time, Milton during these years offers us a more idealized image of the prose writer. Now, he tells us, 'When a man writes to the world, he summons up all his reason and deliberation to assist him; he searches, meditats, is industrious, and likely consults and conferrs with his judicious friends.' His writing – and it is plain from the context that Milton is speaking here of non-fictional prose – is 'the most consummat act of his fidelity and ripenesse', the product of 'his midnight watchings' (*Areopagitica*; YP 2: 532). And so he accommodates himself to his role as prose polemicist.

Milton in 1641–2 was somewhat on the fringes of political controversy, writing to second the arguments of others and, perhaps, to nudge them a little further down the path to root-and-branch extirpation of episcopalian church government. But in 1643–5, with a new notoriety, he stands at the centre of heated argument, both about the heterodox divorce reforms he advocated and about the rights of radicals to express such opinions. Yet still generally on the defensive, and excluded from circles of power and influence, he speaks with a challenging, oppositional voice. By 1649, however, Milton has become the spokesperson of the new ascendancy. Revolutionary independency, the political faction with which he identified himself, had, by the late 1640s, captured the most important institutions of the state. It predominated among the officer cadre of the victorious New Model Army; since Pride's Purge, it had controlled Parliament; and now it was bringing the King to the scaffold and republican government to England. Milton, after several years of silence, thus re-emerges in 1649 as ideologue of a now successful political faction.

His first tract of 1649, *The Tenure of Kings and Magistrates*, is a theoretical justification for Parliament's treatment of the King. Thereafter, he became a paid civil servant of the new regime, as Secretary for Foreign Tongues to the Council of State. Milton's holding this position indicates the *official* and rather corporate nature of the publications for which he was responsible during this period. *Observations upon the Late Articles of Peace* is a response ordered by the Council of State to the Royalists' attempted settlement of Ireland on terms that would permit it to be used as a base for the restoration of Charles II. *Eikonoklastes*, the refutation of the Royalist apologia *Eikon Basilike* (1649), was similarly commissioned by Milton's political masters. In his pamphlet Milton himself stresses that it was a task undertaken, perhaps reluctantly, on behalf of the state: 'I take it on me as a work assign'd rather, then by me chos'n or affected' (YP 3: 339).

Defending the regicide government imposed on Milton a different set of imperatives and obligations from those he felt when, poet by calling, polemicist but for the moment, he lent his talents in support of the anti-prelatical movement. Of course, his earliest tracts were serious contributions to a debate close to the heart of the developing crisis between King and Parliament. But Milton, for all the *élan* of his early writings, functioned in the early 1640s essentially on the fringes of that debate. However, in 1649, particularly in *Eikonoklastes*, Milton achieves a position of pre-eminence as chief adversary of the Royalists' most important propaganda initiative, namely *Eikon Basilike*, which, despite the fact that the republicans had in their hands the whole apparatus of state control of the press, appeared in no less than forty clandestine editions in 1649 alone.

The high seriousness of Milton's tasks in 1649 may well account for the new sobriety of his style. In *Eikonoklastes*, Milton bases his attack on *Eikon Basilike* in part on its 'literary', artful, poetic style, which he adduces as evidence of its remoteness from plain truth. Thus, when King Charles (or his ghost writer, John Gauden) produces an elaborate image, likening the King's withdrawal from Westminster to a man's putting to sea without proper provisioning, Milton responds with questions about literary decorum. The image, he complains, is 'somwhat more Poetical' than the genre permits, and shows that the King thinks more about poetry than about statesmanship. Indeed, 'the whole Book might perhaps be intended a peece of Poetrie' (YP 3: 406). This is quite a shift from Milton's earlier posture, when he would arrest his oratory to beg permission to 'soare' like a poet! Yet his avowed suspicion of 'poetic' prose, while it serves his immediate purpose of blackening the image of the King, also accords well with the austerity of his own practice in 1649.

The final phase in the development of Milton's prose, that further levelling down of lexical creativity which we have already considered, was perhaps no more than the logical extension of the restrained stylistic decorum that informed the pamphlets of 1649. Of course, for the modern reader, the changes must be disappointing. Milton's early prose matches that of any of the great prose writers of his age in the pleasure it can still give.

It rivals the best of Donne and probably transcends all but the best of Browne. To the end of his career, Milton retains his power of syntactical control, and he likewise maintains a tone of savage indignation which anticipates, perhaps, the voice of Dr Johnson at his most incisive. He can still scythe through nonsense and pretension. For example, *Eikon Basilike* claims that the King, when he attempted to arrest Pym and his four colleagues, was 'attended with some Gentlemen'. Milton responds: 'Gentlemen indeed; the ragged Infantrie of Stewes and Brothels' (YP 3: 380). Again, of Charles's well-known cry, 'the birds have flown', Milton asks, 'If som Vultur in the Mountains could have op'nd his beak intelligibly and spoke, what fitter words could he have utter'd at the loss of his prey?' (439). Thus Milton's is a powerful voice still, but the zest of *Of Reformation* is not to be recovered.

For the modern reader, then, the progression of Milton's prose towards ordinariness can be disappointing, though alternatively it can be seen as not so much a falling off as a growing up (see Corns 1982, 102). Milton's early prose seems to presuppose the power of creative writing to fashion opinion and precipitate reform. The sober discourses of 1649 and later seem, by contrast, to recognize the irrelevance of fine writing to the shaping of political events. Yet they are, in several senses, more professional, the work of an increasingly experienced – and, of course, publicly employed – political activist. The earlier brilliance came, perhaps, from the friction of genius and genre, as Milton the poet redirected his energies in the limiting medium of prose. The later work comes from a maturer Milton, securely embedded in the milieu of prose controversy.

Reading list

Corns, Thomas N., 'Obscenity, Slang and Indecorum in Milton's English Prose', *Prose Studies* 3 (1980)

The Development of Milton's Prose Style (Oxford, 1982)

'The Freedom of Reader-Response: Milton's *Of Reformation* and Lilburne's *Christian Mans Triall*', in *Freedom and the English Revolution: Essays in History and Literature*, ed. R. C. Richardson and G. M. Ridden (Manchester, 1986)

Davies, Hugh Sykes, 'Milton and the Vocabulary of Verse and Prose', in *Literary English Since Shakespeare*, ed. George Watson (New York, 1970)

Donne, John, *Selected Prose*, ed. Helen Gardner and Timothy Healy (Oxford, 1967)

Egan, James, *The Inward Teacher: Milton's Rhetoric of Christian Liberty* (University Park, PA, 1980)

Fish, Stanley E., *Self-Consuming Artifacts* (Berkeley, Los Angeles, and London, 1972)

French, J. Milton, compiler, *The Life Records of John Milton*, 5 vols. (New Brunswick, NJ, 1949–1956; rpt. Stapleton, NY, 1966)

Hamilton, K. G., 'The Structure of Milton's Prose', in *Language and Style in Milton*, ed. R. D. Emma and J. T. Shawcross (New York, 1967)

Hill, Christopher, *Milton and the English Revolution* (London, 1977)

Kranidas, Thomas, '"Decorum" and the Style of Milton's Antiprelatical Tracts', *Studies in Philology* 62 (1965)

'Milton's *Of Reformation*: The Politics of Vision', *ELH* 49 (1982)

'Style and Rectitude in Seventeenth-Century Prose: Hall, Smectynmuus, and Milton', *Huntington Library Quarterly* 46 (1983)

Lieb, Michael, and J. T. Shawcross, eds., *Achievements of the Left Hand: Essays on the Prose of John Milton* (Amherst, MA, 1974)

Milner, Andrew, *John Milton and the English Revolution* (London, 1981)

Stavely, Keith W., *The Politics of Milton's Prose Style* (New Haven, 1975)

Webber, Joan, *The Eloquent 'I': Style and Self in Seventeenth-Century Prose* (Madison, Wisconsin, and London, 1968)

Wilding, Michael, 'Milton's *Areopagitica*: Freedom for the Sects', *Prose Studies* 9 (1986); rpt. in *The Literature of Controversy: Polemical Strategy from Milton to Junius*, ed. Thomas N. Corns (London, 1987)

13 Milton and the reforming spirit

The Reformation was an important part of England's national identity in the seventeenth century and an important part of Milton's identity. While England defined itself as a Protestant nation over against the largely Roman Catholic Continent, Milton defined himself over against Protestant opponents at home, turning his antipapal rhetoric first against prelates in the Church of England, whom he called 'more Antichristian than Antichrist himselfe' (YP 1: 850), and later against the Scots Presbyters.

Milton did not consider Luther's break with Rome to be the important watershed in western history it is now regarded, and usually he did not speak of *the* Reformation. In his prose tracts, however, he repeatedly writes of 'reformation', by which he means the work of returning the English Church – and the English nation – to the purity and simplicity of the Gospel. Milton views the work of reformation as a recurring task. In *The Reason of Church-Government*, for example, he refers to the plight of Old Testament prophets 'that liv'd in the times of reformation', to a 'more perfect reformation under Christ', and to the reforming message of the Lollards and Hussites who had anticipated Luther (YP 1: 799, 757). England's role in the modern reformation is for Milton a point of particular pride, and he firmly believes that England has been chosen to complete the Reformation, in which he feels called to participate. Near the beginning of *The Reason of Church-Government*, he explains that he is personally hesitant,

But when God commands to take the trumpet and blow a dolorous or a jarring blast, it lies not in mans will what he shall say, or what he shall conceal. If he shall think to be silent, as *Jeremiah* did, because of the reproach and derision he met with daily . . . he would be forc't to confesse as he confest, *his word was in my heart as a burning fire shut up in my bones, I was weary with forbearing and could not stay.* (YP 1: 803)

Milton goes on to argue that the prelates – especially the bishops and archbishops – are rich, greedy, and corrupt, interested in anything but the care of souls. This hierarchical system of governance, he argues, should be replaced by assemblies of divines *and* laymen – the form of church government that he finds the New Testament advocating. It is, not coincidentally, an arrangement that embodies a cardinal point of Reformation theology – the Priesthood of Believers. Milton says, 'Christians ought to know, that the title of Clergy S. *Peter* gave to all Gods people' until 'the succeeding Prelates took it from them' (YP 1: 838). Therefore he maintains that 'the functions of Church-government ought to be free and open to any Christian man though never so laick' (YP 1: 844).

To advocate complete change in church governance was in Milton's day politically radical because church leaders had been part of the political establishment since the time of Henry VIII. Accordingly, religious discourse was integrated with political discourse in a seamless rhetorical bond that now we have difficulty seeing whole. Milton and the Puritans were not devoid of political or economic motivation, and we catch occasional glimpses of an economic grudge, as when Milton berates the prelates for their wealth and lordliness, even claiming that prelacy 'shall spoil and havock your estates' (YP 1: 851). Nevertheless, public discourse was primarily – and passionately – doctrinal, that is, cast in Protestant categories of thought inherited from the continental reformers – from Luther, Calvin, Melanchthon, among others – and from systematized versions of that thought compiled by English scholastics like William Ames and William Perkins. Milton stands squarely in this evangelical Protestant tradition, as opposed to the more Thomistic Protestant tradition espoused by Richard Hooker and Archbishop Laud.

Little in Protestantism was not already present in the medieval Catholic tradition, but Luther's emphases amounted to a new configuration in which religious life took on a distinctively 'literary' cast. Accordingly, there were marked modifications in how sin was perceived, what composed a sacrament, and what comprised devotional life. One need not be a Protestant in order to read *Paradise Lost*, because the basic story and much of its religious language is common to several religious traditions, the word 'saint' for ordinary believers being one of the few terms given a peculiarly Protestant meaning. Nevertheless, Protestant thought profoundly shaped Milton's poetry and helps to explain its distinctive features. Unlike Dante, Milton represents God by a discursive voice, not by a sensuous symbol. The Virgin is absent from the enthronement scene in heaven, and Purgatory has disappeared altogether from the cosmos.

More particularly, Protestant thought helps explain the shape of Milton's hell and his presentation of evil. The Catholic tradition dealt with a precisely calibrated hierarchy of venial and mortal sins; and though the plan in

Dante's *Inferno* is not exactly a map of the seven deadly sins, it is arranged hierarchically beginning with the most sympathetic sin – adultery between book lovers – and descending in rational sequence toward the bestial and heinous, down to the depths of usury, and finally to Judas and the betrayers. In Milton's hell, however, the terrain is more exegetical than judicial; that is to say, the varied terrain, with its ever burning sulphur and contrasting regions of ice, does not signify gradations of sin, but evidence of the delusional character of the devil's discourse, in particular Belial's assertion that the devils can adjust and become 'inured' to the flames. Although Satan addresses his fellows in misery by titles that seem to presume a ranking by degree – 'Princes, potentates, / Warriors, the flower of heaven' (*PL* 1.315–16) – these titles are primarily honorific and rhetorical. There are effectively only two degrees in Milton's hell – fallen Archangel and his compatriots. The demonic council embodies a two-step hierarchy, rather like a parodic version of the church governance Milton advocated (minister-and-lay-leaders). Dramatically speaking, at least, the orators seem to be peers, differing only in forensic acuity, age, and individual temper. Elsewhere, Milton is explicit about the levelling of evil. There are, he says, but 'two degrees' of evil: 'a reprobat conscience in this life, and hell in the other world' (YP 1: 835).

The elision of degree in hell reflects the Protestant abolition of confession and of precisely calibrated penances. To be sure, Protestants developed their casuists, but their piety purported to erase gradations of sin and concentrate upon the heart's primary orientation. Moral calculus began with faith. The biblical underpinning for this point, cited by Milton as by Luther before him, was Romans 13: 23: 'Whatsoever is not of faith is sin' (YP 6: 639; *Luther's Works* 26: 250). This view no longer localized sin in careful categories, but spread it into all areas of existence, including those normally reserved for virtue. The most 'virtuous' action without faith was sinful; conversely 'sloth' (or merely standing and waiting) might be a most heroic act of faith. This 'either-or' shaping of sin is the most misunderstood point about Milton's devils, who are conspicuous for their virtue. In Book 2 of *Paradise Lost* we see a fearless warrior, a staunch intellectual ('who would lose, / Though full of pain, this intellectual being . . . ?' (2.146–7)), an architectural wizard, and a forensic champion. Unlike the denizens of Dante's *Inferno*, not one devil belongs in a state prison. They are epitomes of sin for one reason only: they lack faith.

Faith, in Milton's tradition, furthermore has an irreducible 'literary' component, for it is defined by reception of divine words that constitute a 'verbal sacrament'. This verbal sacrament is a 'scripture within scripture', or the promise of redemption in Christ in any of the lexical forms in which it recurs throughout the Bible, both in the New Testament and more obliquely in the Old Testament. Indeed, the promise of redemption can be inferred simply by the mention of Christ. The difference between the Catholic and Protestant traditions has often been located in the question of free will, but a more basic distinction concerns authority, which Protestants place, not in the institution of the church or its hierarchy, but in Scripture – 'the only true theologie' (YP 7: 306) – and in the Holy Spirit that makes it 'piercing'.

In a notably Protestant gesture, accordingly, Milton constructs an episode in Book 5 to initiate the entire action of *Paradise Lost* with a pronouncement – a verbal sacrament – paraphrasing Psalm 2: 7:

> This day I have begot whom I declare
> My only Son . . .
> whom ye now behold
> At my right hand; your head I him appoint.   (5.603–6)

The speech concludes with a promissory emphasis: 'Under his great vice-regent reign abide / United as one individual soul / For ever happy' (5.609–11). It is Satan's refusal to accept the sacramental promise, his refusal to 'hear' God's words, that constitutes the primal sin. Once Satan strikes this posture, any virtue or courage he may display partakes of sin. A similar verbal sacrament obtains in the Garden of Eden. Milton takes pains to show that Adam and Eve make glorious love before the Fall, because it is important to show that their primal sin does not derive from sexuality, does not cast suspicion on the goodness of Creation. Rather, their sin, like Satan's, consists in a disregard of divine words. In accordance with the same principle, Adam and Eve's redemption is occasioned by a *reception* of divine words.

The divine promise that comes to Adam and Eve after the Fall, however, is veiled in the sentence of judgment that the Son pronounces in Book 10:

> Between thee and the woman I will put
> Enmity, and between thine and her seed;
> *Her seed shall bruise thy head, thou bruise his heel.* (10.179–81; italics added)

Any well-catechized Puritan would recognize this as a redaction of Genesis 3: 15, known as the *protevangelium*, the first Messianic promise, the first utterance of the Gospel (see YP 6: 515). Adam and Eve, however, do not at first see anything promissory in the *protevangelium*. Only at line 1030, after an emotional reconciliation with Eve – and in response to her suggestion that they abstain from lovemaking to prevent the curse on future generations – does Adam partially solve the *protevangelium*. He seizes upon the right referent for the word *Serpent* in the judicial sentence and instantly grasps that it signifies the death of 'our grand foe Satan' (1033–4).

This moment in *Paradise Lost* is susceptible of several interpretations. Readers in the tradition of Aquinas and Hooker will emphasize an apparent reasoning process in Adam's words, 'then let us seek / Some safer resolution . . . ' (1028–9), whereas readers in the evangelical tradition will emphasize the sudden access of memory and argue that identifying the *Serpent* calls for a daring leap of reference that cannot merely be deduced by the knowledge available to Adam in this scene. In either case, the moment of eureka! marks the passage of the couple from despair to faith. Once Adam sees something of the promise in the *protevangelium*, he begins to see promise in the labour that is to come in the fields, and in childbed.

Adam's experience here also fits the Reformation archetype of a lonely encounter with Scripture and follows the pattern set by Luther's account of how the meaning of Romans 1: 17 ('The just shall live by faith') was for him suddenly transformed – from an impossible demand for goodness into a promise of bestowed righteousness. 'Here I felt that I was altogether born again and had entered paradise itself through open gates', Luther explains (*Luther's Works* 34: 337). The turning point in Book 10 is also very like Christian's experience in *The Pilgrim's Progress* when he is about to commit suicide in the Dungeon of the Giant Despair. Suddenly he remembers that in his pocket he has had the Key of Promise with him all along. He draws it out, turns the lock, and soon is on his way again toward the Celestial City. And so are Adam and Eve, though they still have a great deal more to learn about the *protevangelium* under the tutelage of Michael in Books 11 and 12.

That Milton depicts in minute detail Adam and Eve's experience with God's oracular promise and that he gives it emphasis of place – Books 9, 10, 11 and 12 – is consistent with the assumption in Protestant hermeneutics that Adam and Eve are the first Christians and that, as Milton puts it, the mystical church 'includes people from many remote countries, and from all ages since the creation of the world' (YP 6: 500). Accordingly, Milton's Adam and Eve relate to the sacramental promise in the same way as did Milton's contemporaries, that is, as verbal *report*, albeit an anticipatory one. Milton's choice not to narrate the crucifixion in a poem that includes all time and space reflects the Protestant view that it is the (promise-bearing) *report* of the event, not its repetition in the Mass, that is sacramental. If Milton pushed 'Christian' experience back to the Garden of Eden, he was following in the exegetical footsteps of Luther, Calvin, and other reformers, but he was also making a political gesture, defending Protestantism against the claim that it was a new-fangled religion (Patrides 1982, 102).

If there is no priest in the Edenic Church, who then administers the verbal sacrament? The answer, as Calvin elaborated it, was that the proclamation of God's Promise is made effectively sacramental by the operation of the Holy Spirit. Milton thus presents the *protevangelium* as having no immediate effect upon Adam and Eve during the judgment scene when it is pronounced. Only later in the midst of a marital quarrel is the promise embraced. As the Father explains, their reception of it is a result of 'My motions in him' (*PL* 11.91).

For Calvin, the work of the Spirit was virtually confined to the reception of Scripture, and the sheer fact of belief was the only reliable token of the Spirit's presence. In seventeenth-century England, however, the question of the Spirit's operation was variously understood. For the Cambridge Platonists, the Spirit's work was all but equated with the working of human reason. For the radical sectaries of the 1640s, the Spirit's work was that of prompting a man to specific actions, which might range from choosing a certain text to inciting a bizarre action. For the Quakers, the Spirit was certified both by inner impulse and by a Meeting's consensus, one which might go beyond or counter to Scripture. Milton finds no scriptural warrant for the Holy Spirit as a *Person* within the Trinity, but his *Christian Doctrine* assembles many verses about 'the spirit of God'. Interior 'motions' and the urging of conscience to speak out comprise a prominent theme in Milton's tracts and poetry alike. His shorter poems begin to resolve themselves when a sudden voice supplies an answer. These voices are tactfully designated as 'Patience' in 'When I consider how my light is spent' and as 'Phoebus' in *Lycidas*. In *Paradise Lost*, Adam reveals to Eve the content of the 'persuasion' that grew in him when he remembers the word about the Seed: 'the bitterness of death / Is past, and we shall live' (11.157–8). In *Samson Agonistes* the poet does not supply the content of the 'intimate impulse' that comes to the hero (223, 1382), but in *Paradise Lost* the content of the Spirit's tutelage is fine doctrinal discrimination.

Milton generally refers to the Spirit's work in a restrained and reticent way. Sometimes his assertions seem to identify the Spirit with human reason, as when he insists that Truth should undergo 'the triall and inspection of the Understanding' (YP 1: 830). Sometimes reason and divine prompting seem indistinguishable, as when Milton, on the eve of the Restoration, advocates an unpaid clergy. He writes, 'I promisd then to speak further, when I should finde God disposing me, and opportunity inviting. Opportunity I finde now inviting; and apprehend therein the concurrence of God disposing' (YP 7: 278). At other times the Spirit is implicitly an enemy of reasoning, as when Milton says, 'the quick and pearcing word . . .

throw[s] down the weak mightines of mans reasoning' (YP 1: 827). Sometimes the Spirit is credited only with the task of scriptural interpretation (YP 6: 583). And on occasion, Milton claims urgent divine prompting, as in *The Reason of Church-Government* when he advocates abolishing the entire episcopal system: 'Were it the meanest under-service, if God by his Secretary conscience injoyn it, it were sad for me if I should draw back . . . ' (YP 1: 822). If a 'Secretary' here means one 'entrusted with the secrets or commands of God' (*OED*), then the assertion is a bolder claim to divine intimacy than it first appears.

The question of Milton's inspiration is a vexed one, but it has a bearing upon the dramatic role of the Son, who fights with the 'Sword of the Spirit' in *Paradise Regained*. Milton has been accused of claiming that heavenly dictation supplanted his own writing skill, of claiming that he was privy to God's innermost secrets, or, alternatively, that he was invoking the heavenly muse as a pro forma bow to the epic tradition. The reality lies somewhere between these extremes. As to poetic skills, the role of the Spirit seems to be an additive one – that of a 'supreme inlightning *assistance*'. As opposed to the heat of youth or the fume of wine, Milton claims reliance upon prayer and 'that eternall Spirit who can *enrich* with all utterance' and send a Seraph to purify the lips with a coal (YP 1: 749, 820–1; italics added). What may now seem to be an arrogant presumption of knowing God's mind was, within the Puritan ethos, a witness to faith. Milton's confident tone signals his depth of conviction. When, for example, he claims to be 'incorporate into that truth whereof I was perswaded' (1: 871), he is simply taking the Priesthood of Believers seriously. As he explains in *Christian Doctrine*, the communion that obtained between man and God in his tradition was the kind of union that occurs in 'persuasion' (see YP 6: 471–5): agreement of mind and heart and soul, unity in the Spirit.

One can easily read *Paradise Lost* without being conversant with Protestant theology, because the poem transcends its doctrinal roots. When reading *Paradise Regained*, however, one needs to take account of the 'literary' operations Calvin and Milton credited to the Holy Spirit – belief in the promise of the Redeemer, a faithful interpretation of Scripture, its right application on a given occasion, and the prompting to preach or speak. Calvin, to whom Milton stands closest on 'the question of the Spirit, holds Jesus to be the unique bearer and sender of the Holy Spirit. (Calvin so emphasizes the association between Christ and the Spirit that his position has sometimes been labelled a 'Spirit-Christology'.) In *Paradise Regained* the Father affirms Jesus as his 'son beloved' (1.85) when he rises from the baptismal waters, and this pronouncement initiates the action of the brief epic. The descent of the dove at this moment signals the *full* donation of the Spirit, but Satan sees only a dove, and does not understand that now the hero possesses a secret weapon that will enable him to win any scriptural battle. In short, the hero possesses what Bunyan was to call the Interpreter.

The lack of anything numinous in the hero's presence or his speech tends to mislead us along with Satan, for we expect an emotional effusion to accompany an access of the Spirit. We tend to expect 'heartburnings' of the sort found in Puritan diaries. Instead, the hero's forensic precision is almost chilling, and his failure to defend himself makes him appear emotionally empty. But this absence of the claims of the self is an important indication of the hero's hidden identity as Bearer of the Spirit. As Milton pointed out, to be in the Spirit 'is also called self-denial' (YP 6: 478). In *Christian Doctrine* the Son and the Holy Spirit are both defined by their dialogue: of each, Milton says that he 'never speaks anything of himself' but always refers to the authority of God the Father (YP 6: 259–60). Hence it is revelatory that Satan never manages to engage the hero in discussion as to the 'degree' of his sonship, and that the hero withstands all Satan's attempts to have him speak *as himself*.

Ironically, the Tempter comes very close to the Son's hermeneutic secret when he offers him all the wisdom of the ancients: 'These rules will render thee a king complete / Within thyself' (*PR* 4.283–4). However, Reformation thought considered self-mastery, not sensuality, the quintessence of flesh, to which it opposed self-denial, or self-emptying in favour of the governance of the Spirit. To surrender the egoistic flesh to the governance of the Holy Spirit therefore required, not self-mastery, but an opening of oneself to 'Light from above, from the fountain of light' (*PR* 4.289).

The final temptation on the pinnacle of the Temple demonstrates the supernatural 'inlightning' that helps the hero to defeat Satan. The Tempter's rhetoric presents a dilemma. Once atop the temple spire, he says, 'To stand upright / will ask thee skill' (4.551–2), indicating by his understatement that the feat of standing on the spire is physically impossible. If the hero stands, he will reveal his supernatural identity. Then the Tempter says, 'Now show thy progeny; if not to stand, / Cast thyself down' (4.554–5). The hero must, according to the categories of the natural world, either stand or fall. Yet anything he does will be obeying Satan. The dilemma appears to be an infallible temptation; it invites the despairing conclusion that life in this world necessarily defeats faith. The Son, however, does not betray the smallest tremor of anxiety. He confidently strikes back with a verse from Deuteronomy 5: 16: 'Also it is written, / Tempt not the Lord thy God, he said and stood' (4.560–1). The reply is a denunciation of Satan's perverse application of Scripture, but it is also the most spectacular of all the hero's verbal gestures of self-denial. Once again he refers the Satanic challenge to higher authority, and climactically identifies himself (to those who are doctrinally informed) as a hero fighting with the Sword of the Spirit.

Thus Milton reforms, or recasts, the aggressive warrior-Christ of his first epic into a character more like Abdiel, one who withstands and triumphs over interrogation, verbal attack, and misrepresentation of scriptural truth. The important discriminations in Milton's universe are finally 'literary' ones, for Milton's hell, heaven, 'Edenic Church', and ultimate hero all are defined by the reception of divine words. And that reception, when positive, is credited to the work of a secret agent – the Holy Spirit – whose agency is the beginning of all true reformation.

Reading list

Barker, Arthur E., *Milton and the Puritan Dilemma* (Toronto, 1942)

Calvin, J., *Institutes of the Christian Religion*, ed. John T. McNeill, 2 vols. (Philadelphia, 1960)

Christopher, Georgia, *Milton and the Science of the Saints* (Princeton, 1982)

Danielson, Dennis, *Milton's Good God: A Study in Literary Theodicy* (Cambridge and New York, 1982)

Haller, William, *The Rise of Puritanism* (New York, 1955)

Hill, Christopher, *Milton and the English Revolution* (1977)

Kerrigan, William B., *The Prophetic Milton* (Charlottesville, VA, 1975)

Lieb, Michael, *The Poetics of the Holy* (Chapel Hill, NC, 1981)

Luther's Works, ed. Jaroslav Pelikan and Helmut T. Lehmann, 55 vols. (St Louis, 1955–76)

Patrides, C. A., *Milton and the Christian Tradition* (Oxford, 1966)

  Premises and Motifs in Renaissance Thought and Literature (Princeton, 1982)

Rajan, Balachandra, *'Paradise Lost' and the Seventeenth-Century Reader* (London, 1947)

14 How Milton read the Bible: the case of *Paradise Regained*

Milton read Scripture with a commitment to its themes, genres, and style. He read its two Testaments *thematically* as forming one body of saving truth, consistent but gradually becoming clearer to the understanding. He read it *generically* as consisting of law, story, prophets, and poetry, the poetry divisible into further genres. He read the poetry as composed, *stylistically*, with greater skill and purity than any other ancient national poetry. These three modes of reading influenced his own poems from the beginning to the end of his career, as he took scriptural themes, events, or doctrines for them, adapted scriptural genres to them, and echoed biblical style in them.

The earliest of his poems Milton thought worth saving were English paraphrases of Psalms 114 and 136, the first carrying the headnote 'This and the following Psalm were done by the Author at fifteen years old' (*Poems* 6). The last of his poems, *Paradise Regained*, published when he was sixty-three, was a debate poem like Job, with a plot taken from Luke, expounding an interpretation of Christ's redemptive work drawn from Hebrews, framed by angelic hymns, and foregrounded by human laments modelled on Psalms. That last poem is a particularly good place to see what reading the Bible meant to Milton, since it engages with Jesus at the moment when by his own reading of Scripture he understands his messiahship and holds to it throughout Satan's temptations. At that moment, the New Testament interprets the Old, changing, for Milton, the way the Hebrew Bible should thereafter be understood.

Milton explained how to read Scripture thematically in *De doctrina christiana* in Book 1, the book about beliefs: his analytic method was both comparative and linguistic. He 'proved' his points in that work by arranging citations from the Old Testament in the order of its canonical books and then from the New Testament in the order of its canonical books; he took that canonical order to be the arrangement God made for our understanding of the working out of his providential plan for human beings in history, more or less chronological and increasingly clear if read habitually from beginning to end, Genesis to Revelation. To read in this way is to read *typologically*, subjecting the Old Testament to a Christian hermeneutic, according to which events and persons of the Old are seen as foreshadowing or predicting those of the New Testament (see YP 6: 581; Budick 198–212; Lewalski 1979, 111–44).

In that same chapter 30 of Book 1, Milton also distinguished the Old and New Testament, or as he sometimes called them, the Hebrew and Greek Testament, into broad genres using the terms 'the law of Moses', 'the prophets', and 'the historical books'. In *The Reason of Church-Government*, he not only found lyrical poetry in the Bible, referring to the frequent songs throughout the law and prophets; he also found dramatic and heroic poetry in it, calling The Song of Solomon a divine pastoral with a double chorus, Revelation a tragedy with a sevenfold chorus, and Job a brief model of epic poetry (YP 1: 813). He further distinguished the poetry of the Bible into the genres of psalms in *De doctrina christiana* in Book 2, the book about worship. There he explained that God ought to be worshipped by 'methods which he himself has prescribed' (YP 6: 666), methods found in the Bible patterns or models of such psalm genres as hymn, thanksgiving, lament, and wisdom song (which he called witness, or 'an open profession of the true faith'). Milton thought that God spoke divine truths to chosen individuals who later wrote down what he had said. He knew that certain parts of the Bible showed textual corruption and thought some books lost, but believed the Old Testament better preserved than the New. Of the accuracy of Old Testament history he wrote, 'It is true that the . . . historical [books] cannot be certainly ascribed to a particular date or author, and also that the chronological accuracy of their narrative often seems suspect. Few or none, however, have called in doubt their doctrinal part.' He took the speech formulae of Scripture to offer imitable forms, not prescriptions, explaining: 'Even the Lord's Prayer is a pattern or model, rather than a formula to be repeated verbatim' (YP 6: 670).

Finally, both in *The Reason of Church-Government* as a young man and in *Paradise Regained*, Milton commented on the style of biblical poetry. In the former, he said that the Bible's songs were incomparable not in their divine argument alone, but in their very art of composition (YP 1: 816). In *Paradise Regained*, Satan proposes that Jesus study at 'Athens . . . mother of arts / And eloquence' (4.240–1) in order to 'learn the secret power / Of harmony in tones and numbers hit / By voice or hand, and various-measured verse' (4.254–6). Jesus refuses, having a better model of the power of harmony in mind:

>   if I would delight my private hours
> With music or with poem, where so soon
> As in our native language can I find
> That solace? All our Law and story strewed
> With hymns, our psalms with artful terms inscribed,
> Our Hebrew songs and harps in Babylon,
> That pleased so well our victor's ear, declare
> That rather Greece from us these arts derived;
> Ill imitated, while they loudest sing
> The vices of their deities, and their own
> In fable, hymn, or song, so personating
> Their gods ridiculous, and themselves past shame.
> Remove their swelling epithets thick-laid
> As varnish on a harlot's cheek, the rest,
> Thin-sown with aught of profit or delight,
> Will far be found unworthy to compare
> With Sion's songs, to all true tastes excelling,
> Where God is praised aright, and godlike men,
> The Holiest of Holies, and his saints;
> Such are from God inspired, not such from thee;
> Unless where moral virtue is expressed
> By light of nature not in all quite lost.   (4.331–52)

Jesus commends Hebrew poetry in an imitation of its 'artful terms': the binary rhetorical schemes of balance, antithesis, and parallelism (Alter 3–27; Berlin 18–30, 127–34; Frye 199–214; Kugel 49–58). Jesus thinks that the Old Testament is inspired truth; he thus infers that all its poetical figures too are significant. He treats its parallelism as a device of intellectual complementarity and he praises its purity. He frames a moral antithesis that pits a luxuriant style against a plain style by means of such contrasting pairs as 'remove' : 'compare', 'thick-laid' : 'thin-sown', 'their gods ridiculous' : 'themselves past shame'. He epitomizes the luxuriant by the metaphor of cosmetics and disease ('swelling epithets' are like harlot's varnish) and the plain by the literalized metaphor of clear sight (those praise aright who are inspired by the light of God or the 'light of nature'). His moral antithesis accordingly forms an aesthetic antithesis – good men have good taste and prefer biblical to hellenic poetry.

Milton was habituated to these three modes of reading – thematic, generic, stylistic – and practised them simultaneously. Since he read both Hebrew and Greek and used both the Junius-Tremellius Latin Bible and the *Biblia Sacra Polyglotta* of Brian Walton, he was not committed to a particular translation and did not signal the importance of Scripture to his poetry merely by echoing the language of the King James Version (Sims, in Hunter; Shawcross; but see Sims 1962). What Milton uniquely did among the seventeenth century's great religious poets was to become as far as possible a biblical poet himself, not reproducing the language but reconstituting the themes, genres, and stylistic figures of Scripture within his own religious poetry. What he uniquely did in *Paradise Regained* was to use the lyric genres of Psalms to foreground, highlight, or emotionally colour the important moments in a debate between Satan and Jesus; to take his plot from an event in the life of Jesus as given in Luke's Gospel in preference to the others (Pope); to shape that plot like a judicial debate modelled on the testing of Job (Lewalski 1966); and to centre the debate on a conflict between Jesus and Satan over the interpretation of messiahship derived from the Letter to the Hebrews. The debate instances how Milton read Scripture for its themes.

Theme: Satan and Jesus discuss sonship

In *Paradise Regained* Satan quotes Scripture in his own cause and the Son responds with interpretations that wrest Scripture back from him again. Milton constructs a dramatic conflict by opposing to Satan's literal but worldly reading of the biblical theme of messiahship an evolving higher reading of the theme by the Son (Radzinowicz 1984; Martz 1960). Satan, who apparently has read through the Hebrew Bible with an inquiring but cold eye, makes an adversarial or ironic use of scriptural quotations, seeking to persuade the Son that they define the Messiah as an earthly king, for on that basis Jesus might betray the spiritual values in Holy Writ. Jesus replies with an inspired reading of scriptural quotations to defeat Satan's strategy; he not only eludes entrapment, he enunciates the true meaning of messiahship by his truer hermeneutic.

At the beginning of the poem, Jesus, newly baptized in the Jordan, walks out into the desert in deep thought, reviewing the course of his life. He recollects his first delighted boyhood reading in Scripture and then a further reading, after Mary has told him how at his birth the angels proclaimed him Messiah, 'searching what was writ / Concerning the Messiah, to our scribes / Known partly, and soon found of whom they spake / I am' (1.280–3). What he knows of himself is what has been revealed in the Old Testament. Then Satan comes to the contest with him, straight from a council of the fallen angels called after the baptism, at which he reported that when Jesus rose out of the Jordan a voice from heaven was heard to say, 'This is my son beloved, in him am pleased' (1.85). That proclamation is a mixture of Psalm 2: 7, 'I will declare the decree: . . . Thou art my Son, This day have I begotten thee', and Isaiah 42: 1, 'Behold my servant, whom I uphold; mine elect, in whom my soul delighteth.' What Satan knows of the Son is also what *he* has read in the Old Testament. But since he reads literally Psalm 2: 6, 'Yet have I set my King upon my holy hill of Zion', he construes the next verse, 'Thou art my Son', just as literally: Jesus is of the line of King David: *ergo* the 'decree' is a coronation formula. Hence Satan's attack on the Son is double: one prong is to strike a treaty with the claimant Son; all knees may bow to him, if he will bow to Satan. The other prong is subversive: to alienate Father from Son by showing him unworthy of inheritance. But Jesus already has read:

> that my way must lie
> Through many a hard assay even to the death,
> Ere I the promised kingdom can attain.
> Or work redemption for mankind, whose sins'
> Full weight must be transferred upon my head.　　　　(1.263–7)

He knows, that is, that his messiahship includes priesthood, also an office once dependent on lineage and inheritance (Lev. 8: 1–13) but now on calling and merit (Heb. 5: 4–10). The 'decree' for him is therefore an appointment not to worldly kingship but to high priesthood and self-sacrifice.

The contest between Satan and the Son concludes in the epic as it concluded in Luke 4: 9–13, with a last tussle over Scripture. Satan places the Son on the highest pinnacle of the temple and scornfully invites him to stand:

> For it is written, [God] will give command
> Concerning thee to his angels, in their hands
> They shall uplift thee, lest at any time
> Thou chance to dash thy foot against a stone.　　　　(4.556–9)

That taunting quotation of Psalm 91: 11 assumes that Jesus, only a perfect man, will not be saved by means of angelic levitation. Jesus rebukes Satan from Deuteronomy 6: 16: 'Also it is written, / Tempt not the Lord thy God, he said and stood. / But Satan smitten with amazement fell' (4.560–2). Jesus resists Satan's temptations to abdicate his spiritual mission by constantly rebutting Satan's Scripture-laced arguments through better readings of Scripture. Milton took the pattern for Jesus' self-understanding from Hebrews, having praised its exposition of sonship in *De doctrina christiana*:

'The generation of the divine nature is by no one more sublimely or more fully explained than by the apostle to the Hebrews' (YP 6: 211).

The dispute between Satan and the Son over how to interpret Scripture on the meaning of sonship ranges throughout *Paradise Regained*; but one instance may stand for the whole, that where Satan turns Psalm 82: 6, 'I have said, Ye are gods and all of you are children of the Most High', against the Son. In Book 4 Jesus rejects the kingdoms of the world offered by Satan in exchange for worship of himself, Jesus' indignation being fully aroused by Satan's audacity '[to] offer them to me the Son of God, / To me my own, on such abhorred pact' (4.190–1). In response to that outraged self-identification, Satan quotes Psalm 82: 6:

> Be not so sore offended, Son of God;
> Though Sons of God both angels are and men,
> If I to try whether in higher sort
> Than these thou bear'st that title, have proposed
> What both from men and angels I receive
>
> .   .   .
>
> God of this world invoked and world beneath.   (4.196–200, 203)

Satan reads the verse just as Milton read it in *De doctrina christiana*: it is 'God's own words when he was addressing kings and magnates . . . kings are said to be gods, and yet no one would conclude from this text that the saints were of one essence with God' (YP 6: 213). To Satan too 'Sons of God' is God's formula for the delegation of power, analogous to the titles bestowed on him by men and angels, 'God of this world invoked and world beneath'. Hence when Jesus withstands the terror of the storm, Satan recurs to the verse to test him with a final reading:

> Then hear, O Son of David, virgin-born;
> For Son of God to me is yet in doubt
>
> .   .   .
>
> [I] Heard thee pronounced the Son of God beloved.
> Thenceforth I thought thee worth my nearer view
> And narrower scrutiny, that I might learn
> In what degree or meaning thou art called
> The Son of God, which bears no single sense;
> The Son of God I also am, or was,
> And if I was, I am; relation stands;
> All men are Sons of God; yet thee I thought
> In some respect far higher so declared.   (4.500–1, 513–21)

But Milton went on to say, 'We should notice . . . that the name "God" is by the will and permission of God the Father, not infrequently bestowed even upon angels and men (*how much more, then, upon the only begotten Son, the image of the Father!*)' (YP 6: 233; italics added). Both in Hebrews and to Milton the Psalm does bear one single sense, and Satan's summary of the action reaches that one sense although he himself misreads it:

> [I] have found thee
> Proof against all temptation as a rock
> Of adamant, and as a centre, firm
> To the utmost of mere man both wise and good,
> Not more; for honours, riches, kingdoms, glory
> Have been before contemned, and may again:
> Therefore to know what more thou art than man,
> Worth naming Son of God by voice from heaven,
> Another method I must now begin.   (4.532–40)

To be 'the utmost of mere man both wise and good' stands in Satan's hermeneutic as insufficient evidence that Jesus is 'more than man / Worth naming Son of God'. But that was the evidence by which Hebrews identified the redeemer priest: 'For we have not a high priest which cannot be touched with the feeling of our infirmities; but was in all points tempted like as we are, yet without sin' (Heb. 4: 15). The unique priest is the one who 'Though he were a Son, yet learned . . . obedience by the things which he suffered; and being made perfect, he became the author of eternal salvation unto all them that obey him' (Heb. 5: 8–9). The uniqueness of the Son's priesthood is his willing choice of a life of the most extreme humiliation and suffering. Milton understood the single sense of that heroic self-sacrifice as removing the need of any other mediation, 'if Christians would but know thir own dignitie, thir libertie, thir adoption, and let it not be wondered if I say, thir spiritual priesthood, whereby they have all equally access to any ministerial function whenever calld by thir own abilities and the church' (YP 7: 320).

Milton's thematic consideration of Psalms, Luke, and Hebrews supplied him not only with the language and interpretation for the Son and Satan in their debate over sonship, but also with an interpretation of sonship that emphasized priesthood over kingship, freeing Christians of his own day from the pretensions of the prelates. To follow the trail of his thinking through his biblical sources is to arrive at an understanding of the exemplary and salvatory action of the Son in standing fast against temptation, which makes that action a sufficient atonement and example for all men.

Style: The Old Testament and the Son's dream

In Jesus' preference for Hebrew poetry over Greek, Milton signalled his intention to imitate biblical hymns and psalms in *Paradise Regained* by imitating recognizably scriptural 'artful terms'. The artful terms he chose are the binary structures of balance, repetition, and antithesis, and the rhythms of natural emphasis that reinforce those parallel structures. He imitated a scriptural style in this way throughout the poem, but again one instance may stand for many.

Having rejected the first temptation to turn stones into bread, in Book 2 of *Paradise Regained*, after forty days in the wilderness Jesus for the first time is conscious of hunger as he prepares to sleep, but resolved not to 'mind it, fed with better thoughts that feed / Me hung'ring more to do my Father's will' (2.258–9). Meanwhile Satan, discomfited by the failure of the first temptation, after a second council of his peers skulks nearby with some of them. Surrounded by those hostile beings, Jesus lay down and 'slept, / And dreamed, as appetite is wont to dream / Of meats and drinks' (2.263–5). Satan takes advantage of the dream to bring on the banquet that concludes the temptation to appetite. The banquet scene is a Miltonic invention, not suggested by any of the Gospels; the dream episode, however, is dense with scriptural echoes, and its style is demonstrably parallelistic.

Milton invented the dream episode to exemplify Jesus' sense of mission represented in John 4: 34 – 'My meat is to do the will of him that sent me, and to finish his work' – and thus typologically in the New Testament to complete his earlier use of Deuteronomy 8: 3: 'Man lives not by bread only, but each word / Proceeding from the mouth of God; who fed / Our fathers here with manna' (1.349–51). Milton created the scene from Psalms 3 and 4 translated by him in 1653 (Radzinowicz 1978, 198–208), from two incidents in the life of Elijah (1 Kings 17: 5–6 and 19: 4–8), and from one incident in the life of Daniel (Dan. 1: 3–21).

In Psalm 3, the speaker seeks and receives God's help against enemies surrounding him by night. Its subtitle, 'A Psalm of David when he fled from Absalom his son', linked it to an occasion when David 'passed over the brook Kidron . . . *toward the way of the wilderness*' (2 Sam. 15: 23) pursued by the rebellious army of his son. Milton translated it as a dramatic monologue:

> Lord how many are thy foes
> How many those
> That in arms against me rise

Many are they
That of my life distrustfully thus say,
No help for him in God there lies.
But thou Lord art my shield my glory,
    Thee through my story
    The exalter of my head I count
      Aloud I cried
  Unto Jehovah, he full soon replied
And heard me from his holy mount.
I lay and slept, I waked again,
    For my sustain
Was the Lord. Of many millions
    The populous rout
  I fear not though incamping round about
They pitch against me their pavilions.
Rise Lord, save me my God for thou
    Hast smote ere now
On the cheek-bone all my foes,
    Of men abhorred
  Hast broke the teeth. This help was from the Lord
Thy blessing on thy people flows.

The passionate declamation has a strong forward rhythm. It is divided into four stanzas, each translating two verses of the original, rhyming a a b c c b, with a stress pattern 4 2 4 2 5 4. The poem on the page is not printed in strophes, however, and while the stress pattern is identical in each stanza, the syllabic pattern is very different indeed, running 7 4 7 4 10 8 / 9 5 7 3 10 8 / 8 4 8 5 10 10 / 8 4 7 4 10 8. Because the unaccented syllables are dominated by a strong idiomatic speech-stressing, the rhythmic structure of the verse sounds very much more important than its metrical structure. Spoken English stress and the allowable variations in English prosody over-ride a metre of feet; Milton's translation emphasizes as its musical principle a counterpointed rhythm of natural stress over the rhythm of quantity or feet. His willingness to translate eight psalms in a wide variety of metres suggests that he thought Hebrew verse observed an ancient freedom, privileging rhythm over metre. His version does not echo the words of previous translations; it imitates the parallelism of biblical poetry and its stress-rhythms.

In *Paradise Regained* Milton makes Jesus' beleaguered desert situation – when Satan 'takes a chosen band / Of spirits likest to himself in guilt / To be at hand' (2.236–8) – comparable to that of David in the wilderness; those versicles (4 10 4 syllables rhyming a b a) even pick up the rhythmic effect of his psalm translation. The Son sleeps conscious of hunger. During the night he dreams of God's feeding Elijah and Daniel in the wilderness; the dream is borrowed from Psalm 4, Milton's translation of the relevant verses reading:

> Into my heart more joy
> And gladness thou hast put
> Than when a year of glut
> Their stores doth over-cloy
> And from their plenteous grounds
> With vast increase their corn and wine abounds.
> In peace at once will I
> Both lay me down and sleep
> For thou alone dost keep
> Me safe where'er I lie
> As in a rocky cell
> Thou Lord alone in safety mak'st me dwell.

In the episode in *Paradise Regained*, Milton in effect reverses those two stanzas, imagining a sleep in which joy at God's presence is figured as a dream of receiving food from his storehouse (2.252–78); he fills the gap in the account of David's experience in Psalm 3 between 'I lay and slept, I waked again' with an experience drawn from Psalm 4 which accounts for the emotion with which David in the original and Jesus in *Paradise Regained* awoke: 'I fear not though camping round about / They pitch against me their pavilions.' Satan interprets Jesus' dream literally and provocatively: he reminds Jesus how God fed others who hungered in the wilderness, adding 'Of thee these forty days none hath regard.' The Son challenges his logic – 'what conclud'st thou hence?' – and rebuts it with a pithy antithesis: 'They all had need, I as thou seest have none' (2.315–18).

Milton recounts the Son's dream in the third person as a narrator's summary; he does not enter the sleeper's consciousness, but glosses the dream in advance as wish-fulfilment – Jesus 'dreamed, as appetite is wont to dream'. And he presents it as temptation – Jesus imagines that 'with Elijah he partook'. The summary, although plainstyle, artfully creates complex metrical effects:

> Him thought, he by the brook of Cherith stood
> And saw the ravens with their horny beaks
> Food to Elijah bringing even and morn,
> Though ravenous, taught to abstain from what they brought.   (2.266–9)

The quatrain, three pentameters and one casual hexameter unsupplied with elisions, within the envelope rhyme 'Him thought' : 'they brought', is bound together by the internal rhyme 'thought . . . though . . . taught' and half rhymes 'brook . . . stood . . . food'. Milton then summarizes the feeding of Elijah in an even plainer and pithier style than that of his source. 1 Kings 19: 5–8 reads:

And as he lay and slept under a juniper tree, behold, then an angel touched him, and said unto him, Arise and eat. And he looked, and behold there was a cake baked on the coals, and a cruse of water at his head. And he did eat and drink, and laid him down again. And the angel of the Lord came a second time, and tended him, and said, Arise and eat; because the journey is too great for thee. And he arose, and did eat and drink and went in the strength of that meat forty days and nights unto Horeb the mount of God.

Milton uses fewer than half as many words as the biblical scenario to create the spaceless placeless specificity of dreams in another plain but rhetorically artful passage:

> He saw the prophet also how he fled
> Into the desert, and how there he slept
> Under a juniper; then how awaked,
> He found his supper on the coals prepared,
> And by the angels was bid rise and eat,
> And eat the second time after repose,
> The strength whereof sufficed him forty days.   (2.270–6)

Among its devices are medial and terminal slant rhymes 'prophet' : 'desert' : 'fled' / 'slept'; sound repetitions in 'prophet', 'juniper', 'supper', 'prepared', and 'repose'; anaphora in 'how he fled . . . how there he slept . . . then how awaked', and ploche in 'and eat, / And eat'. Milton adopts the linguistic register of the King James Version – 'juniper', 'coals', 'arise and eat', 'strength', 'forty days' – and extends it – 'fled', 'supper', and 'awaked'. If he seems to have overlooked the most resonant phrase in 1 Kings – 'because the journey is too great for thee' – he has actually reserved it for a later echo and variation. If wish-fulfilment, the dream incorporates Jesus' hope for God's material aid as the faithful in the past received it. The salvation theology of Psalms 3 and 4 makes a different point: God sustains the believer by his inner presence, not by literal food.

Thus 'wore out night'; and Milton glosses the Son's awakening as vulnerable:

As lightly from his grassy couch uprose
Our Saviour, and found all was but a dream,
Fasting he went to sleep, and fasting waked.   (2.282–4)

Satan reads the awakening as disappointed: an angel came to Elijah with food, an unfulfilled dream came to the Son. Then Milton closes his account, rhythmically echoing but overturning the meaning of that resonant line in 1 Kings. Elijah was fed 'because the journey is too great for thee'; the Son's case is different: 'they all had need, I as thou seest have none' (2.318). Whether the Son rest on grassy couch in the wilderness or in rocky cell in exile, the Father fulfils his promise; and in the Son the fulfilment is total trust. His response to Satan has parallelistic pith – 'They . . . had need, I . . . have none'; seconding alliteration in 'They' : 'thou', 'all' : 'as', 'have' : 'had', 'need' : 'none'; and medial near rhyme 'need' : 'seest' : 'none'.

The metaphorical plainness of *Paradise Regained* has been frequently remarked – as have the exceptions in images of light and dark, desert and pastoral life, the society of heaven and the solitude of the wilderness; and in scripturally derived key words that work both literally and metaphorically, nouns like 'hand', 'sheep', 'head', 'root', 'fruit', 'light' and verbs like 'stand', 'fall', 'feed', 'guide' (Robson 124–37; Elliott 227–42; Fowler; Ferry). But the poem's richly biblical parallelism of structure and rhythm has perhaps been insufficiently remarked.

Genre: wisdom song and the Son as autobiographer

Imitating biblical genres, Milton framed *Paradise Regained* within two angelic hymns, based on Luke's New Testament songs conflated with Old Testament psalms. Luke incorporated in the chapters before he treated the temptation in the wilderness four non-canonical psalms made in imitation of Old Testament psalmody (Mowinckel 2: 122–5): Mary's Magnificat, Zacharias's Benedictus, the angels' Gloria, and Simeon's Nunc Dimittis. Milton framed his poem by combining the Benedictus and the Gloria with topoi from hymnic psalms. At the end of the first temptation, he wrote two laments by those closest to Jesus, left behind while he sojourned in the wilderness, one by Mary and one by the disciples, which preface the long second temptation and intensify its emotional power. For Mary's lament, he put the Magnificat in the past and reinforced it by psalmic lament formulae; for the disciples, he used Zacharias's Nunc Dimittis in a similar manner. For the self-characterization of the Son (but see Nohrnberg; Kerrigan), he imitated an Old Testament poetic form, the wisdom song, and his use of that genre may illustrate the value of his generic analysis of the Bible (Radzinowicz 1987).

Wisdom songs are found in Proverbs, Ecclesiastes, Job, Psalms, and many of the prophets. Typically in wisdom song, a learned poet introduces himself as a scribe, refers to his words as a private meditation, confesses that he speaks from his own insight, asks God's approval of his thoughts, and then delivers moral truths, rooting his motive for morality in his fear of God. A blend of wise saws and personal religious awareness, his moral wisdom is typically couched in linked proverbs coupled with exhortations and offered within a stylized autobiography. The scribe emphasizes God's law: its revelation began his enlightenment and he often contrasts his former foolishness with his present understanding by way of the formula 'then I knew'. Sometimes but not often a personality may be discerned behind the stylized autobiography; usually the speaker mentions only his age and general situation. His three main themes are (1) the contrast between the two 'ways', 'roads', or 'paths' of life – worldly, deceitful, and barrenly prosperous versus pious, honest, and ultimately favoured by God; (2) the doctrine of the proper or ripe time or season for human acts and of man's responsibility to discern that time; and (3) the testimony of creation and history to God's justice and concern with man's moral life. Its stylistic signature is the proverb: its pith, clarity with gnomic suggestiveness, memorability promoted often by enumeration (Von Rad 24–53). Elihu (Job 32: 6–10, 18–20) instances its autobiography, proverbs, and themes:

I am young, and ye are very old; wherefore I was afraid, and durst not show you mine opinion.

I said, Days should speak, and multitude of years should teach wisdom.

But there is a spirit in man: and the inspiration of the Almighty giveth them understanding.

Great men are not always wise: neither do the aged understand judgment.

Therefore I said, Hearken to me; I also will show mine opinion.

For I am full of matter; the spirit within me constraineth me.

Behold my belly is as wine which hath no vent; it is ready to burst like new bottles.

I will speak that I may be refreshed: I will open my lips and answer.

So does Jesus in Luke 10: 22, 'All things are delivered to me of my Father: and no man knoweth who the Son is, but the Father; and who the Father is but the Son, and he to whom the Son will reveal him.' Wisdom song is composed to attest to the scribe's personal faith and ethos quite as much as to his learning and reason; in *Paradise Regained*, Jesus' opening 'holy Meditations' (1.196–293) imitate both its witness and autobiography.

Alone, Jesus thinks through the chronological course of his intellectual history, beginning and ending with his present state of mind. He begins with a 'multitude of thoughts' that 'swarm', while he 'consider[s]' what he feels, hears, and knows of his role; and he ends calmly, 'led' by 'a strong motion' that he does not yet understand but accepts, 'For what concerns my knowledge God reveals.' These contrasting states encompass the common wisdom themes, 'where is wisdom to be found?' and 'trust in the Lord', the first seen, for example, in Proverbs 4: 26, 'Ponder the path of thy feet, and let all thy ways be established'; and the last in Proverbs 3: 5, 'Trust in the Lord with all thine heart; and lean not unto thine own understanding.'

Between these moods, Jesus passes through two stages of insight common to sages and then two unique to the Son (Stein 36–47); the stages are intrinsic to wisdom song. The first concerns childhood vocation. When Jesus recalls that as a child 'all my mind was set / Serious to learn and know' and that 'therefore above my years, / The Law of God I read, and found it sweet, / Made it my whole delight' (1.201–8), he divulges a youth much like the psalmist's in Psalm 119: 9, 14, and 16:

> Wherewithal shall a young man cleanse his way? By taking heed thereto according to thy word . . .
> I have rejoiced in the way of thy testimonies, as much as in all riches . . .
> I will delight myself in thy statutes: I will not forget thy word.

His decision to 'do / What might be public good' reflects a second stage in his conception of his role in the world – 'by winning works to conquer willing hearts' (1.203–4, 222) – also much like the psalmist's in Psalm 78: 2 and 72:

> I will open my mouth in a parable: I will utter dark sayings of old . . .
> So he fed them according to the integrity of his heart; and guided them by the skilfulness of his hands.

Wisdom autobiography is impersonal because it claims that the speaker testifies to God, not simply as someone who stepped forward, but as someone sent (Ricoeur 119–54). Jesus' soliloquy of witness follows God's declaration that He sends and inspires the 'humiliation and strong sufferance' of 'This perfect man, by merit called my Son' (1.160, 165). Isaiah 43: 8–10 represents God's calling of a witness (or *martus*):

> Bring forth the blind people that have eyes, and the deaf that have ears.
> Let all the nations be gathered together, and let the people be assembled:
> Who among them can declare this, and show us former things?

Let them bring forth their witnesses, that they may be justified: or let them hear,
and say, it is the truth.
Ye are my witnesses, saith the Lord, and my servant whom I have chosen,
That ye may know and believe me, and understand that I am he.

The witness is a teacher, but more than that he is a servant, ultimately the
suffering servant. Hence the chosen one acknowledges in his impersonal
autobiography that what matters is not how he is a particular human being
(he might be blind or deaf), but that he is a witness (yet he has eyes or ears).
The consequences of accepting the role of witness or *martus* are 'humiliation
and strong sufferance', as in Psalm 44: 22: 'Nay for thy sake we are slain all
the day long, and accounted as sheep for the slaughter.' Hence Milton shows
Jesus move on from the resolve to teach to an acceptance of the role of
witness 'through many a hard assay even to the death' (1.264).

In a final stage of insight in the autobiographical soliloquy, Jesus having
accepted his role as suffering servant – 'Yet neither thus disheartened or dis-
mayed / The time prefixed I waited' (1.268–9) – arrives at the conclusion, 'I
knew the time / Now full, that I no more should live obscure, / But openly
begin' (1.286–8). The Son's cognizance of the ripeness of his time adapts the
final wisdom theme.

As a wise person Jesus learnt about himself and his role by meditating on
the world God created, on his historical moment, and on revelation in
history. He inferred his messiahship and read in it his role both as a wise
teacher and heroic martyr; he witnessed God in those inferences and
proposed for himself a period of wisdom-teaching followed by perfect
obedience in suffering. His inference does not foreclose further revelation;
indeed Jesus anticipates that what he now begins openly as teaching must
end silently and in pain. Milton adapted wisdom song to impersonal autobiography to display the resolution of *two* questions, 'how is man to live?'
and 'who is the messiah?' In *Paradise Regained* it is true both that Jesus
knows, in advance of trial, the essential form of his mission and that he is
capable of attaining to profounder understanding. To hold fast to both these
truths is to respond to Milton's biblicism, which would reject an interpretation of Jesus' life in the poem whereby the search for identity and the
exemplification of moral choice are incompatible alternatives.

For Milton the reading of Scripture in the case of his brief epic confirmed or
authorized his themes as truthful and reasonable; gave him a style expressive
of resilience, toughness, shrewdness, and pith; and put him in touch with a
genre capable also of an abstract serenity conveying the moral equipoise of

purposes long maturing. These effects were the rewards of listening for biblical resonances to the poet who prayed that his last poem would be a

> prompted song else mute
>
> of deeds
> Above heroic, though in secret done,
> And unrecorded left through many an age,
> Worthy t'have not remained so long unsung.   (1.12, 14–17)

Milton's attitude towards his scriptural sources inheres in those words: the poet takes strength from his inspiration to rerecord heroic biblical deeds, and sings them anew for his own times, for in Sion's songs 'God is prais'd aright, and Godlike men.' The spirit that led Jesus into the desert inspires Milton's hoped-for 'Song to Generations' (YP 1: 706).

Reading list

Alter, Robert, *The Art of Biblical Poetry* (New York, 1985)

Berlin, Adele, *The Dynamics of Biblical Parallelism* (Bloomington, IN, 1985)

Boitani, Piero and Anna Torli, eds., *Medieval and Pseudo-Medieval Literatures* (Cambridge, 1984)

Budick, Sanford, 'Milton and the Scene of Interpretation: From Typology toward Midrash', in Hartman and Budick, eds., *Midrash and Literature*

Cook, Eleanor and Chaviva Hošek, eds., *Centre and Labyrinth: Essays in Honour of Northrop Frye* (Toronto, 1983)

Elliott, Emory, 'Milton's Biblical Style in *Paradise Regained*', *Milton Studies* 6 (1974), 227–42

Ferry, Anne Davidson, *Milton's Epic Voice* (Cambridge, MA, 1963)

Fisher, Alan, 'Why is *Paradise Regained* So Cold?', *Milton Studies* 14 (1980), 195–217

Fowler, Alastair, '*Paradise Regained*: Some Problems of Style', in Boitani and Torli, eds., *Medieval and Pseudo-Medieval Literatures*

Frye, Northrop, *The Great Code* (New York, 1982)

Hartman, Geoffrey H. and Sanford Budick, eds., *Midrash and Literature* (New Haven, 1986)

Hunter, William B., Jr, *A Milton Encyclopedia* (Lewisburg, PA, 1978–81)

Kelley, Maurice, ed., *Christian Doctrine*, trans. John Carey, YP vol. 6

Kermode, Frank, ed., *The Living Milton* (London, 1960)

Kerrigan, William, 'The Riddle of *Paradise Regained*', in Woycik and Frontain, eds., *Poetic Prophecy*

Kugel, James L., *The Idea of Biblical Poetry* (New Haven, 1981)

Lewalski, Barbara K., *Milton's Brief Epic* (Providence, RI, 1966)

Protestant Poetics and the Seventeenth-Century Religious Lyric (Princeton, 1976)

'Paradise Lost' and the Rhetoric of Literary Forms (Princeton, 1985)

MacKellar, Walter, ed., *Paradise Regained*, vol. 4, *A Variorum Commentary on the Poems of John Milton* (New York, 1975)

Martz, Louis L., '*Paradise Regained*: The Meditative Combat', *ELH* 27 (1960), 223–47

The Paradise Within (New Haven, 1964)

Poet of Exile: A Study of Milton's Poetry (New Haven, 1980)

Mowinckel, Sigmund, *The Psalms in Israel's Worship*, 2 vols. (Oxford, 1962)

Nohrnberg, James, 'Paradise Regained By One Greater Man: Milton's Wisdom Epic as a "Fable of Identity"', in Cook and Hošek, eds., *Centre and Labyrinth*

Patrick, J. Max and Roger Sundell, eds., *Milton and the Art of Sacred Song* (Milwaukee, 1979)

Pope, Elizabeth Marie, *'Paradise Regained': The Tradition and the Poem* (Baltimore, 1947)

Radzinowicz, Mary Ann, *Towards 'Samson Agonistes': The Growth of Milton's Mind* (Princeton, 1978)

'Paradise Regained as Hermeneutic Combat', *University of Harvard Studies in Literature* 16 (1984), 99–107

'Paradise Inferred and Deferred: Wisdom in *Paradise Regained*', *Journal of English and Germanic Philology*, forthcoming 1988

Rajan, Balachandra, ed., *The Prison and the Pinnacle* (Toronto, 1973)

Revard, Stella, 'The Gospel of John and *Paradise Regained*: Jesus as "True Light"', in Sims and Ryken, eds., *Milton and Scriptural Tradition*

Ricoeur, Paul, *Essays on Biblical Interpretation*, ed. Lewis S. Mudge (London, 1981)

Robson, W. W., 'The Better Fortitude', in Kermode, ed., *The Living Milton*

Shawcross, John T., 'Bibles', in Hunter, *A Milton Encyclopedia*

Sims, James H., *The Bible in Milton's Epics* (Gainesville, FL, 1962)

'Milton and the Bible', in Hunter, *A Milton Encyclopedia*

Sims, James H. and Leland Ryken, eds., *Milton and Scriptural Tradition: The Bible into Poetry* (Columbia, MO, 1984)

Stein, Arnold, *Heroic Knowledge* (Minneapolis, 1957)

Von Rad, Gerhard, *Wisdom in Israel* (London, 1972)

Woycik, Jan and Raymond-Jean Frontain, eds., *Poetic Prophecy in Western Literature* (Rutherford, NJ, 1984)

15   A reading of *Samson Agonistes*

In 1671, when Milton published *Paradise Regained*, he had another piece printed along with it in the same volume. The title page read: 'PARADISE REGAIN'D, A POEM In IV Books. To which is added *Samson Agonistes*'. Although Milton is reported to have composed his brief epic during the four years that had passed since the publication of *Paradise Lost* in 1667, no one knows when he wrote his tragedy. In *Paradise Lost* and *Paradise Regained* we hear the voice of the poet, a strong presence, pursuing 'Things unattempted yet in prose or rhyme' (*PL* 1.16), sharing with us his prayers for inspiration (*PL* 3.1–3) and his judgments of the poem's actions. In *Samson Agonistes*, however, we make no contact with that authoritative voice except in the preface, entitled 'Of that Sort of Dramatic Poem Which Is Call'd Tragedy', a pedagogical note which requests that we read the drama in the context of Aeschylus', Sophocles', and Euripides' works, recognizing the power of ancient Greek tragedy to embody truth.

Even though the poet does not speak to us in the tragedy itself, however, our entry to *Samson Agonistes* is inevitably through the great visionary and doctrinaire epics to which it is 'added'. Milton's preface tells us that in the tragedy we will find ourselves in the same Christian humanist world to which the epics belong – the world as viewed by the philosopher Cicero and 'the Apostle Paul himself' – and that, in submitting ourselves to this tragedy, we will enter an experience graver, more moral, and to our greater spiritual good than even that of *Paradise Lost* or *Paradise Regained*; for the tragedy will work directly on our individual innermost selves, addressing the roots of sin and suffering in us.

To clarify the experience that a reader of his tragedy should expect to undergo, Milton offers the traditional Aristotelian analogy for the experience of tragic art, that of medical 'purging' or 'tempering'. To explain tragic catharsis by a similar analogy from today's medicine we could refer to innoculation: when injected with a controlled dose of the antigen of a disease, our own immune system produces antibodies that restore homeo-

PARADISE REGAIN'D.

A POEM.

In IV BOOKS.

To which is added

SAMSON AGONISTES.

The Author

JOHN MILTON.

LONDON,

Printed by *J. M.* for *John Starkey* at the *Mitre* in *Fleetstreet*, near *Temple-Bar.*
MDCLXXI.

Title page from *Paradise Regained*

stasis (that 'temper and reduce to just measure') and that remain in us to fight powerfully for homeostasis against that disease when we meet it again in its full force and naturally occurring form. What is the 'disease' for which Milton wants his tragedy to prepare his readers once they have witnessed the loss and recovery of paradise? It is 'pity and fear, or terror' and 'such like passions', that is, all pain – both positive (pity) and negative (terror) – that afflicts our emotional life as a result of sin. We should expect, then, that by entering into Samson's experience we will emerge strengthened in mind and spirit to meet such suffering directly in its full and complicated force in our world and in ourselves.

In *Samson Agonistes*, we are not shown heaven or hell or paradise or even the wilderness, but rather a world that we can recognize. It is the world of family (parent, lover, wife); of friendship (colleagues, countrymen); of conventional beliefs and values (religious, societal, political); and of glimpses of our intersection with the divine. It is the world of personal discovery and of commitment to an individual life's meaning; of exhilaration in the achievement of goals against the odds; of betrayal and abandonment; of personal failure and despair; of deep guilt; of the struggle for religious faith; of profound liberation; of the purest individual freedom within the confines of the flow of history.

It is also the political world, and the protagonist's struggle is played out in the context of a difficult international situation. In reading *Samson Agonistes*, we face issues not only of personal spiritual suffering and growth but of corporate humanity's struggle to exist with meaning as well. And finally, we may recognize that these issues were not distant history or myth but lived experience for Milton, who was as deeply concerned for England as were the Judges for Israel: its people had been chosen to act God's will in the world, had failed, and had now to find a way and a will, under oppression, to continue. It is a poem for all times, including our own.

Although the world of twelfth-century BC Palestine is consistently close to us in a way that the worlds of *Paradise Lost* and *Paradise Regained* are not, and although Samson is more ordinarily 'human' than either Christ or Adam, the protagonist we meet at the play's opening is still not someone whom we may readily feel to be 'one of us'. His violent life and his suffering have made him not likeable or even approachable. We meet him – a prisoner of war in forced labour – in rags, filthy, with the stench of 'air imprisoned also', eyes gouged out, living 'a life half dead', his own 'sepulchre, a moving grave' (102). His pain and humiliation are so excruciating, his potential violence so terrifying – poised on the brink of 'sudden rage to tear thee joint by joint' (953) – that when we see him we might wish 'like the choruses of many Greek tragedies, to cry out and to turn away our eyes' (Summers 156).

What we have to do, however, is not to *look* at this play – it was 'never intended' for the stage – but to listen; and with others of the drama's careful listeners over the past three hundred years we will hear the language of the spirit complicating the words spoken by all the characters, words such as 'strength', 'dark', 'light', 'blindness', 'vision', 'prison', 'liberty', 'choice', 'promise', 'reason', 'fool', 'random', 'chance', 'necessity', 'love', 'law', 'deliverance'.

What kind of person is Samson as Milton conceives him? He has been a tremendous military hero but not an effective leader, as evidenced by his own people's disloyalty. The famous battle at Ramath-Lechi (142–5 and 263–6) is a case in point. There two very important events occurred. First, Samson, alone and with only a bone weapon, defeated, indeed slaughtered, an entire well-equipped, top-flight, Philistine army division, clearing the way for Hebrew independence and the end of the Philistine occupation and oppression. Secondly, not one Hebrew tribe or individual followed Samson's lead to capitalize on the successful resistance, and Israel remained a subject nation.

In the course of the tragedy, Samson comes to realize two truths that have impaired his divinely given mission to liberate Israel. The first he has learned before the opening of the play: that his own people have failed their divine national calling, have grown 'to love bondage more than liberty', / Bondage with ease than strenuous liberty' (270–1). Milton had experienced the same abandonment of the revolutionary cause in England where, after twenty years' labour to which he believed God had called him and other great leaders of the attempted Commonwealth, the English people, preferring 'bondage with ease', chose to recall the exiled King from France – just as if, Milton exclaimed in *The Ready and Easy Way to Establish a Free Commonwealth* (1659), the Israelites of the Exodus, for whom God had parted the Red Sea waters, were to call themselves back a captain out of Egypt.

The second truth about his failure, however, comes to Samson as utterly new knowledge. It comes unevenly, in deep pain, and in the course of the tragedy, as Samson, the loyal but unreflecting strong man, enters through his own moral weakness into the spiritual core of his political mission and is thereby reborn as the leader he was destined to be, though only in the moment of his death.

I

Both Milton's Chorus of Hebrews in *Samson Agonistes* and readers of the drama witness Samson's suffering and his regeneration. Milton may well

have intended for his readers, beginning with seventeenth-century English
men and women and extending to ourselves, to measure their own ability to
respond to Samson's experience against the ability of that Chorus of ordinary citizens. These Hebrews are law-abiding and decent. Although they
have not had the clarity of vision or the courage to join Samson in the revolution, they also do not abandon him now; but they remain ignorant of how
to help him or themselves, struggling without success to understand the
meaning of their experience. In the end both witnesses – they and we – are
purged. What are the temperings that occur?

When we first meet Samson, his perceptions are very much like the
Chorus's. He feels the agony of a promise, of his life's mission, betrayed:

> Promise was that I
> Should Israel from Philistian yoke deliver;
> Ask for this great deliverer now, and find him
> Eyeless in Gaza at the mill with slaves.   (38–41)

Although it was God who had promised Israel's deliverance, Samson is
hesitant simply to blame providence for his present plight, considering:
'what if all foretold / Had been fulfilled but through mine own default . . . ?'
(44–5). If he had kept the secret of his strength as God had commanded, he
would still have his sight and his freedom to continue the fight for Israel's
liberation. Yet, he asks, if God had a mission for his great physical strength
to accomplish, why did God create him with such a simple mind and weak
will that he could be won over by a woman's temptations? 'But what is
strength without a double share / Of wisdom? . . . Proudly secure, yet liable
to fall / By weakest subtleties' (53–6). Dalila, Samson feels, though physically 'weakest', had really been too psychologically subtle and emotionally
powerful for him, whose only human resource was his great physical
strength. Why did not God make him wiser? Samson remains, in his suffering, a man of faith and tries not to 'quarrel with the will / Of highest
dispensation' (60–1); but he is prepared at this point in the face of his experience to consider God's will for him, in spite of prophesies, to be 'above my
reach to know' (62). His faith has become blind.

It is worthwhile for readers of *Samson Agonistes* here to recall their reading
of Milton's earlier published work. The idea that God's human creatures
cannot reason toward and know God's will for them is quite contrary to the
spirit of *Paradise Lost*, which was written to 'assert eternal providence'
(1.25). In heaven and in Eden before the Fall, the entire working laws of
their universe are known intuitively to the angels and to the man and woman
who live in harmony with the divine ordering of the worlds in which God has

placed them. Just as material bodies interact with no need to understand the physical laws of nature that underlie their movements, so also in unfallen worlds do rational and spiritual beings interact perfectly with no need to articulate, to separate out and analyze, the moral laws that guide their inter-action. There are no written laws in heaven, the angel Abdiel explains, because 'our reason is our law'; angelic and human minds continually make moral choices in perfect accordance with the universal Good. Milton shows us angelic hymns and dances and Edenic perfection in his epic because he wants our imaginations to reach for a vision of the sheer elegance, at once mystical and mathematical, the heart-stopping beauty of the spiritual whole-ness of God's creation. Only in vision, prayer, and poetry will we glimpse the whole, of course. But having seen it, we are better able to grasp how very fragmented our own moral experience is, and how that fragmentation is reflected by our need for individually expressed laws to govern our behaviour.

After his fall into sin, Adam has trouble imagining how God, who is Perfection, can remain in relationship with sinners. How can Perfection incorporate into itself evil? Adam's question is answered by the Archangel Michael (*PL* 12.280–306); and we need to hold his answer as firmly as possible in our minds when we share Samson's struggle with this same ques-tion. For Milton's God will not send an angel for every crisis; like Samson, we will have to draw on what he has already given us.

Michael answers that God remains in relationship with sinners, rather than abandoning them to evil, by extracting and giving individual expression to selected moral dimensions of the whole law of being, which sin has shattered. These articulated moral principles are given their first expression as the Mosaic commandments, 'so many and so various', which serve first of all to preserve the moral sense, the human capacity for moral awareness. We are given the fragmented, but explicit, commandments so that we can continue to recognize a sin when we meet it. As we have seen in all of Milton's portrayals of temptation, evil's most formidable strength is its ability to be attractive, to assault all of our senses, emotions, and rationality with the powerful claim that it is really not evil but good. God articulates laws for human beings, then, as graspable pieces of reality for them to hold on to in the midst of this assault.

It is no easy contest, however, because what abets the attraction for us of evil is the pain of our own guilt. If only we truly did not know that our actions were sinful, then we would be free from this guilt. But here is the crux of the answer to Adam's question: it is that guilt that keeps the way open for the sinner's relationship with goodness. That very pain is God's loving gift to his people of a continuing awareness of the truth. To remain, after sin, in relationship with God, they must attain a full awareness of their own guilt, or depravity:

> And therefore was law given them to evince
> Their natural pravity, by stirring up
> Sin against law to fight . . .   (*PL* 12.287–9)

Then will come a corresponding awareness of the sheer power of the Good, of God who can take this full awareness of guilt and turn it into faith.

How this process will work out in human history, Michael explains, is through the self-offering of Christ for human sin; his incarnation and atonement will abrogate the Mosaic law. God's people are thus to come through a strict belief that they *must* keep the law to a realization and full admission that they *cannot*. Then the moral depth gained by such an admission will yield the ultimate rational insight: they will understand that this collection of laws itself is imperfect because it can 'discover sin, but not remove' (12.290). The law is still their link to the divine; better to stumble blindly but faithfully in attempting adherence to it, like the Hebrews and Samson, than to live cut off from Truth, without that law and its attendant suffering, like the Philistines. But ultimately, 'in full time', when they have been 'disciplined . . . from flesh to spirit', the law will lead its truest followers to transcend its own limits, taking them from God's 'imposition of strict laws' to their own 'free / Acceptance of large grace'. 'Works of law' – efforts to observe the commandments, those articulated fragments of the world order – are, then, when we have persevered to the attainment of a full awareness of our own impossible but highly desired relationship to perfection, redeemable by God, who makes them acceptable 'works of faith', deeds like those of the unfallen angels, done in genuine harmony with God's will, the divine order (12.301–6).

What is most important for a reader of Milton's tragic drama to understand is that the second function of the law can come into being only after the first function has had its full effect. This does not happen for the Chorus in *Samson*: they are servants under bondage, not yet fully aware of the sin in themselves which the law discovers but cannot remove, pious followers of the Lord, but incapable of faith. Samson, however, reaches the limit of the law and hence is able to transcend and fulfil it. As Samson becomes capable of facing in himself a tremendous sense of guilt, so he proves capable finally of a relentless belief in the existence of that justice which includes within itself the mercy of a chastising Father (see Heb. 8: 5–10).

That belief is hard-won, through a struggle with Samson's own physical, emotional, and moral pain. To such a struggle Milton typically subjects his characters. Their dilemma is always to distinguish pain from evil and good from pleasure. Samson, when we meet him at the play's beginning, feels his own miseries – his blindness, his captivity and slavery, his humiliation – to be 'So many, and so huge, that each apart / Would ask a life to wail' (65–6). His friends and his father Manoa attempt to help Samson ward off a serious psychological depression that would add to his troubles. 'Deject not then so overmuch thyself / Who hast of sorrow thy full load besides' (213–14), the Chorus says; 'wisest men / Have erred, and by bad women been deceived; / And shall again, pretend they ne'er so wise' (210–12). This is the world's wisdom: nobody, after all, is perfect. Manoa, in his own pain, tries to fit God to the world's scheme according to which Samson's suffering is out of proportion to his offence:

> Alas methinks whom God hath chosen once
> To worthiest deeds, if he through frailty err,
> He should not so o'erwhelm . . .
> Be it but for honour's sake of former deeds.   (368–72)

For Samson's spiritual struggle, Manoa's slight impiety, his readiness to argue with the Lord, is more helpful than the attempted worldly wisdom of the Chorus, who views Samson's case as a 'mirror of our fickle state' – just one of those things – and who views God's will for human beings on such an occasion as being 'justifiable', but only inscrutably so.

When he hears his own thoughts reflected in the words of his friends and father, Samson is able to gain some perspective on what they imply. A belief in God's inscrutability is in effect a denial of God's justice. This is a very important insight for Samson. A just God does not reward evil or punish virtue; if a person feels an affliction to be from God – that is, if he experiences a sense during his tribulations of heaven's desertion – then he must accept his suffering as merited, and its justice as comprehensible; he must seek out its cause and its cure. The spiritual fall of a moral creature is always the result of sin.

Instead of accepting an unjust or inscrutable God, Samson is able to continue to look for justice accessible to human understanding; he is thus led to reason back from the magnitude of the punishment to what must necessarily have been the magnitude of his offence:

> Appoint not heavenly disposition, father,
> Nothing of all these evils hath befall'n me
> But justly; I myself have brought them on,
> Sole author I, sole cause: if aught seem vile,

> As vile hath been my folly, who have profaned
> The mystery of God given me under pledge
> Of vow.   (373–9)

The Chorus also looks to the law to discover the causes of Samson's punishment. However, all it can find is a double breach of the law which forbids intermarriage with non-Jews. One consequence of the Chorus's own failure to see how its sin of servility breaches the spirit of the law is its inability to sense how the law embodies the unified 'mystery of God'. The Chorus holds many fragments, the 'letters' of the law, but cannot discriminate higher and lower, central and derivative. It cannot glimpse the law's wholeness, its 'spirit'. The expression it gives to its confusions about the law, however, helps Samson to straighten out his own responsibilities.

Thus, Samson has easily understood that his first non-Jewish marriage – to the Timnan woman – God allowed in order to fulfil the very purpose of the law against intermarriage, that is, to preserve God's people from falling captive to the false gods and morals of the heathens, in this case by seeking Israel's political liberation and religious freedom. Thinking from letter to spirit, Samson is led then to realize that in his second marriage he violently broke the spirit of that same law – not in marrying Dalila, but in revealing to her the secret of his strength. This illumination yields only fuller pain, since he is now able to see more clearly how his breaking ceremonial law in occasioning ritual honour to Dagon, the result of the captivity into which his sin drew him, is a betrayal not merely of ritual, but of his God-given moral relationship to his own people (448–57). For while their political captivity is their own fault and not his, the same moral weakness that binds them in political subjugation renders them all the more vulnerable to a religious confusion from which he, as their leader, has an even greater responsibility to protect them.

At the end of Manoa's visit, both the Chorus and Samson are near despair, but for different reasons. The Chorus suffers fear because it worships a God whom it believes to be, by human ethical standards, unjust (667–709):

> God of our fathers, what is man!
> That thou towards him with hand so various,
> Or might I say contrarious,
> Temper'st thy providence through his short course.   (667–70)

Samson, on the other hand, has clearly seen the depth of his own sin, his betrayal of God's trust; and this guilt is the truth that binds him to God's justice. He is at last ready, in his ensuing encounters with the Philistines, to realize that God himself operates by a law even more perfect than that by which Samson now, truthfully and accurately, judges himself.

II

The Philistine Dalila is an extraordinary woman, a beautiful, passionate, intelligent, life-filled person who is, however, spiritually anchorless and hopelessly adrift, 'the sumptuous Dalila floating' (1072). She has turned her foreign husband over to the authorities of her country, enjoying the role of civic heroine – 'how honourable, how glorious'; 'how meritorious with the gods' – as well as relief from the pressures to which the authorities had been subjecting her. Her public image, her mental ease, her emotional and physical pleasure – these are all good things; and she wants to accumulate the greatest possible number of such goods, to which, she must presume, her very gifted nature entitles her.

Since Samson is in prison, however, she has been frustrated in her attempt to have it all. Wanting Samson back, she recognizes 'I was . . . mistaken / In what I thought would have succeeded best' (907–8). But she has no real sense that she was morally wrong, for Dalila lives outside the law that enables one to distinguish the good from pleasure and evil from pain. Thus she cannot comprehend Samson's notion of freedom when he says: 'This jail I count the house of liberty / To thine' (949–50).

Dalila's relationship to the Mosaic law is ambiguous. Although she is married to a Hebrew, she herself comes from a nation not bound to Jehovah or his decrees. The Hebrew Chorus sees no ambiguity in Dalila's case. According to its interpretation of God's giving the man headship in marriage, the man possesses 'despotic power / Over his female in due awe' (1054–5). Its view of the marriage relationship is an extension of its view of its own relationship to a God whom it is ready to consider likewise despotic, a God who behaves in a contradictory way but is all-powerful and therefore not to be questioned.

Samson, however, is prepared to relate to Dalila not despotically but by requiring of her moral liberty, that spiritual state into which he himself is growing during the course of this drama. Such growth requires that he end the marriage that Dalila has come seeking to resume. Samson's divorce from Dalila is a creative act, a separation and sorting that brings the order of divine law into the chaos their marriage has come to embody. Divorce of this kind Milton had advocated in his tracts written on marriage and divorce in the 1640s. In *Samson Agonistes* we are shown the illumination and healing that a needed separation can bring.

Before his fall, Samson, like Dalila, had unthinkingly believed that he could and should have it all – public glory and private pleasure to match his considerable giftedness. He had been fighting for God and against oppression without understanding the justice of his cause or of his Lord. His actions were not morally contradictory, like Dalila's, but they were unexamined. In examining Dalila's actions now, Samson finds within himself a growing vision of his own God as a universal and not merely national deity; he glimpses the law in its wholeness.

Although he refers to the custom by which a foreign wife adopts the country of her husband, Samson does not make custom the basis of his own thought. Instead, he intuits that Dalila, while his wife, could have retained her 'Philistine' nationality and even her worship of 'Dagon' if those names had represented conditions that were genuinely national and genuinely religious. When her rulers demanded, however, that in service to her nation Dalila should dishonour her own marriage, they – in that very demand – could be seen to violate the right purpose for any government, which is 'to train up a Nation in true wisdom and vertue', as Milton had asserted in *Of Reformation* (1641; YP 1: 571):

> if aught against my life
> Thy country sought of thee, it sought unjustly,
> Against the law of nature, law of nations. (888–90)

Since their request revealed them to be in violation of the universal purpose of government, they were then not to be regarded as valid governors:

> No more thy country, but an impious crew
> Of men conspiring to uphold thir state
> By worse than hostile deeds. (891–3)

From the reasoning by which Samson judges the crime of Dalila and her governors, we can see how his love for her and his campaign against the Philistines might never have been morally contradictory. While he wanted to use his position as Dalila's husband to oppose the Philistine tyranny, he would not have acted against *her*, would not have sought 'aught against [her] life', in violation of his marriage.

As Samson explains to Dalila, the Philistine 'Politician Lords' and not Israel have been Philistia's true foe. If the Philistines had practised true nationhood, permitting religious and civil liberty, Samson's revolution could have ceased; Israel would have been liberated peacefully, and the marriage of Dalila and Samson could have developed a ground for being.

At Dalila's departure, Samson finds himself obliquely aware that God has been at work with him during Dalila's visit: 'God sent her' (999). His second

Philistine visitor is, like Dalila, spiritually adrift. He is 'a storm' (1061); a 'wind hath blown him hither' (1070). Samson's emotional energy is returning, and his wish is to fight this enemy soldier, a desire which he formulates as a proposal to test 'whose God is strongest' (1155). The form which Harapha's refusal takes serves to draw Samson quickly beyond this unthinking stance, however. 'Presume not on thy God', Harapha sneers (1156).

While Samson's service to God before his fall had been loyal, it had also been presumptuous. But the opposite of presumption is not, as the 'tongue-doughty' Harapha hopes it will be, a retreat into despair. Presumption and despair are two sides of the same coin, which is a willed ignorance of God. The opposite of such ignorance is faith, which seeks genuine understanding, trusting that a knowledge of the Truth is attainable.

Harapha seeks to cow Samson with the world's wisdom: 'Is not thy Nation subject to our Lords?' (1182). The rest of Judah had indeed succumbed to this expediency. 'Knowest thou not that the Philistines are rulers over us?' the heads of tribes had said to him before Ramath-Lechi (Judg. 15: 11). This had been the argument of the Royalists at the time of the English revolution: one obeys the King absolutely, even if he is a tyrant, simply because he is the ruler in power. The Royalists had quoted Romans 13: 'There is no power but of God.' Milton had answered them, however, that these words of St Paul 'must be understood of lawfull and just power, els we read of great power in the affaires and Kingdoms of the World permitted to the Devil' (*Tenure of Kings and Magistrates* (1649); YP 3: 209–10).

Your cause is illegal and your God, 'whate'er he be', has disowned you (1156–63), Harapha charges. But Harapha, like Dalila, is God's tool for Samson. In divorcing Dalila, Samson has come to realize how fully his own private sin has fought against his public cause. He is left, at her departure, feeling that not only Dalila, but he also is hopelessly guilty. Now, in the political confrontation with Harapha, however, the other emphasis can be explored. As he defends his past public acts, Samson finds a basis for the hope that God may yet again use him in a public role simply because of the justice of his cause, which exists regardless of his or the Hebrews' unworthiness. And the hope that God will still use him is identical with a hope for Grace: 'Whose ear is ever open; and his eye / Gracious to readmit the suppliant' (1172–3).

The Chorus has been inspired by Samson's courage in the encounter with Harapha: 'Oh how comely it is and how reviving' (1268). But the Chorus is unable to credit Samson accurately for what he has accomplished. For he has proven 'victor' not merely, as it realizes, 'over all / That tyranny or fortune can inflict', but over these also as the appearance of God's desertion

(1290–1). Samson rejects the notion of the arbitrariness of 'fortune', while relentlessly pursuing a full knowledge of his own guilt and that of others. His faith in God's righteousness, moreover, is rewarded with the discovery of what he has gropingly sought, a rationally and morally governed universe. That discovery has brought with it victory over the ultimate enemy, over his own sin and despair. And Samson is ready, from now on, to meet not what 'may chance' (1295), but what God will offer.

With the coming of the next visitor, God speaks at last to Samson directly, though not to the Chorus or to us. A Philistine officer requires Samson's athletic performance at the feast of Dagon. In loyalty to the Hebrew law, Samson refuses. But as soon as he has thought through his options for dealing with this demand, a new sense of the law's wholeness comes upon him in 'some rousing motions . . . which dispose / To something extraordinary' his thoughts (1382–3). His reason has led him to a statement of the hierarchy of values inhering in God's law. God 'may dispense with me or thee / Present in temples at idolatrous rites / For some important cause' (1377–9). Then he knows that he will go to the temple. There, having submitted like a wrestler (an *agonist*) to the Philistines' demand for circus-like shows of strength, in an enormous feat done 'of [his] own accord' (1643), he pulls down the pillars of the temple on all the Philistines' 'choice nobility' (1654) and on himself.

Thus death, for which Samson had earlier prayed as an escape from shame, is given to him instead as the enactment of his own spiritual liberation and glory, as well as the prophesied freeing of Israel. The poet does not let us share that moment with Samson but requires us to stay with the Chorus, against whose reaction we must weigh our own. The men of the Chorus have been sufferers both of the enemy's oppression and, worse, of the fear that God had departed from their leader and from them, leaving no meaning to their suffering. This had been Samson's 'chief affliction, shame and sorrow' (457), that his own sin, in combination with their cowardice, had brought his people to 'diffidence of God' (454), to the brink of spiritual chaos. The Chorus – because it has not faced its own guilt – has not shared Samson's vision of the law's wholeness. It has been purged by its experience; it has acquired a 'calm of mind, all passion spent' (1758). But a more lasting tempering, a stronger immunity to the ravages of pity and terror, will happen for the reader of this tragedy who can share Samson's vision at the pillars.

III

For some readers, however, an obstacle to such a reading is present in the play's catastrophe itself, where the physical vehicle for Samson's spiritual victory involves the violent deaths of hundreds of people. Some of these readers reason that Milton was simply making the best job possible out of primitive material that is basically intractable; he did not have the option of changing the scriptural story's ending (Fell 1953). Others, believing that Milton could not – as a Christian and a humanist – have condoned such violence, argue that Milton intended to show Samson not as the Pauline man of faith after all, but rather as an unthinking strong man bent on a personal revenge which may have been justified by an Old Testament morality but which Milton meant to contrast to the newer humanistic morality of the Christ of his *Paradise Regained*, who patiently endures the onslaughts of his enemy, eschewing violence (Wittreich 1986).

It is sometimes useful for readers to seek modern analogies against which to test their understanding of older literature. With Milton's Samson we may compare a twentieth-century Christian theologian and freedom fighter from the period of the Second World War, Dietrich Bonhoeffer, whose religious and political philosophy resembles Milton's. Bonhoeffer did not believe that Christ calls people to 'a new ethical system'. When we renounce the world's demands on us, he says in *The Cost of Discipleship* (1937; New York, 1963), 'it should not be as though . . . we were exchanging a lower ideal for a higher one'. The law of God is eternally the same. It is 'the call of [God] regarded not as an ideal, but as the word of a Mediator, which effects in us this complete breach with the world' and which calls us to love others, even our enemies; and not just those enemies who hate us as individuals or nationals but those who embody that enmity 'which exists between the People of God and the world' (163), such as the Philistines or the Nazis. 'The will of God . . . is that men should defeat their enemies by loving them' (164). However, for Bonhoeffer as for Milton, such love does not mean passive endurance.

Milton's treatise *Of Civil Power in Ecclesiastical Causes* (1659), which argues against the civil government's penal authority in matters of religious belief and expression, has been read as if it were a pacifist tract. But Milton's argument was against using force in matters of conscience. Samson destroyed the Philistine temple not to force the Philistines' conscience but to stop their evil and to free the Israelites from their religious and political oppression. In this drama it is the Philistines who are 'forcers of conscience', tyrants against whom free people have an obligation to fight. In *Of Civil Power*, Milton discusses Jesus' words in Gethsemane: 'If my kingdom were of this world, then would my servants fight' (John 18: 36). This 'disproves not', Milton warns, 'that a Christian commonwealth may defend it self against outward force in the cause of religion as well as in any other; though

Christ himself, coming purposely to dye for us, would not be so defended' (YP 7: 256–7).

While Bonhoeffer never lost his early belief that 'men should defeat their enemies by loving them', he found no contradiction between this faith and his own activism. 'We must take our full share of responsibility for history . . . because we know that it is a responsibility laid upon us by God', he wrote just before his imprisonment at the end of 1942, ten years after he had made his first public statement of opposition to Hitler's National Socialism and five years after, as a well-known international figure, he had refused asylum in the United States and England and returned to Germany at the outbreak of war to offer leadership to the German church (*Letters and Papers From Prison*, ed. by E. Bethge (London, 1969), 138).

Bonhoeffer's leadership took the form simultaneously of intensive moral and theological teaching and of intensive underground attempts to over-throw the Nazi government. After 1939, he did not believe, as Milton shows the young Christ of *Paradise Regained* imagining, that he could 'make persuasion . . . teach the erring Soul' (1.221–4; see Wittreich 1986, 324). 'Folly', Bonhoeffer wrote in 1944, in reference to the German people's support of Hitler, 'is never amenable to reason . . . it is a moral rather than an intellectual defect . . . the fool cannot be saved by education. What he needs', Bonhoeffer concludes, as does the mature Jesus of Milton's *Paradise Regained*, 'is redemption' (*Letters and Papers*, 139–40).

'At the cost of his own slavery', Milton wrote, Christ 'put our political freedom on a firm foundation' (*A Defense of the English People*; YP 4, 1: 375). Especially during the last years of his own struggle for political freedom, Bonhoeffer wrote on 21 July 1944, he 'had discovered . . . that it is only by living completely in this world ' – not by trying to be an untainted 'saint' awaiting the apocalypse – 'that one learns to believe. It is in such a life that we throw ourselves utterly into the arms of God and participate in his suffer-ings in the world and watch with Christ in Gethsemane' (124–5). These words can be taken as a guide to understanding the relationship between *Samson Agonistes* and *Paradise Regained*. 'How can success make us arrogant or failure lead us astray, when we participate in the sufferings of God by living in this world?' (*Letters and Papers*, 125). Milton's deeply repentant Samson, after 'arrogance' in success and 'straying' in failure, in the end realizes in himself the pure love of God by taking action. How can he know that his rousing motion comes from God? He can know from the depth of his own repentance and his sense of God's return.

Of course, Samson dies, and the success of his cause is short-lived. Where then is his freedom?

'Helpless and forlorn', Bonhoeffer wrote as he foresaw accurately that his own death was imminent upon the failure of the attempt by the German resistance to assassinate Hitler on 20 July 1944, 'you see the end of your deed. Yet . . . you resign your cause to a stronger hand, and are content to do so.' Bonhoeffer's meditation shows how naturally the action undertaken 'of one's own accord', that is, in freedom, is simultaneously of God's accord. 'For one brief moment you enjoyed the bliss of freedom, only to give it back to God, that he might perfect it in glory.' To perfect human freedom in glory is the task of the Christ of *Paradise Regained*. In Milton's brief epic, we see the process by which God's Son invests all deaths – including Samson's and the Philistines' – with the meaning that death held for Bonhoeffer and for Milton's Samson as the last of the 'stations' 'on the road to eternal freedom' (*Letters and Papers*, 161).

Reading list

Crump, Galbraith M., ed., *Twentieth-Century Interpretations of 'Samson Agonistes': A Collection of Critical Essays* (Englewood Cliffs, NJ, 1968)

DiSalvo, Jackie, ' "The Lord's Battells": *Samson Agonistes* and the Puritan Revolution', *Milton Studies* 4 (1972), 39–62

'Intestine Thorn: Samson's Struggle With the Woman Within', in *Milton and the Idea of Woman*, ed. Julia Walker (Champaign, IL, 1987)

Fell, Kenneth, 'From Myth to Martyrdom', *English Studies* 34 (1953), 145–55

Fish, Stanley, 'Question and Answer in *Samson Agonistes*', *Critical Quarterly* 11 (1969), 237–64

Hill, Christopher, *The Experience of Defeat: Milton and Some Contemporaries* (London and New York, 1984)

Hone, Ralph E., ed., *John Milton's 'Samson Agonistes': The Poem and Material for Analysis* (Scranton, PA, 1966)

Kerrigan, William, *The Prophetic Milton* (Charlottesville, VA, 1974), chapters 4 and 5.

Krouse, F. Michael, *Milton's 'Samson Agonistes' and the Christian Tradition* (Princeton, 1949)

Low, Anthony, *The Blaze of Noon: A Reading of 'Samson Agonistes'* (New York, 1974)

Radzinowicz, Mary Ann, *Toward 'Samson Agonistes': The Growth of Milton's Mind* (Princeton, 1978)

Rajan, Balachandra, ed., *The Prison and the Pinnacle* (Toronto and Buffalo, 1973)

Rudrum, Alan, *A Critical Commentary on Milton's 'Samson Agonistes'* (London and New York, 1969)

Summers, Joseph, ed., *The Lyric and Dramatic Milton: Selected Papers From the English Institute* (New York, 1965)

Wittreich, Joseph, *Interpreting 'Samson Agonistes'* (Princeton, 1986)

Wittreich, Joseph, ed., *Calm of Mind: Tercentenary Essays on 'Paradise Regained' and 'Samson Agonistes' in Honor of John S. Diekhoff* (Cleveland and London, 1971)

16 Milton's literary influence

How are we to describe or even measure the 'influence' of a great writer such as Milton on the literary culture of his country? One raw quantitative measure is the continuance of his works in print. *Paradise Lost* has never been out of print. First published in 1667, reissued almost immediately, it went through a second edition in 1674, another in 1688. Complete editions of Milton's works succeeded each other through the eighteenth and nineteenth centuries, from sumptuous subscription sets to cheap octavo reprints. As early as 1732 *Paradise Lost* appeared with the full scholarly apparatus and explanatory notes befitting Milton's stature as a modern 'classic'. In the twentieth century Milton continues to be re-edited (and re-annotated) regularly, even after the publication of the eighteen-volume Columbia 'standard edition' in the 1930s.

Another crude means of gauging influence is to try to establish the number of readers Milton has had, or the proportion of the readers in any given age that he has reached. Though studies of readership have multiplied in recent years, our evidence about Milton's readership is still anecdotal. Those anecdotes would suggest that Milton's fame was established in his own lifetime, spread rapidly after his death, and reached the point by the middle of the eighteenth century that any reader of 'polite literature' would very likely have known of *Paradise Lost*. By the nineteenth century some knowledge of Milton must have been nearly universal among readers of English, and *Paradise Lost* was considered a suitable book for families on pious occasions. By the end of the nineteenth century it was perhaps a book more revered than read. In the late twentieth century, it is probably safe to say that Milton's works are chiefly read by students of English literature, few of whom turn to Milton once they leave school or university. This says little enough about Milton, and perhaps more about contemporary reading habits.

Another way of marking 'influence' is to examine the biographical tradition, and the degree to which biographers have succeeded in creating an enduring image of a writer. Even those who have never read Milton know something significant about him: blind, 'Puritan', 'misogynist', politically prominent, devout. In part because of his extraordinary public career – twenty years in the service of the Commonwealth – Milton very early attracted biographical defenders and detractors, from his nephew Edward Phillips and the Oxford antiquary John Aubrey, to the republican John Toland. Johnson's notoriously partisan 'Life of Milton' (1779) reacted against what he saw as a life of adulatory biographies in the eighteenth century, and itself provoked vehement correctives for several decades. David Masson's seven-volume *Life of Milton Narrated in Connexion with the Political, Ecclesiastical, and Literary History of His Time*, appearing from 1859 to 1894, fixed an image of Milton as the epitome of seventeenth-century Puritanism. More important, perhaps, is that Masson helped identify Milton as a founding father of England's 'Puritan' heritage and its Whiggish political tradition, which rose to dominance in the nineteenth century. In the twentieth century biographers have continued to add to the factual record, from J. M. French's five-volume *Life Records of John Milton* (1949–58) to William Riley Parker's two-volume *Milton: A Biography* (1968). Milton's life continues to fascinate the reader of his poems, the student of English history, or the devotee of biography, perhaps because of the almost mythic tripartite shape of his life: a youth of privilege, early promise, and publicly declared literary ambitions; a middle-age (his thirties and forties) dedicated to a cause for which he fought tirelessly, at the cost of his eyesight and his most productive years; a late maturity in which, the political cause lost, he retired to private life and produced his crowning works, among them the great English epic, dying triumphant but isolated in a world he had failed to remake. He left behind him unusually pure examples of political engagement, moral rigour and self-confidence, and religious fervour. Depending on your angle of vision, Milton is a freedom-fighter or a time-server, a hypocrite or a champion of integrity, a hero of faith or an emblem of repressive Puritanism.

But it is finally his works that have most influenced the literary culture of the English-speaking world. At one time they were so well known that they formed part of what one might call the national consciousness. Generations of literate Englishmen found resonant phrases from Milton on their lips – 'the world was all before them', 'darkness visible', 'fit audience find, though few' – at charged moments. When Sir Joshua Reynolds concluded his inaugural presidential address at the Royal Academy in 1769, Burke could salute him without affectation with words from *Paradise Lost*, Book 8: 'The angel ended, and in Adam's ear/ So charming left his voice, that he awhile /

Thought him still speaking, still stood fixed to hear' (1–3). Our public officials are now perhaps not so classically learned, but it is noteworthy that as late as the *Oxford Dictionary of Quotations* (3rd edn, 1979), Milton is surpassed only by Shakespeare and Tennyson in the number of entries.

Until very recently, one would have said that Milton's literary influence was most acutely felt not in the national consciousness at large, but among the poets. Since Milton's own day his fellow poets have responded to his work, by alluding to it, imitating it, rewriting it, or violently rejecting it (even the last is a sign of potent influence). 'The influence of Milton' has long been studied, but until recently it consisted primarily of tracing signs of Milton in the Latinate diction and syntax or blank-verse religiosity in the poets of the eighteenth and nineteenth centuries. Indeed, it is easy enough to demonstrate, and to deplore, the fact that third-rate writers for two hundred years feebly attempted to reproduce Milton's effects. It is more difficult, and more important, to show how Milton served as a stimulus to the first-rate writers, from Dryden and Pope to Wordsworth and Tennyson. Despite claims in recent years about Milton's allegedly constricting or intimidating influence, few writers, before the modernist movement, failed to make creative use of his work, or would have hesitated to think of Milton as the first of their kind.

The eighteenth century

Traditional studies of Milton's influence have, broadly speaking, fostered three misconceptions about Milton's influence on the eighteenth century. First, that he was, as Eliot put it, a generally 'bad' influence on the century, responsible for the dreary 'Miltonism' of the blank verse poets. Secondly, that he made the epic all but impossible for succeeding generations, and 'used up' or exhausted all the potential of several other genres – the sonnet, classical tragedy, pastoral elegy – and left his heirs with diminished possibilities. Thirdly, that on the whole readers admired Milton's works (especially *Paradise Lost*) but were hostile to Milton's surly republicanism and self-righteous pity. In more recent studies, W. J. Bate (1970) and Harold Bloom (1973) have contended that great writers generally and Milton in particular cast a pall on post-Renaissance English writers, and left them with the sense that there was little left to be done, or otherwise oppressed them with the inimitable magnitude of his achievement. Their arguments, like those of traditional students of 'influence', have misrepresented the literary world that eighteenth-century writers inhabited. A closer look will show that post-Miltonic writers, for all their admiration of their predecessor, found much in his work that they could draw on. It will also show that Milton the man aroused a wide range of responses to his politics and religion. For some he remained a villain, but for many he served as a kind of model of integrity.

Johnson's 'Life of Milton' (1779) is perhaps the best-known account of Milton's politics. Milton's principles, Johnson wrote, were those of a 'surly and acrimonious republican, founded in an envious hatred of greatness and a sullen desire of independence; in petulance impatient of controul, and pride disdainful of superiority'. But Johnson in fact represents an extremist response that few would have shared. For some throughout the eighteenth century the civil war in the seventeenth century was still an unhealed wound, and Milton nothing less than a traitor and a king-killer. Johnson is in fact more psychologically probing than the Milton-haters, and the intensity of his comment is probably a sign that, in his judgment, too many of his contemporaries took an excessively benign view of Milton which simply required a corrective.

Among those who, in Johnson's opinion, idealized Milton's politics were the relatively few who constituted a republican tradition. From the early biographer John Toland to Johnson's contemporary the popular historian Mrs Macaulay, a vocal group of polemicists, editors, and propagandists often cited Milton's political writings as a beacon of light and English liberty in a time of darkness. But more common than either extreme view was the idea that Milton was a sincere adherent of the Parliamentary side, defending what he *thought* was a noble cause. Some who were quite contented with the status quo went on to claim Milton as a founding father of what became the English constitutional system. In 1737 a monument was dedicated to Milton's memory in Westminster Abbey, the national shrine.

But the political world of the eighteenth century was in fact quite different from Milton's mid-seventeenth-century world of civil war. His ideas, even his defenders conceded, were obsolete (except for the defence of freedom of speech in *Areopagitica*). He left no practical model for a reformed polity. His most important political legacy may have been not ideas but the personal example of sincerity and self-sacrifice in a cause he deemed to be just. William Hayley called Milton one of the 'visionaries of public virtue', perhaps too much of an idealist to make a practical statesman (*Life of Milton* (1794), ix). For him politics was a branch of morals. Thomas Newton described him with language usually reserved for heroes: 'he had a soul above dissimulation and disguise; he was neither afraid, nor ashamed to vindicate the truth; and if any man had, he had in him the spirit of an old martyr' (*Life of Milton* (1749), 1: xi).

Milton also appears in the eighteenth-century biographies as something of a *literary* hero. Here there was little disagreement: Milton combined Christian and classical, genius and learning, the rational and the marvellous, in a way that no English writer had before. What is more, his epic matched the achievements of the ancients. The century's pride in Milton suggests too that with him English literature had self-consciously come of age: it now had a national poet to rank with Virgil or Homer. (Shakespeare, a popular dramatist, an untutored genius, was comparable to nobody.) The increasing eighteenth-century interest in 'Britishness' was prompted, in part, by the 'British Homer' who had both equalled his predecessor and had explored a range of heroic 'British' themes.

Though a literary hero, Milton was not obviously a literary model. A recurrent cliché of the age held Milton to be 'inimitable'. Literary historians from Dryden to Thomas Warton found it difficult to chart a line that led from Milton to any immediate successors. This set the problem for the post-Miltonic poet. Some attempted to solve it by superficial imitations of Milton's syntax or diction. The greater poets realized that they had to rethink Milton in order to realize the creative possibilities for them latent in his work.

Conventional literary historians have accustomed us to think of the Restoration and eighteenth century as a literary era distinctly different from the Renaissance. In the usual view, the age was dominated by two new forms, satire and the novel, by a new decorum of wit and correctness, and by new masters, Dryden and Pope. If we look more closely, however, we see a landscape – in poetry at any rate – still permeated by Milton's presence. Milton's achievement commanded admiration, encouraged emulation, and offered opportunities. Broadly speaking, Milton left open or created three kinds of literary opportunities: the post-Miltonic poet might still choose the traditional genres in which Milton had excelled; he might adapt Milton's work for a different medium, style, or taste; or he might find in Milton suggestions that, when developed, lead to a new kind of poem.

In the traditional genres of epic, tragedy, masque, and pastoral, it must be confessed, Milton's eighteenth-century successors did not excel. Can we account for this by invoking the spectre of Milton, who 'used up' the old genres, or frightened off the best poets, and attracted only the weak and timid? With hindsight we might think so. But the working poets of the day thought differently. The epic enjoyed great prestige; its conventions were understood; the greatest poets – Dryden and Pope among them – aspired to write epic. They abandoned early epic projects, and turned to translation of Virgil and Homer, though Pope was planning *Brutus* at the end of his career.

If it is difficult to explain why a particular form should prosper in a given age, it is more difficult to explain why it should not prosper. On the whole, however, it seems likely that poets in the period felt increasingly that epic – originally a primitive and military poem – was not suited to a polite and enlightened age. If Milton exerted influence on epic aspirations, it was not to deter the would-be epic poet but rather to keep the idea of epic alive, or to turn the thoughts of writers toward domestic heroism, increasingly the subject of the novel.

Milton's *Samson Agonistes* seems to us the last great 'Greek' tragedy in English, but it would be a mistake to say that the idea of the form died with Milton. Thomas Rymer at the beginning of the eighteenth century and William Mason at the end forcefully urged the use of a Greek model for tragedy. Racine's success in France encouraged Dryden to project a tragedy 'according to the manner of the Grecians' ('A Parallel Betwixt Painting and Poetry' (1695)). Audiences in England thrilled to the looser classicism of Joseph Addison's *Cato* (1713). Despite some modern misconceptions, playgoers in the century were perfectly capable of appreciating tragedy (witness David Garrick's career as a Shakespearean actor). If Milton's *Samson* did not inspire a great flowering of classical tragedy, it may have been because Milton's play was conceived and executed in defiance of what he considered a debased theatrical tradition.

The lesser forms of masque and pastoral likewise continued to attract attention. Dryden still wrote masques to be presented at court in the 1680s, but the form was gradually absorbed by the public playhouse, where it survived as opera or the Restoration prologue 'To the King'. It was probably a change in audience taste and theatrical convention, together with a change in the monarchy's view of itself, that eventually made the masque seem an outdated form. Pastoral would probably have followed the same path in the eighteenth century if Milton had not written *Lycidas*. Though some pastoralists imitated Milton's monody, most reclassicized the form, looking back to Theocritus and Virgil, and wrote sets of eclogues in a style that aimed at 'simplicity, brevity, and delicacy'. The best pastorals in the century – by Pope and John Gay – owe little to Milton.

Comus and *Samson Agonistes* may not have led to a tradition of masques and tragedies, but they themselves had a vigorous life in the eighteenth century, not on the page but the stage. *Comus* was successfully adapted for the musical theatre in 1738, and stayed in the repertoire for thirty years. *Samson* was turned into an oratorio by Handel in 1743, and was second in popularity only to his *Messiah*. In part as a result of such adaptations, Milton reached far wider audiences: *L'Allegro* and *Il Penseroso*, once obscure, were made 'universally known' (so Joseph Warton claimed, with some exaggeration) by Handel's settings in 1740. Milton was likewise adapted by a long line of engravers and painters (Blake is the best known), who provided illustrations for editions of Milton's works or, like Henry Fuseli, displayed an entire 'Milton Gallery' in 1799–1800. Such adaptations both honoured Milton and made him more accessible, as did the many 'translations' of Milton into Latin or into English prose (or rhymed couplets). If the former recognized Milton's status as a 'classic', the latter helped him reach readers who had some difficulty in following Milton's syntax.

We can also reasonably infer that a number of new eighteenth-century literary genres – the tetrameter hymn, the mock-epic, and the evening poem – were inspired or at least encouraged by Milton's poetry. *L'Allegro* and *Il Penseroso* led to a tradition of meditative-descriptive poems with a distinctive light tetrameter rhythm, addressed to a personified abstraction. Sometimes called hymns and more commonly odes, they include some of the best work of Collins, the two Wartons, Akenside, and Langhorne. One of the best minor genres of the period is typified by Collins's 'Ode to Evening'. Though Milton himself wrote no such ode, his evocative descriptions of calm and beneficent evenings in *Paradise Lost* are frequently echoed in the eighteenth-century evening-ode. He likewise wrote no mock-heroic, but planted the seed for one within his own epic, by making Satan a kind of mock-hero, subject to divine ridicule. Eighteenth-century satirists had other examples of mock-heroic in Italy and France, but Milton provided a model closer to home of how one might parody traditional epic values. Allusions to Milton's Satan in mock-epic may in fact have been designed not to bring out the evil of Achitophel or Cibber so much as their fraudulence and impotence.

Finally, Milton's creative pressure can be detected in the century if we look at the ways in which poets made use of Milton's most important bequest – the myth of a lost garden paradise. Milton himself offered soberly qualified hopes about the recovery of the lost paradise. Eighteenth-century writers permitted themselves stronger hopes that a paradise might indeed be regained, either a contemplative paradise within, or an earthly paradise in England's green and pleasant land. One way to recover paradise, so the poets suggested, was to retreat from the world into contemplative (often rural) solitude, and to celebrate it in a 'retirement' poem. Such poems, from Henry Vaughan's 'Retirement' (1704) to John Pomfret's 'The Choice' (1704) and Lady Winchelsea's 'Petition for an Absolute Retreat' (1713) all show – in their phrasing or their conception – the presence of Milton. Another means was through the exercise of enlightened perception. Mark

Akenside's *Pleasures of Imagination* (1744) suggests that Milton's unfallen world is accessible to man's imagination. Edward Young's *Night Thoughts* (1744) suggests by contrast that the paradise regained will be a heavenly one, but he is confident that it will be happier than the unfallen Adam's: 'Death gives us more than was in Eden lost', a better Eden, a 'Paradise unlost'.

For contemporary georgic writers paradise might be found in the natural world of agricultural England, as evidenced by consistent Miltonic allusion in John Philips's *Cyder* (1708) and John Dyer's *The Fleece* (1757). Even landscape gardeners encouraged their clients to see the world through Milton's eyes, and to think that as they walked through Stowe or Stourhead they had recovered some of the original innocence of Eden. For those not wealthy or meditative enough to retreat to their own rural Eden, a more common way lay open: marriage. Celebrants of the married state from Sir Richard Steele to Samuel Richardson looked back to Milton's descriptions of marriage in Eden as their model of conjugal love, and suggested that a modern marriage, with proper care and discipline, need never go through the domestic hell of the Fall and the subsequent mutual recriminations of *Paradise Lost*, Books 9 and 10.

Milton's creative influence can be found widely dispersed in the century; it can also be found concentrated, in some of the best work of the greatest writers. Dryden, for example, a younger contemporary of Milton, spent much of the middle of his career experimenting with Miltonic heroic materials. An admirer of Milton, though occasionally ambivalent and even evasive in clarifying Milton's achievement in relation to his own, Dryden also aspired to write heroic poetry himself. Though he never wrote his projected epic on Arthur, he wrote a series of poems in the 1670s and 1680s – *The State of Innocence* (his operatic version of *Paradise Lost*), *MacFlecknoe*, *Absalom and Achitophel*, and *The Hind and the Panther* – in which he freely appropriated Miltonic language and situations for his own witty (and consciously unMiltonic) epic narratives.

The State of Innocence (1674) recasts Milton's epic as drama. Dryden pared away much of Milton's cosmic action and focused (as later adapters would) on the domestic situation, Adam and Eve's quarrel, separation, and reconciliation. At the same time, Dryden subverted the ground of Milton's justification of God's ways. Dryden's vigorous debate on free will, foreknowledge, and predestination leaves the issue problematic. In the world of *Absalom and Achitophel* politics is not practical theology (as in Milton) but the art of the possible. And David is not a divinely ordained redeemer so much as a skilful manager of men. *The Hind and the Panther* at one point (2.498–514) recalls a key scene in *Paradise Lost* (when Christ volunteers to redeem man) as an analogue for the Roman church's unique claim to 'unfailing certainty', thus asserting the authority of a church that Milton himself had thought heretical.

Like Dryden, Pope seems to have been free of any anxiety of Miltonic influence. Inspired by Milton to do some of his best work, he discovered ways of using Miltonic materials for his own purposes. Though wholehearted in his admiration of Milton, who was already established as a classic when he began to write, Pope could still aspire to equal Milton's greatness, but knew that he breathed different air and would have to take a different path: he could aim for Miltonic amplitude but he would also have to be 'correct'. His early poems – the *Pastorals*, *Windsor Forest*, and *Rape of the Lock* – all solicit comparisons with *Paradise Lost*, acknowledge their indebtedness, but finally declare their independence. Pope's pastorals are reclassicized; his georgic is a declaration, in Philips's fashion, that Eden had survived; his mock-epic is a sophisticated parody that takes seriously a world of social ritual that in Milton's epic world is merely trivial. Pope's later poems might also be said to 'rewrite' Milton. *An Essay on Man* broadly alludes to *Paradise Lost* to advertise Pope's radical departure: his limited focus on 'man as he is' effectively leaves out of consideration the Fall and the Redemption; his expository stance of easy confidence contrasts with Milton's solemn reverence. *The Dunciad*, long recognized as Pope's version of the Miltonic sublime, should perhaps be seen rather as his farce-epic, a kind of satiric afterpiece to epic tradition. Its allusions to Satan serve more to belittle the dunces than to aggrandize them: Cibber the 'Antichrist of Wit' is a court buffoon, like his original Camillo Querno (as Pope's note makes clear). For that matter, the *Dunciad* helps remind us that even Milton's devil is an ass.

A lesser writer, James Thomson, might stand as the characteristic Miltonic poet of the century: he knew and admired Milton's work, often borrowed or alluded, but did not set himself up as rival or emulator. And yet he shows no sign of intimidation or anxiety in Milton's shadow. *The Seasons*, his greatest work, begins as a Miltonic hymn, and grew into a theodicy but with a difference: Thomson's poem has no fall and no Satan. He is reluctant to think that our world of mixed joy and woe is irrevocably separated from Eden. Like Philips and Dyer, Thomson suggests in his descriptions, especially of evenings, that paradise is not entirely lost. Thomson's blank verse, as Johnson noted, is not simply warmed-over Milton: 'his numbers are of his own growth'. And more than most readers have noticed, Thomson's manner often approaches the mock-heroic. Miltonic allusions help him to convey both detached amusement and rapturous wonder.

The nineteenth century

Literary historians used to suggest that the Romantic attitudes toward Milton, like their attitudes toward literature itself, represented a total repudiation of the eighteenth century. We can now see this to be a crude oversimplification. Just as Johnson's suspicions of Milton's character do not represent the eighteenth century, so it is inaccurate to assert that the Romantics were the first to see Milton as a moral or political hero. Wordsworth's 'Thy soul was like a Star, and dwelt apart' builds on a long eighteenth-century tradition. The other commonplace about Milton and the Romantics – that Blake and Shelley discovered Satan to be the hero of *Paradise Lost* – likewise needs considerable qualification. And contrary to Harold Bloom's more recent argument that some of the Romantics, like Keats, felt oppressed by Milton's achievement, there is clear evidence to suggest that for most writers of the period Milton was more liberator than oppressor.

Throughout the eighteenth century Englishmen had hailed (and reprinted) *Areopagitica*, Milton's tract in defence of the liberty of the press. And in the years around 1790 his political tracts aroused some renewed attention, from conservatives concerned about their dangerous influence and radicals concerned to fan the fires of 'liberty'. But Milton's reputation as a symbol of republican ideals and resistance to tyranny during the French Revolutionary period should not be overstated. When Wordsworth in 1802 declares 'Milton! thou should'st be living at this hour', he is not simply calling for a political saviour. 'Give us', Wordsworth continues, 'manners, virtue, freedom, power.' What biographers like William Hayley (1794) and others emphasize is not Milton's partisan politics but his 'steadfastness and resolution', his 'energy and intrepidity of mind', and his 'integrity'.

One of Hayley's early readers and friends was Blake, who represents in the most visible way the powerful impact Milton made on the Romantic imagination. From 1801 to 1825 Blake produced some ninety illustrations to *Comus*, *L'Allegro* and *Il Penseroso*, the Nativity Ode, two sets of watercolours illustrating *Paradise Lost*, and a set of designs for *Paradise Regained*. As many commentators have suggested, Blake's work does not simply illustrate Milton: it also interprets. During the years 1804–8 Blake wrote a long prophetic poem, entitled *Milton*, in which the older poet descends from heaven to inspire and to redeem a world from Satan and 'Death Eternal'. But Blake's best-known response to Milton is one of his earliest remarks: the 'Note' in *The Marriage of Heaven and Hell* (1790–3) that Milton was 'of the Devil's party without knowing it'. On this narrow foundation, and Shelley's later remark about Milton's 'bold neglect of a direct moral purpose', has been raised an edifice of 'Satanist' interpretation. But few Miltonists have in fact looked closely enough at what Blake and Shelley actually wrote.

Without question the early Blake and the mature Shelley thought contemporary Christianity psychologically repressive and politically tyrannical, and they found Milton's God the Father to embody the worst aspects of the Old Testament heritage. When critics in the twentieth century discovered Satan to be the real hero of *Paradise Lost* or went on to deplore Christianity itself, they enlisted Blake and Shelley as ancestors. In the narrow technical sense, Satan had long been thought the 'hero' of *Paradise Lost*, since, as Dryden had said, he triumphs (at least in the short run). But Blake and Shelley in fact did not take the next step of finding Satan a *moral* hero. When Blake said that Milton 'wrote in fetters when he wrote of Angels & God, and at liberty when of Devils and Hell', he may well have been making no more than what Bloom calls an 'aesthetic' judgment. In any case, we should not overlook the fact that *The Marriage of Heaven and Hell* is a deliberately provocative and satiric work – designed to unsettle the complacent – and furthermore that the statements in it are delivered by 'The voice of the Devil', who might well be expected to be partisan. We should not assume that Blake and 'the Devil' are one.

Shelley went so far as to say in the *Defence of Poetry* that Milton's Satan was 'superior' to Milton's God 'as a moral being'. But it is not always observed that Shelley seemed to have found both Satan and God to be morally reprehensible. The latter 'in the cold security of undoubted triumph inflicts the most horrible revenge upon his enemy . . . with the alleged design of exasperating him to deserve new torments' (this is the difficult doctrine of hardening the sinner's heart, which many Miltonists – and Christians – find painful). The former, for all his perseverance, is without question in Shelley's mind an evildoer. Insofar as Satan is 'subdued', we may perhaps find him 'ennobled'. But insofar as he himself is a 'victor' over Adam and Eve, Satan's own 'implacable hate, patient cunning and a sleepless refinement of device to inflict the extremest anguish on an enemy' are 'not to be forgiven'. So as to leave us in no doubt Shelley declared: 'These things are evil.' Shelley elsewhere found Satan, unlike his own Prometheus, tainted with 'ambition, envy, revenge, and a desire for personal aggrandizement' (Preface to *Prometheus Unbound*).

Finally, Bloom's argument that the Romantics felt oppressed by Milton, and did their best work when they resisted his influence, has been rightly challenged. Keats's famous 'Life to him would be death to me', and his abandoning of the too-Miltonic *Hyperion* should not be over-generalized.

They do not represent the full range of Keats's own responses. The equally famous 'Fine writing is next to fine doing the top thing in the world' is followed immediately in Keats's letter by 'The Paradise Lost becomes a greater wonder.' At the time Keats was at work on *The Fall of Hyperion*, which, as Stuart Sperry has argued (314), shows Keats's more mature appropriation and 'assimilation' of Milton's language and conception of human history. The opening scene of Keats's poem is Milton's paradise, after the Edenic meal has been completed and the principals have departed. But a 'feast of summer fruits' remains: there is still a Miltonic harvest to be gleaned. Keats tastes, and dreams. And when in the dream he ascends the steps of Moneta's temple he again recalls the moment when Adam ascends the hill of vision of *Paradise Lost*, Book 11.

Wordsworth, despite his great admiration, did not hesitate to criticize Milton or express a hope that he might even equal him. Wordsworth seemed untroubled by the mighty dead, and muses in the beginning of the *Prelude* on the poems that still remain unwritten, 'some British theme, some old / Romantic tale, by Milton left unsung' (1.179–80). As some have argued, the *Prelude* may be seen as Wordsworth's own personal or interiorized epic, a replay of Miltonic themes of the Edenic freshness of youth, fall, renovation, and recompense, in a natural rather than a supernatural world and mode. Wordsworth's sonnets similarly renew a Miltonic tradition. Like eighteenth-century poets before him, Wordsworth seemed to see Milton not as a pre-emptor or a blocking figure, but an inspiration and a resource, 'the grand store-house of enthusiastic and meditative Imagination' (1815 *Preface*).

Milton exerted, then, a powerful and multiform influence on the Romantics. He offered forms which they might still use, encouraging them to aspire to epic amplitude in their long narrative poems. For other writers, like Mary Shelley, *Paradise Lost* also offered a model which might inspire imaginative recreation. *Frankenstein*, with an epigraph from *Paradise Lost*, is a reconsideration of the middle books of Milton's epic. The narrative invites a rethinking of the relationship between a creator and a creature who wants to be an unfallen Adam but is treated like a Satan (or Adam in the fallen world), and is excluded from bliss. Like Adam, the monster wants an Eve, and even reads *Paradise Lost* as a 'true history' of his own heart. More important perhaps was Milton's stance as a poet. Insofar as Wordsworth, or any other Romantic poet, conceived of himself as a prophet or visionary, he was taking a place in what Wittreich has called (1975a, 141) 'the line of vision', a Miltonic tradition of prophecy, in which the poets 'regarded themselves as the spiritual men who would usher in a new order and a new age'. As Thomas De Quincey, one of the last Romantics, wrote in 1848, 'What you owe to Milton is not 'knowledge' but 'power' – that is, 'exercise and expansion to your own latent capacity of sympathy with the infinite' (Wittreich 1970, 492).

Milton remained the great English poet throughout the nineteenth century. If anything, his influence was probably even more widely dispersed than before, both in England and in America. In 1846 the transcendentalist Margaret Fuller honoured Milton as one of the 'fathers' of that new idea – Puritanism – which 'agitates the sleep of Europe, and of which America would become the principal exponent'. In 1894 Augustine Birrell wrote that 'no other poem can be mentioned which has so coloured English thought' (Nelson 4). John Ruskin claimed that not the Bible, but 'Milton's poem, on the one side, and Bunyan's prose, on the other, formed the English Puritan mind' (Nelson 74). No doubt Masson's seven-volume biography helped establish Milton as 'the genius of Puritan England' (6: 840), and thus the forefather of a strong strand in English culture. One might still feel, as Matthew Arnold did, that Puritanism was not an unmixed blessing, for a culture or for a poet. Milton, he wrote, 'paid for' his 'Natural affinities with the Puritans' by his 'limitations as a poet', by which Arnold seemed to mean his 'asperity and acerbity, his want of sweetness of temper, of the Shakespearian largeness and indulgence', Hebraism rather than Hellenism. Still, Arnold could say with admiration that Milton was England's one 'first-rate master in the grand style' (*Complete Prose Works*, ed. R. H. Super, 8 (1972), 185, 169, 183).

There is some evidence to suggest, as the nineteenth century wore on, a 'shift in interest and emphasis' (Nelson 127) from Milton's 'matter and thought to his manner, style, and prosody'. Perhaps because of mid-Victorian doubts about the truth of Genesis, or of religion itself, prompted by Darwin or the 'higher criticism', the theology and the moral issues of *Paradise Lost* commanded less attention. But the poets continued to find Milton an aesthetic teacher. Tennyson is perhaps the greatest of Victorians to learn from and to imitate the music or sonority of the 'mighty-mouth'd inventor of harmonies' (Nelson 106). A life-long admirer, Tennyson was famous for his recitations of Milton (from memory) and for his unparalleled technical understanding of Milton's handling of the pauses and vowels of blank verse. A poet as different as Hopkins called Milton 'the great standard in the use of counterpoint' (Thorpe 372). And Robert Bridges, later to be Leavis's whipping boy, said Milton had been 'the strongest and most

enduring of all influences on the subsequent progress of English poetry'
(Nelson 149). For him, that accounted for much that was good; for Leavis,
it explained what had gone wrong.

The twentieth century

Milton's influence in 1900 can be judged by Sir Walter Raleigh's *Milton*,
published in that year. *Paradise Lost*, Raleigh wrote, is a 'monument to dead
ideas', but Milton's style is 'the most distinguished in our poetry . . . a more
consistent and unflagging elevation than is to be found elsewhere in literature' (Thorpe 142). Milton's matter is obsolete – narrow theology and out-
worn myths – and he is read and admired above all for his style. Raleigh himself thinks that no poet since Milton's day has been able to rediscover the
'secret' of that musical style of 'large utterance'. Despite the elegiac tone of
Raleigh's tribute, Milton has continued through the twentieth century to be
a 'living' writer. It is possible to distinguish three separate phases. For a
short period during and just after the First World War Milton exerted a
powerful pressure on the makers of a new poetry. For nearly three decades –
from Leavis's essay in 1933 until about 1960 – the so-called 'Milton controversy' divided the worlds of literary criticism and scholarship, and called
forth a good deal of sharply argued debate. And since 1960, though the controversy has died down, Milton scholarship has burgeoned, and Milton's
central position in English literary history has become firmly established.

The first phase is properly associated with the names of Pound and Eliot,
and with their efforts to define and promote a new modern poetry different
from that of their Victorian ancestors. Milton's style may have been
unrecoverable, but in Pound's view that did not prevent poets from trying
to write like Milton. In a 1914 essay ('The Renaissance') concerned about
providing models for the contemporary poet, Pound complained in his
characteristically outspoken manner that Milton was 'the worst sort of
poison . . . the worst possible food for a growing poet'. Always alert to literature as a living tradition that grows and renews itself, Pound identified
Milton's 'contribution' as 'developing the sonority of the English blank-
verse paragraph'. But 'sonority' pursued too far becomes the sound of
'bombast'. In a 1917 essay on translating the classics, Pound warns that 'we'
(by which he seems to mean both writers and readers of poetry) 'have long
fallen under the blight of the Miltonic or noise tradition, to a stilted dialect
in translating the classics, a dialect which imitates the idiom of the ancients
rather than seeking their meaning' (Pound, *Literary Essays* (1968), 216–17,
232). What Pound wanted from modern poets was apparent in his Imagist

anthology of 1915: a spare and direct poetry presenting concrete particulars in common speech.

Eliot, working closely with Pound during these years, extended the campaign for a new poetry by identifying models in the English tradition in a series of critical essays beginning in 1919. In the early essays Eliot promotes the metaphysical poets (especially Donne) and the blank verse of the Elizabethan dramatists. Though he wrote no essay on Milton until 1936 Eliot made clear in some often-quoted critical tags that it was the 'Chinese wall' of Milton's blank verse that aggravated the 'dissociation of sensibility' in the late seventeenth century. Eliot's campaign continued until his 1936 essay, 'A Note on Milton's Verse', addressed specifically to 'practitioners' of poetry. Here Eliot gestures toward Milton's 'greatness', but explicitly declares Milton's 'bad influence' on the future course of English poetry, 'an influence against which we [practising poets] still have to struggle', in the modern effort to overcome a powerful Miltonic pressure and achieve particularity, a conversational tone, and to follow actual speech or thought.

Although Eliot's remarks are well known and often discussed, it is worth making three brief points: first, that his essay (and Pound's earlier attacks) indicate that Milton's ghost had *not* been laid to rest. Old poets without influence do not need to be rejected. Secondly, it is perhaps the rare modern poet who chooses to articulate in a critical essay his masters or his sources of power. Yeats, Hart Crane, and Wallace Stevens continued reading Milton, though they say little about him, and would appear to draw on a complex Miltonic heritage of sound, rhythm, theme, and epic amplitude in poems as different as those in *The Tower* (1928), *The Bridge* (1930), and *Notes Toward a Supreme Fiction* (1942). Thirdly, the Eliot–Pound attack was relatively short-lived. By 1947, when Eliot returns to the subject of Milton, the urgency is gone. Though his second essay has been considered by some a recantation of earlier anti-Miltonic views and by others as a reaffirmation disguised by critical evasiveness, one thing is plain: Eliot now thinks that the 'revolution in poetic idiom' has been accomplished, and that Milton might now safely be offered for study. But the recommendation is so cautious that one senses the real centre of the debate about Milton has shifted – to the issue of Milton's stature as a classic. One senses too that Milton's stature – and not his influence on young poets – was perhaps the issue all along.

In any case, the critical campaign first associated with Pound and Eliot was taken up in the 1930s by F. R. Leavis and directed to a wider audience, not the practitioners but the critical readers of modern as well as traditional poetry. Like Eliot, Leavis was concerned with 'new bearings in English poetry' (see his 1932 book of that title). His 1933 essay on 'Milton's Verse', drawing heavily on the 'critical asides' in Eliot's early essays, assumes Milton's 'dislodgement' from his seat of literary 'predominance'. Leavis's assumption was a little premature, as the ensuing 'Milton controversy' testified. Leavis himself continued to argue for twenty-five years that Milton had been admired uncritically and thus overrated. According to his own 'revaluations', Milton is far less impressive than Shakespeare, and also lesser than Donne, Marvell, and Pope, who comprise for Leavis the 'line of wit'. But Leavis and his associates encountered considerable resistance and reaction, at first largely from traditional literary scholars. Indeed, the controversy tended to divide the literary world into historical 'scholars' and 'critics'; Christian apologists and secular sceptics; and to some extent Americans and British (though the British could be found on both sides of the question, Americans tended largely to be defenders of Milton). The other chief documents in the 'controversy' are probably C. S. Lewis's *Preface to Paradise Lost* (1940), A. J. A. Waldock's *Paradise Lost and Its Critics* (1947), and William Empson's *Some Versions of Pastoral* (1935), though Empson's attack, as his later *Milton's God* (1961) suggests, is not directed at Milton himself.

By the early 1960s the 'controversy' had run its course. Its end might be marked by a collection of essays compiled by Frank Kermode in 1960 tellingly entitled *The Living Milton* and the appearance in 1963 of Christopher Ricks's *Milton's Grand Style*, which presented the strongest and still most influential counter-argument to the claims by Leavis and others that Milton's style was 'grand' but insensitive and unsubtle. Milton's stature as a great poet – in the minds of critics as well as scholars – was secured. But with his reinstatement has come a certain diminishing of creative influence.

Milton seems to have had little effect on modern poetry since the end of the great modernist movement in poetry about 1945. By the early 1960s Milton had ceased being the sort of controversial writer who demanded a response from anybody concerned with English poetry or with critical standards. There is little evidence to suggest that Milton has once again won an audience of 'common' or 'general' readers (perhaps in part because the audience for poetry itself has dwindled). Paradoxically, it is precisely during this period that Milton's academic reputation has reached its greatest heights. Milton scholars and critics never stopped writing books, but the pace of the Milton 'industry' has increased markedly since 1960. In the sixties Miltonists produced about 100 books and articles per year. By the early seventies the average had risen to about 140 per year (partly as a reflection of the expansion of the academy), and has remained at that level in the eighties, about twice the annual amount of published work on such poets as Blake or Yeats. Much of the work is of a specialized nature, and of interest largely to Milton specialists. But some is designed for a broader audience: Milton has been used as a lens to examine the English Revolution, the rise of companionate marriage, and the dynamics of literary influence. Since Sandra Gilbert's controversial 1978 essay on 'Milton's Bogey', feminist claims of Milton's patriarchal bias and its effects on later women writers have also been a topic for much debate.

Milton now reaches unprecedented numbers of students. As recently as 1962 B. A. Wright could complain that 'young men and women go up to the universities to read Honours English without having read a line of [Milton], for their teachers have told them that they need not bother with a poet of exploded reputation' (*Milton's Paradise Lost* (1962), 9). But in the 1980s Milton is a canonized set text for almost every examination board in Britain, and figures prominently in the best-selling English literature anthologies in America. This guarantees at least a certain influence on captive audiences in university communities. Many of those readers, to be sure, come to Milton without the deep grounding in the English Bible and the Greek and Latin classics which Milton could assume in his first readers, and which his 'general' readers probably enjoyed until the beginning of this century. But Milton's work, and especially *Paradise Lost*, still seems to have the power to arouse fresh response in new students more than three hundred years after his death.

Reading list

Bate, W. J., *The Burden of the Past and the English Poet* (Cambridge, MA, 1970)

Bloom, Harold, *The Anxiety of Influence* (New York, 1973)

Eliot, T. S., *On Poetry and Poets* (London, 1957)

Gilbert, Sandra, 'Patriarchal Poetry and Women Readers: Reflections on Milton's Bogey', *PMLA* 93 (1978), 368–82

Good, J. W., *Studies in the Milton Tradition* (Urbana, 1915)

Grierson, Herbert, *Milton and Wordsworth* (Cambridge, 1937)

Griffin, Dustin, *Regaining Paradise: Milton and the Eighteenth Century* (Cambridge, 1986)

Havens, R. D., *The Influence of Milton on English Poetry* (Cambridge, MA, 1922)

Hunter, W. B. Jr, gen. ed., *A Milton Encyclopedia*, vol. 4 (Lewisburg, PA, 1978), 103–46; contains four essays on Milton's literary influence.

Johnson, Samuel, 'The Life of Milton' (1779), in *Lives of the Poets*

Labriola, Albert C., and Edward Sichi, Jr, eds., *Milton's Legacy in the Arts* (University Park, PA, 1988)

Leavis, F. R., *Revaluations* (London, 1936)

Nelson, James G., *The Sublime Puritan: Milton and the Victorians* (Madison, 1963)

Saurat, Denis, *Blake and Milton* (London, 1935)

Sharma, K. L., *Milton Criticism in the Twentieth Century* (New Delhi, 1971)

Shawcross, John, *Milton [1628–1731]: The Critical Heritage* (London, 1970)
   Milton 1732–1801: The Critical Heritage (London, 1972)
   Milton: A Bibliography for the Years 1624–1700 (Binghampton, NY, 1984)

Sperry, Stuart, *Keats the Poet* (Princeton, 1973)

Thorpe, James, ed., *Milton Criticism: Selections from Four Centuries* (New York, 1950)

Wittreich, Joseph A., *Angel of Apocalypse: Blake's Idea of Milton* (Madison, 1975b)
   Visionary Poetics: Milton's Tradition and His Legacy (San Marino, 1979)
   Feminist Milton (Ithaca, NY, 1987)

Wittreich, Joseph A., ed., *The Romantics on Milton* (Cleveland, 1970)
   Milton and the Line of Vision (Madison, 1975a)

17 Milton's place in intellectual history

Intellectual historiography as it has commonly been practised is devoted to the formidability of tradition. It seeks to identify enduring suppositions – world-pictures, cosmological principles, models of nature, mind, time, and God – and to view their elasticity over great expanses of cultural history. It does not shy away from apparent examples of radical change. Indeed, some of these examples are its stock subjects – the seeming break between Christianity and antiquity, the rise of scientific empiricism, the self-proclaimed specialness of the various romanticisms. But, armed with concepts such as the 'unit ideas' of Arthur O. Lovejoy and the 'reoccupied positions' of Hans Blumenberg, intellectual historians have generally preferred to craft stories about gradual renovation and substitution rather than rupture and novelty. It is telling in this respect that in *The Legitimacy of the Modern Age*, a work of tremendous scope and originality, and probably the most distinguished contribution to intellectual history in recent years, Blumenberg should keep returning to the oddly provincial point that the idea of progress does not derive from a secularization of Christian history: for a historian of ideas, the challenge of modernity is to get straight on its tradition. It can sometimes seem, in the light of this discipline, as if the course of Western thought were the internal conversation among fifty or so intellectuals dedicated to solving each other's problems while doomed to pass on new versions of them. This vision of thinking as the grandest of human games, self-generated and self-regulating, is responsible for a marked decline today in the authority of classical intellectual history. At the extreme of this suspicion, in the popular new Marxisms, the entire project of intellectual history, the boundary that constitutes its subject matter, appears wishful. Intellect is too flimsy and extravagant, too uneconomical, to have so grim and massive a thing as a history. Ideas are the forms ideology takes when forgetful of its purpose, and intellectual history dissolves into the forces at work in history at large.

Whatever the future may hold for intellectual history, its popularity as an

Peter Paul Rubens (1577–1640), *The Fall of the Damned into Hell*

approach to Milton's work, especially *Paradise Lost*, shows no signs of exhaustion. For one thing, *Paradise Lost* is built of the very same materials intellectual historians delight in studying. Other poems take place against the backdrop of a universe. Milton's makes one, producing rather than pre-supposing its structuring principles: his is an intellectual universe composed of theories, causes, explanations, arguments. Where but to intellectual history, long familiar with these matters, should we turn for enlightenment about this thoughtful poem and its famous puzzlements, such as the appearance of Galileo in a universe that is none the less terracentric and finite? Moreover, the ambitious world-weaving of the epic has as its complement Milton's unrelieved erudition, or it might be better to say, his knowingness. He used with precision, and in the primordial contexts afforded by his myth, those large treacherous words like 'author', 'reason', 'nature', and 'grace' that intellectual history at its most impressive has warned us not to receive naïvely, since they bear vast networks of interlocking assumptions. These words flowed from every Renaissance pen, of course, but Milton was not off-hand. His frame of reference was *the* frame.

Much like Dante, then, whose work bears a similar affinity to the programme of intellectual history, Milton has repeatedly been 'placed' on the grids of this discipline. We know a good deal about his relationship to science (Curry; Svendsen; Nicolson; Kerrigan), to the various Platonisms, and above all to Protestant and patristic theology. I want to suggest, with all due respect, two difficulties with this approach to *Paradise Lost*.

The mere extent of this knowledge, coupled with the sense of coherent tradition with which it has customarily been offered, encourages us to regard the poem in a certain fashion – as, let us say, a very nice museum. *Paradise Lost* gathers into one text many odd and wonderful snatches of ancient lore, and annotating curators keep enlarging the exhibits. Thus Lactantius, to open yet another exhibit in the name of one of Milton's favourite church fathers (see Hartwell), contended that man alone among creatures was created upright with a swivelling neck so that he could know the heavens. Recounting his birth, Milton's Adam tells of the first use he made of his propitiously hinged head:

> Straight toward heaven my wondering eyes I turned,
> And gazed a while the ample sky, till raised
> By quick instinctive motion up I sprung,
> As thitherward endeavouring, and upright
> Stood on my feet.   (8.257–61)

Milton packs the Lactantian nexus of neck, heavenly knowledge, spiritual aspiration, uprightness, and righteousness into a single fluid action: the first action in human history. We have adduced the source; the exhibit is open. But the achievement of intellectual history in such cases does not serve the vitality of the poem, which is ultimately the vitality of its readers, if it leads us to believe that interpretation is now complete.

Often the procedures of intellectual history assume that while passages in *Paradise Lost* are mysteries in need of interpretation, the sources discovered for them are not. Illumination flows in one direction only, from source to poem, and the implied relationship of poem to source becomes the placid one of mere duplication. Should it be made to appear that the meaning of Lactantius is the meaning of Milton's use of Lactantius, we face tradition at its apex of coherence: repetition. But the pieces of lore embedded in Milton's beautifully complex design are extended, questioned, cross-referenced with other themes and symbols. To understand the moment when Adam first leaps to his feet we must work out connections with many other passages; a partial list would include the golden roof of Pandaemonium (1.717), the bowed heads of bedazzled angels (3.381–2), the broken heads of proud angels (6.840), Eve's curiosity about night (4.657–8), the apparent limits placed on human curiosity about the heavens in Book 8, the story of aspiration Satan invents for the snake (9.571–612), the uprightness of the snake (9.494–503), and the punishment God imposes on the uprightness of the snake (10.175–81). There are intriguing metaphorical transformations here. Reaching for knowledge of the stars seems to prefigure reaching for the forbidden fruit. Curiosity about the heavens becomes entwined with the question of the sufficiency of man's original happiness, wealth, and intellectual endowment. Milton sets the gifts of the creator against our problematic need to seek more than we already have, which may itself belong to our endowment, yet also appears to lay down the plot of our depravity. It is above all this interwovenness, the constant pressure of the entirety upon the part, that renders Milton's place in intellectual history a treacherous subject. We have stumbled into a common thicket: how is poetry related to philosophy? Milton's epic is not simply an instance of this general problem. As I will later suggest, *Paradise Lost* actively and deliberately stages the ancient battle between poetry and philosophy.

A second disappointment with the contribution of intellectual history to Milton studies is its relative lack of interest in articulating his position with respect to subsequent philosophy, despite the impressive start made in this direction by one of the early triumphs of modern Milton criticism, Denis Saurat's *Milton, Man and Thinker*. Milton lived at a time when philosophy, theology, science, and poetry were just beginning to feel the extent of their mutual antagonism. A century later the various systems of Romantic philosophy would try to suspend in a unity the fragments of an exploding intellectual universe, and philosophy would establish itself as the queen of disciplines, charged with determining the ultimate sense and good order of the others (see Rorty). As M. H. Abrams demonstrates in his magisterial *Natural Supernaturalism*, philosophies of the self-perfected subject in one sense conquered, but in a profounder sense reinstigated departed Christian myth by claiming as their own the old story of oneness, exile, and return. In figures like Schelling and Hegel, Spirit – the mind in its potential for self-consciousness – traverses its own salvation history. Philosophy must begin somewhere; and in this tradition it wants to set out in the truth, from the rational Eden of an apodictic ground. But the piecemeal business of philosophical exposition must proceed in exile from this initial oneness with the truth. The goal of the system is to recover at the end of its long detour into the partialities of exposition the 'absolute' from which it presumes to have arisen. Viewed in this context, Milton chose to dilate the great cycle of salvation history – to write of 'all', as Marvell noted in his commendatory verses – on the threshold of a major mutation in the history of this myth.

Since the myth survived philosophically in non-incidental metaphors that cannot be dissociated from the conviction Romantic thought both exemplified and inspired, *Paradise Lost* provides us with a master exploration of these key philosophical tropes. Consider, for instance, the summary symbol created by the action of the epic and named in its title. There are three paradises by the time we have arrived at the concluding Expulsion: Eden, the lost paradise; the eschatological 'Paradise' (12.464) toward which Christ leads us; and in between the 'paradise within' (12.587), the interior soul of mortal man cultivated by Christian virtues. At the Expulsion, man bears within him a symbol born of paradise lost and pointed toward paradise regained. In Romantic idealism (to follow Abrams once again) the two paradises on either side of the interior one reappear in the naïve oneness prior to systematic thought and the sophisticated oneness regained at its completion. The break characteristic of twentieth-century philosophy occurs when the two framing paradises drop away, leaving us only a paradise within, the symbol of a home that reason never had and can never hope to find. There is just wandering, just discourse or *écriture*.

Exile then becomes the sole condition of thought. Alienation or homelessness, the philosophical afterlife of Milton's summary symbol, is among the pervasive signs of modern culture. We find it in Marxism, in Freudian ideas such as 'displacement' and the 'uncanny' (*unheimlich*, 'un-homely'), in Derrida's 'deferral', 'difference', and '*différance*', and conspicuously in early

Heidegger, the ponderous magician of philosophical symbolism who preached alienation with an almost Gnostic intensity.

It is impossible to understand the point of *Being and Time*, its evocation of historical crisis, without appealing to texts like *Paradise Lost* as horizons against which to measure its strange, godless reassertion of traditional theological ideas. Who is Heidegger's *Dasein?* Imagine an Adam for whom the arc of time stretches from the throw of birth to the oblivion of death. Expulsion is his life. He visits rather than dwells, for how can he be at home in a world he must leave? Here is Heidegger preaching a secular sermon on Novalis's 'Philosophy is strictly speaking a homesickness':

> We are without a native land and are restlessness itself, living restlessness: it is because of *this* that it is necessary for us to philosophize. And this restlessness is *our* confinement, we who are finitude itself. And we are not allowed to let it pass away, to comfort ourselves in an illusion about totality and a satisfactory infinitude. We must not only bear this restlessness in us, but accentuate it, and when we are not only confined but entirely isolated, only then do we strive more to incite ourselves to be important, civilized; only then are we in a position to be 'gripped'. And when we thus make ourselves grippable, by handing ourselves over to reality, our homesickness makes us into human beings. (Quoted in Naess 174)

If, for 'restlessness' and 'homesickness' in this passage, we substitute 'the philosophical fate of Milton's symbolism of paradise', we see where we are in modern thought, which is not to say that Milton's vision yields Heidegger's merely by substraction. For the gesture by which Heidegger converts this homesickness into an opportunity for authentic existence in the resolute grip of life's finite possibilities is recognizably a version of the therapy Milton's God designs in order to prepare Adam and Eve for their Expulsion: accepting loss and privation as our own, and not as fates chosen once in a mythical past and ever after suffered passively, makes us human beings able to choose a place of rest in the possibilities of our history. Writing a theodicy in the absence of God, early Heidegger resists the illusion of religion while affirming the conventional theological imperative to own up to our privation, dispelling the 'forgottenness' of comfortable repose in this world. It is difficult to see why this sort of reading, breaking into modern thought with Milton and into Milton with modern thought, should be considered less truly critical, and less a matter of historical concern, than the approach through classical and patristic texts. Looking ahead to the mutations of its myth permits the epic to seem, not a museum, but the poem Milton wanted to create, 'so written to aftertimes, as they should not willingly let it die' (YP 1: 810).

By some measures the author of *Paradise Lost* was not a particularly philosophical man. I doubt whether he read Descartes. He does not seem to have felt the seventeenth-century urge to nip scepticism in the bud by supplementing Scripture with rational proofs for things divine, although in *Paradise Lost* he follows the fashion of his day in suggesting, with Edward Herbert, Descartes, and the Cambridge Platonists, that God is an innate idea, even that, in a plausible interpretation of the final two books, the Bible as an inspired record still in need of construction is an idea innately planted in fallen man. It is useful in fixing Milton's positions to refer to famous landmarks of seventeenth-century intellectual history, such as the Hobbes–Bramhall debate on free will. Yet I do not think Milton would have had the patience to get down to brass tacks with Hobbes on subjects like this. An almighty God and a free human will were true for Milton because they had to be true, because the meaning of the world he both derived from and imposed on the Bible demanded they be true. 'No man who knows ought', he grumbled in *The Tenure of Kings and Magistrates*, 'can be so stupid to deny that all men naturally were borne free' (YP 3: 198). Many, on this view, were his stupid contemporaries. After conceding the sometime complexity of words like 'naturally', we do well to remember that these are also the words used for beliefs impervious to objection. Sheer conviction probably outweighs proposition in Milton's prose. The result is not what we normally think of as rational argument: it is ridicule, Milton describing how stupid opponents look from the point of view of his own exasperated certainty. The compatibility of God and freedom, which has vexed many Christian thinkers, is only a problem in Milton's epic for philosophical devils, and God says all there is to say on the matter in his first speech (3.80–134). When Eve murmurs after her fall, 'for inferior who is free?' (9.825), the entire poem rises up as one voice to shout back at her: 'Everyone free in this universe (save God) is also inferior!'

But Milton does of course have an argument, and a great one. He fuses narrative and theodicy in *Paradise Lost* – a two-sided intention neatly epitomized in the doubleness of the word *argument*, meaning both plot and proposition. The effect of theodicy on such a scale is very near to a recentring of Christianity about the justification of God; and in fact, Christianity in *Paradise Lost* is invented before our very eyes in response to theodical antinomies brought about by the foreseen fall of man. Dennis Danielson has shown how the early Protestant endorsement of predestination led to seventeenth-century controversies over the power and goodness of God. It is important for modern readers to grasp this background sympathetically, because they are almost certain to bring Enlightenment suspicions to Milton's great argument. Theodicy inevitably takes up the theme of this world's relation to other possible worlds; to justify God means to defend some vision of how things are against other visions of how things might be. The relation of possible worlds to the actual world is a subject of such rarefied difficulty in a theological context that Duns Scotus, its scholastic proponent, had become a laughing-stock to many seventeenth-century thinkers (though not to Milton; see Rumrich), and by the late eighteenth century the fate of Leibniz, author of the most influential theodicy in Renaissance philosophy, was not dissimilar. Voltaire, repelled by the smug hubris of drawing-room theodicy, remarked that God must have given us noses so that we could put spectacles on them. The barb goes deep, since Christians have a longstanding habit of making facts into occasions for appreciating divine wisdom – witness Lactantius on the neck.

In his essay 'On the Failure of All Philosophical Attempts at Theodicy', Kant proposed that insofar as theodicies presume to know the ways of God to men, 'which are inscrutable', all such arguments exemplify the premier human vice of insincerity. We are not sincere with ourselves about knowing and believing. The mind is so prone to self-deceit in the matter of knowledge that many people spend their entire adult lives congratulating themselves on having achieved it: 'In the carefulness to be conscious to one's self of this believing (or not believing), and not to give out any holding-true, of which one is not conscious, the very formal conscientiousness, the ground of veracity, consists' (Kant 181). Kant had not read Milton. Yet he brilliantly articulates the grudge that Milton's opponents old and new tend to hold against him. There is no theodicy without presumption, and Milton was unquestionably a presumptuous man – by Kant's definition an insincere man, convinced that he knew what no man can know.

Intellectual history should instruct us here. The impressive thing about Milton's case of Kantian insincerity is that we do not find it nakedly before us in the form of unconceded presumption, but marked, pointed out, by an elaborate prophetic stance, which could be thought of as a way of confessing within a Christian framework that the argument is beyond human capacity, 'invisible to mortal sight' (3.55). Nor is theodicy for Milton, or for his century, the sugared enhancement of moral complacency it became in the next. Seventeenth-century Protestants did not ask about God's justice as one might the sum of the angles of a triangle or the implications of rebounding billiard balls. Milton reanimated theodicy because he felt that good men, in the current or future state of the world, would be compelled to enquire into the moral vision of the deity; and the impulse to worship, adore, and celebrate God as noble creatures worthy of being his creations could not last if this enquiry were to be denied in principle – denied as Kant was to deny it. What Kant leaves out is sincerity about our need for theodical assurance. Milton's was an argument taken up in the heat and sorrow of disappointment, in the face of apparent evidence of divine injustice. So Milton argues, narrating and contending. At stake is the justice of God, and beyond that the momentous question of whether religion can be made answerable to our moral dispositions.

Sometimes Satan and the divine speakers in *Paradise Lost* seem to be trading rejoinders like warring pamphleteers who will do almost anything for a score and show little interest in the mutual articulation of their positions. This quality has often been noted in Satan's improvised reproaches to God, but it can also be found (the taunt of lowering the stairs of heaven as Satan flies by, the derisive metamorphosis at Satan's return to hell) on the righteous side. Some readers, moved by this spirit of controversy, take up the cudgels for one party or the other. Some in the spirit of Kant find the theodicy pretentious. Yet the grand justification taken in its entirety, which is the entirety of our experience of the poem, is astonishingly tight. Any arguer must be allowed some givens. Once you grant Milton a Christian premise or two, there are not many good ways out, which may be one of the things that drove Blake mad and transformed William Empson into a picky lawyer. The theodicy of *Paradise Lost* is a consummate example of impassioned argument. More than this, like no other argument with which I am familiar, the epic delivers its meaning so as to produce a friendly competition between (Milton might not have used these terms) poetry and philosophy.

That Milton's epic is, in one sense or another, highly 'philosophical', we have the valuable testimony of Lovejoy: 'Now *Paradise Lost* is not merely, as the schoolboy noted with surprise, full of familiar quotations: it is also full of ideas' (3). Milton probably seems to us a more philosophical poet than Spenser, but this judgment has more to do with what seems to us philosophical than it does with the intellectual character of either poet. Spenser's notion of what constitutes philosophically serious talk descends in the main from Italian Neoplatonism. Though generally shunned in Renaissance universities, this philosophy attracted Elizabethan poets in large part because it already resembled poetry. It spoke of cosmology by allegorizing classical myth, and sought to display creation's order in corresponding lists of hierarchical kinds. Its harmonies were often generated through numerology: beholding reflections and graded repetitions in the world demands analogies, and number is the readiest sanction for analogies; anything may be related to anything else simply because there are three of them, or seven, or ten, cosmic homology without end. The early Milton, who would 'unsphere / The spirit of Plato', fell partially under the spell of this tradition. Spenserian allegory remained an alluring model for philosophical poets of the seventeenth century such as Henry More and Edward Benlowes; in his *Conjectura Cabbalistica*, an exegesis of Genesis, More used the numerological tradition to construct an up-to-date Cartesian hexameron. But in philosophy proper these neoplatonic strains were dying out, which is to say that people like Descartes himself were establishing a new idea of 'philosophy proper'. Toward the end of the century we find Leibniz proclaiming that Plotinus and his follower Ficino had responded only to the fanciful Plato, downplaying his severer rationalism, reifying his myths, and freely debasing his thought with curious additions (Cassirer 155). At last the Platonic tradition, for centuries lagging behind the Aristotelian in the practical matters of textual transmission and plausible commentary, was getting its house in order. This insistence on keeping a distance from myths and magic numbers, which was to culminate in Enlightenment thought, dovetails with the sort of exercise Milton set himself in the *Christian Doctrine*, the work of systematic theology and biblical exegesis that occupied him before and during the composition of *Paradise Lost*.

This treatise proceeds in a medieval manner by proposing flat, gnomic, unmetaphorical *sententiae* which are then broken apart into constituent phrases and justified by proof texts. This is hardly Cartesian philosophy, but in its banishment of cosmological myth, in its suspension of 'literary' elements such as myth and parable, and in the emphatically unintoxicated tone of its exposition, it is far closer to Cartesian philosophy than to Marsilio Ficino. One doubts whether Spenser possessed, or thought it important to possess, such a catalogue of scrubbed axioms for the design of the Christian world. In the preface to *Christian Doctrine* Milton calls the work 'my dearest and best possession' (YP 6: 121).

As a poet, however, Milton had in some manner to remythologize these stark doctrines. At times in *Paradise Lost* the factual or philosophical appears almost separate from the figurative or poetic, dividing for a moment the two ambitions linked in the word 'argument'. Thus Chaos is represented first as a wild sea of embryonic atoms and then as a senile monarch. For the reader this is a fateful crossroads. What is the relationship between philosophy and poetry? Are the two representations of Chaos equivalent – semantic twins, each the mirror of the other? Associating the propositional with the truthful, we are disposed to assume that the atoms interpret the senile monarch. But could it be the other way around? Does the symbolic Chaos tell us something that the propositional one does not?

It is at moments like this, when we are invited to reach into Milton's representations and make our own sense of them, that *Paradise Lost* transcends philosophy as we have come to know it. For in its journey from Ficino to Descartes, Hobbes, Locke, Hume, and Kant, philosophy gradually aspired to transparency, a clear and explicit language requiring no special act of interpretation because its interpretation is already conveyed in its sense, *is* its sense; allegory, which requires decoding but seeks to stipulate its correct interpretation, could be viewed as the literary analogue of this dream. But if we decide, as I think we will, that Chaos as personification is not the semantic double of embryonic atoms, then Milton's monarch has broken loose from the moorings of conventional allegory, and becomes – I can think of no better phrase – an authentic symbol. Interpretation in Milton always comes up against realms of adventure. If we have read Augustine, we know in propositional form the argument about evil as privation or non-being. Arguing in two senses, Milton in the opening books of his epic embodies or emplots this idea by appropriating the old literary convention of the parodic devil. Never before has the convention been so charged with intellectual weight, and never before has the idea been so richly imagined. As we watch Satan and hell imitating God and heaven, we strike beneath metaphysical abstractions to recognize in the literary mode of parody, which turns against its source, a way to be while hating being; we see the hard pathos of a rivalry in which the detested God is also the devil's most coveted ideal. Formulations in philosophy proper do not feel like this. After noting that Milton had many ideas, Lovejoy went on to say, 'Scarcely one of them is original with him, though many of them receive a special twist or coloring, or enter into novel combinations, in consequence of personal characteristics of his' (4). The intellectual historian treads softly here. He wants to say that Milton is philosophical, but does not want to say that Milton ranks with the philosophers he has borrowed from. The adjective befits him, yet not the honorific noun. Because Lovejoy assumes that literary texts, when they are full of ideas, duplicate or strive to duplicate philosophy proper, he underestimates the intellectual power of this poet.

A doubleness of meaning, similar to the one that parts Chaos, emerges in Milton's similes. Epic comparisons are 'focused' in that, unlike metaphors and ordinary similes, they state expressly the terms of the analogy. So Satan on the burning lake is 'in bulk as huge / As . . . ' (1.196–7. Bulk, we are told as we enter the simile, is the unknown to be determined. These are our instructions: learn how huge Satan is. When we exit from the first simile of *Paradise Lost* thirteen lines later, Milton reiterates the initial lesson plan with the implication that the unknown is now well known: 'So stretched out huge in length the arch-fiend lay' (1.209). But what are we to do with the wealth of information seemingly extraneous to the determination of Satan's size – the story of the slumbering leviathan, the mistaken pilot, and the ominous lack of closure in this story, which does not say how the beast reacted to that anchor in its scaly rind? Reading has its slavish side. Presented with the signifiers, we adduce the signifieds, and bear the sense of the syntax variously from line to line. But we have no instructions concerning the semantic overspill of the simile. We are, as Milton punningly suggests a few lines later, 'at large' (1.213), freed from the bonds of explicit sense. We have the freedom to make our own rules, and the responsibility to argue about our results with other readers. Look again on the protean face of Chaos. Whatever is said about the incoherence of the atoms, the personification does speak, does express, which might be thought to question creation's claim to a monopoly on Logos; and whatever is implied in *Paradise Lost* or stated in the *Christian Doctrine* about the moral neutrality of the embryonic atoms, the personality of Chaos makes an alliance with Satan (see Schwartz), whose own face, reminding us of his senile partner, undergoes contortions of rage and despair when he lands on earth (4.114–17). The bulk of Satan is to the extraneous story of the pilot what the atoms are to Chaos personified. Meaning in both cases has a double structure, one explicit and one a challenge. As he welcomes ideas into *Paradise Lost*, Milton invites us to rescue them from their calcified formulations in discursive philosophy.

Since our interpretations will translate the surplus of the simile or the symbolic representation of Chaos into new discursive forms, which may then require fresh interpretation of other discursive and symbolic passages in the epic, the meaning of *Paradise Lost* seems forever beyond us, unsettled and in process. Stanley Fish (36) argues that the drama of the mistaken pilot refers to the careless reader who finds a safe harbour in the exposed surface of Satan. I have been suggesting, in line with this view, that the crucial difference in the first simile between what is seen naïvely and what is submerged betrays a difference throughout *Paradise Lost* between the stated, overt, or discursively known and the symbolized or implied that must be hunted out in the depths of the epic. This second dimension of excess and uncertainty, while allowing Milton's poem to outwit as well as absorb philosophy, brings with it the threat of monstrous chaos. A protean uncertainty of meaning could demote or dismiss truths secured on the discursive surfaces of the work. For this very reason, after all, philosophy has tended to banish literature from its own language, or to enslave it via allegory and example. A major exception to this generalization is the dialogue form, which puts discursive achievements back into process. Suggestively, this is the philosophical genre Milton adapts in the middle and final books of his poem.

Philosophy, in sum, is discourse with a limit. Poetry is chaos. (Philosophy and poetry have other facets in the epic; we are coming in at an angle.)

It might be objected that the effects I have described are common to all instances of philosophy's intrusion into literature. Fair enough: I have been maintaining the inadequacy of the orthodox account of their relationship. But *Paradise Lost* is distinguished by the controlled lucidity with which it releases the double power of 'argument' to fix and free, joining philosophy and literature to their mutual enrichment. The poet is wiser than the philosophers he uses and anticipates. Milton's distinct value in intellectual history derives from the fact that his epic argument is *not* philosophy only, and with respect to the transmutation of sacred history in Romantic idealism, from the fact that his story is *not yet* philosophy. His dictum in *Of Education* that poetry is 'more simple, sensuous, and passionate' than logic (YP 2: 403) has often been quoted to discourage readings that might issue in philosophical praise for his literature on the assumption that they would be more likely to uncover philosophical embarrassment. The metaphysicians themselves, however, have taught us that simplicity is the most complex idea of all.

Once, in a metaphysical mood, I played with the notion that Milton's representation of how Adam arrives at God could be reduced to Cartesian epigrams (Kerrigan 230): I think, therefore I am; I am, therefore I was created; I was created, therefore I am religious; I am religious, therefore I am poetic. The severe compression of this pleases me. But Adam's wondering desire for a maker as he springs upright into the hesiodic space between earth and heaven reveals more about identity and certainty than any attempt to string out Descartes's unimpeachable mental nugget will reveal. As it happens, history presents us with this very choice.

Rhyming Milton's blank verse in *The State of Innocence*, Dryden also tried to regularize his thought. The Adam of *Paradise Lost* bounds to his feet in health and happiness, looks 'about me round' at the landscape and its other inhabitants, inspects his body, exercises in 'lively vigour', and then, aware that he does not know 'who I was, or where, or from what cause', discovers speech in naming and finally addressing his surroundings, searching for the maker who put him there (8.257–82). Dryden knew that this Adam wants for logic. As Wallace Stevens was to note several centuries later, 'Adam / In Eden was the father of Descartes' ('Notes toward a Supreme Fiction'). Immersed in the novelty of how things are, Milton's Adam leaves out a step – a thought he does not make explicit, but necessarily presupposes.

Dryden's Adam will not be permitted to elide this truth more certain than the sun, the hills, the rivers, the animals, the body, curiosity or speech. He awakens a professional philosopher:

> What am I? or from whence? For that I am,
> I know, because I think;   (Dryden 3: 431)

This Adam is off on the right foot, and before long may be expected to discover the categorical imperative. It can be said in Dryden's favour that he was miltonically correct in placing the *cogito* after the interrogative quest for what and whence; as in *Paradise Regained* (3.106–7), identity is above all else a recognition of having been made. But the passage seems fatally aware of the usual complaint that literature dilutes philosophy. It wants to serve this master impeccably. Giving over the first indicative thought of the first man to the *cogito* of an anxious seventeenth-century Frenchman produces thumping banality because, like all strict allusions, it signals limiting redundance. It says: 'This line means what Descartes means in his *Meditations*'. It implies: 'Descartes figures out this moment in the primordial history of Everyman'.

The poet who designed with palpable relish the Athenian temptation of *Paradise Regained* was never so submissive to philosophy, to the explicit in general. He is a better teacher than Descartes or Kant. They are islands of rock. He is leviathan.

Reading list

Abrams, M. H., *Natural Supernaturalism: Tradition and Revolution in Romantic Literature* (New York, 1971)

Blumenberg, Hans, *The Legitimacy of the Modern Age*, translated by Robert W. Wallace (Cambridge, MA, 1983)

Cassirer, Ernst, *The Platonic Renaissance in England*, translated by James Pettegrove (Austin, 1953)

Curry, Walter Clyde, *Milton's Ontology, Cosmogony and Physics* (Lexington, 1957)

Danielson, Dennis, *Milton's Good God: A Study in Literary Theodicy* (Cambridge, 1982)

Dryden, John, *The Dramatic Works*, ed. Montague Summers, 6 vols. (London, 1932)

Fish, Stanley, *Surprised By Sin: The Reader in 'Paradise Lost'* (New York, 1967)

Hartwell, Kathleen, *Lactantius and Milton* (Cambridge, MA, 1929)

Kant, Immanuel, *An Enquiry Critical and Metaphysical into the Grounds of Proof for the Existence of God, and into the Theodicy*, translated by John Richardson (London, 1836)

Kerrigan, William, *The Sacred Complex: On the Psychogenesis of 'Paradise Lost'* (Cambridge, MA, 1983)

Lovejoy, A. O., *Essays in the History of Ideas* (New York, 1960)

More, Henry, *Conjectura Cabbalistica* (London, 1662)

Naess, Arne, *Four Modern Philosophers*, translated by Alastair Hannay (Chicago, 1968)

Nicolson, Marjorie Hope, *John Milton: A Reader's Guide to his Poetry* (New York, 1963)

Rorty, Richard, *Philosophy and the Mirror of Nature* (Princeton, 1979)

Rumrich, John, 'Milton, Duns Scotus, and the Fall of Satan', *Journal of the History of Ideas* 46 (1985), 33–49

Saurat, Denis, *Milton, Man and Thinker* (New York, 1925)

Schwartz, Regina, 'Milton's Hostile Chaos: " . . . and the Sea Was No More" ', *English Literary History* 52 (1985), 337–74

Stevens, Wallace, *The Collected Poems of Wallace Stevens* (New York, 1964)

Svendsen, Kester, *Milton and Science* (Cambridge, MA, 1956)

18   Reading Milton: a summary of illuminating efforts

The volume of Milton criticism has grown so great – nearly 10,000 items in the twentieth century alone – that it daunts even the most stalwart scholar. It prompted one renowned critic to write disparagingly of the 'Milton industry'. Another rose at a conference a few years back, iconoclastically, to suggest that all one needs to do to find a project is randomly to choose any idea or literary figure, plop 'Milton and' in front of it, and set to work.

Despite the overwhelming volume, however, such cynicism is unwarranted. It ignores two important facts, the first of which is Milton's capaciousness. Milton's writing is so elaborately inwrought with learning that it needs a great deal of careful scrutiny.

The second consideration is that great works, almost like persons, always transcend interpretation, however brilliant or accurate, and our understanding and appreciation of them constantly need revitalizing. Admittedly, not everything published is of equal merit, but the opportunity for everyone to contribute to the 'great conversation' about books is necessary for magisterial studies to emerge.

The purpose of this bibliographical overview is to provide some help to the beginning scholar in choosing from the available wealth. Of necessity it includes only a small portion of what is worthy of attention. Nor does it exclusively cite only the best criticism. It simply gives standard, useful, or provocative sources on a variety of topics, and tries to be descriptively rather than just assertively evaluative.

We are fortunate to have these many fine shoulders to raise us up. However, we need occasionally to remind ourselves to stand, not rest, on these shoulders. Criticism is secondary – a beast of burden – and should not steal upon the attention belonging to the poetry and prose.

Texts

The only edition of the complete poetry and prose, F. Patterson, gen. ed., *The Works of John Milton* (also known as the Columbia Milton), 18 vols.

(1931–8), translates the Latin works on contiguous pages and records textual variants but is without explanatory notes, making it of somewhat limited usefulness for beginning readers. Its prose, especially the translation of *Christian Doctrine*, has been superseded by D. Wolfe, gen. ed., *Complete Prose Works* (known as the Yale Prose), 8 vols. (1953–82), which has full, scholarly introductions and erudite notes. Still the most quoted single-volume edition, M. Hughes, *Complete Poems and Major Prose* (1957), conveniently offers over four hundred pages of prose, informative introductions, and judicious notes. The most useful edition of the poetry, however, is J. Carey and A. Fowler, eds., *Poems* (1968). The introductions are comprehensive and insightful, and the notes, copious, thorough, and highly illuminating. Intended as a classroom text, D. Bush, ed., *Complete Poetical Works* (1965) has modernized spelling and simple annotations. Another useful school edition that is only half completed is J. Broadbent, gen. ed., *Cambridge Milton for Schools and Colleges* (1972–); both the introductions and notes are generally good. In contrast, H. Darbishire, ed., *Poetical Works*, 2 vols. (1952–5), reconstructs Milton's spelling and bases its text of *Paradise Lost*, though divided into twelve books, on the 1668 edition. Both J. Shawcross, ed., *The Complete Poetry*, rev. edn (1971), and B. Wright, *Complete Poems*, introduction G. Campbell (1980) are equipped with briefly informative notes intended for the general reader. The prose collections – J. Patrick, ed., *The Prose* (1967) and C. Patrides, ed., *Selected Prose*, rev. edn (1985) – are both excellent. Patrick includes lucid annotations, a chapter-by-chapter précis of *Christian Doctrine*, and an introduction on Milton's modernity. The annotations in Patrides are less elaborate, but the selections more ample and the bibliography nearly comprehensive.

Bibliographies and general reference works

D. Stevens, *Reference Guide* (1930) and H. Fletcher, *Contributions to a Milton Bibliography* (1931) list all the relevant scholarship from 1800 to 1930; and C. Huckaby, *Supplement* (1960) extends the list to 1957. The standard bibliography of modern criticism is Huckabay, *An Annotated Bibliography, 1929–1968*, rev. edn (1969), containing 3,932 entries. It is well organized and carefully indexed, but the annotations are somewhat spare. A very convenient classified listing is J. Hanford and W. McQueen, eds., *Milton*, 2nd edn (1979).

For tracing Milton's word usage, consult W. Ingram and K. Swaim, *A Concordance to the English Poetry* (1972), and L. Sterne and H. Kollmeier, *A Concordance to the English Prose* (1985). A good short guide to Milton's vocabulary, allusions, characters, and contemporaries is E. LeComte, *A Milton Dictionary* (1961). Also see his *A Dictionary of Puns in Milton's English Poetry* (1981).

An incomparably fine source on virtually any aspect of Milton is W. Hunter, gen. ed., *A Milton Encyclopedia*, 9 vols. (1978–83). Also excellent is the half-completed (vols. 1, 2, and 4 – minor poetry and *Paradise Regained*) M. Hughes, gen. ed., *A Variorum Commentary* (1970–), which provides extensive line-by-line notes and thorough histories of criticism.

J. Boswell, *Milton's Library* (1975) deduces the books Milton owned on the basis of allusions to them in his works. C. Pecheux, *Milton: A Topographical Guide* (1981) provides information on places – chiefly his residences – that are of importance to Milton's life and works.

There are several good handbook introductions to Milton. J. Hanford, *A Milton Handbook* (1970; first edn, 1926) is arguably the best, though J. Carey, *Milton* (1969) is the most stimulating in asserting that *Paradise Lost* is great because of its 'objectionableness'. M. Nicolson, *A Reader's Guide* (1963) is generally informative, though sometimes oversimple. D. Daiches, *Milton* (1957), D. Bush, *John Milton: A Sketch of His Life and Writings* (1964), and D. Miller, *John Milton: Poetry* (1978) provide straightforward information and basic interpretations. Of the two illustrated introductory guides, L. Potter, *A Preface* (1971) is more reliably informative than D. Wolfe, *Milton and His England* (1971), which is attractively entertaining – 119 illustrations interspersed by brief glosses.

Biography and reputation

The standard biography is W. Parker, *Milton: A Biography*, 2 vols. (1968), a monumental undertaking that touches upon nearly every major issue of Milton scholarship. It is the first comprehensive attempt at a 'life' since the massive D. Masson, *Life of John Milton: Narrated in Connexion with the Political, Ecclesiastical, and Literary History of His Time*, 7 vols. (1859–94). Although excellent, Parker is for true lovers of Milton. J. Hanford, *John Milton, Englishman* (1949) is more accessible to non-specialists and can still claim to be the most reliable short biography. A. Wilson, *John Milton: A Life* (1983) is delightfully readable but in places sacrifices accuracy for dramatic effect. On Milton as a human being as reflected in his major characters, see E. Wagenknecht, *The Personality of John Milton* (1970). A similar, but wiser and profounder, study is J. Thorpe, *John Milton: The Inner Life* (1983), which lucidly explores Milton's values, ambitions, drives, and sense of self-esteem, particularly his relationship to God and his sense of virtue and poetic mission. J. Diekhoff, *Milton on Himself*, rev. edn (1965) also examines Milton's self-perception but through the explicitly self-referential passages. Milton's school career is excavated in D. Clark, *John Milton at St. Paul's School* (1948), and his Cambridge University career in H. Fletcher, *The Intellectual Development of John Milton* (1951–61). H. Darbishire, ed., *The Early Lives of Milton* (1932) collects the biographies by Aubrey, Wood, Phillips, and Richardson. An important resource is J. French, ed., *The Life Records of John Milton*, 5 vols. (1949–58). Finally, a thoughtful but forgotten appreciation is R. Macauley, *Milton* (1933).

For the reaction of other ages to Milton, consult J. Thorpe, ed., *Milton Criticism: Selections From Four Centuries* (1950), which contains an excellent introductory essay on Milton's reputation down to the middle of the twentieth century; and J. Shawcross, ed., *Milton: The Critical Heritage* (1970 – excerpts from 1628 to 1731); and *Milton, 1732–1801* (1972). W. Parker, *Milton's Contemporary Reputation* (1940) provides an analysis and list of seventeenth-century allusions to Milton, and B. Rajan, *'Paradise Lost' and the Seventeenth-Century Reader* (1947) looks at Milton and his epic through the eyes of his first audience. Milton's influence and reputation in the nineteenth century are amply considered in L. Brisman, *Milton's Poetry of Choice and Its Romantic Heirs* (1973), which analyzes the different ways in which the Romantics imitated Milton. J. Wittreich, *The Romantics on Milton* (1970) is a rich collection of comments by major Romantic writers; and *Angel of the Apocalypse* (1975), also by Wittreich, treats Blake's conception of Milton in detail and offers a view of Milton as a 'revolutionary' poet. J. Nelson, *The Sublime Puritan* (1963) exhaustively analyzes Milton's reputation among, and treatment by, the Victorians. P. Murray, *Milton: The Modern Phase* (1967) provides a thorough review of modern criticism with particular attention to the objections to *Paradise Lost*. Finally, as an example of how literary judgment can change even within a few years, see T. S. Eliot, *Milton: Two Studies* (1948).

General studies (involving several of Milton's works)

Of the studies that span Milton's writings, the following are among the most illuminating and provocative. L. Martz, *Poet of Exile* (1980) is an elegantly imaginative interpretation of the 1645, 1667, and 1671 volumes as a triptych in which *Paradise Lost* sings of exile by blindness and political defeat and *Paradise Regained* and *Samson Agonistes* dramatize strategies for dealing with the past. It contains a wonderful example of how poetry (St John Perse) can illuminate poetry. Equally provocative (and imaginative in its use of twentieth-century sources – Karl Popper, Anders Nygren, the experience of Berkeley in the 1960s) is H. Richmond, *The Christian Revolutionary: John Milton* (1974), which argues that Milton repudiated his faith in ratiocinative reform for acceptance of original sin surrendering faith, a transformation which, Richmond argues, accounts for the three major poems. By contrast, E. Tillyard, *Milton*, rev. edn, (1966) contends that Milton saw in the Incarnation a device for the idea of 'spiritual' regeneration. C. Hill, *Milton and the English Revolution* (1977) believes that Milton chiefly drew his inspiration and ideas from the radical underground, making his poetry a map of the radical and political movements of his day. In *The Experience of Defeat* (1984), Hill analyzes the effect of the Revolution's failure on not only Milton but other seventeenth-century writers. A. Milnar, *John Milton and the English Revolution* (1981) also pursues the theme of defeat in the three major poems, but from a pronouncedly sociological and Marxist perspective. In contrast, focusing on the intellectual and aesthetic dimensions of Milton's work, G. Christopher, *Milton and the Science of the Saints* (1982) finds him not only a Puritan but one who shares Luther's and Calvin's interests in speech as a reflection of The Word; it intriguingly suggests that any new insight achieved from this perspective must be understood 'as the work of the Holy Spirit'.

Several studies have also been done of Milton's sense of prophetic calling and apocalyptic urgency. W. Kerrigan, *The Prophetic Milton* (1974) argues that Milton deliberately imitated the biblical prophets, 'sharing the burden of woe which accompanied this divine authority' in order to unify private revelation and public authority, passive recording and active creation, intuition and rationality, celestial praise and vigorous rebuke. J. Wittreich, *Visionary Poetics* (1979) discusses Spenser's and Milton's recovery of the principles of prophecy with special attention to *Lycidas* as a prophetic paradigm.

On Milton's language and prosody, consult S. Sprott, *Milton's Art of Prosody* (1953); A. Oras, *Blank Verse and Chronology in Milton* (1966); and R. Evans, *Milton's Elisions* (1966). Especially informative is R. Emma and J. Shawcross, eds., *Language and Style in Milton* (1967); the essays cover a broad range of topics from the style of God's speech to Milton's pronunciation. Two very fine studies, which demonstrate that Milton's style has greater depth and diversity than is sometimes thought, are C. Ricks, *Milton's Grand Style* (1963), which focuses exclusively on *Paradise Lost*, and A. Burnett, *Milton's Style* (1981), a sophisticated work presenting meticulous linguistic analyses of the minor poems, *Paradise Regained*, and *Samson Agonistes* in the context of recent criticism.

On Milton's imagery, T. Banks, *Milton's Imagery* (1950) and R. Tuve, *Images and Themes in Five Poems by Milton* (1957) are solid, but more stimulating is R. Frye, *Milton's Imagery and the Visual Arts* (1978), which locates artistic references for Milton's epic imagery. In addition to 269 illustrations and useful iconographic history, it discusses Milton's visual imagination and his knowledge of art. S. Budick, *The Dividing Muse: Images of Sacred Disjunction in Milton's Poetry* (1985) locates Milton within the tradition of religious symbolism and argues that theological meaning is 'repeatedly renewed in the imagination's own acts of discrimination and division'. R. Daniells, *Milton, Mannerism and Baroque* (1963) attempts to discern parallels between two artistic eras and Milton's poetry.

Studies of Milton and other writers are numerous: I. Samuel, *Plato and Milton* (1947); R. DuRocher, *Milton and Ovid* (1985); D. Harding, *Milton and the Renaissance Ovid* (1946); T. O'Keeffe, *Milton and the Pauline Tradition* (1982); J. Arthos, *Dante, Michelangelo, and Milton* (1963); I. Samuel, *Dante and Milton* (1966); H. Cory, *Spenser, the School of Fletchers and Milton* (1912); J. Guillory, *Poetic Authority: Spenser, Milton, and Literary History* (1983); M. Quilligan, *Milton's Spenser* (1983); R. Helgerson, *Self-Crowned Laureates: Spenser, Jonson, Milton, and the Literary System* (1983); P. Stevens, *Imagination and the Presence of Shakespeare in 'Paradise Lost'* (1985); R. Frye, *God, Man, and Satan* (1960; on pattern in Milton and Bunyan); E. Tillyard, *The Metaphysicals and Milton* (1956); A. Ferry, *Milton and the Miltonic Dryden* (1968); P. Fiore, *Milton and Augustine* (1981); K. Hartwell, *Lactantius and Milton* (1929); A. K. Hieatt, *Chaucer, Spenser, Milton: Mythopoeic Continuities and Transformations* (1975); J. Grierson, *Milton and Wordsworth* (1937); M. Williams, *Inspiration in Milton and Keats* (1982); J. Wittreich, ed., *Milton and the Line of Vision* (1975; covers from Chaucer to Wallace Stevens). Also see, J. Mulryan, *Milton and the Middle Ages* (1982) and G. Sensabaugh, *Milton in Early America* (1964).

Milton's use of, or relationship to, various ideas and traditions has also been extensively investigated. On Milton and the Bible, see J. Sims, *The Bible in Milton's Epics* (1962) and J. Sims and L. Ryken, eds., *Milton and the Scriptural Tradition* (1984), which has a fine essay on new critical approaches to Milton and the Bible and good studies of biblical epic models in *Paradise Lost* and of the Gospel of John and *Paradise Regained*. Milton's relationship to Judaism is studied in H. Fletcher, *Milton's Semitic Studies and Some Manifestations of Them in His Poetry* (1926) and *Milton's Rabbinical Readings* (1930). See also T. Stroup, *Religious Rite and Ceremony in Milton's Poetry*

(1968); G. Whiting, *Milton's Literary Milieu* (1939); K. Svendsen, *Milton and Science* (1956); and R. West, *Milton and the Angels* (1955).

There are several good anthologies of criticism covering Milton's entire canon: A. Barker, ed., *Milton: Modern Essays in Criticism* (1965; first rate); *Critical Essays on Milton from ELH* (1965); L. Martz, ed., *Milton* (1965); J. Summers, ed., *The Lyric and Dramatic Milton* (1965); A. Stein, ed., *On Milton's Poetry* (1970); C. Patrides, ed., *Milton's Epic Poetry* (1967); F. Kermode, ed., *The Living Milton* (1960); and G. Williamson, *Milton and Others* (1965).

For analogues to Milton's major poems, consult W. Kirkconnell, *The Celestial Cycle* (1952; on *Paradise Lost*); *Awake the Courteous Echo* (1973; for *Comus*, *Lycidas*, and *Paradise Regained*); and *That Invincible Samson* (1964).

Paradise Lost

Of the many fine studies of *Paradise Lost*, there are a few magisterial ones that reward periodic rereading. J. Summers, *The Muse's Method* (1962) provides elegantly sensitive readings of the epic opening, the characters, Edenic life, the Raphael narrative, the Fall and judgment, and the vision of history. C. S. Lewis, *A Preface to 'Paradise Lost'* (1942) lucidly discusses epic tradition, Satan, Adam and Eve, and central themes. H. Gardner, *A Reading of 'Paradise Lost'* (1965) concentrates on the distinctions the epic draws between the particular and the universal, the human and cosmic. Taking Milton's announced purpose seriously, D. Danielson, *Milton's Good God* (1982) examines the precision and vitality of Milton's justification of God while clarifying such difficult matters as free will, predestination, pre-lapsarian and postlapsarian life, creation and chaos. With somewhat less philosophical sophistication, D. Burden, *The Logical Epic* (1967) pursues the same ground, arguing that *Paradise Lost* is disciplined by the 'best sense' of Genesis.

These studies largely, though indirectly, answer the attack that was launched against Milton for supposed inconsistencies between his art and his theology. A. Waldock, *'Paradise Lost' and Its Critics* (1947) contends that Milton's sympathetic rendering of Satan and the Fall contradict his theodical purpose and result in evasiveness, literalism, and contradiction. Similarly, but with Miltonic polemical passion, W. Empson, *Milton's God*, rev. edn (1965) asserts that Milton's epic is actually an argument in defence of eating the apple and against worshipping God.

D. Bush, *Paradise Lost in Our Time* (1945) eloquently justifies Milton by showing how every feature of the epic evinces relevant ethical principles, but readers who take Milton's purpose seriously should consult (in addition to Summers, Lewis, Gardner, Danielson, and Burden) W. Hunter, C. Patrides, and J. Adamson, eds., *Bright Essence: Studies in Milton's Theology* (1973); highly technical, but most illuminating, it discusses Milton's theories of the Godhead, the Trinity, creation, the Incarnation, and accommodation. C. Patrides, *Milton and the Christian Tradition* (1966) surveys some of the same ground from a historical perspective while asserting the essential Protestant nature of the epic. H. MacCallum, *Milton and the Sons of God: The Divine Image in Milton's Poetry* (1986) analyzes the presentation of Christ and Adam within the context of reformed theology. Two helpful studies of Milton's use of hexameral literature (accounts of creation and prelapsarian life) are I. Corcoran, *Milton's Paradise with Reference to the Hexameral Background* (1945) and J. Evans, *'Paradise Lost' and the Genesis Tradition* (1968).

A stimulating, though sometimes misleading, book-by-book guide is J. Broadbent, *Some Graver Subject* (1960). L. Ryken, *The Apocalyptic Vision in 'Paradise Lost'* (1970) astutely analyzes the means by which Milton renders transcendental reality persuasive. B. Berry, *Process of Speech: Puritan Religious Writing and 'Paradise Lost'* (1976) examines Milton's thinking in comparison with Puritan tracts and homilies. L. Babb, *The Moral Cosmos of 'Paradise Lost'* (1970) points to how everything in the epic reflects the divine will. D. Hamlet, *One Greater Man: Justice and Damnation in 'Paradise Lost'* (1976) suggests that justice in the epic is redemptive and merciful rather than punitive and legalistic. M. Lieb, *Poetics of the Holy* (1981) argues that the experience of holiness is so fundamental in the epic that it even redeems Milton's iconoclasm and polemicism.

Four major studies have been written on Milton's narrative strategy. The first, A. Ferry, *Milton's Epic Voice* (1963), successfully refutes the notion that the narrative commentary is an afterthought indicating Milton's uneasiness over his poetic effect; it shows that narrative and action are in agreement. S. Fish, *Surprised by Sin* (1967) ingeniously argued the questionable thesis that *Paradise Lost* recreates the Fall in the reader and that the narrator's function is to alert readers to their distance from original innocence. W. Riggs, *The Christian Poet in 'Paradise Lost'* (1972) sees the narrative presence as central to Milton's effort to explore what it means to be a Christian poet; the narrator's ordeal is intended as a microcosm for all humanity. A. Stein, *The Art of Presence* (1977) more conventionally considers how the Miltonic presence affects the reader and shapes theme, description, and drama.

On the form of *Paradise Lost*, the most ambitious study is J. Webber, *Milton and His Epic Tradition* (1979), which demonstrates that Milton's epic, like its predecessors, reports a major turning-point in the history of consciousness and culture. It also offers the intriguing thought that the reason we have had no epic since Milton is that we have yet to exhaust its vision. F. Blessington, *'Paradise Lost' and the Classical Epic* (1979) focuses more on the formal elements that *Paradise Lost* shares with Homer and Virgil. J. Steadman, *Epic and Tragic Structure in 'Paradise Lost'* (1976) suggests that the plot, with its major elements of reversal, recognition, and 'scene of suffering', is the epic's organizing principle; in *Milton's Epic Characters* (1968), he examines the characters in the light of classical and Renaissance ideas of heroism. J. Demaray, *Milton's Theatrical Epic* (1980) turns to a different set of genres, analyzing Milton's borrowings from pageants, spectacles, masques, and musical dramas. C. Grose, *Milton's Epic Process* (1973) contends that the epic gives formidable expression to the issues that concerned Milton in his early poetry. However, the most integrated interpretation of the rich panoply of forms is B. Lewalski, *'Paradise Lost' and the Rhetoric of Literary Forms* (1985). It argues powerfully that Milton exploited the 'moral values associated with the several kinds, as a means of imagining his unimaginable subject, and as a rhetorical strategy to educate his readers'.

The internal structures of the epic are intriguingly explicated in G. Crump, *The Mystical Design of 'Paradise Lost'* (1975). Also useful are A. Gilbert, *On the Composition of 'Paradise Lost'* (1947), and M. Lieb, *The Dialectics of Creation: Patterns of Birth and Regeneration in 'Paradise Lost'* (1970).

On the war in heaven, see S. Revard, *The War in Heaven* (1980), which interprets the rebellion in the context of theological treatments of Satan's fall and Renaissance hexameral poetry; and J. Freeman, *Milton and the Martial Muse* (1980), which analyzes the critique of war in *Paradise Lost* against the bellicose tradition of the Renaissance. Somewhat broader in its concern is R. Fallon, *Captain or Colonel: The Soldier in Milton's Life and Art* (1984).

On the portrayal of Edenic life and the Fall, see J. Duncan, *Milton's Earthly Paradise* (1972), which provides a comprehensive history of literary treatments of the paradisial state. J. Knott, *Milton's Pastoral Vision* (1971) demonstrates that in transforming the Arcadian ideal into a theological reality, and in making *it* rather than the battlefield the main epic stage, Milton replaced heroic values with pastoral ones. Taking Raphael and Michael as points of departure, K. Swaim, *Before and After the Fall* (1986), contrasts 'psychological and spiritual conditions before and after the fall'.

A. Stein, *Answerable Style* (1953) analyzes Milton's effort to discover a style 'answerable' to the problems of evil, paradise, and the Fall. D. McColley, *Milton's Eve* (1983), in focusing on Eve and the iconographic and literary traditions behind her, illuminates nearly all the major issues of prelapsarian and postlapsarian existence. Finally, a very good reading is E. Marilla, *The Central Problem of 'Paradise Lost': The Fall of Man* (1953). Collections of essays on *Paradise Lost* include A. Dyson and J. Lovelock, eds., *Milton 'Paradise Lost': A Casebook* (1973); C. Patrides, *Approaches to 'Paradise Lost'* (1968); T. Kranidas, *New Essays on 'Paradise Lost'* (1969); and B. Rajan, *A Tercentenary Tribute* (1969).

Paradise Regained

If any study approaches the definitive, it is B. Lewalski, *Milton's Brief Epic*, (1966) which establishes the validity of the brief-epic genre, locates Milton's poem within that tradition, and interprets Christ's temptations as directed at his offices as prophet, priest, and king. Although superseded by Lewalski's work on background, E. Pope, *'Paradise Regained': Tradition and the Poem* (1947) is useful for its examination of the temptations as variations of the world–flesh–devil triad. P. Cullen, *Infernal Triad: The Flesh, the World and the Devil in Spenser and Milton* (1974) argues in even greater detail for the triad as the backbone of both *Paradise Regained* and *Samson Agonistes*. A. Stein, *Heroic Knowledge* (1957) contends that both *Paradise Regained* and *Samson Agonistes* are about attaining 'heroic knowledge', the right combination of magnanimity and humility that tries to act out 'the likeness of the divine image' while recognizing the difference between God and man. A fine study of the intricate patterns of *Paradise Regained*, with a searching critique of the many attempts to define the poem's structure, is B. Weber, *Wedges and Wings* (1975). A highly original analysis of the interrelationships of the three temptations is J. McAdams, 'The Pattern of Temptation in *Paradise Regained*', *Milton Studies* 4 (1972); and two fine studies of the narrative technique are L. Martz, '*Paradise Regained*: The Interior Teacher', in *The Paradise Within* (1964), and R. Sundell, 'The Narrator as Interpreter in *Paradise Regained*', *Milton Studies* 2 (1970).

Samson Agonistes

The major studies of *Samson Agonistes* have all, to some degree, touched upon the trinity of incongruities the drama presents: Hebraic hero and Greek form yielding a Christian drama. After an exhaustive survey of the Samson tradition from the patristic period to the Renaissance, F. Krouse,

Milton's Samson and the Christian Tradition (1949) interprets Samson as a type of Christ who resists temptations of the flesh, the world, and the devil. W. Madsen, *From Shadowy Types to Truth: Studies in Milton's Symbolism* (1968) also gives a typological reading, but rather than emphasizing the similarities between Samson and Christ it focuses on dissimilarities: Samson is similar to Christ only in victory. It also contains a good discussion of *Samson Agonistes*'s place in the canon. M. Radzinowicz, *Toward 'Samson Agonistes': The Growth of Milton's Mind* (1978), an intricate, highly illuminating study (arguably the best) of the drama as a culmination of Milton's intellectual and poetic development, considers *Samson Agonistes* in relation to Milton's use of dialectic and his conception of history, politics, ethics, theology, and poetics. W. Parker, *Milton's Debt to Greek Tragedy* (1937) enumerates *Samson Agonistes*'s specific debts to the Greek tragedians and also comments on its 'spirit' and relationship to the Book of Judges. Samson's heroism and villany are argued skilfully in A. Low, *The Blaze of Noon* (1974) and J. Wittreich, *Interpreting 'Samson Agonistes'* (1986). Low gives a detailed reading of the drama as one of regeneration and offers judicious insights on the form, spirit, theme, ironies, and characters. Wittreich, on the other hand, contends that when viewed in its biblical, Renaissance, and Miltonic contexts, *Samson Agonistes* frustrates any regenerative interpretation and dramatizes not only the futility of violence, but, specifically, the failure of the Revolution.

Minor poems

The only study encompassing all the minor poetry is J. Leishman, *Milton's Minor Poems*, ed., G. Tillotson (1969), which was composed as a course of lectures. In addition to background, it gives detailed commentaries. On the sonnets, E. Honigmann, *Milton's Sonnets* (1966) is a useful edition containing extensive commentary and an introduction which suggests that the images, themes, and sequence of the sonnets give them a rough coherence. A. Nardo, *Milton's Sonnets and the Ideal Community* (1979) extends Honigmann's suggestion, arguing that 'the principle of community – the relation of the individual to himself, home, friends, country, mankind, and God' – organizes the sonnets into 'a comprehensive scheme of man and his offices'. On *Lycidas*, C. Hunt, *Lycidas and the Italian Critics* (1979), the most original study, contends that under the inspiration of the Italian critics Milton refashioned the pastoral elegy to achieve tragic and epic effects. J. Evans, *The Road From Horton: Looking Backwards in Lycidas* (1983) considers how the pastoral and elegiac traditions provided Milton with the ideal means to confront his frustrations about his future. D. Berkeley, *Inwrought with Figures Dim* (1974) suggests that the poem's fundamental structure is typological. C. Patrides, ed., *Milton's Lycidas: The Tradition and the Poem*, rev. edn (1983) conveniently collects soundly informative commentaries on the pastoral tradition and Milton's adaptation of it.

On *Comus*, J. Demaray, *Milton and the Masque Tradition: The Early Poems, Arcades, and Comus* (1968) securely establishes Milton's work as a masque rather than a drama. M. McGuire, *Milton's Puritan Masque* (1983) treats its Puritan elements, and W. Hunter, *Milton's Comus: Family Piece* (1983) considers the interest and excitement the masque gains when read as a commissioned piece. The most intriguing study is A. Fletcher, *The Transcendental Masque* (1971), which argues that the 'themes of chastity and virginity give structure' to Milton's concern with freedom and that the Lady's virginity has an 'affinity' with 'the power of God'.

The prose

Two informative general 'reference' works are H. Fletcher, *The Use of the Bible in Milton's Prose* (1929) and R. Mohl, *John Milton and His Commonplace Book* (1969). J. Egan, *The Inward Teacher* (1980) examines Milton's modifications of Renaissance prose genres in the interest of more effectively arguing for Christian liberty. K. Stavely, *The Politics of Milton's Prose Style* (1975) 'traces the steady movement of Milton's prose toward an idealistic denigration of politics and affirmation of the "paradise within"'. Two very fine but somewhat forgotten studies are W. Gilman, *Milton's Rhetoric: Studies in His Defense of Liberty* (1939), which analyzes structure and the use of ethos, pathos, and logos in five tracts; and R. Weaver, 'Milton's Heroic Prose', in *The Ethics of Rhetoric* (1953), which contends that Milton's arduous style is the result of his giving primacy to the 'concept' rather than to 'conventionalized expository patterns'. A very fine study of the lexical and syntactic characteristics of Milton's prose is T. Corns, *The Development of Milton's Prose Style* (1982). The classic 'analysis of the progressive definition' of Milton's social, political, and religious ideas and the impact of the Revolution on his thinking is A. Barker, *Milton and the Puritan Dilemma, 1641–1660* (1942). M. Lieb and J. Shawcross, eds., *Achievements of the Left Hand* (1974) is a very fine collection of essays covering such topics as the figure of the orator in the prose, the relationship of *Areopagitica* and *Paradise Lost*, and the theological context of *Christian Doctrine*. It also contains a comprehensive survey of editions, contemporary reactions, and scholarly discussions.

Periodicals

Both *Milton Quarterly* and *Seventeenth-Century News* (also issued quarterly) specialize in brief articles, notes, reviews, abstracts, and announcements of current events. *Milton Studies*, issued annually, contains from eight to twelve high-quality essays.

A final word

There is a much better response to this plethora than the cynicism noted in the introduction:

Reading *Paradise Lost* is a form of communion. We may do it separately, but not alone. Our delightful task stirs up what Milton called a gust for Paradise, not only by making us desire the life of active goodness his poem figures forth with such beauty and interest, but also by creating a community of readers for whom its radiant cosmos is a deeply shared experience. Students of Milton can always say with pleasure, 'This enterprise, many partake with me.'   (McColley, Milton's Eve, i)

Index